The Basics of American Government

Edited By
Ross C. Alexander
and
Carl D. Cavalli

Contributors:
Maria J. Albo, Ross C. Alexander, Carl D. Cavalli,
Barry D. Friedman, Craig B. Greathouse, Jonathan S. Miner,
Brian M. Murphy, K. Michael Reese,
and Charles H. "Trey" Wilson

UNIVERSITY PRESS OF
NORTH GEORGIA

University Press of North Georgia

North Georgia College & State
University
Dahlonega, GA

Published by:
The University Press of North Georgia
Dahlonega, Georgia

Publishing Support by:
Booklogix Publishing Services, Inc.
Alpharetta, Georgia

Cover Photograph "U.S. Mint at Dahlonega" Courtesy of Hancock & Harwell, Atlanta, GA

Cover Design by Lee-Anne Elliott
Book Design by April Loebick & Matt Pardue

ISBN: 978-0-9792324-6-6

Printed in the United States of America, 2011

For more information, please visit: http://www.upnorthgeorgia.org
Or e-mail: upng@northgeorgia.edu

UNIVERSITY PRESS OF
NORTH GEORGIA

Table of Contents

Preface

This book is a collaborative effort among eight current and one retired North Georgia faculty members in the Department of Political Science and Criminal Justice with extensive experience teaching and conducting academic research in the field of American politics. All of these professors were concerned with both the rising cost and lack of academic rigor among American government texts on the market. So, they decided to write their own.

The purpose of this book is twofold. First, it provides a thorough, no-frills overview and analysis of the American political system. Second, most chapters include a work of original academic scholarship that demonstrates or highlights the chapter content. In addition, all chapters provide questions for discussion and several feature a "civic engagement exercise" designed to spur students to become more involved in the political system. Ultimately, this book combines the best aspects of both a traditional textbook and a reader, presented in a concise, low-cost format. The reader will see that the "basics" of the American political system are all addressed. However, in addition, this text devotes entire chapters to topics not found in most texts on the market, i.e. state and local government and civic engagement. Unlike other textbooks, but consistent with political science research, this book is presented utilizing the APA format, with in-text citations. A secondary goal of the authors is to familiarize the reader with scholarship in the field, making it easier to locate the sources used to craft the chapters.

The authors hope you enjoy the book and are inspired to learn more about the American political system.

Ross C. Alexander & Carl D. Cavalli, editors

Acknowledgements

We would like to thank Dr. Kerry Stewart, Gainesville State College, and Dr. T. Casey LaFrance, Western Illinois University, who diligently reviewed each chapter in the text. We are also grateful for the feedback from our discussion panel at the 2010 Georgia Political Science Association annual meeting. Lastly, we are grateful for the people at the University Press of North Georgia–including the director, Bonnie Robinson, and editors, April Loebick and Matt Pardue–for taking a chance on an unusual idea and turning it into a reality. The corrections, edits, and suggestions of all of the aforementioned made *The Basics of American Government* a better finished product.

Thanks also to Maria Albo's summer 2011 American government class for their feedback on a draft copy of this book.

Ross Alexander and Carl D. Cavalli

June 2011

The Basics of American Government has an Online Companion. Please visit http://www.upnorthgeorgia.org/amergovt/ to access this material.

Derek Sutton, Content Editor

Chapter One
Theories of Democracy and Types of Government
Ross C. Alexander

Learning Objectives
After covering the topic of theories of democracy, students should understand:

1. How democracy has evolved in the historical and contemporary sense.
2. How democracy in America functions, comparing and contrasting it with other systems around the world.
3. How foundational pieces in political philosophy influenced the establishment of our republic, most notably the contributions of John Locke.

Abstract

What is democracy? How does it differ from other political structures and systems that have existed over the past two millennia? In this chapter, we will address these foundational questions, in addition to others, to provide a solid framework for the remainder of the book. By examining those thinkers, philosophers, and scholars who have had an impact on the American political system, we can define democracy in the American sense and contrast it with other systems today and throughout time. To accomplish this end, this chapter will offer an in-depth examination of Locke's Second Treatise of Government *to determine its effect on the American brand of democracy.*

Introduction—Toward a Definition of Democracy

Most texts addressing the American political system invariably begin with an attempt to define democracy, which is vaguely understood as "rule by the people." But what, exactly, does that mean? How does democracy differ from other systems of government? Philosophers, thinkers, politicians, and students have been trying to address and answer these questions for hundreds, if not thousands, of years with little consensus. Over 2,500 years ago, Aristotle, the godfather of western political thought, in *The Politics*, offered a discourse on different systems of government, and outlined six possible forms—three positive or "good" and three negative or "bad"—each linked with another. For example, with regard to rule by one individual, **kingship** was the positive form; **tyranny,** the negative. With regard to rule by few in society, **aristocracy** was desirable, while **oligarchy** was undesirable. Finally, concerning rule by many in society, **polity** was the positive outcome, and **democracy** the negative. To fully understand Aristotle's distinctions, his terminology must be defined. His view of kingship was one of an enlightened, benevolent monarch ruling in the best interests of his people. Conversely, if kingship would erode into tyranny, the tyrant would function as a self-interested despot who would do anything to stay in power. For Aristotle, aristocracy was not rule by the rich, but rather rule by the most capable in society, whether it be the most educated, most experienced, or most enlightened. Conversely, as aristocracy devolved into oligarchy, power would fall into the hands of the power-hungry few. Finally, Aristotle viewed a polity as a representative democracy, where citizens would elect qualified leaders to carry out their wishes in government. As polity devolved into democracy, Aristotle envisioned rule by the mob which is different than the modern view of democracy. For Aristotle, this constitutional cycle was inevitable. Every enduring society would experience all these systems of government as it progressed or evolved (Aristotle, 1984).

So, if democracy is not simply "rule by the people," what is it? For Aristotle, democracy had a negative connotation and was marked by mob rule, chaos, and disorder. From a modern perspective, many political scientists and theorists have attempted to define the notion of democracy. E.E. Schattschneider defined democracy thusly: "Democracy is a competitive political system in which competing leaders and organizations define the alternatives of public policy in such a way that the public can participate in the decision-making process" (Schattschneider, 1960, 141). Schmitter and Karl viewed the concept as the following: "Modern political democracy is a system of governance in which rulers are held accountable for their actions in the public realm by citizens, acting indirectly through the competition and cooperation of their elected representatives" (Schmitter and Karl, 1991, 76). Vanhannen contended that "Democracy is a political system in which different groups are legally entitled to compete for power and in which institutional power holders are elected by the people and are responsible to the people" (Vanhannen, 1997, 31). Perhaps the CIA World Fact Book defines the concept of **democracy** best, with the following: "a form of government in which the supreme power is retained by the people, but which is usually exercised indirectly through a system of representation and delegated authority periodically renewed" (CIA World Fact Book, 2010). So, while it is impossible to offer an authoritative, singular definition of democracy, the common components of these various definitions seem to be concepts such as competition, accountability to the public, election of representatives, respect for the law, equal opportunity, encouragement and respect for debate, and involving the people in political decisions.

Since the 19th century, most "democracies" are better described as republics. A **republic** is an indirect democracy, a representative democracy whereby eligible voters (the electorate) choose representatives to carry out their wishes in the government. Most republics throughout the world function as **constitutional democracies**, meaning that the government draws its legitimacy from some authoritative document (a **constitution**) that defines the nation's system of government, its laws, and usually the rights of citizens (CIA World Fact Book, 2010). The United States is, of course, a constitutional democracy or **constitutional republic**. In most republics and democracies today, the basic functions of government could include the following: 1) protecting citizens, 2) providing public goods such as education, parks, roads, sanitation, and health care, and 3) ensuring some degree of equality among its citizens. With regard to the American style of constitutional democracy, our relative degree of "success" is due in large part to many factors, including the relatively high level of affluence in the U.S. which contributes to governmental and societal stability, a high level of education among the populace which encourages participation, and plentiful resources with which to create jobs. To better understand the American political system and its governmental structure, it is helpful to compare and contrast it with other systems throughout history and today.

Other Systems of Government

When the U.S. Constitution was written in 1787 and ratified in 1789, most forms of government throughout the world were either **monarchies**—whereby a single sovereign (a king or a queen) exercised rule over a given populace and territory with power transfer based upon heredity, but in which laws and rights were established—or **absolute monarchies**—whereby the sovereign ruled with absolute power and authority with no defined laws or rights. Throughout the 19th century, during the industrial revolution, communism and socialism took root as a backlash against oppressive economic and social conditions in society created largely by industrialization. **Marxism**, based upon the writings of Karl Marx, espoused the inevitability that the working classes in society (who were the overwhelming majority), would shrug off the oppressive yoke of the capitalist industrialists who were exploiting them, and set up a classless society in which goods would be shared by all people with the guidance of an authoritarian ruling party, which is what came to be known as **communism**. In most cases, including the Soviet Union, China, Cuba, and North Korea, communism devolved into **totalitarianism**, where the state controlled all aspects of life, including the economic, political, social, and cultural spheres, and where any dissent was quickly punished by the ruling party elite. This system functioned very much like a **dictatorship**, in which a single person or small group exercises absolute power, like Iraq under Saddam Hussein or Uganda under Idi Amin. In **theocracies**, there is no separation of church and state, and the church, in effect, constitutes or controls the government, such as is the case in several Islamic republics in the Middle East today.

In the 19th century, **socialism** functioned like, or was aligned with, Marxism or communism. In the 20th century and today, socialism functions differently. In those nations that utilize socialist systems, most notably the Scandinavian nations of Sweden, Norway, and Denmark, the state provides many public goods such as universal health care and public education and also controls the economy or "means of production." Yet, citizens enjoy many of the same rights and liberties as those living in democratic republics, including freedom of speech and expression, freedom of the press, and freedom of religion, to name a few. The primary distinction between socialist nations and capitalist nations is the level of taxation. Obviously, taxes are much higher in socialist nations where the state controls the economy and provides more public goods to its citizens. Finally, **anarchy** is the unfortunate situation in which no government authority exists whatsoever with total chaos ensuing.

Democracy in the United States—Separating Myth from Reality

Are there certain characteristics and experiences that are unique to Americans or the American political experience? Do Americans have a unique political culture or common set of values shared by all? In his famous examination of Americans and the American political system in the early 19th century, French author Alexis de Tocqueville contended that Americans were individualistic, pragmatic, hard-working, freedom-loving, and industrious among other qualities. In his treatise, *Democracy in America*, he argued that these common American qualities allowed its people to form a government that reflected these values which, at the time, were unique in his estimation. So, was de Tocqueville correct? Are these qualities uniquely and exclusively American? Do they apply to all Americans, or just some? Can they be applied to other cultures in other nations as well? These questions are difficult, if not impossible, to answer. So, what is myth, and what is reality? What constitutes *American* democracy?

Political culture influences the political system. Individuals voting in elections determine the nature of government, or so most are taught. This notion of **political equality**, or one person, one vote, is often cited as a cornerstone of the American political system. The notion that everyone's vote counts equally regardless of race, gender, sexual orientation, socioeconomic status, or religious affiliation is something taught to students in schools beginning at a very young age. Is political equality myth or reality? Do all citizens have an equal ability to impact the political system? Some would argue yes, others no. Both would be correct. In a practical sense, citizens can only cast one vote per election, seemingly resulting in political equality. However, some have more ability to impact the political system than others, largely through money, influence, power, or connections to policymakers, which would shatter the notion of political equality. The previous exercise sheds light on the nature of the American political system and its unique brand of democracy. There are many questions and few simple answers. If political equality does not exist, the myth does endure. How about **equality of opportunity**?—does it exist? The "work hard and you'll get ahead" myth has been ingrained in the American experience for generations, but is it accurate? Do we all have equal opportunity to succeed? Again, some would argue yes, others no. Those arguing "yes" would be quick to point out that we have relatively equal access to public goods such as a free education, as well as equal freedoms of speech, association, and expression. Those arguing "no" would contend that some in society are inherently better off than others, having access to better schools, business connections, nicer neighborhoods, and even more stable families. Who is correct? Both sides. Again, there are no easy answers.

Ultimately, these opposing forces have shaped and forged the American republic. The common perception of the American political system that students learn in elementary, middle, and high school is that the majority of citizens, voting in elections, determine the nature of government. Is that accurate? Is the United States a system governed by individuals exercising **majority-rule democracy**, or does this model exist only in a textbook? Can the *individual* shape the American political system? Perhaps. Does the individual, exercising his or her political rights, have the ability to cause change at the national level? Probably not. Does this same individual have the ability to cause change in his or her community by becoming involved in political matters at the local level? Probably.

If individuals do not substantively shape or influence the political system at the national level, what forces do? In our system, in the modern sense, groups exercise a tremendous amount of power and exert significant influence over the political system, largely through money. This notion of groups having a profound impact on the political system is referred to as **pluralism**. Groups donate significant amounts of money to finance the campaigns of politicians, including members of Congress, the Senate, and the president. These "special interests" lobby policymakers to enact laws and regulations that benefit their interests and will be discussed in much greater detail in Chapter 5. Groups are able to exert this level of influence for many reasons, most notably because they possess constitutional protection that allows them to lobby government. The First Amendment to the U.S. Constitution reads, "Congress shall make no law respecting an establishment of religion, or prohibiting the free exercise thereof; or abridging the freedom of speech, or of the press; or the right of the people peaceably to assemble, *and to petition the Government for a redress of grievances*" (italics added). While the shifting of power towards interest groups has surely had negative consequences, including an over-emphasis on the interests of groups with the most money, there have been positive outcomes as well, such as those groups advocating for social and educational policy influencing lawmakers to pass bills in those arenas. While the functioning of government in the United States has become pluralistic in nature, it is by no means exceptional compared to democracies and republics throughout the world, where special interests also have tremendous degrees of power.

In sum, the myths of the development and functioning of the American political system can be separated from the realities in some cases, but not others. While much of what students learn about the system in grade levels is over-simplified and inaccurate, some is not. The founding and development of the American political system is a complex and fascinating case, but it can be compared to other nations' development as well. Furthermore, it is difficult to offer an authoritative set of political values that all Americans share or treasure, which is why American politics are so fascinating.

Case Study—The Influence of John Locke on *The Declaration of Independence*

To gain a better understanding of the American political process and the nature of American democracy, we need to examine the influences on the founding fathers during the colonial and Revolutionary War eras. When Thomas Jefferson authored the *Declaration of Independence* in 1776 under the guidance of Benjamin Franklin and John Adams, he demonstrated the degree to which he had been influenced by other great minds. Jefferson, like most of the delegates present in Philadelphia in 1776, was an educated, well-read man who had studied the classics (the writings of Greek and Roman historians and philosophers), as well as the works of the **Enlightenment Period** of the previous century. Arguably, the author who influenced Jefferson most was John Locke. Locke's ideas are woven throughout the *Declaration*. What follows is an in-depth examination of Locke's most famous writing and the impact that it had on Jefferson and the *Declaration of Independence* in particular.

John Locke (1632-1704) was an English political philosopher, commentator, and thinker who wrote during a time of great political change and upheaval when the monarchy was being challenged in England before the "Glorious Revolution" in 1688 and during the Enlightenment Period. Locke was considered one of the greatest minds of the Enlightenment era along with such luminaries as Voltaire, Rosseau, and Hobbes. Locke proposed and discussed many radical political beliefs during this period of upheaval and political change which dealt with the responsibilities of government, the rights of common men, and the philosophical basis of government in general (Laslett, 1988, 16-20). Unlike previous generations, and contrary to the very nature of monarchy, Locke believed that men were born free (in a state of nature) and possessed inherent, inalienable rights that could not be arbitrarily removed by the government (the king). Locke assumed that the rights of man were bestowed not by the monarch, but by their creator (God), which was a radical idea at the time (Locke, 1988).

Locke's most famous work, *The Second Treatise of Government,* contains the passages and ideas that were most influential to Jefferson and are easiest to identify in the *Declaration of Independence.* As Jefferson advocated the *Declaration,* Locke believed in limited government. For Locke (and Jefferson), man's freedom was his greatest right, bestowed on him not by government, but by God (an inalienable right). For Locke, men are born natural, reasonable, and free, beholden to no one, possessing inherent civil liberties and natural rights, including freedom and self-determination (Locke, 1988). Furthermore, man is able to acquire wealth from his labor, which is best evidenced through the accumulation of **private property.** For Locke, then, the primary duty of government is to preserve man's property, noting, "...whereas Government has no other end but the preservation of Property" (Locke, 1988, 94). For Locke, government exists to preserve man's life, liberty (freedom), and property, a theme paraphrased by Jefferson in the *Declaration* as, "That all men are created equal; that they are endowed by their Creator with certain unalienable rights; that among these are life, liberty, and the pursuit of happiness..." (Jefferson, 1776).

Another Lockean theme that influenced Jefferson was the notion that citizens consent to be governed—that the people create, craft, and mold the government because they allow it to exist—which was an extremely radical supposition at the time. The idea that government exists to serve the people and only exercises power over them because the people allow it to was contrary to the very ideals of monarchy. The impact this idea had on Jefferson is observable in the *Declaration*: "...governments are instituted among men, deriving their just powers from the consent of the governed; that whenever any form of government becomes destructive of these ends, it is the right of the people to alter or abolish it, and to institute a new government..." (Jefferson, 1776). Ultimately, according to Locke and Jefferson, man and government enter into a **contract** of sorts, each with duties, responsibilities, and obligations. Government's obligation to its citizens is to exercise power in a limited fashion securing the life, liberty, and property of the people. The obligations of the people involve following the laws set forth by the government (which the people create) and respecting the rights and property of others. If government violates this contract, according to Locke, the people have the right to: 1) change the government, 2) leave society (keeping their property and wealth), and 3) revolt, an idea which especially appealed to Jefferson (Locke, 1988).

Locke's influence on Jefferson and the *Declaration of Independence* is profound and easily observable. Locke's radical teachings from the century before the founding period had far-reaching effects on the establishment of our republic (and others, such as France). Lockean teachings and principles are found in the *Constitution* as well, even if they are a bit harder to find at first glance. For example, Locke strongly advocated for separation of powers, which is a hallmark of our constitutional system. Locke wrote, "Therefore, 'tis necessary there should be a *Power always in being,* which should see to the *Execution* of the Laws that are made, and remain in force. And thus the *Legislative* and *Executive Power* come often to be separated" (italics in original) (Locke, 1988, 365). Ultimately, Locke believed that people were inherently good. Furthermore, because of their inherent "goodness," they should not be constrained by government. Therefore, the responsibilities and duties of government were the following:

1. to provide a universal application of the laws to all men, regardless of class,
2. making laws that are designed for the common good of the people,
3. ensuring low taxes, with tax increases being approved by the people or their representatives, and
4. ensuring that the power of government, especially with regard to lawmaking, resides in the legislature, because they are representatives of the people (Locke, 1988).

As can be plainly seen, Locke's ideals have impacted our republic since its founding, and still do so today.

Discussion Questions
1. Which definition of democracy do you prefer? Craft your own definition and compare it to the one you chose.

2. Which form of government is most similar to democracy? The most different? What positives and negatives do you see in each?
3. With its emphasis on pluralism, has the United States moved too far away from the ideal form of democracy? Do interest groups have too much power in our system?
4. In your opinion, how would Locke view our democracy today? Which of his ideals do we see reflected in our political system?

References

Aristotle. (1984). *The politics.* (C. Lord, Trans.). Chicago, IL: University of Chicago Press. (Original work published 350 B.C.E.).

Central Intelligence Agency. (n.d.). [Information on the history, people, government, economy, geography, communications, transportation, military, and transnational issues for 266 world entities]. *The World Fact Book.* Retrieved from https://www.cia. gov/library/publications/the-world-factbook/index.html

de Tocqueville, A. (1945). *Democracy in America.* New York, NY: Alfred A. Knopf, Inc.

Jefferson, T. (1776). *Declaration of Independence.* Retrieved from http:// avalon.law.yale.edu/ 18th_century/declare.asp

Locke, J. (1988). *Two treatises of government* P. Laslett, (ed.). New York, NY: Cambridge University Press. (Original work published 1690).

Schattschneider, E.E. (1960). *The semisovereign people.* New York, NY: Holt, Rinehart and Winston.

Schmitter, P. C., & Karl, T. L. (1991). What democracy is...and is not. *Journal of Democracy, 2*(3), 75-88.

Vanhannen, T. (1997). *Prospects of democracy: A study of 172 countries.* New York, NY: Routledge.

Chapter Two
The U.S. Constitution
Ross C. Alexander

Learning Objectives
After covering the topic of the U.S. Constitution, students should understand:

1. How forces during the Revolutionary War era led to the writing and ratification of the Constitution.
2. The basic structure and functioning of the U.S. government as laid out in the Constitution.
3. How the flexibility of the Constitution has allowed it to endure, but also resulted in debate and controversy.
4. How the framers of the Constitution stated their case to the American people in *The Federalist*.

Abstract
    The Constitution is a revered, enduring document that provides the framework for our democratic republic, but it is not without controversy. It is brief, flexible, and open to interpretation, just as the framers intended. As a result, the document has been able to remain largely intact in its original form for over 220 years. The Constitution provides both the theoretical and practical framework for our government, providing insight into the intentions of the framers during the Revolutionary and Founding Periods. In a practical sense, the document provides a framework for our branches of government, means by which they check and balance each other, and the scope and limits of the power of the national government. The Constitution was a product of events and forces culminating throughout the Colonial and Revolutionary War eras, not something that was produced in a vacuum in 1787. This chapter not only describes and analyzes the Constitution itself, but also the historical events leading up to it. It also examines the legacy of the document and the reasons for the controversy it has caused.

The Events leading to the Constitution
The Revolution
    The **American Revolution** raged from 1775, when shots were first fired at Lexington and Concord, until 1783 when the Treaty of Paris formally ended the war (even though the final battle was fought at Yorktown

in 1781). Students learn in school that the Revolution was brought about by freedom-loving patriots who desired self-governance, shedding off the oppressive yoke of British rule. This story is partly true. The causes of the Revolution are varied and complex, and by no means did the entirety of the population of the colonies support the uprising. Many were fighting for the right to self-rule and determination while others were fighting for largely economic reasons (they were sick of paying high taxes to fund the various wars of the British empire or they did not want to pay off their British creditors) while others yet were fighting for adventure. Some, especially along the western frontier of the colonies, paid little attention to the war in the east as it did not directly affect them. Finally, many colonists remained loyal to the crown and even fought side-by-side with their British cousins against the rebels. Regardless of their politics, loyalties, and motivations, most would have agreed that the chances of a rag-tag, loosely associated, underfunded, diverse group of colonies defeating the strongest military empire in the world would have been slim at best.

Discontent with British rule had been culminating for at least ten years before the skirmishes at Lexington and Concord. The British viewed the resource-rich colonies as a cash-cow that could be exploited and taxed to fund their extensive wars and campaigns around the globe. These increasing taxes on goods such as stamps and tea resulted in the beginnings of organized dissent, like the Boston Tea Party in 1773. Coupled with these high taxes was the reality that the planter classes in the middle Atlantic and southern colonies owed more and more to their British creditors for goods bought on credit–something that George Washington and Thomas Jefferson understood and experienced first-hand. A small, influential group of citizens believed that the colonies would be better as a sovereign, self-governing entity, divorced from British rule and control. These influential few echoed the sentiments of many who saw themselves as British citizens, but did not have the rights and privileges of those living in Britain. That is, they paid taxes to the British crown yet had no representative voice in Parliament. This notion of "taxation without representation" was a rallying cry for many itching for rebellion.

The Declaration of Independence

On July 4, 1776, 56 delegates to the **Second Continental Congress** signed the **Declaration of Independence** (including Lyman Hall and

Button Gwinnett from Georgia). The treatise was penned by Thomas Jefferson, one of the youngest and brightest delegates to the Congress, under the tutelage of the more experienced John Adams and Benjamin Franklin. The document is one of rebellion, not reconciliation. It is written almost as a personal letter to King George III of England and explains in detail the reasons for rebellion against the crown. Jefferson borrowed liberally from many contemporary and historical sources, most notably John Locke's *Second Treatise of Government*, where Locke's "life, liberty, and property" became Jefferson's "life, liberty, and the pursuit of happiness." In the document, Jefferson argues for a limited government that exists at the consent of the governed: the people, who possess these "inalienable" rights. Those who signed the Declaration were literally putting their lives on the line. Had the Revolution been lost, these men would have been tried (and probably executed) for treason. The Declaration is one of our sacred founding documents largely because it articulates the philosophical basis for our political system.

The Articles of Confederation

After we had formally declared our independence from Great Britain, one of our first orders of business was setting up some sort of government, largely in order to effectively wage war. The 13 former British colonies did not necessarily view themselves as one nation. Rather, they viewed themselves as 13 independent, sovereign countries, loosely-affiliated, but working together (somewhat ineffectively) to fight the Revolution. The idea of one "United States of America" had not yet taken hold. However, some sort of government had to be created to coordinate the activities of all the former colonies. In November 1777, the **Articles of Confederation**, written by John Dickinson, was established. The hallmark of this new government was that the national government possessed very little real power. Rather, the true power remained with the states. A confederation is just that—a loose association of independent or quasi-independent states. The national government under the Articles was so weak that it could not levy taxes, wage war, regulate commerce, or issue a uniform currency among all the states. It contained no executive branch, which resulted in relatively poor leadership. Rather, the power that did exist was concentrated in the Congress, or legislature. However, passing legislation or amending the Articles was onerous and difficult, requiring a unanimous vote of all 13 members (Kammen, 1986, pp. 10-18). It quickly became apparent that the Articles was an inefficient, ineffective system of government and was created in a haphazard fashion. It was not even formally ratified by the states until 1781. The result was that funding the Revolution was uncoordinated and ineffective, making the American victory even that more impressive. Nevertheless, the Articles was our first system of uniquely American government and existed until the late 1780s. It should also be noted that it is within the Articles that the words "United States of America" is mentioned for the first time, which is a rather odd coincidence considering the weak nature of the national government provided by the document.

The Great Compromise

By 1787, many in the new nation realized the inherent inefficiencies of the Articles of Confederation. They argued that such a weak national government could leave the new nation exposed to financial ruin or ripe for future foreign invasion by Great Britain, France, or Spain, all of whom still laid claim to vast stretches of the North American continent. However, others argued that there was no need for more government beyond what the states and the weak national government provided. Both sides tended to agree that the Articles could or should be amended to function better. That was the charge of those delegates who met in Philadelphia in the summer of 1787—to amend the Articles, not create a new system of government. That is, however, exactly what they did. Twelve states sent delegates to the **Constitutional Convention**, every one except Rhode Island. The meetings occurred in secret; the windows were nailed shut, and sentries were posted at the doors and entrances. The framers very quickly understood that they would be proposing a brand new government, one which looked radically different from what existed under the Articles. They also understood that such a development would not be without controversy.

Two Plans of Government

Many delegates from the various states made speeches and proposals as to what the new government should look like. However, the proposals of two factions soon became the most popular and seriously considered. The Virginia delegates, proposed the **Virginia Plan** or Randolph Plan, which was written by James Madison, who had come to the Convention with the proposal already written for the most part. The Virginia Plan proposed a radical new form of government, one in which the national government was significantly more powerful than that found under the Articles. If accepted, the states would be ceding a great deal of power to the national government. The plan proposed a bicameral or two-house legislature with representation in both houses based on population which favored the large population states such as Virginia, Pennsylvania, and Massachusetts. The people would choose members of the lower house, while state legislatures would chose members of the upper house (www. ourdocuments.gov). The plan proposed a fusion-of-power or parliamentary system, whereby the legislature would choose the chief executive (this is the type of arrangement present in Britain, and with which the framers were familiar) (Kammen, 1986, pp. 22-25). With regard to the judicial system, the Virginia Plan proposed a type of "supreme court" chosen by the upper-house of the legislature (www.ourdocuments.gov). In a philosophical sense, the Virginia Plan viewed governmental power as being derived from one, unified American "people," rather than from the states; much different than the Articles, which was state-based in terms of power.

In contrast, the New Jersey delegates proposed the **New Jersey Plan**, or Paterson Plan. This plan looked very similar to the Articles, because it proposed a unicameral or one-house legislature with equal representation regardless of state population and favored the small population states such as New Jersey and New Hampshire. It proposed a multi-person chief executive chosen by the legislature (Kammen, 1986, pp. 25-30). In a philosophical sense, the New Jersey plan assumed that national government power would be derived from the states, not the American people as a whole. In our Constitution, there are elements of each proposal with more weight given to the Virginia Plan. After much debate, a compromise was reached by the framers, which came to be called the **Great Compromise** or **Connecticut Compromise**, because it was largely brokered by the Connecticut delegation. The proposal that resulted from the Constitutional Convention represented a radical departure from the government under the Articles.

The Document

The United States Constitution possesses seven articles, the first three of which detail the various branches of government. Article I outlines the powers of Congress (who would pass the laws); Article II the powers of the President (who would execute the laws); and Article III the powers of the Judiciary (who would interpret the laws). The framers chose this sequence deliberately, intending that Congress, the legislature, be the strongest branch of government. They were familiar with how a strong legislature functioned (British parliament) and were wary that the President (which had never before existed) would become tyrannical or king-like, and they had just had a bad experience with a king leading up to the Revolution. Some among the framers (like Alexander Hamilton) even advocated that the President *should* possess powers similar to a king, serving a life-term and functioning as the strongest entity in the government, yet they were over-ruled. Rather, they reasoned, a bicameral (two-house) legislature possessing the most power would best articulate the wishes of the people. Therefore, Article I is long and detailed. Conversely, Article II, which deals with the presidency, and Article III, which addresses the Courts, are brief and less detailed. Neither a president nor an independent judiciary had ever existed and the framers were not exactly sure how either would function.

The document provides for a bicameral legislature; the lower house, the **House of Representatives**, is directly elected by the people. Representation in the House is based upon state population; the more people in a state, the more representatives it has in the House. However, representation in the upper house, the **Senate**, is equal with each state possessing two, regardless of population. According to the Constitution, *state* legislatures choose each state's Senators, a provision in place until the passage of the **17th amendment** in 1913, which resulted in the direct election of Senators by the people. House members serve two-year terms, must be 25 years old, and must be U.S. citizens for a minimum of seven years. Senators serve six-year terms, must be 30 years old, and have been U.S. residents for at least nine years. Both House members and Senators must reside in the state they represent. Today, there are 435 members of the House of Representatives (13 from Georgia); (Georgia will gain one more Representative as a result of the 2010 census, raising the number to 14) and 100 members of the Senate (two per state).

According to the Constitution, the president must be 35 years of age, a natural born U.S. citizen, and a resident of the U.S. for the previous 14 years. The president serves a four-year term of office and is not limited to any specific number of terms. Presidents for over nearly 150 years served a maximum of two terms not because of any Constitutional regulation, but rather because it was the precedent set by George Washington. Franklin D. Roosevelt was the only president to break with tradition having been elected to four terms of office–1932, 1936, 1940, and 1944–during the Great Depression and World War II. In 1951, Congress passed the **22nd Amendment**, which now limits the president to two terms of office.

The framers were not common men. Rather, they were the elite, the powerful, the educated, the aristocrats of the new nation. As such, they were a bit wary of giving too much power to the common people, and they structured the presidential election procedure uniquely. We do not directly elect the president as we directly elect members of Congress. Rather, when we vote for president, we are technically voting for a "slate of electors" who, in turn, several weeks after the general election, vote for the president. Therefore, the true mechanism for choosing the president is this Electoral College. Electors are chosen by their respective political parties to serve this role. Representation in the Electoral College is based upon population. A state's total number of electors is the sum total of its Representatives plus its Senators (Kimberling, 1992). For example, in Georgia, this number is 14 (with Georgia gaining a seat in the House after the 2010 census). Therefore, states with more people have more electors in the college. Today, the total number of electors is 538–which is the total number of Representatives (435) plus the total number of Senators (100) plus three representing the District of Columbia. In all states except Maine and Nebraska, the candidate who wins the majority of the popular vote receives all that state's electors. For example, if candidate A receives 60% of the popular vote in a state and candidate B receives 40%, candidate A would receive 100% of the electoral vote. For a candidate to win the presidential election, he or she must receive a majority (270) of the votes (Kimberling, 1992). Therefore, candidates for the presidency are wise to gear their elections toward those states with high numbers of electoral votes (CA, TX, NY, FL, IL, PA, OH, GA, etc.). Because of the Electoral College, the person receiving the majority of electoral votes (not popular votes in the general election) becomes the president. In fact, four times, most recently in 2000, the "victor" actually received fewer votes than the "loser," but received more votes where it counted–the Electoral College.

While no federal rule requires electors to choose the candidate determined by the general election, a quirk referred to as a "faithless elector," many states have such rules. However, no faithless elector has ever been punished. There have been a few such electors in recent elections, the last one occurring in 2004.

Impeachment is the formal means of removing the president from office. It is a two-step process involving both houses of Congress. First, the House of Representatives conducts an investigation to determine if the president has committed some sort of crime. If so, "Articles of Impeachment" can be voted against the president, requiring a simple majority vote. The "Articles" then go to the Senate for the formal trial of the president. Here, the Senators serve as the jury, and the Chief Justice of the Supreme Court oversees the proceedings. For the president to be convicted and forced to leave office, he must be found guilty of "High Crimes and Misdemeanors," requiring a super-majority (two-thirds) vote. Two presidents, Andrew Johnson and Bill Clinton, have had Articles of Impeachment voted against them, but neither was convicted of High Crimes and Misdemeanors.

Article III established the **Judicial Branch** of government, or the courts. An independent judiciary had never existed, so Article Three is very vague. In it, the framers described the parameters of the highest court in the land–the Supreme Court. Today, the Court has nine members. However, the Constitution does not require a specific number of justices. The most controversial aspect of this Article is the notion that federal judges receive life appointments, serving as long as they are deemed to be in good standing.

Article V of the Constitution describes the formal **amendment** process. The U.S. Constitution is amended infrequently, only 27 times in total. The first 10 amendments serve as the Bill of Rights (adopted in 1791). The process of both proposing and ratifying an amendment is onerous and requires more than a majority vote. There are two methods of proposing an amendment to the Constitution. The more common method is by a two-thirds vote in both houses of the U.S. Congress. The less common method is at the request of two-thirds of the state legislatures. With regard to ratifying a proposed amendment, the more common method is by a three-quarters vote of all state legislatures. The less common method of ratification is by three-quarters of the states in a special convention. With respect to both the proposal and ratification process, a relatively small minority can block the will of the majority, which has resulted in only 17 amendments being ratified since 1791.

Slavery

The word "slave" or "slavery" does not appear in the Constitution, yet the framers were very aware of the controversial nature of the institution. Slavery is addressed indirectly, most notably by the **three-fifths compromise.** Article I, Section Two, Paragraph Three of the Constitution describes how slaves would be counted as three-fifths of a person in terms of representation, when determining the total number of persons in a state. The slave-holding states of the south argued that slaves should be counted in terms of representation, resulting in more representatives in the House for those states. The non-slave-holding states contended that they should not count as "persons" because they were considered property. The resulting compromise was that slaves would be counted as three-fifths of a person.

Many founding fathers were slaveholders, including Washington and Jefferson. Others were abolitionists who abhorred the practice and desired to see it ended immediately. Most, however, understood that ending slavery would be difficult, as the many southern states depended upon it economically. Had slavery been outlawed in the Constitution, it would probably not have been ratified, because many southern states would have withdrawn their support. Valid arguments can be made saying that the framers should have outlawed slavery at the founding. The counterargument that ending slavery at that time would have resulted in the Constitution not being ratified is also valid. There are no simple or authoritative answers on this subject.

Controversy

Enumerated v. Implied Powers

The framers understood that they could not possibly predict the challenges that the Constitution would have to face, yet they wanted to create a document that would endure and be applicable for future generations. To that end, they crafted a purposefully ambiguous product that could be molded, changed, and applied somewhat differently by future policymakers. One mechanism they included to allow for this constitutional evolution is found in Article I. Article I, Section Eight of the U.S. Constitution is referred to as the **Necessary and Proper Clause.** This clause, sometimes referred to as the "Elastic Clause," allows for the future expansion and evolution of the power of the federal government. It reads, "To make all Laws which shall be necessary and proper for carrying into the Execution the foregoing Powers, and all other Powers vested by this Constitution in the Government of the United States, or in any Department or Officer thereof." This relatively simple provision, which leaves open-ended the power of the federal government, has sparked a great deal of controversy about the limits of its authority.

At the time of the founding, and even today, many argued that the powers of the federal government should be limited to those specifically listed, or enumerated, in the Constitution – no more, no less – and that the powers of the federal government are not open-ended. Rather, they argued, the states should possess those powers not listed in the Constitution. These states' rights advocates also looked to the Constitution and the Bill of Rights to substantiate their case. The 10th Amendment to the Constitution is referred to as the **Reserved Powers Clause,** which simply states: "The Powers not delegated to the United States by the Constitution, nor prohibited by it to the states, are reserved to the states respectively, or to the people."

These two clauses, one found in the Constitution and one found in the Bill of Rights, are contradictory in nature. The Necessary and Proper Clause assumes that the federal government possesses **implied powers** beyond what are listed in the Constitution. Conversely, the Reserved Powers Clause assumes that the federal government possesses **enumerated powers,** or those listed in the Constitution, with all others being given or reserved to the states. This ambiguity has caused a great deal of debate, confusion, conflict, and even rebellion over the past 200 years, resulting in events leading to the Civil War and conflicts between the states and the federal government ever since. What did the framers actually intend? It is impossible to know exactly. They purposely crafted and envisioned a flexible document that is open to interpretation by future generations. However, they also understood the need for strong state governments.

Federalists v. Anti-Federalists
The ratification of the Constitution was not a slam-dunk. Many were

opposed to its passage. Mostly, they were fearful of a tyrannical national government that would take all power away from the states, causing them to wither away. These anti-Constitution forces were largely fearful of what was referred to at the time as consolidation of power, or the notion that all governmental power would be concentrated in one level of government (the national level in this case). Rather, they contended, power should be decentralized across two levels of government—the national and the state—leaving the states with considerable power and authority. The forces in favor of the Constitution were dubbed **Federalists**, while those opposed to it were called **Anti-Federalists**.

The Federalists included such dignitaries as James Madison, John Adams, Alexander Hamilton, and George Washington—those who had attended the Constitutional Convention and played a large part in the crafting of the document. The Federalists saw the need for a strong, energetic, and efficient national government that would unify the new republic as one nation. They assumed that power would be somewhat consolidated under the national government, but realized that states would play a major role in this power-sharing arrangement. The Federalist base of support was much stronger in New England and the Middle Atlantic States, in the cities, and among intellectuals, merchants, and scholars. Conversely, the Anti-Federalists believed that the states should remain strong, that they be at least co-equal players with the national government, and that power should be dispersed among these levels of government. The Anti-Federalist base of support was stronger in rural areas, the south, and among farmers, frontiersmen, and individualists.

Case Study—Marketing the Constitution: *The Federalist*

Once the Constitution had been written, it needed to be ratified by the states. To become the law of the land, nine of the thirteen states had to support it. To ensure passage, the framers needed to explain to the states, and more importantly, to the people, why the Constitution was in their best interests. The primary method they chose to sell the Constitution to the people was through a series of periodic essays published in newspapers throughout the states, laying out in simple terms, the basic provisions of the Constitution. These 85 essays, collectively called *The Federalist*, appeared in newspapers and were widely circulated in 1787-88. Not only did they explain how the Constitution was structured and how it would function, the essays provided insight into the framers' philosophical and theoretical reasoning when crafting the document. Three men wrote the 85 essays, James Madison, Alexander Hamilton, and John Jay. Madison and Hamilton penned the vast majority. Overall, Madison's essays are probably the most famous, because he laid out a commonsense, nuanced, and balanced argument, which respectfully addressed the concerns of the Anti-Federalists.

Hamilton, on the other hand, was more direct and less conciliatory towards the Anti-Federalists. The framers reasoned that if people could read these essays and understand their reasoning, that they would ultimately support the new Constitution. The Anti-Federalists wrote a number of rebuttal essays that in many cases provide excellent arguments against the Constitution. However, because the Constitution ultimately is ratified and the Federalists "won," the Anti-Federalists' essays have been largely marginalized or forgotten. Throughout this year-and-a-half, Madison and Hamilton would publish an essay under the pen-name "Publius" and various Anti-Federalist writers, many of whom would also use a pen-name, would respond with a counter-essay. What follows is an analysis of some of the most famous essays of *The Federalist* – those that lay out the argument of the Federalists best. Collectively, the 85 papers that comprise *The Federalist* are probably the third-most important set of documents of the founding era, behind only The Declaration of Independence and the Constitution. These three pieces comprise the basis of American political philosophy.

Federalist #10, written by James Madison, is probably the most famous and influential of all the essays. It best summarizes the Federalists' collective argument in favor of the Constitution. In this essay, Madison primarily addresses the issue of factions, what we would call special interests or interest groups today. With incredible foresight into the development of the modern American political system, Madison explained that if a strong, energetic government was not established, factions would dominate the system, alienating the people and negatively influencing the crafting of legislation and public policy (which, many today would argue, is exactly what occurred). Madison defined factions as "...a number of citizens, whether amounting to a majority or minority of the whole, who are united and actuated by some common impulse of passion, or of interest, adverse to the rights of other citizens, or to the permanent and aggregate interest of the community" (Madison, 2001, p. 92). Madison explained that factions would always exist, but government should ensure that their effects are tempered or diminished. To accomplish this end, he reasoned, a strong national government, a republic, must be established to safeguard the liberties and will of the people. He further argued that too much freedom and liberty can result in too much faction: "Liberty is to faction what air is to fire" (Madison, 2001, p. 92). Madison further explained that the best system of government to limit the power and influence of factions is a republic, a representative democracy. Echoing Rousseau and others, Madison understood that democracy was predisposed to breeding faction. However, he reasoned, the United States, with its large territory and population, was uniquely situated and comprised to limit factions. Factions were inevitable, but could be marginalized in a large, vast republic. Madison envisioned a system whereby the people would choose the best, brightest, and most capable members of society to represent them in government. He, in fact, advocated for a "natural" aristocracy that would represent the people in government. Like the rest of the framers, he was an aristocrat, an educated man who felt that some were better fit to lead than others. Throughout #10, and in other essays, the authors refer to "men of fit character" who would govern in the best interests of the people.

Federalist #39, also penned by Madison, addresses the primary concern of the Anti-Federalists–that the proposed Constitution would result in a consolidated government whereby all power would be concentrated in the national government, and the states would lose all or significant power, causing them to wither away. Madison does concede that the states would lose some power, but would remain very important partners in this unique power-sharing arrangement that the Constitution proposes, where there are multiple levels of sovereign government existing at the same time, which is the definition of **federalism**. Today, we use the terms «federal» and «national» almost interchangeably. To Madison, they were different. In explaining how the states would retain power under the Constitution, he made a detailed distinction between «federal» and «national.» Madison explained that the government would function simultaneously as federal and national in nature. When governmental authority flowed from the states, it was federal in nature. However, when governmental authority flowed directly from the people, it was national in nature. Therefore, the proposed Constitution viewed its power as derived from sovereign states individually as well as from the American people collectively. For one of the first times, the nation was beginning to view itself as one, unified entity.

Most of the essays written by Hamilton are not nearly as delicate as Madison's. In fact, at times, they tend to even contradict Madison. In *Federalist #15*, Hamilton also addresses the issue of consolidation of power and is not nearly as conciliatory to states' rights advocates, explaining that a powerful national government is the best guarantee of national progress and health as a nation. He even refers to the Articles (which guaranteed the strength and power of the states) as a "national humiliation." In this essay, Hamilton argues that the fledgling nation needs to be grounded on firm financial footing and possess an ability to defend itself, something that can only occur through the establishment and leadership of a strong national government. He argues that the states had proven to be ineffective in either of these areas. Hamilton also argues strongly for consolidation, even at the expense of state power: "...we must resolve to incorporate into our plan those ingredients which may be considered as forming the characteristic difference between a league and a government; we must extend the authority of the Union to the persons of the citizens—the only proper objects of government" (Hamilton, 2001, p. 111). Here, Hamilton is advocating that the government rightly serves all Americans as individual citizens of one nation, not the interests of the states. Until then, he reasoned, the new nation would remain financially insolvent, fractured, and ripe for foreign invasion.

A Civic Engagement Challenge—Draft a Constitution

Are there aspects to the Constitution that do not seem just or fair? Did the framers err when drafting certain articles that left the document open to interpretation and speculation that did not mirror their intent? Would you like to see certain amendments made to the Constitution? Here's your chance. Break into groups of five or so students and draft your own Constitution for a nation you have created. Be sure to include the following: a brief description of your society or nation; a Preamble or "mission statement;" and 10-12 realistic, detailed, specific changes and/ or provisions your group would like to seen enacted. Your document can be focused at a national, state, community, or even campus level. After you have finished, trade papers with another group to see what they have crafted. Be serious, but have fun!

Discussion Questions

1. Are the Declaration of Independence and the Constitution compatible documents? How are they similar? How are they different?
2. How do you think the framers would react to the evolution of the power of the president over the past 200 years? Has the office become too powerful? Was that their intent?
3. Should the federal government be more limited to the enumerated powers found in the Constitution or is it inevitable that it assumes implied powers over time? What are the consequences or implications? What did the framers intend?
4. Should the framers have ended the institution of slavery in the Constitution? Why or why not?
5. If you were alive in 1787, would you have been a Federalist or Anti-Federalist? Why? What were their basic differences?

References

Declaration of Independence. (2010, June 30). Retrieved from http://www.loc.gov/rr/program/bib/ourdocs/DeclarInd.html

Hamilton, A., Jay, J., & Madison, J. (2001). *The Federalist* G. W. Carey & J. McClellan (eds.). Indianapolis, IN: Liberty Fund. (Original work published 1788).

Kammen, M. (ed.). (1986). *The origins of the American Constitution: A documentary history.* New York, NY: Penguin.

Kimberling, W. C. (1992). *The electoral college.* Retrieved from http://www.fec.gov/pdf/eleccoll.pdf

Locke, John. (1988). *Two treatises of government* Peter Laslett, (ed.). New York, NY: Cambridge University Press. (Original work published 1690).

Our Documents. (n.d.). Retrieved from http://www.ourdocuments.gov/ index.php?flash=true&

United States Constitution. (n.d.). Retrieved from http://topics.law.cornell. edu/constitution. (Original work published 1878).

Chapter Three
Federalism
Charles H. "Trey" Wilson III

Learning Objectives

After covering the topic of federalism, students should understand:

1. What federalism is and how the U.S. Constitution allocates powers to both the national and state governments to create a federalist system in the United States.
2. The evolution of American federalism from inception to its modern manifestations. The concepts of "dual federalism," "cooperative federalism," "New Federalism," and "New Age Federalism."
3. The future of federalism in light of recent Supreme Court decisions affecting the distribution of power between the national and state governments.

Abstract

Federalism in the United States refers to a governmental system outlined in the Constitution in which power is distributed between the national government and the state governments. The U.S. Constitution allocates power to the national government chiefly through the enumerated powers, the implied powers, the power to tax, and the Supremacy Clause, and to the state governments through the "Reserved Powers Clause." The nuances of federalism have evolved and changed in the U.S. as views altered over time about how power should be shared between the federal government and state governments. Political scientists routinely use labels such as "dual federalism," "cooperative federalism," "New Federalism," and "New Age Federalism" to describe the various incarnations of federalism. The future of federalism may be dynamic depending upon how the U.S. Supreme Court chooses to adjudicate cases in which the distribution of power in government is at issue.

Introduction

Federalism may be defined as a political system in which power is divided between a central government and multiple constituent, provincial, or state governments. While the U.S. Constitution never expressly states anything like "the United States will have a federalist system," various provisions in the document confer or deny powers to the national government while others reserve or withhold powers for the fifty state governments. In this way, a federalist system was created for America. This system has evolved and changed over time and continues to do so today, as a kind of tension has grown to exist between the central and the state governments over which will exercise power. Understanding this system and its nuances is requisite to fully grasping American government, since federalism is at the heart of how government is organized in the United States.

Why Federalism?

For the framers, federalism was a kind of middle ground between two other systems of government that had proven to be unsatisfactory for Americans. In one such system (called a **unitary** system by political scientists), a centralized, national government retained virtually all governmental power, as in the case of the British monarchy. Many colonists believed they had been subjected to tyrannical oppression at the hands of the king, and so were wary of conferring too much power on what they feared would become a distant and unfamiliar national government. However, the opposite extreme of government was equally undesirable. While the **confederal** system created by the Articles of Confederation did create a national government, the Articles gave relatively little power to that central government and instead reserved most governing power for the several states. While this provided for a great deal of local autonomy, the result was a puny national government. Indeed, this national government was too weak and ill-equipped to respond to even internal crises such as Shays' Rebellion (a minor uprising of Massachusetts farmers angered over an ailing economy), let alone external threats from powerful neighbors. A **federal** system empowered to some extent both the state and national governments, thereby combining the benefits of both.

Creating a Federalist System
Empowering a National Government

Four items contained in the U.S. Constitution serve to confer the lion's share of power on the national government: the "enumerated powers," the "implied powers," the "Supremacy Clause," and the power to tax.

To enumerate something simply means to count it off, one by one, as in a list. Hence, the **enumerated powers** are essentially contained in list form in the U.S. Constitution, specifically in Article I, Section 8. This text gives "Congress," which should be taken to mean the national government, the power to do many specific things, including coining money, establishing post offices, and maintaining a navy, among others.

While the enumerated powers specify many things that the federal government can do, the framers knew that they could never create an exhaustive list of powers for the Congress. After all, times change, and much would doubtlessly occur in the future that they could not even anticipate, let alone write about. Consequently, the framers included language in Article I, Section 8 which has come to be known as the **Elastic Clause**, so-called because it lets the federal government expand and stretch its power under certain circumstances. The Elastic Clause provides that Congress shall have the power to make all laws which are "necessary and proper" for executing any of its enumerated powers (The Elastic Clause is sometimes referred to as the "Necessary and Proper Clause" because of this language). The result is that, providing Congress can demonstrate that a law it likes is both necessary and proper, it may be able to do something that might, at first glance, seem beyond the scope of its enumerated powers. Of course, determining exactly how "necessary" and "proper" should be defined in any given circumstance is often a matter of fierce debate in government, and anyone who does not like the law in question will certainly argue that it is unnecessary and improper. Political scientists refer to powers the national government derives from the Elastic Clause and the enumerated powers as **implied powers** since, while they are not overtly stated, such powers may be fairly construed to exist.

Article VI of the U.S. Constitution contains what is referred to as the **Supremacy Clause**. Occasionally, both the federal government and one or more state governments might each claim some power to do something—for example, the power to regulate the issuance of monopolies on steamboat ferry transportation across the Hudson Bay (see the Supreme Court case of *Gibbons v. Ogden* later in the chapter). The Supremacy Clause states that in these conflicts, the federal government shall be presumed to win out over the state government(s). Chief Justice John Marshall put it more eloquently in the judicial opinion he wrote in 1819 for the U.S. Supreme Court case of *McCulloch v. Maryland*. Marshall declared, "the

Constitution and the laws made in pursuance thereof are supreme…they control the constitution and laws of the respective States, and cannot be controlled by them." The framers included this provision because they had seen first-hand under the Articles of Confederation how the nation could suffer under an impotent national government.

Finally, the national government derives much of its power from the ability to tax. To avoid the myriad problems of inadequate revenue that surfaced under the Articles of Confederation, the framers empowered the federal government with the ability to levy charges against such things as activities, products, and, with the Sixteenth Amendment, income. The power to tax can be a powerful tool to shape public policy. Consider, for example, consumption or "sin" taxes imposed by government on everything from alcohol to tobacco products to "gas guzzling" vehicles. Proponents of such taxes hope tacking on additional expenses to the cost of taxed products will discourage people from acquiring them and, eventually, make the products so unattractive to consumers that they disappear from the market.

Empowering State Governments

Like the federal government, state governments derive power from the U.S. Constitution. Regarding state power, Supreme Court Justice Hugo Black once wrote that federalism meant, "a proper respect for state functions, a recognition of the fact that the entire country is made up of a Union of separate State governments, and a continuance of the belief that the National Government will fare best if the States and their institutions are left free to perform their separate functions in their separate ways" (*Younger v. Harris*, 44). Indeed, having lived for a decade with the Articles of Confederation under which states maintained virtually all governmental power, it would have gone without saying for many of the framers that states would retain power under the U.S. Constitution. Consequently, relatively little is stated outright regarding state power in the Constitution's articles. However, Anti-Federalist concerns over the national government usurping too much power eventually led to the inclusion of the Tenth Amendment in the U.S. Constitution. It states, "The powers not delegated to the United States by the Constitution, nor prohibited by it to the States, are reserved to the States respectively, or to the people." Political scientists refer to this bit of text as the **Reserved Powers Clause** and these powers as "reserved powers" or, alternatively, "police powers." While the latter term might conjure up images of men and women in blue brandishing pistols and handcuffs, think of it more broadly. Besides being a noun, "police" can also be a verb. To "police" something essentially means to keep something maintained in good order. In the context of federalism, a state's "police powers" let it exclusively regulate within its borders things like law and order, health, safety, and morality as it sees fit and prohibits the federal government from interfering with state interests in these areas. This explains why some states may permit some practices (such as same-sex marriage or capital punishment), while others do not. Each state is exercising its reserved powers autonomously.

Powers Shared Between (and Denied to) the Federal and State Governments
We have seen how the U.S. Constitution confers power onto the national government and onto state governments to create America's federalist system. However, to completely grasp how federalism functions, we must also understand the concepts of concurrent powers (or shared powers) and prohibited powers (or denied powers). **Concurrent powers** are powers that are held by both the federal and the state governments. For example, both the federal government and the several state governments have the power to establish a court system. This is why the United States has a federal Supreme Court, just as each state has its own state supreme court of last resort for cases moving through the state judicial system. Another example of a shared power would be the power to tax. If you have not already begun doing so, every year around mid-April, you will submit your Federal Income Tax Return, probably the (in)famous I.R.S. Form 1040. In most states, such as Georgia, you will also submit an income tax return to the state you live in around this time as well. Some states, such as Florida, Nevada, and New Hampshire, do not have a state income tax. As the name implies, concurrent powers may be exercised by the states and the national government simultaneously. However, note that states may exercise these shared powers only up to the point that they do not violate or conflict with national law. For example, while the state of Georgia does have the power to tax, the state could not begin taxing goods slated to be exported to other countries through its shipping ports. This is because the U.S. Constitution contains a clause that prohibits export taxes from

being used (note that Georgia and other states can tax *imported* goods—providing they obtain approval from Congress to do so).

The prohibition on export taxes is a good example of a "prohibited power." As the name implies, a **prohibited power** is one that is denied to either the federal government, the state governments, or, at times, denied to both governments. For example, the Constitution contains a clause that reads, "No Title of Nobility shall be granted by the United States." Hence, as nifty as they might sound, there will never be a "John Jones, Duke of Dahlonega" or "Susan Smith, Duchess of Dawsonville"—at least not officially, anyway. Another example of a prohibited power relates to what are called *ex post facto* laws. "*Ex post facto*" is Latin for "after the fact." An *ex post facto* **law** is one that would criminalize some action for the purpose of prosecuting it *after* someone had already performed the action at a time when it was legal to do so. Vengeful politicians in neither the federal government nor any state government can enact such laws. Examples of powers prohibited to only state governments would include the power to make treaties or to coin money. Examples of powers prohibited to only the federal government could include things like establishing a drinking age or setting the age of consent for marriage, since these would be considered state police powers protected from federal government intrusion thanks to the Tenth Amendment.

"Horizontal Federalism" and Relations between the States

The foregoing material describes how the U.S. Constitution allocates (or does not allocate) powers to the national and state governments. Some political scientists qualify this as **vertical federalism** since it describes a dynamic occurring between government on two different levels, federal and state. Just as important, however, is how power is shared *between* the several different governments that all inhabit the state level.

To many people, part of what makes the United States a remarkable country is the heterogeneity of its fifty states. The size, population, resources, natural environment, and political culture of no two states are exactly alike. What is it that keeps big California with its population of over 35 million people and vast resources from trying to throw its weight around against other, smaller states? In fact, several provisions of the Constitution serve to put all the states on one level (i.e., horizontal) playing field. Four of the most significant of these provisions of **horizontal federalism** are the Full Faith and Credit Clause, the Privileges and Immunities Clause, and the Interstate Rendition (a.k.a. Extradition) Clause, which are all contained in Article IV, and interstate compacts.

The **Full Faith and Credit Clause** requires each state to respect "the public Acts, Records, and judicial Proceedings of every other State." Practically speaking, this statement means that contracts and judicial orders arising out of one state will continue to be binding in other states, mostly because it better facilitates national commerce. It is the reason a couple can drive cross-country all night, get married at a 24-hour wedding chapel in Las Vegas, and then return home, still married, even though their ceremony occurred several states away. Assuming the marriage contract was valid in Nevada, the Full Faith and Credit Clause requires that other states recognize it as well. Incidentally, this kind of situation might one day pose an interesting problem: What if Nevada decides to legalize same-sex marriage, just as many other states have amended their state constitutions to prohibit it? Would a state whose constitution specifies that marriage can only occur between a man and a woman be obligated to recognize a same-sex marriage performed for two of its residents in Nevada in light of the Full Faith and Credit Clause? When questions like this come up, the U.S. Supreme Court may be asked to settle the matter. Indeed, Article III of the Constitution states that when a dispute between two states arises, the Supreme Court may exercise original jurisdiction to hear the case, one of the few instances when the Court does not act in an appellate capacity.

Like the Full Faith and Credit Clause, the **Privileges and Immunities Clause** also serves to equalize power distribution between states. This clause guarantees that citizens of one state shall be deemed to possess the same fundamental rights as citizens of all other states. It is occasionally referred to as the "Comity Clause" because it prevents any state from discriminating against visiting citizens from another state in certain respects, which would tend to preserve harmony as people travel between states ("comity" means a friendly social atmosphere, which probably would better come about if everyone thought they were on equal footing with everyone else). Note that this clause applies only to basic constitutional rights such as those discussed in Chapter 11. So, for example, a state might legally charge residents one price to enter a state museum but charge non-state-residents a higher price since museum-going is not a fundamental right protected by the U.S. Constitution.

Interstate Rendition (or perhaps more commonly, if not entirely correctly, referred to as "extradition") occurs when a fugitive apprehended in one state is handed over to the authorities of another state for prosecution for crimes committed in that latter state. To preserve interstate comity, when rendition occurs, it typically does so without much incident. However, occasions have arisen when one state may not want to turn over a fugitive to another state. Perhaps the most celebrated instance of this in recent years came in the legal case of *Puerto Rico v. Branstad*. In this case, an Iowa governor declined to extradite a man charged with homicide in Puerto Rico who had fled to Iowa while released on bail. The man (who was white) stood accused of killing a Hispanic woman, and the governor did not believe he could get a fair trial owing to racial circumstances. The case eventually reached the U.S. Supreme Court, which ruled that federal courts have the power to force states to hand over fugitives thanks to the Extradition Clause in Article IV, Section 2, Clause 2. (See *Puerto Rico v. Branstad*, 483 U.S. 219 [1987]).

Interstate compacts are discussed in Article I, Section 10 of the U.S. Constitution and also serve to harmonize relationships between states. These compacts are legally binding agreements between two or more states to do something that must be approved by Congress before taking effect. They can be on any subject, but often revolve around natural resources (such as lakes and rivers) that touch or flow through multiple states. Signatories to these compacts agree to share power and resources to maintain the common natural resource and prevent any one state from polluting or overusing the resource.

Ultimately, these several provisions of the U.S. Constitution do much to help the fifty states get along. Except for one unfortunate period from 1861 to 1865, horizontal federalism has worked for over two hundred years. This track record should argue powerfully that horizontal federalism is just as important as federalism in the vertical sense when it comes to American government.

The Evolution of Federalism
Early Years: The "Supremacy" Period

Our present understanding of federalism and the manner in which power is allocated between the state governments and the national government did not spring into being overnight. Rather, this understanding has changed over the last two hundred-plus years. This process began with the writing of the U.S. Constitution. The framers meant for that text to communicate much about how power would be distributed; hence, we have the enumerated powers, the implied powers, the reserved powers, etc., discussed earlier. At the same time, the framers meant for their words to be interpreted by future generations. They understood that times would change and that phrases such as "necessary and proper" and words like "supremacy" would have to be qualified in the future to be meaningful in light of those changes. The job of qualifying this constitutional language typically falls to the United States Supreme Court. How that language has been qualified over time by the Court in response to changing times is the evolutionary process of federalism.

This evolution of federalism really commenced in the early 1800s when Chief Justice John Marshall, a very talented jurist, headed the U.S. Supreme Court. In 1819, the Marshall Court heard a case called *McCulloch v. Maryland*, which is often referred to as "the bank case" for reasons soon to become apparent. In a simplified version, things began when Congress chartered a national bank and located a branch office of this bank in Baltimore. Maryland's state legislature, which doubtlessly disliked the idea of added competition for state-owned banks within its borders, responded by levying a steep tax on all banks operating in the state that had not been chartered by Maryland. When James McCulloch, the head of the Baltimore branch of the federal bank, received the tax notice, he refused to pay. The state of Maryland sued McCulloch in state court and, unsurprisingly perhaps, won. McCulloch appealed to the U.S. Supreme Court.

There were two central issues in the case that the Supreme Court was asked to decide, and both related to federalism. The first was, "Did Congress have the authority to charter a bank?" Maryland pointed out that the U.S. Constitution never mentioned such a power; indeed, the word "bank" never even appeared in the document. However, the Supreme Court sided with the federal government's argument on this issue. That argument asserted that it was reasonable to *imply* that Congress should have the power to charter a bank thanks to the Elastic Clause. After all, the Constitution did expressly give Congress the power to issue currency, collect taxes, and to borrow money in the enumerated powers. A bank could assist with doing these things—indeed, the U.S. government claimed it was *necessary* to have a bank to do them efficiently. Also, a national bank was not some arcane, complicated contraption that Congress conjured up out of nowhere. Many countries had national banks of one form or another even back then. Hence, one could say that having a national bank was *proper* as well as necessary for a nation like the United States to thrive. The Supreme Court decided that the federal government had made its case that the national bank was "necessary and proper" to the exercise of Congress's enumerated powers involving revenue and currency. And, according to the Elastic Clause, if something Congress wants to do can be deemed "necessary and proper," then that something is a constitutionally permissible exercise of federal government power.

The second question presented for resolution in *McCulloch v. Maryland* related to taxation. Maryland argued that, assuming the national bank could exist, nothing should stop the state from taxing it. After all, the bank was on Maryland soil and so was potentially a burden to the state, albeit a minor one. The tax would compensate the state for its trouble. The Supreme Court did not buy it. Chief Justice Marshall, who wrote the majority opinion in the case, invoked the Constitution's Supremacy Clause and held that a state law taxing the bank must be trumped by a federal law permitting the bank to operate freely.

McCulloch v. Maryland is an important case in the evolution of federalism because of how the Supreme Court interpreted the Elastic Clause and the Supremacy Clause. In both instances, the Court read the U.S. Constitution in such a way that opened the door for the expansion of the federal government's power. Consider that the Court *could have* qualified "necessary and proper" in such a way that would have made it very difficult for the federal government to characterize anything as either necessary and/or proper. It did not. Rather, the Court put the entire country on notice that satisfying the parameters of the Elastic Clause was something doable. Likewise, the Court could have adopted a more limited definition of "supremacy." Again, it chose not to, sending in the process a clear signal to states that their laws would fare poorly in competition with federal statutes (See *McCulloch v. Maryland*, 17 U.S. 316 [1819]).

Another landmark case affecting federalism came before the Marshall Court only a few years after *McCulloch*. In 1824, the Court heard **Gibbons v. Ogden**, which has come to be known as the "steamboat case"—again for reasons that will soon become apparent. Though the case eventually turned out to be somewhat complicated on several levels, the main issues in dispute were actually fairly simple. Aaron Ogden, who had ties to Robert Fulton, the inventor of the steamboat, had secured exclusive rights from the New York State legislature to operate a steamboat passenger ferry service on the Hudson River between New York and New Jersey. About the same time, Thomas Gibbons, a former business partner of Ogden's, also secured exclusive rights to do roughly the same thing—but his license came from Congress, not a state legislature. Ogden sued to protect his monopoly.

Before the Court, the case turned chiefly on how the **Interstate Commerce Clause** of the Constitution would be interpreted. This clause states that Congress, not the states, shall have the power "To regulate Commerce with foreign Nations, and among the several States, and with the Indian Tribes." No one much disputed that the two steamboat services were operating "among" states. However, the parties to the lawsuit differed over how the word "commerce" in the clause should be defined. Ogden argued that commerce should amount to what people probably typically think of when they think of commerce—namely, exchanging money for goods. Since Ogden's steamboat ferry provided a service, not goods, in exchange for money, he argued that what he did fell outside of the definition of commerce. And, if what he did was not commerce, then the Interstate Commerce Clause could not apply to give Congress the power to issue anything.

The Supreme Court demurred. Justice Marshall wrote that commerce should be broadly defined to include "intercourse, all its branches." So, you would be engaging in commerce if you swapped money for goods, money for services, services for goods, goods for goods, etc. Hence, the Congressional license granted to Gibbons was the valid one since the national government and not the state of New York was constitutionally empowered to regulate commercial activities that involved more than one state, which the steamboat ferry service did. This broad interpretation of what constituted commerce would let Congress use the Interstate Commerce Clause as a rationale to regulate many things over the next two centuries, much to the chagrin of many states. While during this time period the Court would occasionally reformulate its ruling on the matter (sometimes contracting when the clause could apply only to re-expand it at a later time), the clause has still always remained a powerful resource for the federal government (see *Gibbons v. Ogden*, 22 U.S. 1 [1824]).

The final truly significant Supreme Court case that qualified federalism during its age of supremacy was that of *John Barron v. The Mayor and City Council of Baltimore*, which was decided in 1833. Barron owned part of a lucrative wharf in the Baltimore harbor. He sued Baltimore for damages, claiming that when the city had diverted the flow of several streams to facilitate road work, the diversion caused sand and silt to collect around his wharf. Barron asserted that this hurt his business by making the water around the wharf too shallow to accommodate many big vessels that sought to dock and unload their cargos there. Barron won the suit in the lower court, but Baltimore appealed the ruling, eventually all the way up to the Supreme Court.

The key issue in the case was whether or not state government takings of private property for public use (known in the law as "eminent domain," which, essentially, this was) required just compensation to individuals deprived of property. The Court held that while the Fifth Amendment of the U.S. Constitution did require this, the requirement only applied to the *federal* government and not the several state governments. Importantly, the Court essentially ruled that the freedoms guaranteed by the Bill of Rights did not restrict the state governments but, rather, applied only to the federal government. This qualifier was important in the development of federalism because it furthered a divide between federal and state governments (see *Barron v. Mayor of Baltimore*, 32 U.S. 243 [1833]).

The Era of "Dual Federalism"

While the Supreme Court's rulings in both *McCulloch* and *Gibbons* interpreted constitutional language in such a way that favored the federal government over the states, this would not always be the outcome. Over the next several decades following these decisions, the Court would be asked many times to decide just how far federal government power extended. The justices occasionally ruled against the federal government, thereby firming up the power of state governments.

Perhaps the most (in)famous instance of this occurred in the 1857 case of *Dred Scott v. Sandford*. In this dispute, an African American slave sued for his freedom after moving with his owners from the slave-holding South to a free state in the North, believing his residence on free soil had ended his slave status. In an extremely controversial opinion, the Court held that Scott and other slaves should be "regarded as beings of an inferior order" not considered citizens of the United States, and so prohibited from filing suit in federal court. From a federalism standpoint, the case is significant because the Court declared that Congress lacked the power to ban slavery in the western territories such as Kansas and Nebraska, something it had attempted to do with the Missouri Compromise of 1820. States, then, and their citizens, would determine the fate of the "peculiar institution" within their borders, not the federal government (see *Dred Scott v. Sandford*, 60 U.S. 393 [1856]).

Supreme Court rulings like that in *Dred Scott* that conferred power on state governments or rulings like those in *McCulloch* and *Gibbons* that conferred power on the national government collectively created what political scientists refer to as **dual federalism**. Under this scheme, the federal government and the state governments are viewed as each having their own "sphere of influence" in which each exercises power and into which the other may not encroach. The national government derives its power to control everything in its sphere largely from the expressed and implied powers of the U.S. Constitution. The state governments control their spheres and keep the federal government out of their business largely thanks to the Reserved Powers Clause in the Tenth Amendment.

A time-honored model used by American government students to visualize the arrangement of dual federalism is a two-layer-cake. Think of the federal government as being the top layer and the state governments as being the bottom layer. Each otherwise identical layer of cake is analogous to a sphere of influence and each is separated from the other by a thick layer of gooey icing, an insulating confection whipped together by the U.S. Constitution.

The basic belief in dual federalism controlled American constitutional jurisprudence until the 1930s. Despite the notion of duality, the federal government's overall power as compared to the states arguably, if gradually, increased during this interval. Perhaps the biggest factor for this increase was the Civil War. Ironically, this conflict that started out to increase the power of state governments ended up augmenting the national government's power in many ways. For example, the federal income tax came into being. This taxation gave the national government a revenue source it had not possessed before. The tax would eventually become a permanent fixture in American life with the ratification of the Sixteenth Amendment and provide the federal government with vast capital resources (see U.S. Dept. of the Treasury, "History of the U.S. Tax System").

Also out of the Civil War came the Thirteenth, Fourteenth, and Fifteenth Amendments to the U.S. Constitution. These so-called "Civil War Amendments" all dealt with race and sought to uplift free-blacks in whatever state they lived. However, judicial rulings like *Plessy v. Ferguson* (discussed in detail in Chapter 11) often thwarted this aim by returning power to states to make their own civil rights laws.

Some years after the war, another kind of fight would increase the federal government's power. Congress enacted the Sherman Antitrust Act in 1890 to combat the growth of corporate monopolies in America. This act permitted the federal government, not the states, to regulate many aspects of business and commerce in the name of protecting consumers from anti-competitive practices.

While the Civil War Amendments and the Sherman Act empowered the federal government, not everything during the era of dual federalism was a loss for state governments. Supreme Court rulings in some cases, like *Plessy*, empowered states. For example, states enjoyed relative autonomy to legislate in the areas of voting and civil rights within their own separate spheres.

The Era of "Cooperative Federalism"

Dual federalism became old news in 1933 with the advent of the New Deal. "New Deal" was the name given to a collection of radical government programs championed by President Franklin Roosevelt to get the United States out of the economic quagmire that was the "Great Depression." Almost any problem one could think of (unemployment, crime, etc.) loomed large in America during this age. About the only entity anyone believed was sizable enough to even stand a chance at combating these ills was the federal government. Congress enacted law after law, creating new federal agencies geared toward promoting some aspect of economic recovery. These agencies had names like the Civilian Conservation Corps or the Tennessee Valley Authority, but were more often known by their initials. Collectively, history somewhat jokingly knows the CCC, the TVA, and others as the "Alphabet Soup Agencies." The laws that created them demanded cooperation from multiple levels of government.

The laws associated with the New Deal demanded that multiple levels of government (federal, state, and, now for the first time, often municipal governments) work together on implementation. For example, the federal government might do something like provide funds to a state that would then hire some of its unemployed citizens to, in turn, complete a roadwork project for a city. Because of the governmental interconnectedness inherent in this arrangement, political scientists refer to this as **cooperative federalism**. Recall that under dual federalism, the different levels of government operated autonomously within their separate spheres of influence—little cooperation there, to be sure. With the advent of this new kind of federalism, the lines between governmental spheres blurred and became more fluid.

Of course, this changing federalism requires a change of metaphor as well since a slice of layer cake will always reveal two distinct parts separated from each other by frosting. Think of cooperative federalism as being illustrated by a piece of marble cake instead. A slice of that confection—when viewed from the side—reveals a swirling, intermixing of light and dark cake. Just as it is difficult to discern precisely where one cake starts and the other stops in a marble cake, cooperative federalism accepts that the boundaries of power for federal, state, and local governments are no longer fixed and distinct.

You will probably have surmised that the shift from dual federalism to cooperative federalism was a radical one. Many people feared this unprecedented growth of the federal bureaucracy and some filed legal challenges to New Deal legislation that made it all the way to the Supreme Court. Initially, the Court overturned much of the legislation. The justices often agreed with challengers that aspects of the New Deal conferred too much power on the national government.

President Roosevelt fumed. In private, he derisively referred to the justices as the "nine old men." Publically, he proposed a plan that would essentially have given him and a sympathetic Congress the power to expand the Supreme Court from nine to fifteen justices. Of course, the additional jurists he would install would be New Deal supporters.

Roosevelt's **court-packing plan**, as it came to be known, proved to be largely unpopular with the American people, who resented his effort to tamper with the judiciary. However, merely proffering the plan may have had the effect FDR desired. Perhaps a bit spooked by the court-packing threat, the high court began ruling in favor of much New Deal legislation starting around 1935. These rulings cleared the way for Congress to increase its sway over states (see William Leuchtenburg's essay for more on court-packing).

Since the New Deal era, the primary tool employed by the federal government to induce states and municipalities to do their share of the cooperating in cooperative federalism was something called a **categorical grant**. A grant is simply an assignment of funds—usually a lot of funds when it is a federal program in question. The federal government had provided a few grant programs to states over the years prior to the Great Depression (such as the Morrill Land Grant Act of 1862, which gave states federal land to establish public colleges), but these were nothing compared to New Deal grant programs in either size or scope. The term "categorical" is meant to describe how Congress doles out federal dollars to states to accomplish distinct things in some particular area—as opposed to giving states money to spend however they might wish.

Using categorical grants, Congress can, for all intents and purposes, regulate just about anything. Indeed, even though the Tenth Amendment reserves some powers to states, Congress can often tempt states with grants to induce them to police something in a way desired by the federal government. For example, there was a period of time during the 1970s where many oil-rich Arab countries instituted an oil embargo against the United States, mostly to punish Americans for historical support of Israel. Gasoline prices spiked, hours-long lines at pumps were common, and many places ran out of gas entirely as refinery oil supplies dwindled. The federal government wanted the nation to drive slower to conserve fuel. However, setting speed limits is a classic police power and lowering them is something only individual states could do thanks to the Tenth Amendment. Still, the federal government would get its way. It offered states large grants of highway improvement money if they would only lower their interstate speed limits to 55 mph. Hungry for those highway funds, virtually all did so in a relatively short time. Hence, the national government accomplished its goal almost just as if it had regulated things directly (see Edward Weiner's essay for more on the history of the national speed limit).

Beginning in the 1960s, the tone of cooperation between the states and the federal government began to change. Prior to that decade, most states had been generally content to work with the federal government under the terms of categorical grants, believing as they did that the two levels of government shared common aims. However, as the federal government advanced programs to combat poverty and discrimination under the Kennedy and Johnson administrations, many states—particularly in the South—abandoned this view. This occurred largely because the national government found ways to bypass state legislatures en route to achieving national objectives. Local governments and even community organizations received much federal funding, since Congress believed they would be more likely than several staunchly conservative states to spend money in ways benefitting African Americans and other marginalized groups. From many states' points of view, the cooperation in federalism had disappeared.

Equally vexing for states was the fact that many of the federal government programs that did emerge in the 1960s and 1970s contained what are known as **unfunded federal mandates**. Put simply, this term means that the federal government enacted some regulation that states were required to abide by but gave no money to states to spend for this purpose. For example, in 1974, Congress passed the Safe Drinking Water Act. Essentially, this act stated that public water sources had to meet Environmental Protection Agency standards of purity within a given time frame. While everyone will agree that clean drinking water is a good thing, Congress left to the states and local governments the responsibility and expense of getting water supplies tested and of removing pollutants and impurities if any were found. Governments that did not comply with the act faced stiff federal penalties and, in extreme circumstances, could be forced to find some other water supply—however inconvenient or expensive doing so might be. State and local governments, already short of time and money, bristled at what they saw as unreasonable burdens imposed by SDWA. This and other unfunded federal mandates would eventually be amended or repealed so as to lessen the burden on state and local governments; however while they were in effect, relations between these governments and the federal government strained.

"New Federalism" and Beyond

Ronald Reagan assumed the presidency in 1980 with an eye toward vastly curbing federal government power that had increased thanks to the growth of unfunded mandates and the deterioration of cooperative federalism. Reagan, a conservative political thinker dubious of big government, served as governor of the state of California from 1967 to 1975. He had experienced first-hand the frustration visited upon states by the federal government and unfunded mandates. Reagan sought to shrink federal government power and return more autonomy to the states by greatly reducing unfunded mandates and by changing how federal grants operated. In doing so, he would be building on groundwork laid by another Republican president, Richard Nixon, who had initiated a practice of "revenue sharing" in 1972 in an effort to shift some power and responsibility back to state and local government through a federal assistance program.

Political scientists refer to what Reagan ushered in as **New Federalism** because of its novelty. It had several key features. Soon after assuming office, President Reagan rallied public opinion to urge Congress to make drastic cuts in both federal domestic programs and in income tax rates. This action created an environment in which the federal government took in less revenue and had fewer programs to utilize in disbursing what it did collect to the states. Consequently, state and local governments had to become more self-sufficient, which lessened the power the federal government had over them.

But things did not stop there. Another key feature of New Federalism was a heavy reliance on **block grants**. Recall that in cooperative federalism, the federal government offered states and municipalities categorical grants. These grants came with many strings attached and required states to spend any federal dollars they received doing very specific things. Block grants are very unlike categorical grants because states and local governments receive sums of money along with better flexibility in determining how the funding can be spent. Additionally, federal government oversight or monitoring of block grant funds is relatively light. All of these actions had the effect of reducing the influence of the federal government over state and local governments since the power of the purse is effectively transferred to the latter. While block grants had been around in one form or another since the 1960s or so, New Federalism employed them with a gusto not yet seen in the United States to give states increased agency in governing areas ranging from healthcare to education to transportation, etc.

The trends of New Federalism and the downsizing of the federal government generally continued to some extent for many years after President Reagan left office in 1989. For example, when Bill Clinton assumed the presidency in 1993, his administration began championing something some political scientists have come to refer to as **New Age Federalism**. The name may be a somewhat tongue-in-cheek label. "New Age" refers to a modern spiritual movement that stresses peace and introspection. Under New Age Federalism, Washington, D.C. supposedly gently encouraged states to explore new ideas and options for policymaking—yet, ultimately, had no trouble imposing federal solutions on problems that states failed to solve.

Perhaps in response to President Clinton's policies, in 1994, Republicans gained a majority in Congress while advancing something they referred to as the "Contract with America." This "contract" was essentially a collection of campaign promises and priority statements, many of which related to decreasing the size of the federal government. Some provisions of the Contract would eventually become law; many would not. Political scientists and other political commentators differ on just how much the Contract succeeded in curtailing the size and power of the federal government, but such was certainly its aim.

While President George W. Bush campaigned on a platform of continuing to return power to state and local governments in 2000, the events of September 11, 2001, made doing so largely infeasible. Rather, the federal bureaucracy and the power wielded by it swelled as America fought enemies foreign and domestic and, later, grappled with natural disasters and economic crises. The direction federalism will take under the administration of President Barack Obama is not yet clear. By mid-2010, the White House had overseen passage of a historic health care bill and a huge overhaul of financial regulation. Critics asserted that such measures could only lead to bigger national government, claims Obama supporters denied. Time will tell what impact these administrations will exert on the evolution of federalism.

Federalism and the Modern Supreme Court: A (Slow) Return to States' Rights?

For most of the twentieth century, the U.S. Supreme Court generally sided with the federal government when adjudicating legal questions of federalism. Consequently, the power of the national government expanded just as that of the various states contracted. This judicial trend would shift somewhat beginning in the 1980s. As part and parcel of New Federalism, President Reagan appointed jurists who attempted to return some power to states through their legal opinions. On topics ranging from gun control to abortion to gambling on Indian reservations to physician assisted suicide, the Supreme Court handed down decisions that restricted Congress's power and rendered the states more sovereign. The Court's reversal has not been absolute, however. For example, in a pair of cases decided in 2004 and 2006, the justices ruled that under the Americans with Disabilities Act, Congress could require states to make their courthouses and prison facilities reasonably accessible to handicapped individuals. Whether these holdings herald a return for the Court to old habits or are merely aberrations along a path toward recognizing greater state sovereignty remains to be seen.

Civic Engagement and Federalism

The sheer size and scope of the United States government has doubtlessly prompted more than one person to ask, "What difference can a single individual possibly make in governing?" Indeed, unless that one person happens to be the president of the United States, a Supreme Court justice, or the like, it will probably be difficult to directly influence national policy to any great degree. However, thanks to federalism, other opportunities for civic engagement actually exist for just about anyone. Federalism encourages democratic participation by dividing government powers and responsibilities between different levels of government—and some of those levels are very accessible. The trick is to know what level of government to approach about any given issue. Given the overlapping complexity of government, discerning the layers can oftentimes be difficult. However, with diligence and an understanding of how federalism operates, one can tease out the correct federal, state, or local entity to approach about virtually any problem. The Internet can be a citizen's best friend in accomplishing this task. While the mechanics of federalism are still fresh in your mind, make it a point to visit the websites of your local, state, and federal governments. As you browse those pages, you will begin to get a sense of what agencies and departments deal with what and, just as importantly, how you can contact them. Do this and you will be doing some good, since, as Thomas Jefferson observed, "Whenever the people are well-informed, they can be trusted with their own government."

Discussion Questions

1. What is federalism? What powers does the U.S. Constitution confer on the national government? What powers does the U.S. Constitution confer on the several state governments? What powers are shared by and denied to both the federal and the state governments?
2. What is "horizontal federalism" and what are the parts of the U.S. Constitution that function to place all states on a level playing field?
3. How were the Supreme Court rulings in the cases of *McCulloch v. Maryland* and *Gibbons v. Ogden* important for federalism?
4. Compare and contrast "dual federalism," "cooperative federalism," "New Federalism," and "New Age Federalism."
5. What is the current state of U.S. Supreme Court jurisprudence on the topic of federalism?

References

Leuchtenburg, W. E. (1969). Franklin D. Roosevelt's Supreme Court 'Packing' Plan. In H. M. Hollingsworth & W. F. Holmes (Eds.), *Essays on the New Deal* (69-115). Austin, TX: University of Texas Press.

"Safe Drinking Water Act (SDWA)." (P.L. 93-523), *United States Statutes at Large.* 88 Stat. 1660.

U.S. Dept. of the Treasury. (2010, December 5th). *History of the U.S. tax system.* Retrieved from http://www.treasury.gov/resource-center/faqs/Taxes/Pages/historyrooseveltmessage.aspx

Weiner, E. (1992). *Urban transportation planning in the US - A historical overview/Nov 1992.*Retrieved from http://ntl.bts.gov/DOCS/utp.html.

Court Cases

Younger v. Harris. 401 U.S. 37. (1971).

McCulloch v. Maryland. 17 U.S. 316. (1819).

Puerto Rico v. Branstad. 483 U.S. 219. (1987).

Barron v. Mayor of Baltimore. 32 U.S. 243. (1833).

Dred Scott v. Sandford. 60 U.S. 393. (1856).

Gibbons v. Ogden. 22 U.S. 1. (1824).

Chapter Four
Political Socialization and the Media
Maria J. Albo and Barry D. Friedman

Learning Objectives

After covering the topic of political socialization, students should understand:

1. The impact of political socialization on our norms, values, and expectations of government.
2. The universal values that all Americans share, and how we differ in applying those values.
3. The various ways in which Americans participate in the political process and why.
4. The connection between public opinion and public policy.
5. The role of the communications media in the political socialization process and policymaking.

Abstract

In every nation, people are subjected to a process that political scientists and sociologists refer to as political socialization. Through this process, children are coaxed into embracing the belief that the political system is legitimate, and then learn how to be participants in the political system. In the United States, children learn to show respect for the American flag and to recite the Pledge of Allegiance, and their parents and teachers exhort them to recognize the legitimacy of government officials and institutions that make and enforce laws. Mechanisms of political socialization endeavor to reinforce these behaviors and beliefs throughout adulthood. There is significant evidence that the political socialization cues to which affluent children are exposed differ from those to which working class children are exposed: Affluent children are guided to participate and lead, while working class children are geared toward passivity and compliance. Hence, the political socialization process has the additional effect of restraining the social forces that might otherwise disturb the existence of significant economic inequity.

Americans and Government

In virtually all political science courses, we learn about the complex institutions of governmental and political activity. In an "American Government" course, we, for the most part, focus on American political institutions and their role in our society. But in this chapter we examine what Americans think about politics, and how this thinking affects our political behavior. Many Americans will advocate passionately that their political beliefs are superior to the beliefs of others, that their political party and its candidates are superior to other parties and candidates, and that their country is better than other countries. Without necessarily evaluating whether these declarations are true or not, we nevertheless observe that people usually develop their opinions and affiliations by adopting the opinions and affiliations of their parents, their schoolteachers, their classmates, their friends, their coworkers, and the communications media.

Americans are a patriotic group; a 2006 poll showed that 85 percent of Americans were either "extremely proud" or "very proud" to be Americans. According to researchers, "studies consistently show that the percentages of people expressing their enthusiasm and pride for their country are, in fact, higher in the United States than in any other country" (Bresler et al., 2007, p. 135). This deep attachment is not an accident, but a result of **political socialization**, "the process by which an individual acquires attitudes, beliefs and values relating to the political system of which he is a member and to his own role as citizen within that political system" (Greenberg, 1970, p. 165). The implications of political socialization are a sense of patriotism and support for the government that continues throughout life. This loyalty is apparent throughout our country and is demonstrated in values that are shared by most Americans.

Political socialization is a lifelong process. It begins virtually from birth when the very small children taught that they are Americans and that they ought to be enormously proud of that fact. In school, "civics" education begins at the elementary level—in fact, in kindergarten or first grade. It is likely to be the very first day of school when the pupil is taught to recite the Pledge of Allegiance to the U.S. flag. The teaching of the "Star Spangled Banner" follows almost immediately. Symbolism is a subtle but key instrument of political socialization. Children are shown photographs of Mount Vernon when they learn about George Washington: They see the stately mansion, and develop respect for the Father of our Country. They are shown photographs of historic, famous members of Congress, appearing statesmanlike in debate. Images of the Lincoln Memorial, Washington Monument, and U.S. Capitol are all intended to build reverence among American children and adults for government institutions and leadership. Political socialization is necessary to instill feelings of patriotism and love for one's country in citizens. This process exists in all cultures and is crucial for the continuation of national identity. Political socialization takes place throughout childhood. Dawson, Prewitt, and Dawson (1977, pp. 21-23) describe the stages by which political socialization takes place in a child. During the *politicization* stage, the child begins to recognize that authority figures other than her parents have to be taken into account. During the *personalization stage,* a child begins to recognize the president of the United States as the personification of government (symbolic "chief of state") and learns to respect his role as the "head of government." The *idealization stage* follows, in which a child perceives the president as "protective, helpful, trustworthy, intelligent, hardworking, persistent, correct in his judgments, and well qualified as a leader." Finally, during the *institutionalism stage,* a child's idealization is transformed into support for the political system. While adult opinions are understood as the end product of youthful political socialization, the process continues throughout life.

Agents of Socialization

There are several actors involved in the political socialization process, collectively known as **agents of socialization.** Some of the most common agents of socialization are family, schools, religious institutions, peer groups, and the communications media. Each plays a unique and important role in the political socialization process.

Family

Socialization began on the day you were born and were assigned a pink or blue blanket. Parents are responsible for passing along widely accepted norms and beliefs so that children can become functional members of society. Therefore, most childhood socialization is deliberate on the part of parents (e.g., having good manners), but political socialization is often not deliberate as children are generally not "taught" politics, unless one's family happens to be very politically motivated or part of a political legacy, such as the Kennedy family or the Bush family.

In reality, most of our initial perceptions and ideas about political matters come from overhearing adult conversations and observing adult behaviors. We may have heard Mom discussing an upcoming election with a friend or heard Dad complaining about paying taxes every April. All of these experiences shape our early views and expectations of government, which stay with us for our lifetime. This idea is known as the **primacy principle,** which states that what is learned first is learned best (and retained the longest). The **structuring principle,** on the other hand, states that what is learned first structures later learning that generally occurs in schools. While both theories have merit, researchers acknowledge that the role of the family is important but is also limited and competes with the other agents of socialization that enter later in life. However, party identification and opinions about major issues are usually transmitted from parents to children, much like religious beliefs.

Schools

Following the family, the next major agent of political socialization is school. It is in school where you likely got your first formal lesson in civics education when you were taught to recite the Pledge of Allegiance, sing the "Star Spangled Banner", and recognize key national landmarks. These demonstrations of patriotism are necessary exercises designed to instill American norms and values into the nations' schoolchildren while creating a lifelong bond to the nation. This step is essential for the preservation of the state and is practiced in all countries. Easton and Dennis (1965, p. 41) note, "But for the fact that each new generation is able to learn a body of political orientations from its predecessors, no given political system would be able to persist."

While our schools are remarkably effective in promoting loyalty and patriotism in students, the influence of the schools is limited. First, schools tend to promote a president-centered view of American government. The president is idealized and understood to be very powerful, benevolent, and protective. The president is a critical point of control for a child in the political socialization process, and a presidency-centered view of government lingers throughout adolescence. While this is an essential component of national pride, the president-centered view focuses on government as an "all powerful" institution and suggests the authoritative role of the government. Second, while the schools will stress the importance of voting, very little attention is given to the role of an individual in a democracy. Hess and Torney (1967) explain that most civics education does not involve the structure, institutions, and processes of national, state, and local government; rather, most of that instruction involves compliance with rules and authorities. According to Hess and Torney, "the school focuses on obligations and the right to vote but does not offer the child sufficient understanding of procedures open to individuals for legitimately influencing government. Nor does it adequately explain and emphasize the importance of group action to achieve desirable ends" (1967, p. 218). Indeed, schools mostly promote a **duty-based model of citizenship,** which is discussed in detail in Chapter 15. Schoolteachers purposefully avoid controversial political issues and discussion of the shady side of politics in the classroom. This lack leaves students with an idealized view of government and unprepared to navigate the complicated political world.

Peers and the Workplace

Peer groups rarely have a substantial influence on political views, as young people tend to affiliate with acquaintances of the same socioeconomic status and probably just reinforce the opinions and attitudes of the family. The main exception to this rule is when a public policy issue is specifically relevant to young people (e.g., Vietnam War, drinking age). When these types of issues dominate the public policy agenda, peers can be very influential on each other in mobilizing collective action.

Religious Groups, Interest Groups, and Professional Associations

Although the United States has no "state church," which obstructs the development of a moral consensus, religious institutions and organizations regularly seek input into policymaking through direct lobbying efforts by influencing congregants and members. The role of religious organizations in the life of Americans is prominent. The Roman Catholic Church has taken a stance on abortion issues and the Christian Right has instituted a conservatism movement; both have been influential in policymaking.

Individuals may also join interest groups or professional associations for a wide variety of reasons including affiliation, a sense of purpose, fulfillment of duty, determination to have influence, opportunity to exert leadership, or desire for membership benefits. These groups can be very influential over their members, but members will have little input in policy. For more information, refer to Chapter 5.

The Communications Media

As the final agent of socialization, the communications media have taken on an increasing role in our lives both socially and politically, as the average American spends hours each day reading the newspaper, watching television, listening to the radio, and surfing the Internet. Television especially has exposed more people to information and institutional symbols than previous generations experienced. Listening to the radio or watching the television was the forerunner of what we now call "multi-tasking." As a reporter reads the news, the telephone rings, dinner is served, and the children are made ready for bed. Therefore, the hallmark of radio and television news reporting has always been simplicity and brevity. The words, sounds, and images of broadcast news are fleeting; even if listeners and viewers try to concentrate, they will fail to absorb some of the words and names. Also, in terms of time duration, a radio or television news report will typically last no more than 30 minutes, less the amount of time necessarily set aside for commercial advertisements. Journalism professor Charles H. Brown once wrote:

> *In comparison with the newspaper, both radio and television suffer because they lack completeness and comprehensiveness in their coverage. Both tend to skim the surface of the news. The typical radio and television news program gives only the highlights of an event, frequently only a half-minute or minute of time being devoted to the report. People who want fuller details, and there are many of them, have to go to a newspaper. . . [T]he newspaper can be read anywhere and anytime. A radio or television newscast, once given, is gone forever. . .* (Brown, 1957, pp. 292 293)

The opportunities for being misunderstood are more numerous for radio and television than they are for the newspaper. The chief factor that leads to misunderstanding in spoken journalism is that the listener has only one chance to grasp the meaning. In reading the newspaper a person can go back over material and figure out the meaning of a word or sentence if it is not clear at first, but in listening to a broadcast a second chance is denied him

As Americans' lifestyles have changed—for example, the role of "housewife" is essentially extinct—a frantic schedule has evolved, leaving little time for the luxury of reading a newspaper. The afternoon metropolitan newspaper is a thing of the past, and morning newspapers appear to be in their death throes. Increasingly, Americans are obtaining their news from the airwaves, cable, and the Internet, and sources of news are adapting to Americans' shortened attention spans. The result can be described as a theater of the absurd. A news report that cannot be accompanied by some kind of action-oriented video, like the president debarking from Air Force One, is unlikely to survive the final production meeting. In 1982, disgruntled CBS News reporters leaked the network executives' decision to convert the Tiffany Network's news program from serious news to "infotainment." Observers have complained that television reporters, given the choice between reporting the content of a candidate's well-thought-out speech about foreign affairs or presenting video showing the candidate trip on a step as he leaves the platform, will highlight the candidate's mishap.

The rise of 24-hour news stations has further increased this influence, as we now have unlimited access to news. Despite the fact that the average American watches over three hours of television daily, individuals who depend on the general news media for their information are most likely to be uninformed about political matters (Anderson, 2011, p. 65). Any hope that Ted Turner's invention of the 24-hour cable news channel—i.e., CNN (Cable News Network)—would bring about more comprehensive coverage of political news has vanished, as the cable news channels have become dominated by highly partisan, inflammatory commentary. The commentators, such as Glenn Beck, Sean Hannity, and Keith Olbermann, seek out viewers of the same ideological inclination, question the character of political rivals, and introduce panelists whose job (if they want to be invited back) is to entertain the viewers with overheated rhetoric. The result is not an informed electorate. Rather, the bombast creates a highly agitated, alarmed public that is highly suspicious of anyone who is trying to craft bipartisan solutions to pressing national problems. The president is under continuous, withering attack, which weakens his ability to persuade other policymakers to cooperate.

Polarized America?

If you watch the news, it may seem that Americans just cannot agree on policy issues. While our current political climate would suggest otherwise, as Americans we are not really all that different from one another. In actuality, Americans are, for the most part, a remarkably cohesive group. The political socialization process is very successful in deeply rooting a sense of universal pride and emotional attachment to the United States. Every time you watch a fireworks display on Independence Day, sing the national anthem at a baseball game, or sit down to Thanksgiving dinner, you are demonstrating pride for your country. In addition to these universal displays of patriotism, there are four uniquely American characteristics that are valued from coast to coast. These universal American values are the belief in political equality, the value of individual freedoms, the mandate of consent of the governed, and faith in the free-enterprise system.

The concept of **equality**, the idea that "all men are created equal" and should, therefore, have equal access to the political system, may have been a theme of the Declaration of Independence but was not a reality until the mid-twentieth century with the enactment of the Civil Rights Act of 1964 and the Voting Rights Act of 1965. The United States government is founded on the principle that every American is entitled to participate in political activity. As Thomas Jefferson stated in the Declaration of Independence:

> *We hold these truths to be self-evident, that all men are created equal, that they are endowed by their Creator with certain inalienable Rights, that among these are life, liberty and the pursuit of happiness. That to secure these rights, Governments are instituted among men, deriving their just powers from the consent of the governed. That whenever any form of Government becomes destructive to these ends, it is the Right of the People to alter and abolish it, and to institute new Government, laying its foundation on such principles and organizing its powers in such form, as to them shall seem most likely to affect their Safety and Happiness.*

Today the basic premise of political equality, the idea that all citizens should have input in government, is widely accepted. However, while we can reach a consensus that political equality is an ideal principle, we know in practice that this has not traditionally been the case. Are all men truly created equal? The answer is not as simple as yes or no. Individuals are born under various circumstances (children of illegal immigrants, children born to poverty, children with disabilities, etc.), which inherently limit their ability to reach full equality. Therefore, the government has, from time to time, created policies designed to offer protections and create opportunities for minority groups in an effort to promote equality. These programs tend to be very controversial and are subject to much debate in our system.

In addition to equality, Americans strongly value **personal freedoms,** the belief that individuals should be able to decide what is best for themselves and exercise those decisions with limited government interference. This philosophy is evident in the Bill of Rights, which protects states and individuals from national government legislation that abridges personal freedoms. While we may universally value individual freedoms, personal freedoms need to be limited as well. While individuals should be able to act as they choose, we must protect citizens from being hurt by other citizens. The old saying says, "Your right to swing your fist ends where my nose begins." In addition, it is at times necessary to limit our freedoms as a society in times of crisis for national security reasons, as we saw following the 9/11 attacks with the passage of the controversial USA PATRIOT Act and Homeland Security Act. Americans disagree somewhat when faced with decisions on what freedoms to support: for example, recent studies have indicated that 76% of Americans would favor a constitutional amendment to permit prayer in public schools, while the Supreme Court has found that school prayer impairs the rights of members of religious minority groups (Bresler et al., 2007, p. 140). It can be difficult to balance our desire for personal freedoms with the limits necessary to maintain a safe society.

The concept of **consent of the governed** means that government gets its power from the people and a government exists only because people want it to. It is the consent of the governed that keeps government accountable to the people (via the election process) in a representative democracy that utilizes the "majority rules" principle as a guide for public policy. However, governments in free countries provide protections to all citizens and do not operate on a simple "majority rules" principle, as there must be protections for the minority.

In the United States, we operate under a predominately capitalist system, which represents our final universal American value—support of the "free enterprise" system. We strongly support the value of hard work, respect the right to own property, and favor the right of business to make profits. The so-called "Protestant work ethic" further promotes the free enterprise system by viewing hard work as a virtue that deserves to be rewarded and sees laziness as an individual shortcoming. According to Bresler et al., "Americans believe that competition brings out the best in people and that the most successful competitors deserve the greatest rewards. Americans' preference for freedom over equality manifests itself in the economic as well as the political sphere" (2007, p. 138). However, free enterprise in practice is not a realistic arrangement in a democratic society, and, therefore, policymakers must balance our predominately capitalist system with "redistributive policies," policies that distribute resources to lower classes of society. According to James Anderson, "in American society redistributive policies ultimately involve disagreements between liberals (pro) and conservatives (con) and tend to be highly productive of conflict" (2011, p. 15). Edelman argues that some sort of welfare system is essential in capitalistic societies. As Edelman explains, "Welfare is essential in recessions, in places where there are no jobs, in circumstances where women have special care giving responsibilities, where there is functional disability, and in a manner that supplements unemployment insurance" (2003, p. 94). Critics of welfare policies maintain that ongoing welfare promotes a "culture of dependence" and does not provide an incentive to join the workforce. Public-assistance programs that predominately benefit the poor (such as cash aid, food stamps, and Medicaid) are not as politically popular as social insurance programs (such as Social Security and unemployment compensation) that favor the middle class (Dye, 2008, p. 108).

As you can see, Americans are alike in many ways, yet there is much conflict over public policy issues. Mainly, these differences are due to a conflict of **political ideology,** the conflict on *how* to establish policy. According to Bresler et al., "Americans do not question the fundamental concepts of American political life, but they differ on matters of emphasis and degree" (2007, p. 109). In other words, we disagree about how to apply these generally established principles—not about the principles themselves. Political ideology is often portrayed as a controversy between liberals and conservatives, but differences in ideology are often more complex than that. Differences in ideology are fundamentally different ideas about the role of government in our everyday lives. Some people believe that government should take an active role in our lives, while others favor limited government interference. Americans' responses to political issues are influenced by a number of factors, including an individual's upbringing and background. No two people will have the same view of political matters. As Rufus Miles said, "Where you stand depends on where you sit."

The News Media and Political Attitudes

The First Amendment to the Constitution guarantees "freedom of the press." The courts have interpreted this right as expansively as possible, especially for newspapers, drawing the line only at libel and grotesque pornography (obscenity). With respect to radio and television, the Federal Communications Commission had a "Fairness Doctrine," but abandoned it in the 1980s, so that almost anything can be broadcast. Very rarely does the FCC intervene; only an apparent sociopath like New York radio's Howard Stern will arouse the FCC sufficiently to take adverse action.

This means that newspapers, radio, and television can legally slant the news as they please. The rule for readers, listeners, and viewers is *caveat emptor*—buyer beware. Government makes no certification as to the accuracy or reasonableness of the contents. Some readers, listeners, and viewers express concern for the accuracy, fairness, and objectivity of the news they receive. Media critics act as "watchdogs" to expose prejudicial news reports.

Conservative Republicans are virtually unanimous in claiming that the news media are biased toward progressive Democrats. Sean Hannity insists as much on a regular basis. The conservatives' accusations are supported by surveys showing that most reporters are Democrats (or, at least, vote Democratic most of the time). From 1968 to 1980, a period when Republican candidates won three out of four presidential elections, 80 percent of leading reporters and editors voted Democratic (Press & VerBurg, 1988, p. 94).

Everett Carll Ladd Jr. and Seymour Martin Lipset, in *The Divided Academy: Professors and Politics* (1975, pp. 2-3), explained:

> *Another sphere of activity in which the elite show clear signs of being influenced by ties to the university world is the mass media; the people who write for major newspapers, magazines, and news services, and who direct network broadcasting, have values and political orientations similar to academics. It may be argued that those who have risen to prominent positions in the media seek acceptance as intellectuals and along with theologians look to faculty as a primary reference group. A. James Reichley of Fortune has described this development in the outlook of journalists:*

> "Since World War II the old reporters of the Front Page school, whose attitudes were at least as much anti-intellectual as anti-government, have gradually disappeared. The new journalists have tended to be better educated and more professional and strongly influenced by prevailing currents of opinion in the academic community. The part played by the Ivy League in the intellectual establishment has no doubt been exaggerated, but it is worthy of note that almost one third of the nation's most influential journalists who are not college graduates . . . operate in a milieu in which liberal intellectual attitudes are pervasive. The suggestions of one critic that many national journalists now function as a kind of 'lesser clergy' for the academic elite is 'not far from correct.'"

Progressive Democrats dispute the conservatives' accusations, and argue that the news media are biased in the opposite direction. They cite the ownership by wealthy corporate owners who are threatened by progressive, anti-business, pro-regulation politics. Editorial-page sentiment was quite favorable to Nixon in 1972 and to Reagan in 1980 and 1984. New-left activists charge that the news is written to discredit the radical left and those who lead progressive social movements. Instead, the news favors *status-quo* policy approaches. The press glorifies most foreign-policy adventures and rarely exposes imperialistic initiatives of the U. S. government. Walter Cronkite was a cheerleader for the NASA space program when social activists were questioning it as a budget priority. And, clearly, the news media treated Reagan with great deference, to the joy of his media advisors (Hertsgaard, 1988, p. 3).

These perspectives can be reconciled. Reporters, for the most part, serve to the people what they want to read and hear. Page and Shapiro (1992, p. 346) state that television news commentary is an indicator for other contemporary influences on public opinion and may simply track the climate of opinion in the country as a whole. They also state (pp. 341 342) that the news media are aware that people prefer to receive news from politically compatible sources. When it comes to political analysis, most people delegate most of the work to people they trust as like-minded agents. So reporters show preference for popular candidates. Reagan's 1984 opponent, Walter Mondale, recalls viewing television news reports in which he was featured, and thinking to himself, "I would have voted against the fool, too."

Furthermore, reporters have a natural attraction for attractive or charismatic personalities. They gravitated toward John F. Kennedy and Reagan alike. According to Press and VerBurg (1988, p. 97), Stephen Hess calls this "style bias." He observes that reporters prefer a Kennedy or a George Will to a Jimmy Carter or a Gerald Ford. "It is possible for a 'liberal' press to be anti-George McGovern and pro-William Buckley."

Another question about media bias ought to be addressed here: Do reporters systematically undercut government officials? A story disseminated by Reid Irvine's right-wing Accuracy in Media organization tells of a Cuban editor who was interviewed after Fidel Castro came to power in January 1959. Miguel Angel Quevedo, editor of the Cuban magazine *Bohemia*, reflected on the part that he and his fellow journalists had played in Castro's triumph over the regime of Fulgencio Batista after a 5½ year revolt. Quevedo lamented that Cuban journalists had worn the "hateful uniform of systematic oppositionists." Regardless of who was president of the Cuban republic, Quevedo explained, he "had to be attacked" and "he had to be destroyed." A few months after giving the interview, Quevedo committed suicide.

Vice President Spiro T. Agnew had similar observations about the news media in a memorable speech entitled "On the National Media" that he delivered in Des Moines, Iowa, on November 13, 1969. Agnew complained that every televised speech by the president was followed by so-called "instant analysis" by news commentators in which they would criticize what the president had just said even before the viewers were able to digest the speech. Once the president concluded his speech, his image would fade from the screen to be replaced by the image of some three to five network commentators who would proceed to question everything from the president's integrity to his sanity. Agnew observed that the spontaneity of the analysis was patently phony, recalling the confusion into which the commentators were thrown on the evening in 1968 that President Johnson announced unexpectedly that he would not seek reelection. Agnew's speech seemed to hit its mark; the era of "instant analysis" abruptly ended.

Presidents find this sort of treatment to be humiliating. As Nixon complained: "Scrubbing floors and emptying bedpans has as much dignity as the presidency." President Reagan's spokesman, Larry Speakes, criticized the American news media for the "steady denigration of the president [that] has gone on for two decades."

In 1977, Michael Robinson wrote, "[T]he network news has emerged as 'the loyal opposition' more so than even the party out of office. *It is now the networks that act as the shadow cabinet.*" In 2011, the cable-news commentators whose ideological affiliation differs from that of the president subject him to daily rhetorical bombardment, portraying him as inept and insincere.

Surely, this confrontational approach is consistent with the history of the free press in the United States. Still, some critics object that the news media are not confrontational enough, that the news media parrot government officials without critical analysis. Only the appearance of scandal mobilizes the press.

Implications of American Political Socialization

We have already determined that the political socialization process makes children receptive to government in their lives. Young children perceive government officials and institutions to be powerful, competent, benign, and infallible. Children trust government officials to offer protection and help. This sense of trust, Hess and Torney (1967, p.135) say, appears to be compensatory: It develops because the child sees himself or herself as inferior and vulnerable, and needs to reassure himself or herself that powerful public authority is not dangerous. As the child matures, he or she develops a sense of realism about government officials and institutions. Nevertheless, the support for government lingers, at least in principle. This support is especially strong for the Executive Branch, as schools tend to focus on a president-centered view of the government.

In reality, the president has little influence over policy after his honeymoon period (the first six to eight months of his term of office) ends. The president is influential early on because, just a few months earlier on Election Day, he provided an impressive demonstration of brute political strength by doing what no one else could do—win a national election! After the honeymoon is over and the memory of his victory has faded, his influence declines. The irony, according to Michael Nelson, is that it is not until the new administration has been in office for two years or so that it knows what it is doing—but the honeymoon is over and the president's influence on policymaking has evaporated. Fleishman and Aufses (1976, p. 37) point out that, as effective as FDR was in getting bills through Congress during his honeymoon period, popularly known as the "Hundred Days," he was just as powerless to get bills through afterwards through the rest of his lengthy presidency.

A noteworthy result of the political socialization process is its perpetuation of privileges of the elite class. One of the intentions of the framers of the U. S. Constitution in drafting the document in 1787 was to create a national governmental system that could intervene in any localized effort to undermine the right to property ownership. Clearly, the failed Shays' Rebellion of 1786-1787, an effort by debtors to eliminate the state government that routinely enforced debts, was on the framers' minds. At the same time, the Constitution created an electorate that, theoretically, had the power to use the ballot box to hamper the right of the affluent class to control a disproportionate share of the nation's wealth. As Louis Hartz chronicles in *The Liberal Tradition in America* (1955), the electorate chose, instead, to ratify the right of the wealthy to accumulate even more wealth.

This acquiescence to the right of the richest Americans to become richer, while others endure deprivation, became a fundamental principle of American political thought. Complaints by Americans who have struggled to make ends meet have been fended off with the offer of conditions that supposedly allow for free movement from one socioeconomic class to the other:

- Those who complain about their deprivation are instructed to be proactive to change their economic status. They are advised that they can be successful through hard work. They are advised that they can be successful if they get an education. These arguments portray the conditions that have given rise to a person's economic struggle as being his own deficiencies, in so far as he has not worked hard enough and not obtained a sufficient level of education. Holsworth and Wray (1987, p. 56) wrote: "Education is widely assumed to provide what might be called 'secular salvation.' Those wishing to move up the social ladder must 'get a good education.' Educational opportunity appears to be democratic and meritocratic. It seems open to everyone on a more or less equal basis, and it is widely believed that people rise through the educational system according to their intellectual merit and their willingness to work. Education is probably the closest thing we have to a national religious faith."
- State governments, including Georgia's government, advertise incessantly about how gambling, specifically purchasing lottery tickets can propel an ordinary person to life on "Easy Street."

Therefore, members of the lower class do not perceive themselves to be "stuck." Said Edward Everett (quoted in Hartz, 1955, p. 112), "The wheel of fortune is in constant revolution, and the poor, in one generation, furnish the rich of the next."

On occasion, in the course of events in the United States, conditions agitate the working class to the extent that it appears possible that the working class might reject the mythology of free movement between socioeconomic classes. When the level of tension rises to the point that government leaders fear an uprising, whether a rebellion at the ballot box or mass rejection of the power structure, government leaders may then be motivated to institute reform. For example, the spectacle of industrial monopolists cornering their respective markets and amassing spectacular fortunes created the pressure for Congress to enact the Sherman Antitrust Act in 1890. The Sherman Antitrust Act allows the national government to obstruct the efforts of an individual or a business to monopolize the market for a particular product. As another example, President Franklin D. Roosevelt, fearing the survival of the system of liberty, the free market, and property rights, decided to reform the relationship between business owners and laborers by empowering labor unions, giving them the legal right to collectively bargain on behalf of workers. Therefore, he championed the enactment of the National Labor Relations Act of 1935. Other reforms have included the establishment of minimum-wage levels, maximum lengths of workdays and work weeks, restrictions on child labor, and worker-safety standards. Each of these policies was designed to dampen public agitation against the power of business owners.

In this country, the process of political socialization reinforces the belief that businesses should be free of interference by the government. Page and Shapiro (1992, p. 378) explain:

> *In the information Americans receive about both foreign and domestic issues, we believe there is a pervasive procapitalist slant. American schools, besides training manageable workers, teach the virtues of free enterprise. . . . Corporate advertising trumpets the capitalist gospel. . . . Most news organizations are themselves owned by large corporations; more than half the newspapers and TV media were owned by just 29 corporations in 1986. . . .The media take the superiority of capitalism for granted, even while investigating and publicizing malfeasance by particular firms.*
>
> *The average American is bombarded throughout his or her life by messages about the productive power and efficiency of "free enterprise," the high standard of living it has provided, and the personal liberties it promotes. Rare is the voice that seriously questions the fairness*
>
> *of the system (for example, its relation to poverty and inequality) or explores economic and social alternatives.*

Because of the combination of the political socialization cues and the government's occasional intervention to stabilize an unstable system, the

American public acknowledges the right of the affluent class to control a disproportionate amount of the nation's wealth. On the other hand, the affluent class acknowledges few rights of the lower class. Therefore, political socialization operates separately for the children of the two classes. The children of rich parents are socialized to actively participate in public affairs and to prepare to be leaders of the government and captains of industry. The children of poor parents are socialized to obey laws and to be respectful (and sometimes fearful) of authority figures. At the extreme, such children are taught, "You can't fight city hall," which is usually enough to extinguish any possibility that the child will assert her right to pursue equality and justice.

Edgar Litt (1963) found that schoolteachers taught upper-middle-class and upper-class children that they were not only to obey the laws, but also that they could play an active role in shaping the laws. Meanwhile, Litt discovered, children in working-class schools were taught only that a good citizen obeys laws.

Trained to be subservient, members of the lower- and middle-class are unlikely to do anything either to attempt to change the political and economic system or, even, to affect the distribution of power in the communities and organizations of which they are a part. Thus, in a neighborhood association or in the workplace, the minority can assume control and direct the majority of participants, who are unaccustomed to trying to exert their influence. In the workplace, workers have long since come to understand the peril of defying management, regardless of which of them outnumber the other. Lindblom (1977, p. 48) writes:

> *A person whose style of life and family livelihood have for years been built around a particular job, occupation or location finds a command backed by a threat to fire him indistinguishable in many consequences for his liberty from a command backed by the police and the courts.*
>
> *In most societies the law broadly prohibits one person from inflicting injury on another. . .But it leaves one great exception: injury through termination of an exchange relation [such as the relationship between an employer and an employee]. It is easy to see why it must allow the*

*exception if a market system is to persist. But it is an
exception, one to which classical liberal theory is blind.*

It is a common phenomenon that blue-collar (and, often, even white-collar) workers stream out of the factories and offices at quitting time and head for bars, whereupon they get themselves drunk in order to forget the indignities that they have endured. Holsworth and Wray (1987, p. 82) write:

> *Many people do not like to talk about their work. Leaving the work at the office is often regarded as a sign of mental health. It is increasingly clear that, to reduce the damage that work does to personal lives, people are segmenting their lives, giving to work the absolute minimum that is possible and then trying to forget it during the remaining portion of the day. Stand outside any factory gate or office building at day's end and notice the mad scramble to get away from work. It is not an accident that bars across the United States have designated the 5-7 p.m. time as "happy hours."*

Once these employees get home, they explain to their children that there is nothing to be gained from challenging authority. The result is the deference of the majority of Americans to the elite class, which maintains its minority control of society's opportunities and resources.

Introduction to Political Participation

Political participation is defined by Conway as "activities of citizens that attempt to influence the structure of government, the selection of government authorities, or the politics of government" (Conway, 1991, pp. 3-4). Political participation is a learned behavior. While our civics education in schools tends to focus on voting as a major instrument of political participation, there are many ways in which individuals can participate politically. According to Gant and Luttbeg, "While voting is probably the easiest, and therefore the most common, form of political participation, citizens have available to them a wide variety of alternative forms of political activity. These range from writing to a government official about some particular problem or issue, to contributing money to a political party, to running for public office" (Gant & Luttbeg, 1991, pp. 106-107). Listed below are ways in which citizens can participate in the political process:

- Registering to vote
- Voting
- Joining a political party
- Joining a political interest group
- Working on a candidate's campaign
- Working for a political party
- Working for an interest group
- Writing a letter to a government official
- Writing a letter to the editor
- Marching in a rally or protest march
- Donating to a campaign or party
- Running for public office
- Wearing a campaign button
- Putting a bumper sticker on a car
- Persuading friends, coworkers, relatives, etc., to vote for a candidate
- Reading newspaper articles about politics

All of these activities are important and set the stage for lifelong political participation and civic engagement. There are many factors that influence political participation. **Political efficacy** is defined as a person's sense of being able to accomplish something politically (Bresler et al., 2007, p. 153). Individuals with high political efficacy are more likely to participate politically, while those with low efficacy are at risk for minimal participation. Another motivator for political participation is a sense of patriotic duty. These individuals see their participation as a part of citizenship and likely have a very strong party identification. **Party identification**, strong allegiance to a political party, is itself a strong motivator for political participation. Finally, there may be social motives for political participation. In certain circles, it is simply socially unacceptable to not participate in the political process, so participation occurs in response to social pressures.

Who Votes?

Voting is by far the most common and basic form of political activity. The right to vote should be taken seriously and is arguably the most essential for the political system to persist. Yet, we have a voting crisis in the United States. There are various factors that determine voter turnout. Gant and Luttbeg, citing the "American Voter" study (1991, p. 99), state that the following factors influence voter turnout:

- Individuals with strong partisanship are more likely to vote than weak partisans and independents.
- Republicans are more likely to vote than Democrats.
- College graduates are more likely to vote than those without a high-school diploma.
- Those with annual income above $25,000 are more likely to vote than those with annual income below $10,000.
- Professional and technical workers are more likely to vote than unskilled laborers and the unemployed.
- Persons 45-70 years old are more likely to vote than persons 18-24 years old.
- White persons are more likely to vote than non-white persons.
- Jews and Catholics are more likely to vote than Protestants.

In addition, Anthony Downs, in *An Economic Theory of Democracy* (1957), argued that voting is a rational act and voters make their decisions based on "utility"; that is, they will vote for the candidate who can best maximize their wealth. The act of voting comes at a cost—it involves time, money, and ideally educating oneself in political matters. Many citizens simply do not see any benefit in voting and, thus, choose not to engage in this important part of political participation.

Downs used an equation form by Riker and Ordeshook to determine what makes an individual likely to vote: $R = PB - C + D$ where,

R = expected new utility from voting

P = probability that the individual's vote will make a difference in the outcome of the election

B = benefit an individual receives if his or her preferred candidate or party wins the election

C =cost of voting
D =social satisfaction derived from voting

The most important part of this equation is "D" because "P" is actually very small, especially in presidential elections. The social satisfaction an individual derives from voting is clearly a result of successful political socialization, which promotes compliance with the norm that good citizens always vote, satisfaction derived from the maintenance of the political system, and the enjoyment derived from the involvement in the political process. Otherwise, the average citizen has very little incentive to participate in the political process.

Opting Out

Political participation, when it works, benefits the entire citizenry as it creates support for the democratic system, the belief that participation and voting are essential to the democratic process, and approval of government policies and administration. When these attitudes do not materialize, political alienation has occurred, which is dangerous to the system.

There are four varieties of **political alienation**:

- *Political powerlessness*: Individuals with low political efficacy often feel separated from the government and limited in their ability to influence government actions. Political powerlessness is often experienced by disadvantaged groups in society.
- *Political meaninglessness*: Individuals who believe there are no predictable patterns to political decision making and, therefore, no way to influence the political system, may give up. These individuals cannot rationalize certain government behaviors, such as government spending in the face of deficits, civil liberties for accused felons, and a perceived lack of government attention to ongoing social problems.
- *Political normlessness (anomie)*: Individuals conclude that government and its officials are violating widely accepted norms leading to a breakdown of the political system. These individuals become distrustful and cynical of government officials, resulting in a breakdown of the political system. Tax loopholes for the very wealthy, complaints about welfare recipients, and scandals and

policies that appear to promote the breakdown of family values are all related to anomie.

- *Political isolation:* This occurs when an individual rejects current norms as "unfair and illegitimate," and, therefore, withdraws from political life. According to Gant and Luttbeg (1991, p. 125), "this form differs from anomie in that anomie suggests that an individual perceives that others are violating norms which he accepts. But in the case of political isolation, an individual rejects the norms themselves and is not concerned with whether leaders are adhering to them or not."

It is unfortunate that this disconnection from the political system develops. Adoption of these feelings simply creates further barriers between the citizenry and government.

Public Opinion and Public Policy

When it is strong and clearly expressed, public opinion has a substantial influence on public policy. Historically, social movements resulting in major policy changes were due to changes in public opinion. The black civil-rights movement, for example, was a combination of persistent collective action that pushed issues on to the policy agenda and a shift in public opinion that could no longer justify racism. When the Supreme Court handed down the *Brown v. Board of Education* decision in 1954, school boards throughout the South ignored the mandate and actively resisted any attempts at integration. Many Southerners considered the decision illegitimate and, therefore, politicians were loath to implement it. While we tend to credit the success of the black civil-rights movement to the charismatic leadership of Dr. Martin Luther King Jr., it is important to acknowledge that the changes in public opinion began with the actions that took place in the background. The arrest of a frail Rosa Parks, the persistent non-violent protests, and the senseless murders of African-American school girls in Birmingham that led the public to demand change and resulted in public opinion moving in favor of integration (Bianco & Cannon, 2009, pp. 511-514). However, in general, Americans have little direct control over public policy because policy decisions are plagued by a number of constraints that must be reconciled by policymakers.

The Communications Media and Public Policy

The communications media have an important **agenda-setting function**, and are able to put something on the public policy agenda by bringing attention to a problem. In addition, the media have great influence over how the public perceives political events and helps shapes political attitudes. The media serve as a **vehicle** of direct communication, allowing policymakers to communicate directly with the public. In addition, the media act as **gatekeepers and spotlights** for policy problems by singling what the public should know and care about.

Journalists have the following impacts on public policy:

- Political campaign coverage signals to voters which campaign events are most important. By emphasizing events and reporting them repeatedly, the news media signal the public that the events are important. The news media relegate other events to the background (Yeric & Todd, 1989, p. 60).
- The news media do not create basic attitudes, but they may activate attitudes. Patterson says that political candidates are aware of the invulnerability of most basic attitudes: "Even the candidates seldom try to overturn basic attitudes, but work instead to create perceptions that they feel will elicit those attitudes beneficial to their candidacies" (quoted in Yeric & Todd, 1989, p. 60).
- Television news creates *short-term* changes in public opinion. It does not account for instantaneous or glacial changes in public opinion (Page & Shapiro, 1992, p. 344).
- Editorials have much more influence on public opinion that news reports have. ". . . We have been surprised by the remarkably strong estimated impact of news commentary. . . . We found a large effect of editorial columns" (Page & Shapiro, 1992, p. 345).
- Press and VerBurg (1988, p. 62) state that editorial endorsements are most effective when any of these conditions applies:
  - The newspaper's position already fits readers' predispositions.
  - Voters' ties to both major political parties are weak.
  - Voters have few other cues or guidelines (especially in nonpartisan elections, referenda, or long ballots).
- People who follow national politics entirely on television are

significantly more *confused and cynical* than those who use other media as well (Press & VerBurg, 1988, p. 92).

- The less knowledge the public has prior to a media report, the more likely it is to be affected by it (Yeric & Todd, 1989, p. 61).
- Television may have a more significant effect on public opinion than newspapers do when the subject is dramatic and the event is short-term (Yeric & Todd, 1989, p. 61).
- Leaders and experts communicate with each other through news commentaries (Page & Shapiro, 1992, pp. 364 365).
- The news media place some issues on the agenda of public policy. "Advocacy journalism" is influential in this context. Problems like child abuse and spousal abuse, which might have been ignored for centuries, can be brought to the public's attention by television more effectively than by any other information source.

Case Study: Political Socialization in a Polarized America

During the 2009 school year, while President Barack Obama prepared to deliver the annual "back to school" message from the White House, controversy regarding the president speaking directly to schoolchildren was brewing. What would the Democratic president say? Would he discuss the benefits of his health-care plan? How dare he use schoolchildren to promote his political agenda! Predictably, the much anticipated "indoctrination" speech was simply a "pep talk" to our American schoolchildren reinforcing basic societal norms: work hard in school, education is important, etc. Yet the controversy surrounding this tradition was puzzling. How could the president delivering a simple speech to our nations' youngest citizens become a battleground for political debate? Have we become so extreme in our views that simply hearing a speech from the president is viewed as unacceptable in public schools? According to James Wilson, Americans have become so polarized that the ideological gap between Democrats and Republicans was twice as strong in 2004 as it was in 1972. Wilson asserts, "As for the extent to which these extremist views have spread, it is probably best assessed by looking not at specific issues but at enduring political values and party preferences. It seems that Americans are increasingly intolerant of varying political views. In 2004, only 12 percent of Democrats approved of George W. Bush while in earlier periods three to four times as many Democrats approved of Ronald Reagan,

Gerald Ford, Richard Nixon, and Dwight D. Eisenhower" (Wilson, 2006, p. 9). The effects of our current polarized political environment on civic education and political socialization should be considered. It is evident that we have a civic engagement problem in this country. Robert Putnam (2000) argues that civic engagement has been on a downward trend since World War II and continues to decline. Meanwhile, researchers argue that the schools, as an agent of socialization, can be instrumental in reversing this trend by promoting engaged citizenship in classrooms. This idea makes sense, as the classroom is likely where children first learn about government institutions, yet civic education in schools is ridden with controversy in our current explosive political environment which hinders its ability to create engaged citizenship.

Public schools have been used as training grounds for democracy since their inception. According to Galston, "Education for citizenship was one of the major motives for the creation of public schools" (Galston, 2001, p. 231). Frischler and Smith state that, to some, civic education is "merely knowledge of the institutional features of government: the function of local, state and national governments; the role of the legislative, executive and judicial branches; voting requirements, etc" (Fritschler & Smith, 2009, p. 8). While this understanding of the nuts and bolts of government is important, it does not focus on how everyday people can influence their government through active citizenship (e.g., marching in rallies, writing letters to the editor). In contrast, schools focus on passive citizenship (e.g., following political campaigns, voting), as the curriculum of social-studies courses emphasizes nationalistic values and stresses national patriotism while avoiding ideological disagreements. Courses in history emphasize events that reflect national glory, as unattractive aspects of U.S. history and politics are downplayed. Despite the fact that democratic values are held up in admiration, there is an emphasis on obedience and compliance with seemingly petty regulations (e.g., dress code, movement in the halls) rather than the promoting of citizen participation.

Intense partisan politics make it difficult for teachers to effectively teach about government without being accused of "indoctrination." Youniss explains, "As party politics have become decidedly divisive, public schools have been burdened with the dilemma of having to teach about the political system while remaining neutral and skirting over controversial issues. An accusatory watchdog climate has cast a chill over the classrooms so that, for example, it is easier to teach about homelessness by engendering empathy, but it is less safe to have students delve into the responsible political policies, for instance, regarding affordable housing, mental health services, drug rehabilitation and job retraining" (Youniss, 2005, p. 360). Educators are discouraged from going beyond the assigned curriculum to avoid ideological controversy which results in instruction being limited to widely accepted views—even though those values involve an ideological point of view. As Dawson, Prewitt, and Dawson note, "A school lesson celebrating the free enterprise economy would be viewed as civics education by the Chamber of Commerce, but as political indoctrination by the Socialist-Labor party" (Dawson et al., 1977, p. 141). Therefore, indoctrination is fairly inevitable. The question, therefore, becomes *whose* indoctrination? Teachers who depart from the traditional approaches of capitalism and equality of opportunity are roundly denounced. While this is an effective method of promoting patriotism, it limits the students' ability to understand complex problems and differences in ideology. Therefore, by limiting the curriculum, schools are not being effective educators in civic education. Hocutt explains, "Although education transmits knowledge useful to the individual, indoctrination has another, decidedly different aim—promoting loyalty to the group. Thus, education in engineering helps students prosper, while indoctrination in a false ideology helps only the ideology prosper" (Hocutt, 2005, p. 37). Therefore, while teachers are supposed to be neutral in their lectures, they must promote "universal values" including democracy, liberty, the two-party system, equality, and capitalism. Schoolteachers must balance all of these ideas by stressing ideal norms yet not dealing with the unpleasant factors of political life. When new materials are introduced in schools to encourage independent thinking, they are met with fierce controversy.

A democracy depends on having an informed electorate, yet our schools are limited in the information that they can hand down to students. Recently, the Texas Board of Education mandated the use of textbooks that promote a conservative, Christian bias. We have to wonder what long-term implications this will have on the political-socialization process as these ideas limit the greater understanding of political matters necessary for engaged citizenship.

FOR MORE INFORMATION ABOUT JOURNALISM IN THE UNITED STATES

This chapter contains excerpts of co-author Barry Friedman's description of journalism in the United States. For the longer essay, which includes a history of American journalism, please see chapter 4 on this textbook's website at http://www.upnorthgeorgia.org/amergovt/.

Discussion Questions

1. What is the role of political socialization in forming our values and expectations of government in the United States? How does this experience vary among American schoolchildren? What is the implication of these divergent approaches to political socialization?
2. Identify and describe the various ways in which Americans can participate in the political process. Which types of political participation are the most effective and why?
3. Describe the influence of the communications media in the public-policymaking process. How do the communications media help set the policy agenda?
4. What is the influence of public opinion on policy outcomes? Is public opinion important? Why?

References

Anderson, J. E. (2011). *Public policymaking*. (7th ed.). Boston, MA: Wadsworth.

Bianco, W. & Canon, D. (2009). *American politics today*. New York, NY: W.W. Norton & Co.

Bresler, R. J., Friedrich, R., Karlesky, J., Stephenson, D. G. Jr., & Turner, C. C. (2007). *Introduction to American government*. (4th ed.). Redding, CA: Best Value Textbooks LLC.

Conway, M. M. (1991). *Political participation in the United States*. (2nd ed.). Washington, DC: CQ Press.

Downs, A.. (1957). *Economic theory of democracy.* New York, NY: HarperCollins.

Dawson, R. E., Prewitt, K., & Dawson, K. S. (1977). *Political socialization: An analytic study.* (2nd ed.). Boston, MA: Little, Brown and Company.

Easton, D. & Dennis, J.. (1969). *Children of the political system: Origins of political legitimacy.* New York, NY: McGraw-Hill.

Edelman, P. (2003). The Welfare Debate: Getting Past the Bumper Stickers. *Harvard Journal of Law and Public Policy,* 27(1), 93-100.

Fritschler, A. L. & Smith, B. L. R. (2009). Campus Engagement in Civic Education Remains Weak: Opportunities and Challenges Exist on Many Fronts. *Phi Kappa Phi Forum,* 89(3).

Hocutt, M. (2005). Indoctrination v. Education. *Academic Questions,* 18(3), 35-43.

Galston, W. (2001). Political Knowledge, Political Engagement and Civic Education. *Annual Review of Political Science,* 4, 217-234.

Greenberg, E. S. (Ed.). (1970). *Political socialization.* New York, NY: Atherton Press.

Hartz, L. (1955). *The liberal tradition in America.* New York, NY: Harcourt Brace Jovanovich.

Hess, R. & Torney, J. (1967). *The development of political attitudes in children.* Chicago, IL: Aldine Publishing Company.

Holsworth, R. D. & Wray, J. H. (1987). *American politics and everyday life.* (2nd ed.). New York, NY: MacMillan Publishing Company.

Lindblom, C. E. (1977). *Politics and markets: The world's political economic systems*. New York, NY: Basic Books.

McKinley J. Jr. (2010). Texas Conservatives Win Curriculum Change. *New York Times*. Retrieved from http://www.nytimes.com/2010/03/13/education/13texas.html.

Page, B. I. & Shapiro, R. Y. (1992). *The rational public*. Chicago, IL: University of Chicago Press.

Putnam, R. (2000). *Bowling alone: The collapse and revival of American community*. New York, NY: Simon & Schuster.

Tanenhaus, S. (2010). In Texas Curriculum Fight, Identity Politics Leans Right. *New York Times*. Retrieved from http://www.nytimes.com/2010/03/21/weekinreview/21tanenhaus.html?_r=1&ref=education

Youniss, J. (2005). Much to Learn about New Agents of Political Socialization. *Human Development*. 48, 356-362.

Wilson, J. (2006). How Divided Are We?. *Commentary*. Retrieved from http://www.commentarymagazine.com/viewarticle.cfm/how-divided-are-we--10023?search=1.

Chapter Five
Interest Groups
Carl D. Cavalli and Barry D. Friedman

Learning Objectives

After covering the topic of interest groups and political participation, students should understand:

1. The history of and reasons why interest groups exist.
2. Why we join interest groups, and their structure, their organization, and the "free-rider" problem.
3. The mythology and reality of interest groups.
4. The influence of interest groups on public policymaking, including the various methods of influence.

Abstract

The framers' hostility to "factions" was addressed not by restrictions, but by encouraging proliferation, creating what today is referred to as a pluralist system. While groups offer potential members many social and economic reasons for joining, obtaining active support is often difficult because of the "free-rider" problem. Modern literature challenges the popular myth of benevolent groups alleviating inequities in society. Instead, Roberto Michels speaks of an "iron law of oligarchy" and E.E. Schattschneider warns of a strong upper-class bias. Data on federal spending by lobbyists support this theory about bias. Groups use many methods to influence public policy. These methods include lobbying, direct access through "iron triangles," litigation, direct grants of power from governments, "going public," and electoral activity. Government regulation of groups' electoral activity has resulted in the formation of many types of organizations, including political action committees, "527" organizations, and, most recently, "SuperPACs."

Introduction

Watching each others' backs

In the feudal systems that once dominated European countries, lords, as the saying goes, "watched each others' backs." For that matter, so did the serfs. The feudal system placed all individuals into automatic, life-long affiliations with their peers. In case of trouble, help was on the way.

The European immigrants who came to North America to populate the colonies had a common, middle-class background. Besides, while the shortage of land in Europe was part of the rationale for feudalism, once they arrived here, the immigrants discovered an abundance of land. Imitating feudalism in North America was, quite simply, out of the question.

But the choice of individualism came with a new challenge: Each individual, faced with some sort of problem, could not automatically rely on any association for assistance. For example, if someone's barn was burning down, it would be problematic to endeavor to put out the fire alone. Therefore, the colonists learned to create associations for collective benefit—associations like volunteer fire departments. As a matter of fact, it was Benjamin Franklin who founded the first such association, known as the Union Fire Company, in 1736 in Philadelphia. The stage was set for the creation of innumerable interest groups in the United States.

In *Federalist* #10, James Madison reflects the distaste of the framers toward what he called "factions" (see Chapter 2): "The friend of popular governments never finds himself so much alarmed for their character and fate, as when he contemplates their propensity to this dangerous vice [i.e., factions]" (Madison, 2001, p. 92). We generally understand his term "factions" to encompass political interest groups, political parties, and other instruments whose purpose is to cultivate political influence. Conventional wisdom states that the delegates to the Constitutional Convention were still in some kind of shock over **Shays' Rebellion**, the recent incident in Massachusetts during which debt-ridden farmers set out to topple the state government in Boston so that there would be no instrument to enforce their debts. Although the rebellion failed, the affluent delegates to the convention must have feared imitators and, thus, the possibility that private property would not be secure. In so far as the *Federalist* papers were intended to advocate the ratification of the proposed Constitution, Madison took on the challenge of showing that the document would manage the threat posed by factions. Did the delegates to the Constitution Convention decide to *outlaw* factions? No, says Madison; they did not outlaw them by "destroying the liberty which is essential to [their] existence." That, he acknowledges, would be "worse than the disease" itself. Instead, he explains, the framers did something much cleverer: They decided to "extend the sphere"—i.e., they transformed the system of 13 separate political systems into *one large*, *national* system.

And then they set the stage for factions to proliferate. Then, he boasted, there would be so many factions in this one national system that they would cancel each other out, rather than creating the conditions under which one faction would eventually prevail.

By the time that the French observer Alexis de Tocqueville toured the United States in the early 1830s, the creation of clubs and associations had clearly become second nature to Americans. His observation was that Americans form associations at the drop of a hat. Subsequently, scholars in the field of American government found many reasons to celebrate the proliferation of interest groups. Tocqueville himself referred to the spectrum of clubs and associations as "great schools, free of charge, where all citizens come to be taught the general theory of associations," in which Americans learn to make proposals, debate them, vote on them, and accept the majority decision (Tocqueville, 1835/2000, p. 497). In 1951, David B. Truman referred to interest groups as the "balance wheel in a going democratic system" (p. 514). The existence of innumerable interest groups, and each American's affiliation with a variable number of such groups, amounted to a system of **pluralism**, whose net effect is considered to be the moderation of individual Americans and, as a result, of the entire political system.

The Basics
What are they and why do they exist?

Quite simply, interest groups organize to influence government. This makes them purely *political* entities, as they seek to affect public policy. However, these groups generally are not interested in all policies. Typically they focus on a single area, remaining uninterested in others (except to the extent those others may affect their interest). This focus leads many to refer to them as *special-* or *single*-interest groups.

While the framers' distaste for "factions" included interest groups as well as political parties, this single focus distinguishes them from political parties, which generally seek to mold policy in *all* areas. Another distinction is that, in general, while interest groups are focused on *influencing* government—largely from the outside—parties want to get their members elected to government in order to *run* it (see Chapter 6).

Democracy, Diversity, and Division

While not an absolute requirement, *democracy* helps explain the existence of interest groups. Democratic governments are set up to listen to public input, and an organized group is more easily heard than a scattered collection of individuals (Think of a chorus versus a crowd).

Another explanation is found in *diversity*. There would be little reason for groups to form if the entire population possessed the same beliefs, desires, and needs. Indeed, in *Federalist* #10, Madison notes that one way of "removing the causes of faction" is to give everyone "the same opinions, … passions, and … interests" (Madison 2001, p. 92). He quickly dismisses this as impossible. So–factions happen!

One other less appreciated but equally important explanation for the existence of interest groups is *division*. More precisely, our government is fragmented–divided in many ways. Implementing the constitutional principle of separation of powers leads to a divided government–three branches (Executive, Legislative, and Judicial) in each of three levels (national, state, and local). In addition, each branch at each level usually has multiple agencies with many individuals within it. This diversity creates numerous **access points** for interest groups to contact. In addition to lobbying Congress for favorable legislation, they may also lobby executive agencies for favorable regulations as well as accessing the legal system to affect laws, regulations, and their implementation. All of these may be pursued at the state (governor, state legislature, state courts) and local (mayor, city council, municipal courts) levels as well.

The Rationale for Forming or Joining Groups

Clubs and associations originate because of their founders' perception of self-interest. Others join these organizations to advance their self-interests, too. While one cannot rule out the possibility that those who establish an association are doing so for purely altruistic reasons, systematic observation suggests that such an event is a rarity. People join groups for some of these reasons:

- People may join an organization in order to obtain a *material benefit*. For example, one may join AARP–the organization for people 50 years of age and older–to obtain health insurance at a discounted group rate or to obtain discounts when checking into a hotel.

- People may join an organization in order to feel good about themselves . They may volunteer their unpaid labor to helping a free-soup kitchen so that they can get some *personal satisfaction* out of feeding hungry people. They may join a museum organization to feel as though they are doing something worthy by being a patron of the arts.
- People may establish or affiliate with an organization in order to obtain *employment.* Clubs and associations employ millions of Americans. The most successful organization executives even in the nonprofit charitable sector command generous salaries, sometimes exceeding $1 million.
- People or business enterprises may affiliate with an organization in the hope that the organization will attempt to persuade legislators and others who possess government authority to make decisions that will promote the well-being of the members' industry or other *common interest.*
- People may affiliate with an organization because of their intention that the organization's ideological program or policy preferences would, if transformed into public policy, *benefit the individual* or, at least, create the kind of society that they prefer.

Organization

There are more *potential* interests than most of us may comprehend. Your interests may stem from any number of factors related to you or your surroundings, including sociological factors (race, ethnicity, nationality, religion, sexual orientation), political factors (partisanship, ideology), behavioral factors (activities, personal and consumer habits), demographic factors (gender, age, location, income, occupation, education), and even physical characteristics (height, weight, health issues). However, not all interests gain the attention of government. The key to gaining this attention is *organization*. Organization is what separates interests from interest *groups* (recall the earlier analogy: a chorus versus a crowd).

Any interest wishing to influence government must have some sort of structure, consisting most basically of *leadership* and *membership*. The leadership provides direction and (along with the staff) usually accounts for much of the group's activities. The membership may account for some activity (e.g., picketing, protesting, writing to or calling government officials), but in many instances provides mainly financing and popular support.

In general, organized groups cannot achieve significant success without a sound *financial structure*. Most organizations rely on membership dues along with additional contributions from supporters (including charitable foundations and think tanks—i.e., other groups). Many groups also benefit from federal and state funding. This funding is not *supposed* to be used to support their attempts to influence government. However, funding in the form of research or project grants—often providing data in support of a group's aims—may help them succeed nonetheless.

The "Free-Rider" Problem

As noted above, people join groups for many reasons. In general, it makes sense to say that we look to obtain some sort of benefit from our memberships. In turn, groups need our support in order to function effectively. Yet many groups find it difficult to obtain that support. Interestingly, this difficulty generally increases with the size of a (potential) group. You might think that the broader the interest, the easier it is to organize, collect resources, and take action. You would be wrong! Broad interests face a **free-rider problem**. Mancur Olson (1982) describes the logic:

> *The successful boycott or strike or lobbying action will bring the better price or wage for everyone in the relevant category, so the individual in any large group with a common interest will reap only a minute share of the gains from whatever sacrifices the individual makes to achieve this common interest. Since any gain goes to everyone in the group, those who contribute nothing to the effort will get just as much as those who made a contribution. It pays to "let George do it," but George has little or no incentive to do anything in the group interest either, so ... there will be little, if any, group action. The paradox, then, is that (in the absence of special arrangements or circumstances ...) large groups, at least if they are composed of rational individuals, will not act in their group interest. (p. 18)*

In other words, groups that pursue **collective, or public, goods**, cannot limit them only to those who contribute time and resources to the cause (see Samuelson 1954). National defense is one of the purest examples of a collective good. It is impossible to divide: If it is provided at all, it is provided for everyone. Contrast this with largely private goods–like typical consumer goods–that are bought and sold through individual transactions. You must pay for that iPod you want! On the other hand, much of the regulations regarding the manufacture and sale of iPods (material and manufacturing quality, limitations on the use of hazardous materials, required disclosure of radiation levels) are closer to public goods that exist (or not) regardless of your individual actions. If you benefit from these goods whether you contribute or not, it is not rational for you to contribute to any groups seeking these benefits. Groups seeking these regulations often will struggle to build support. You will just "let George do it" (which, of course, he will not because he has no more incentive than you!). In small groups (such as a local union seeking a pay raise for a company's workers), you may quickly realize that if you and George do not act, you may not receive any benefit. This realization may spur you to action. However, in large groups (such as consumer, environmental, social, and issue groups), there are lots of other Georges, at least some of whom (you are likely to assume) will act. Yet again, they have no more incentive than do you. This lack of action is the problem.

Governments may address this problem through compulsory action. National defense is funded through tax revenues. You pay taxes or you go to prison (assuming you are caught). Interest groups, however, do not have that compulsory power. So how do groups overcome this problem? Two words: **selective incentives** (or selective benefits). These are benefits that *can* be limited in their distribution. As Olson (1971) says,

> ... *group action can be obtained only through an incentive that operates ... selectively toward the individuals in the group. The incentive must be "selective" so that those who do not join the organization ... can be treated differently from those who do* (p. 51).

These are the kind of benefits mentioned earlier, including material benefits like access to or discounts on consumer goods or other resources or information, and social benefits like entertainment, travel, and other group activities. Regardless of what George does, you are more likely to contribute your time and money to the group if it means that you can get a t-shirt with the group's logo on it, or a magazine with information on the group's accomplishments and activities, or a discount on tickets to a Yankees game or on an insurance policy, or if you can attend a group party or lecture, or go on a Caribbean cruise with group members.

The Mythology and the Reality
The Myth: Inequities Are Alleviated

The spectrum of communications-media sources that discuss American life in general contains a significant amount of mythology about groups, organizations, associations, and so forth. The traditional mythology describes these collectivities in mostly flattering terms. They are said to contribute to the spirit of American democracy. They are described as effective instruments of political participation. Charitable organizations are rhapsodized as instruments by which socioeconomic inequities are alleviated because the charities redistribute wealth from generous haves to appreciative have-nots.

That there is such a mythology is somewhat ironic, given the clear skepticism among the framers of the U. S. Constitution about such collectivities. To Tocqueville, the participation of Americans who, he said, organized clubs and associations at the drop of a hat, in such groups gave the public experience with the idea of democracy: The members would learn to make a proposal, debate it, vote on it, and abide by the results of the majority vote. Thus, he said, these groups served as training grounds for democracy. While Madison considered "factions" a threat to the republic, Tocqueville considered associations to be its very mainstay.

The Reality: Oligarchy, the Upper Class, and Corporations

As the twentieth century proceeded, the literature of political science, following the direction of the literature of sociology, gradually departed from the mythology of popular publications about the value of interest groups, but for reasons that were different from Madison's rationale. In 1915, French sociologist Roberto Michels made this chilling observation: "Who says organization, says oligarchy" (1915/1958, p. 418). His "iron law of oligarchy" suggests that, in *any* organization, a clique of some sort will inevitably rise to the top and assume control. The automatic process that determines who will become the leaders recognizes charisma, strength, leadership ability, intelligence, wealth, access to influential individuals, and so on. When, in 1966, Grant McConnell studied special-interest groups in the United States and their influence on public policy, he rediscovered Michels' "iron law," and complained: "If private associations themselves should be undemocratic [because of the iron law of oligarchy], ... how can they be essential to democracy?" (pp. 122-123).

The further development of the literature of political science explores with increasingly greater sophistication and alarm the actual effect of groups. The effect is not, as Tocqueville surmised, the empowerment of the common man as his participation in groups makes him an effective participant of the political system, but, rather, to solidify the dominant position of those who are already affluent and influential. Evaluating the celebrated idea of American "pluralism," which heralds the role of groups as, in the words of David Truman, the "balance wheel in a going political system like that of the United States," (1951, pp. 514), and E. E. Schattschneider lamented, "The flaw in the pluralist heaven is that the heavenly chorus sings with a strong upper-class accent" (1960/1975, p. 34-35). Theodore J. Lowi decried the influence of special-interest groups in American policy-making as a distortion of democratic decision-making that he called "interest-group liberalism" (1979, p. 50).

Even though groups of various kinds tend to promote the interests of the wealthy, their insatiable appetite for funds causes them to solicit dues and donations from people of modest means. These groups certainly include political parties, ideological groups, and election candidates' campaign committees. While, to be sure, political leaders tend to be wealthier than the average American, they send desperate solicitations to the masses to send money lest their political opponents inflict irreversible damage on the United States. The solicitations, written by shrewd fund-raisers, contain shrill, disingenuous messages to alarm and inflame the recipients, who proceed to write checks as donations to the organizations. Undoubtedly, an immediate effect of these transactions is to transfer wealth from lower-middle and middle-class Americans to wealthier political operatives and fund-raising professionals. Most vulnerable to these appeals are elderly citizens, who, confronted by the question, "What kind of country are we going to leave for our children and grandchildren?" write generous checks that they can often ill afford. Even the most casual observer can see that this economic activity has done little to create a better country, but it certainly has depleted the resources of working-class and retired Americans somewhat while it has allowed the organizations' managers to prosper.

In addition, this upper-class "accent" leans in a clearly corporate direction. This leaning can be demonstrated by examining the spending done by lobbyists at the federal level. Compiling data from the U.S. Senate Office of Public Records, OpenSecrets.org ranked various sectors of society by how much they spent on lobbying (see http://www.opensecrets. org/lobby/top.php?indexType=c). In 2010, definably corporate sectors– agribusiness, communications/electronics, construction, defense contractors, energy, finance/insurance/real estate, health (dominated by pharmaceutical companies), lawyers/lobbyists, transportation, and other business interests–spent approximately $3 billion on lobbying while non-corporate interests–ideological, single-issue (e.g., environmental, human rights, social issues), labor, education, public sector, and religious interests–spent less than $500 million. In other words, corporate interests spent about six times as much as did non-corporate interests.

The Nonprofit Sector: A Case Study

Where the divergence between the mythology and the reality is widest probably involves the nonprofit sector, which encompasses educational, cultural, and religious organizations and a countless array of charities. The national, state, and local governments generously subsidize the activities of these organizations by exempting them from the payment of income, property, and sales taxes. Section 501(c)(3) of the Internal Revenue Code even permits donors to most of these organizations to deduct their donations when they calculate the amount of income on which they must pay taxes. Americans are then inundated with appeals to give, give, give. These appeals come in the mail, they are delivered by e-mail, and they are communicated incessantly by television and radio stations and newspapers. *Much less frequently*, the news media get around to reporting about the unattractive activities and behaviors that are common in the nonprofit sector, such as the generous salaries that many nonprofit executives draw. In 1992, William Aramony, president of the United Way of America, resigned under pressure when the news media finally revealed that he "was earning $463,000 a year in salary and other benefits, was flying first class on commercial airlines, had occasionally booked flights on the supersonic Concorde and avoided cabs in favor of limousines." As Aramony arranged, the United Way "created and helped finance several taxable spin-off organizations that provided travel, bulk purchasing and other services to local chapters. One of these companies acquired a $430,000 condominium in Manhattan and a $125,000 apartment in Coral Gables, Fla., for business use by Aramony and his associates" (Duffy, 2001). But these revelations usually reach the public only when the greedy conduct has become grotesque, as it did in Aramony's case supposedly because, according to his lawyer, his cancer and brain atrophy impaired his judgment. After the journalists do their civic duty of reporting these scandals on rare occasions, their television and radio stations and newspapers go back to their routine of promoting the charities and imploring viewers, listeners, and readers to give away as much of their money as they can be persuaded to donate. This occurs even though the journalists, their editors, and the corporate owners who employ them know very well that the charities they are promoting are run by executives who are living very comfortably on the salaries that the donations are financing.

Consider the case of the annual "telethons" that support the Muscular Dystrophy Association. In each television "market," one television station will agree to donate about 21 hours of its air time beginning on the evening before Labor Day for the specific purpose of continuously soliciting the public for donations. Repeatedly, during the national broadcast hosted by MDA national chairman Jerry Lewis and during the occasional presentations from the studio of the local television station featuring the station's news anchors and weather and sports reporters, the viewers' attention will be drawn to a scoreboard that appears to be tallying the viewers' pledges. At the end of the telethon, the scoreboard displays a total amount in excess of $60 million. The perception that the pledge total is growing gradually over the 21-hour broadcast undoubtedly incites many viewers to call in a pledge. *None of the journalists who are involved in this spectacle* thinks that it is newsworthy to report that, in fact, most of the $60 million has already been raised *before the telethon even goes on the air*, despite the fact that the "tote board" falsely shows a beginning amount that is negligible or even zero when the broadcast begins. MDA executives feed the pre-telethon donations into the "tote board" *gradually* over the course of the 21-hour begging marathon to create the illusion that the viewers' interaction with the telethon activity is causing the donation total to build along with the nail-biting excitement (Bakal, 1979, pp. 354-360). MDA's president claimed $402,000 of the organization's 2008 revenue for his salary. Put another way, the $25 donations of *16,080 donors* to the MDA that year were needed to pay for the president's salary. The question must arise: What possible motivation does a wage-earner who earns $50,000 per year have to donate $25 to the MDA in order to pay 1/16,080[th] of the president's generous salary? But such individuals *do* make these donations, making one suspect that the donors do not have enough information to make an informed, rational decision.

While television, radio, and newspaper personalities like Atlanta's Clark Howard explain to viewers, listeners, and readers how to practice the vigilance of *caveat emptor* ("let the buyer beware") in their purchasing transactions, these communication outlets contrarily plead with the public to give their money away spontaneously and injudiciously to charities. The result of this relentless manipulation is that Americans, chronically, are too gullible to make intelligent decisions concerning charity. Charities and religious organizations (such as those that sponsor television broadcasts hosted by such televangelists as the Rev. Pat Robertson) have manipulated countless elderly people to provide their bank-account numbers so that the organizations can *debit their accounts monthly* (an exploitation that their adult children often discover only when the elderly parents become enfeebled or die). A group of journalists and academic researchers conducted a study to determine just how gullible Americans might be when they are solicited for charitable donations (Bakal, 1979, pp. 289-290). The group set up fund-raising tables in front of stores, with jugs for the collection of money and signs identifying charities (however, the charities were the results of the researchers' fertile imaginations and sense of humor). Shoppers stopped at the tables and deposited money into the jugs to help these nonexistent charities:

- "Heroin Fund for Addicts."
- "American Communist Refugee Fund"
- "National Society for Twinkletoed Children."
- A fund to "Help Buy Rustproof Switchblades for Juvenile Delinquents."

- "National Growth Foundation for African Pygmies."
- "The Fund for the Widow of the Unknown Soldier" (Bakal, 1979, pp. 289-290).

The nonprofit sector, sometimes referred to by economists as the "Third Sector" of the economy, appears to be a collection of needy little organizations struggling to help poor and sick people. Actually, the U.S. nonprofit sector is a formidable economic engine, accounting in 2006 "for 5 percent of GDP, 8 percent of the economy's wages, and nearly 10 percent of jobs" (Urban Institute, n.d.). The term "nonprofit" suggests that the organizations are living hand to mouth and giving away their revenues as quickly as they receive them, but nothing could be further from the truth. The term "nonprofit" merely means that the organizations have no *owners* (such as proprietors or stockholders) who anticipate profit. Nothing in the Internal Revenue Code or other statutes prohibits a "nonprofit" organizations from collecting more revenue than it expends for programs. It just calls the difference a "surplus." As Bennett and DiLorenzo (1994) report, organizations like the American Cancer Society, the American Heart Association, and the American Lung Association, which plead for donations in solicitations that claim the urgent need to help patients and fund vital research, have on hand in their investment accounts at any given time an amount of money equivalent to *an entire year's revenue*. This they can use later on to build more impressive office buildings containing office suites suitable for their executives. If all of these charitable organizations are combined with other nonprofit (although not tax-exempt) organizations, such as business and political interest groups, we are examining a mammoth economic complex that collects much of the nation's wealth, provides generous salaries and benefits to its leadership and management, and redistributes wealth in various directions. Far from being a mechanism that takes from the haves and gives to the have-nots, the nonprofit sector inconspicuously redistributes wealth from the working class to the wealthy with surprising frequency, as it does when it collects a donation from a working-class individual and uses it to pay a salary of hundreds of thousands of dollars to a charity executive. The tax-deductibility provision of Section 501(c)(3) often has this effect as well. When affluent individuals make $10,000 donations to art museums, they deduct the $10,000 from their taxable income when they file their income-tax returns. The effect of the deduction is that wealthy taxpayers may reduce their tax payment by, say, $4000. This is $4000 that would otherwise go into the public treasury to fund such programs as children and family services. The government has given them the $4000 benefit, even though their donations went to a museum whose visitors are almost all similarly wealthy people. How many working-class people go to a museum? Likewise, consider a $10,000 donation from an affluent alumnus of Harvard University to the university's endowment. Harvard University's endowment stands at *$25 billion.* Now, after the donation is made, Harvard University has an endowment of $25,000,010,000 to support the education of upper-class children, and the government sacrifices $4000 of revenue to fund such programs as children and family services. The rich-get-richer phenomenon is clearly alive and well.

Many of these organizations invite ordinary people to enroll as members, which involves a payment of membership dues. The member may receive a membership card as an acknowledgment of the payment. In most organizations, the award of "membership" is a meaningless gesture. The governing documents of most national organizations restrict actual voting and decision-making to a small group, such as a board of directors. Some organizations have as few as three members of the decision-making board. The members of the board of a charity do not receive any pay. They will, however, usually ratify the recommendations of the paid executive, a person with a title such as president, executive vice president, or executive director. The ordinary donors who possess membership cards tend to get no vote at all. This is the clear pattern of national organizations: The organizations appeal to the masses of supporters to give and give and give, but have no particular interest in the supporters' opinions about how the organization ought to be run. It is not unusual that the founder of such an organization will develop the organization's governing documents to disenfranchise the supporting masses from the outset. However, if the founder happens to have a democratic orientation, her successors will inevitably conform to Michels' "iron law of oligarchy" by adjusting the governing documents to confine decision-making to a select few. A charity's field volunteers (as distinguished from the volunteer board members)–i.e., those individuals who have been attracted to the charity to provide labor without pay–will usually discover in a short period of time that their opinions about how the organization should operate are unwanted. Attempts by such individuals to affect policy-making will often be met with a firm rebuke and, at the extreme, excommunication, as this chapter's co-author, Barry D. Friedman, experienced and reported in his 1997 exposé entitled, "Cracking Down on Red Cross Volunteers: How American Red Cross Officials Crushed an Insurrection by Agitated, Mistreated Volunteers in Northeast Georgia." In trying to address mistreatment of Red Cross volunteers in White County, Ga., Friedman sought information about the organization's governing bodies, which Red Cross managers refused to divulge. Instead, they terminated his 9½-year-long volunteer affiliation. Friedman concluded: ". . . [T]he Red Cross wants *your* money, unpaid labor, blood, and bone marrow but for its part *it prefers to operate in secrecy* and to be governed by committees shrouded in anonymity" (See http://faculty.northgeorgia.edu/bfriedman/studies/REDXcd.htm.)

Objections to the activities of the nonprofit sector are also expressed by business people in the profit-making sector when they find themselves in competition with nonprofit organizations that are invading their markets. One of the most visible examples of a nonprofit organization competing with the profit-making sector is the sale of Girl Scout cookies. The Girl Scouts sell cookies with a total annual sale of $700 million. This amount is about 9 percent of the total American market for cookies, estimated at $6 billion per year. Competing companies such as Keebler (now a subsidiary of the Kellogg Company) have to compete head-on with the scouts, but the scouts have two impressive advantages: (a) the fact that the Girl Scouts do not have to pay taxes and (b) the fact that the Girl Scouts do not have to pay the sales force! This competition is most definitely not on a level playing field. Testing laboratories for electrical devices complain about the tax-exempt status of their nonprofit competitor, Underwriters Laboratories, asking how they are supposed to compete fairly (in terms of pricing) with an enterprise for which taxes are not a cost of doing business.

In conclusion, far from being a humble segment of American society and the indefatigable source of relief for the poor, the massive assortment of interest groups, charities, and other associations has proved to be *most* effective in promoting the interests of the influential, mostly well-to-do people who control and manage them.

The Influence of Groups in Public Policymaking

Lobbying

Countless interest groups have been established to influence public policymaking in the national government. If you plan to visit Washington, D. C., consider taking a walk along K Street. Enter the buildings, and look at the list of groups that appear on each building's directory. You will notice that a lot of the groups that occupy space in the buildings are called "American _____ Association" and "Center for _____." These groups have set up shop in the nation's capital to lobby Congress and other government officials and to obtain public policies that will benefit or satisfy them. Of course, maintaining an office in Washington and staffing it are costly matters, so that the upper class is disproportionately represented in this competition to influence policymaking. The business community is amply engaged at numerous points of contact in this frenzy of lobbying activity.

One of the challenges facing these groups is knowing how to play the game. All the money, expertise, and effort a group has may go to waste if they do not know the whos, hows, and whens of lobbying. To assist them, an entire community of professional lobbying firms also line K Street. These firms are not dedicated to any causes–their value lies in both their knowledge of the policy process and (more importantly) their connections to it. They are populated with highly paid former members of Congress and ex-congressional and Executive Branch staffers. What makes these people so valuable is their knowledge of the process and *especially* their connections to current members of the Legislative and Executive Branches. A former member of Congress has access to many places in the Capitol to which others do not. This advantage gives them a chance to buttonhole current members that ordinary interest-group members do not have. The "revolving door" of legislators and staffers going from government to lobbying firms (and back again) has become a regular feature in Washington, D. C. The high price of these professional lobbyists also limits their availability to upper-class and corporate clients.

LOBBYISTS HELPING LOBBYISTS

Sometimes, interests and their lobbies form unlikely allies. T.R. Reid (1980) describes a situation in the late 1970s in which railroad lines and environmentalists both favored a waterway user charge for barge lines and opposed funding to rebuild a major Mississippi River Lock and Dam in Alton, Ill. The environmentalists were concerned about the ecological impact while the railroads were battling a competitor in the transportation business. The railroad companies were flush with lobbying cash while the environmentalists were not (see the earlier discussion of the free-rider problem). Yet railroads were hesitant to spend a lot for fear of being dismissed as a self-interested competitor with a financial stake. They thought that environmental lobbying could have a greater impact because these groups had no direct financial or business interest in the policies. However, the railroads could not contribute funds directly to the environmentalists because they were as big (if not *bigger*) polluters as were the barge lines. Environmental groups would not take their money. The railroads' chief lobbyist got an idea.

> *He conjured, out of thin air, a new organization, for which he created a name (The Council for a Sound Waterways Policy), an address (a vacant office down the hall in the Western Railroads Building), and a bank account. Each month he transferred some money from the railroads' lobbying fund to the Council, and the Council, in turn, transferred a monthly grant to environmental groups lobbying for waterway charges and against the Alton project... For the environmental groups, this arrangement was just right. They could continue their work without ever acknowledging that they were accepting money from a major polluter.* (Reid 1980, pp. 50-1)

The funding for the non-corporate environmentalists was now coming in large part from a major corporate interest. So, the corporate bias discussed earlier is likely even greater than the data may indicate.

Interest Groups in the Iron Triangle

Truman (1951) maintained that interest groups have an extensive influence in public policymaking in the United States (see a detailed description of his analysis in Chapter 12). Another analysis is widely known among scholars and students in the field of political science. This analysis features the "subgovernment model of public policy." Cater and

Freeman discussed this theory in their 1964 and 1965 works, respectively. This subgovernment model states that, in each area of public policy, there is a subgovernment that dominates policymaking in that policy area. The famous illustration of subgovernment is the **iron triangle** (see Figure 5.1).

Figure 5.1: Iron Triangles

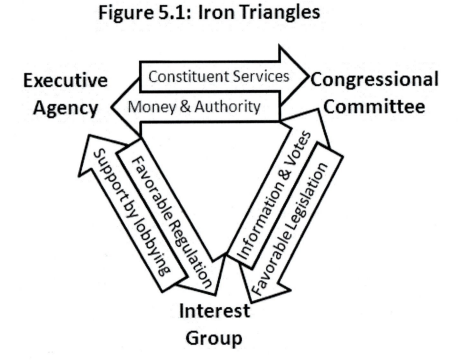

For example, in the policy area of agriculture, the partners in the iron triangle are as follows: congressional committees, the standing Agriculture Committees; executive agency, the Department of Agriculture; and interest groups, the American Farm Bureau Federation, among others. The theory is that these partners take control of policymaking in the policy area of agriculture, while other officials and citizens pay little attention to the making of agricultural policy.

Meanwhile, other iron triangles dominate policymaking in other areas. In the policy area of veterans' benefits, the partners are as follows: congressional committees, the standing Veterans' Affairs Committees; executive agency, the Department of Veterans Affairs; and interest groups, the American Legion, the Veterans of Foreign Wars, and others. Again, these partners take control of policymaking in the policy area of veterans' benefits, while the partners in the agriculture iron triangle pay little attention to the making of veterans'-benefits policy.

If this model is accurate—and many political scientists have found it to be very persuasive over the years—the motivation of people to establish and operate interest groups becomes perfectly clear. Participating in an iron-triangle partnership can be extraordinarily beneficial for the partners, while those who are not involved in these mutually beneficial arrangements are condemned to pay the taxes that finance the benefits that the iron-triangle partners are enjoying. No enterprising individual or group will be content for very long to be left out of the process by which the pie is divided and the pieces are distributed to those who are actively playing the game.

Interest Groups and Litigation

Many groups—notably **public-interest groups**—set out to influence policy by going "over the heads" of the president and Congress, and filing lawsuits in the judiciary. This tactic accounts for much of the influence that public-interest lawyer Ralph Nader and his "Public Citizen" public-interest law firms have been able to exert. While Nader's interests have been far-reaching, he is best known as an activist for consumer protection. For example, when in 1972 Nader was "bumped" from a flight that Allegheny Airlines (the forerunner of U. S. Air) had deliberately overbooked, Nader retaliated against the airline by filing a lawsuit in the case of *Nader v. Allegheny Airlines, Inc.*, 426 U.S. 290 (1976), accusing the airline of concealing its policy of overbooking. Nader collected $25,000 in punitive damages, as did an organization of his creation–the Connecticut Citizens' Action Group–whose meeting Nader, the would-be guest speaker, was unable to address when Allegheny refused to board him. Today, of course, an airline will do anything within its power to find "volunteers" who are willing to give up their seats to ticket-holders whose travel plans are inflexible. Many policies in the areas of consumer protection, worker protection, environmental protection, and so forth have come about through litigation filed by interest groups.

Delegations of Raw Government Power

Congress and the state legislatures sometimes delegate raw government power to certain kinds of interest groups. This occurrence happens most commonly when one of these legislatures empowers a professional association of some kind to determine who will be licensed to practice the profession.

> *Often . . . the exercise of licensing powers is delegated to "private" associations, even though the coercive power involved is that of a state. In the clearest case of this sort an association receives direct delegation; in other cases professional or trade associations are given the power to nominate personnel, virtually as a form of representation, to official licensing boards (bar associations, for example) and, on occasion, to policy-making boards.* (McConnell, 1967, p. 147)

The licensing power is an extremely significant form of influence over economic activity. For example, the American Bar Association has a keen interest in the licensing of lawyers and the accreditation of law schools, for such reasons as erecting barriers to entry into the profession in order to limit competition and sustain the levels of their fees. McConnell writes:

> *The practice of giving public authority—sometimes formally but often in practice—to private associations of professionals is quite old. As early as 1859 the North Carolina legislature enacted that "the association of regularly graduated physicians . . . is hereby declared to be a body politic and corporate," with "power to appoint the body of medical examiners."* (1967, p. 188)

While one might find the licensing of physicians and dentists to have some justification as a method of protecting the public from incompetent practitioners, the practice of licensing, often controlled by the members of the profession and trade, extends into a variety of fields for questionable reasons.

> *... [T]he list of activities frequently given state authority to regulate the qualifications of their members also includes barbers, hairdressers ("cosmetologists"), dry cleaners, funeral directors, cemetery salesmen, and many others. Even garage mechanics have attempted to gain such standing. Clearly, protection of the job market, which has been behind much trade unionism, forms a large part of the motivation to establish under state authority licensing systems effectively controlled by members of a given vocation.* (McConnell, 1967, p. 189)

Going Public, Grassroots, and "Astroturf"

Legislators may or may not listen directly to interest groups (who may sometimes be discounted or dismissed as unrepresentative of the general population), but they will *frequently* listen to public opinion. The quest for reelection means constantly pleasing the voters. Recognizing this idea, many groups attempt to influence public opinion in addition to trying to directly influence government. In the age of modern media, "going public"—as it is often called—is an increasingly popular strategy that may take several forms:

- *Advertising*: Trade and issue groups will try to build a favorable public image through advertising. One of the more successful ad campaigns is the dairy industry's "Got Milk?" ads (e.g., see http://www.gotmilk.com/). Look carefully at the ads. They are not designed to sell one company's brand of milk. They are designed to build support for the overall dairy industry. Their hope is that these ads will pressure governments to support policies favorable to a "popular" industry. Other ad campaigns may involve more naked attempts to pressure governments for favorable action. In 2010, the National Association of Manufacturers (http://www. nam.org) ran a series of ads to pressure the federal government into enacting tax policies favorable to their industry. Their ads raised the specter of job losses and other calamities if Congress did not do what they wanted (see: http://www.nam.org/Special/ Energy-Tax-Ads/Landing.aspx).In addition to broad advertising, groups may try to build support with narrower direct mail or

E-mail campaigns in which they obtain lists of customer addresses from companies that they believe their potential supporters will patronize (e.g., if you subscribe to the *Wall Street Journal*, you are a good target for business, Republican-leaning, and conservative groups), and send out information to those customers.

- *Letters, phone calls, and E-mails*: As they build favorable public opinion, groups will also encourage supporters to take action. One of the simplest forms of action is to have supporters contact government officials by mail, phone, or E-mail. The New York branch of the AIDS policy organization ACT-UP explains the value of letter-writing campaigns:

> *Letter-writing and post card campaigns, like phone and fax zaps, are a direct means of letting public officials and others know how you feel about a particular issue and what you want them to do. Like phone calls, they are counted and often used by politicians or agency heads to justify their actions. Without taking personal responsibility, they can then claim they were "responding to their constituencies."* (ACT-UP New York, 2000).

Notice ACT-UP's suggestion that this kind of contact not only helps pressure government officials into action, but also provides them with some cover as well. Phone calls and E-mails work much the same way.

- *Rallies and protests*: As with letters, phone calls, and E-mails, rallies and protests are a way of turning public support into action. They are often used by groups with fewer resources, as the main costs–time, transportation, bullhorns, and hand-signs–are much less expensive than media ads, billboards, and professional lobbyists. The purpose of most rallies and protests is to gain both the attention of government officials *and* the news media in the hopes of building further support for a cause. It should also be noted that, in many instances, these gatherings provide as much of a cathartic experience for their participants as anything else.

WISCONSIN UNION PROTESTS–AN EXAMPLE: In February 2011, the governor of Wisconsin and a supportive legislative majority were poised to quickly enact legislation curtailing the collective-bargaining rights of many state employees. Union members representing state teachers and other employees quickly flocked to the state capitol to protest the proposal, and thousands of protesters (and counter-protesters supporting the governor) filled the capital (Reiss, 2011). With lawmakers opposed to the legislation deliberately out of state to prevent formal action on the bill, the protests continued for weeks. Similar protests erupted in other states considering legislation curbing union rights (McPhee, 2011).

• *"Grassroots" and its evil twin, "Astroturf"*: Sometimes the public seemingly will act on its own, with little or no aid from organizing groups. This type of spontaneity is known as **grassroots** activity (as in, from the bottom up). Grassroots activity generally consists of the letters, phone calls, E-mails, rallies, and protests described above. New laws or proposed legislation may energize people to contact their legislators in support or opposition. They may gather in public to protest, as did many of the public employees in Wisconsin. Interest groups may encourage these activities or use them as a springboard to their own activities.

Grassroots activities may appear to be democracy at its purest– but sometimes appearances can be deceiving. Knowing the value of public opinion to lawmakers, interest groups may try to artificially generate activity that appears to be grassroots. That is, what look like grassroots letter-writing campaigns or spontaneous protests may actually be carefully planned and orchestrated by interest groups. These activities have been derisively (but not inaccurately) referred to as "Astroturf" (get it? fake grass!). In a 1996 PBS documentary, Hedrick Smith interviews the head of a professional public-relations firm that generates these kinds of campaigns (Smith, 1996):

HEDRICK SMITH [VOICE OVER]: Usually, business is targeting congress.
JACK BONNER/PRES., BONNER & ASSOCIATES: They want 100 phone calls, 20 calls into a senator, 25 letters, 200 letters to a particular member of the House.

SMITH: So you have 300 phone lines, that means you can have 300 people out of here at one time?

BONNER: The biggest thing we ever did we were doing six thousand patch through phone calls a day to the Hill.

HEDRICK SMITH [VOICE OVER]: Patch through phone calls are a hot item for Bonner and leading edge lobbyists. Bonner's staff phones ordinary citizens, sells them on a client's issue, and when successful, immediately patches the call through to their senator or house member, while the mood is hot.

SMITH: If they're on the side of the issue your client wants, they get patched through?

BONNER: Right.

SMITH: if they're on the other side of the issue, what happens to them?

BONNER: What's your guess?

SMITH: They get dropped.

BONNER: That's right.

[*Source:* http://www.hedricksmith.com/site_powergame/files/uneltrans.html.]

So be wary. What appears to be grassroots activity may be democracy at its purest–or it may be Astroturf at its most artificial!

Groups and Election Campaigns

One way in which groups may increase their chances of obtaining favorable policies is to help put the "right" people in office in the first place by getting involved in election campaigns. The further benefit of this is that officials who arguably owe their election to groups' support may feel gratitude for that support. This gratitude, in turn, may influence their policy positions in ways beneficial to the groups.

The most common electoral strategy is campaign spending. This spending may take the forms of either contributions to parties and candidates or direct spending in support of candidates. To address the concern among many Progressives in the early 1900s that politicians were "bought" by corporate money, the 1907 Tillman Act outlawed corporate campaign contributions. The 1947 Taft-Hartley Act also outlawed labor-union contributions. In addition to those laws, many others in the first half of the twentieth century established a patchwork of regulations on money in elections. Following the 1968 presidential election and in the midst of the 1972 election and the Watergate scandal, there was still public concern regarding the influence of wealthy individuals and groups over elections.

Congress enacted a set of laws known as the Federal Election Campaign Acts (FECA) in the early 1970s to

- Set strict limits on individual and group contributions to parties and candidates.
- Require the public reporting of contributions.
- Require groups to register with the federal government before they can contribute.
- Limit the spending of presidential and congressional candidates.
- Set up a system of public funding for presidential elections.
- Create an independent agency, the Federal Election Commission (FEC), to administer and enforce the regulations.

See Chapter 6 for more details on the FECA.

Political Action Committees

While law forbids corporations and unions from contributing to candidates' campaign committees, the FECA formalized their *members'* ability to create **political action committees** (PACs) for the purpose of raising money to contribute to campaigns. These PACs (the legislation actually refers to them as "multi-candidate committees") must register with the FEC before they can raise and contribute money, and they are limited to contributing a maximum of $5,000 per candidate, per election. To qualify as a PAC, they must support at least five candidates.

The number of PACs has grown dramatically, from fewer than 1,000 in the mid-1970s to over 4,000 today, with the bulk of that increase coming in trade association and non-connected (ideological and issue-oriented) PACs (Federal Election Commission, 2009a). Consistent with the upper-class and corporate biases discussed earlier, the greatest amount of spending on campaigns by far comes from corporate and trade-association

PACs. FEC data from 2006 indicate that corporate and trade-association PACs spent more than twice as much as labor and non-connected PACs combined (Federal Election Commission, 2009b).

FOLLOW THE MONEY

PACs differ in their goals and strategies. Paul Herrnson (2008) describes three different PAC strategies: access, ideological, and mixed. The bottom-line goal of access PACs is to influence legislation. They like winners, so they contribute most often to incumbents and to sympathetic candidates in close elections (where the extra money may make the difference). They do not wish to waste resources on challengers with little chance of getting elected. Most corporations pursue an access-oriented strategy. Ideological PACs wish "to increase the number of legislators who share their broad political perspective or position on specific, often emotionally charged issues..." (Herrnson 2008, p. 141). Most of their contributions go to sympathetic candidates in close elections, but they are far more likely than access PACs to contribute to sympathetic challengers as well. Most non-connected (issue or ideological) PACs pursue this strategy. PACs pursuing a mixed strategy will make some contributions to candidates sharing their views, and some contributions to incumbents "to improve their access to legislators" (Herrnson 2008, p. 143). Most unions pursue a mixed strategy.

Beyond PACs: "Soft Money", 527 Groups, and "Super PACs"

Restrictions placed on political-party spending by the Bipartisan Campaign Reform Act (BCRA) of 2002 (see Chapter 6) opened the way for vastly increased spending by groups in recent elections. The law restricted the ability of parties to raise and spend unregulated "soft money," and restricted their ability to run "issue ads." However, no such restrictions were placed on interest groups. Party activists, now restricted by BCRA, simply shifted their activity to outside groups. Given the exponentially growing costs of campaigns, PACs were not an attractive alternative, given their $5000-per-candidate, per-election limitation. Activists found their answer in tax-exempt "527" groups (named for Section 527 of the Internal Revenue code). These groups are technically not allowed to engage in campaign activity.

However, FEC and court decisions established that soft money and issue ads do *not* amount to campaign activity as long as they do not expressly advocate the election or defeat of candidates. What seals the deal is that these decisions also said that candidate names and images could be used in soft-money-funded issue ads without violating the campaign restriction.

In recent years, whole new classes of groups have formed to keep interests involved in the big-money world of modern campaigns. The latest creation is the "Super PAC." These are officially known as independent expenditure-only committees, and they

> *may raise unlimited sums of money from corporations, unions, associations and individuals, then spend unlimited sums to overtly advocate for or against political candidates. Super PACs must, however, report their donors to the Federal Election Commission on a monthly or quarterly basis—the Super PAC's choice—as a traditional PAC would. Unlike traditional PACs, super PACs are prohibited from donating money directly to political candidates.* (OpenSecrets.org, 2011)

In addition, the restrictions placed on corporations (and presumably unions) have been upended by the 2010 Supreme Court decision in *Citizens United v. Federal Election Commission* (130 S.Ct. 876). The court said that corporations have a First Amendment right to spend money from their own treasuries to expressly support the election or defeat of candidates, which the BCRA had forbidden (though they are still forbidden from contributing to campaigns, and their members' PACs still face contribution limits).

Other Activities

While spending dominates the election-related activity of interest groups, there are other ways in which members may get involved. Group members may volunteer their time and effort to candidates. Supportive candidates may recruit volunteers for groups to help with information and get-out-the-vote (GOTV) activities. This often involves staffing phone banks, or operating computers, or stuffing envelopes. Given their place among the workforce, union members are especially able to help candidates they support by going door-to-door throughout their communities, encouraging residents to vote for their candidates.

Other Forms of Participation
　　The participation of individuals and groups in public life extends well beyond the activities of interest groups. For a discussion of other forms of civic participation, see Chapter 15.

Discussion Questions
1. Discuss the history of interest groups. Why do they exist at all?
2. Tocqueville said that America is a nation of joiners. What did he mean? Investigate other nations to see if they differ from the United States.
3. Contact a local interest group or the local chapter of a larger group. A number of groups may be found at this site: http://www. twyman-whitney.com/americancitizen/links/lobbies.htm. What are their goals? What are their strategies for achieving those goals?
4. Examine the data on the "revolving door" by going to the OpenSecrets.org Web site. Under the "Influence & Lobbying" menu, click on "Revolving Door." On the left-hand menu, click on "Lobbying Firms," and select one of the firms. You will see a list of their lobbyists. Examine the lobbyists' employment timeline and history. In addition, there are tabs for information on the industries they represent and their expertise. Examine several lobbyists' profiles. What do you see? Did they spend time in government service before their current employment as a lobbyist? If so, explore their time in government. Does it appear related to their expertise and/or their clients? Can you make the case that their past government work constitutes a current asset to their lobbying work?

References

ACT-UP New York. (2000). *Letter Campaigns*. Accessed February 22, 2011, at http://www.actupny.org/documents/LW.html.

Bakal, C. (1979). *Charity U.S.A.* New York, NY: Times Books.

Bennett, J. T. & DiLorenzo, T. J. (1994). *Unhealthy charities: Hazardous to your health and wealth.* New York, NY: Basic Books.

Cater, D. (1964). *Power in Washington.* New York, NY: Random House.

de Tocqueville, A. (1945). *Democracy in America.* New York, NY: Alfred A. Knopf, Inc.

Federal Election Commission. (2009a). Number of Federal PACs Increases [Press release]. Accessed February 23, 2011 from http://www.fec.gov/press/press2009/20090309PACcount.shtml.

_____. (2009b). PACs Grouped by Total Contributions to Candidates – 2005-2006 [Press release]. Accessed February 23, 2011 from http://www.fec.gov/press/press2009/20090415PAC/documents/7groupbycontrib2006.pdf.

Freeman, J. L. (1965). *The political process.* New York, NY: Random House.

Herrnson, Paul. S. (2008) *Congressional Elections: Campaigning at Home and in Washington.* 5th ed. Washington, D. C.: CQ Press.

Lowi, T. J. (1979). *The end of liberalism: Ideology, policy, and the crisis of public authority.* (2nd ed.). New York, NY: W.W. Norton.

Madison, J. (1788/2001). The Utility of the Union as a Safeguard Against Domestic Faction and Insurrection. *The Federalist.* G. W. Carey & J. McClellan (Eds.). Indianapolis, IN: Liberty Fund.

McConnell, G. (1966). *Private power and American democracy.* New York, NY: Albert A. Knopf.

McPhee, E. (2011, February 22). Union Disputes Spread to Indiana, Ohio. *RealClearPolitics.* Accessed February 23, 2011, at http://realclearpolitics.blogs.time.com/2011/02/22/union-disputes-spread-to-indiana-ohio/.

Michels, R. (1911). *Political parties: A sociological study on the oligarchical tendencies of modern democracy*. Tübingen, Germany: J.C.B. Mohr.

Olson, Mancur. (1971) *The Logic of Collective Action: Public Goods and the Theory of Groups*. Cambridge, Mass.: Harvard University Press.

_____. (1982) *The Rise and Decline of Nations*. New Haven, CT: Yale University Press.

OpenSecrets.org. (2011) *Super PACs*. Accessed February 23, 2011, at http://www.opensecrets.org/pacs/superpacs.php?cycle=2010.

Reid, T.R. (1980) *Congressional Odyssey: The Saga of a Senate Bill*. New York: W.H. Freeman & Company.

Reiss, D. (2011, February 21) With Wisconsin's Protesters: A Cold Night in Madison. *Time*. Accessed February 22, 2011, at http://www.time.com/time/nation/article/0,8599,2052884,00.html.

Samuelson, P. A. (1954) The Pure Theory of Public Expenditure. *Review of Economics and Statistics* 36(November): 387-389.

Schattschneider, E. E. (1960/1975). *The semisovereign people: A realist's view of democracy in America*. Hinsdale, IL: Dryden Press.

Smith, Hedrick (producer). (1996). The Unelected: The Media & The Lobbies. *The People & The Power Game*. PBS. Online transcript accessed February 22, 2011, at http://www.hedricksmith.com/site_powergame/files/uneltrans.html.

Truman, D. B. (1951). *The governmental process: Political interests and public opinion*. New York, NY: Albert A. Knopf.

Urban Institute. (2010) "Nonprofits." Accessed February 18, 2011, at http://www.urban.org/nonprofits/index.cfm.

Chapter Six
Political Parties, Voting, and Elections
Carl D. Cavalli

Learning Objectives
After covering the topic of political parties, elections, and voting, students should understand:

1. The evolution, organization, and functions of the two major political parties.
2. The role of "third" or "minor" parties and the hurdles they face in our system.
3. The history of suffrage in America and the rules governing registration, voting, and elections.
4. The prominent role of money in contemporary elections.

Abstract

As noted in chapters one and two, our government is a democratic republic, and the centerpiece of all such governments are elections in which eligible voters select candidates to represent them. The organizing of voter preferences through political parties is central to the electoral concept. Not only did the framers not foresee this, but they were actually hostile[1] to the concept. This lack of foresight may have been their biggest failure. A strong case may be made that our two-party system traces its roots to the nation's founding. This system is sustained by our most common electoral rules: single-member district, plurality (or "SMDP") rules. Not only do these rules affect our party system, but there is strong evidence that they can affect the outcome *of individual elections. Other rules affecting elections include campaign finance regulations.*

Introduction
Political parties seek to control government through elections. As such, their existence is closely tied to the electoral process.

Political Parties
What is a political party? It is an organization that *selects* candidates for office to represent the party's ideals, conducts *election* campaigns to get their candidates into office, and *organizes* government to facilitate

---

1 See especially *Federalist* # 10 (http://thomas.loc.gov/home/histdox/fed_10.html) as well as George Washington's farewell address (http://www.ourdocuments.gov/doc.php?doc=15&page=transcript).

achievement of its goals. Selection includes recruiting (searching for and encouraging) candidates to run, and then conducting a nominating process to formally select a nominee among all competing candidates. In election campaigns, parties provide services (e.g., advertising, polling) for their nominees, and will also encourage turnout to support them. Examples of organization include majority party leadership in Congress (see chapter 7) or state legislatures, and presidential or gubernatorial appointments to the executive and judicial branches (see chapter 8). All of this is toward the goal of implementing a broad *policy* agenda. In addition, political party labels serve as "cues," or shortcuts to help us as voters decide whom to support in elections.

Unlike other multi-party democracies, we have sustained a system of two major parties for most of our history. This fact is interesting because the framers did not anticipate their formation. Indeed, they were actively hostile to the idea. James Madison devotes *Federalist #10* to a discussion of controlling the effects of factions. He defined a faction as "a number of citizens...united...by some common impulse of passion, or of interest..."–a definition in which all modern interpreters include political parties (Madison 1787). Additionally, in his farewell address as president, George Washington warned us "against the baneful effects of the spirit of party."

However, the formation of political parties was in the air, and that air portended *two* political parties from the start. Every major issue surrounding the formation of the government provoked two opposing sides: national versus state power, commerce versus agriculture, North versus South, and when it came down to it, pro-Constitution versus anti-Constitution. Moreover, these were not random divisions. Those on one side of any issue tended to be consistently on the same side of each of the other issues. Two *big* factions.

Elections

Why conduct elections? With elections, we can reward elected officials who appear to serve us well (by re-electing them to office), and punish elected officials who fail to serve us well (by kicking them out). That is, we can hold them responsible for their actions. This ability also provides the public with a sense of *influence* (as debated in chapter 1). One might actually make the case that voting replaces violence as the main means of political participation (consider: if you cannot vote politicians you dislike out of office, then how do you *get* them out?).

From the viewpoint discussed above, elections represent a bargain, both in the sense that they are (at least in theory) a good deal for us *and* in the sense that they represent an *exchange* between us and the government. What is the bargain from the government's standpoint? They concede our right to participate – to influence their composition – in exchange for gaining *stability* and *legitimacy*[2]. What is the bargain from our standpoint? We concede other means of altering the government (for example, *violence*) in exchange for the sense of influence discussed above.

Basics: Parties
Formation

As noted in the introduction, political parties were neither anticipated nor welcomed by the framers. However, the stage was set from the founding for a two-party system. The two big factions mentioned earlier developed, at first, into the Federalists and the Anti-Federalists.

The Federalists

The better organized faction at our founding was the Federalists. The framers were largely Federalists. They felt the Articles of Confederation was a failure (see chapter 2) and so wrote an entirely new constitution. They favored national power over local power – in large part because they felt co-ordination at the national level was required to promote and develop the nation's commerce and industry (e.g. see Wood 1998). Most were northerners, probably because most of the nation's commerce and industry was located in the north.

The Anti-Federalists

At least as numerous, but less organized were the Anti-Federalists. With many located in the agricultural South, they feared a powerful national government and the industrialization it might bring. They wanted to maintain the nation's agrarian roots. Throughout the states, opposition to centralized national power was found most often in areas "in which small, self-sufficient, and often debtor farmers were most numerous" (Main 2006, p.112).

2 That is, we will respect and obey the laws they create, even if we disagree with them. Disagreement becomes a catalyst for voting (and other forms of participation), and *not* for violence.

From the Anti-Federalists to the Democrats

The Anti-Federalists formed the first true American political party. They recognized the value of coordinating their efforts to win elections throughout the nation and to help bridge our system of separation of powers. Under the leadership of Thomas Jefferson and James Madison, they called themselves Republicans[3]. By the election of 1800, their organizational efforts paid off and they began to win huge majorities in Congress (Senate Historical Office 2010, Office of the Clerk 2010) as well as an unparalleled seven consecutive presidential elections.

Among intra-party divisions in the 1820s, Andrew Jackson came to lead the party and attempted to preserve its Jeffersonian roots. It was at this time they began to call themselves Democrats. Even though some left the party, perceiving Jackson's leadership to be autocratic, they continued to win elections. Including their Jeffersonian Republican forebears, they won all but two presidential elections from 1800 through 1856, and maintained control of Congress for all but a few years during that time.

After a period of dominance by the new Republican Party (see below) in the late 19th and early 20th centuries, the Democratic Party regained its majority in the 1930s under the leadership of Franklin Roosevelt. They maintained this majority largely intact into the 1970s. It was a changed party, however.

From its Anti-Federalist forebears, it came to be the party of the "common man." While the party maintains a similar focus today as the party of workers, minorities, and women, its view of government has changed drastically. Franklin Roosevelt's Democratic Party was quite different from Jefferson's and Jackson's. Gone were the Anti-Federalist fears of national government. Roosevelt's "New Dealers" believed in using the power of the national government to fight economic distress and inequality (e.g., see: http://www.democrats.org/agenda.html).

From the Federalists to the Whigs to the Republicans

Though our founding was dominated by Federalists, their dislike of political parties proved to be their downfall. The electoral system they created worked to the advantage of organized parties. By the time they realized this and organized into a Federalist Party, it was too late. In the

---

3 This is not the modern Republican Party (see next section). To distinguish this party from the modern one, the terms "Democratic-Republicans" or "Jefferson's Republicans" are often used.

elections of 1800, they lost out to their better-organized opponents (see above) virtually everywhere. By the early 1800s, they were finished as an organized group. Their sympathizers did not disappear, however. A combination of former Federalists and Democrats (who feared what they saw as autocratic rule in the election of Democrat Andrew Jackson to the presidency) formed the Whig Party. They were quite successful in the 1830s and 1840s, electing several presidents and building congressional majorities (Senate Historical Office 2010, Office of the Clerk 2010). The thorny issue of slavery split and ultimately destroyed the party in the early 1850s.

At that time, a new party arose from anti-slavery elements in both the Democratic and Whig parties. To emphasize their belief that they were truly fulfilling the Founders' vision, they called themselves the Republican Party. Under the leadership of John C. Fremont and Abraham Lincoln, they quickly rose to major party status. From the mid-1850s through today, they have competed with the Democrats as one of the two major political parties in America.

Consistent with their Federalist roots, the Republicans have historically been the party of business and commerce. However, unlike their forebears who saw a strong national government as the key to commercial development, modern Republicans often take a dim view of federal power. More like the Anti-Federalists, modern Republicans generally place more trust in local government. The modern Republican Party supports free-market commerce (i.e., it opposes much government regulation of businesses and industries), small and localized government, and a socially conservative ideology (e.g., see: http://www.gop.com/index.php/learn/what_we_believe/).

Three-Part Structure

As noted earlier, parties exist to select and elect candidates and to organize government. This idea suggests a three-part structure to parties as we know them. Not only is there the *party organization* itself, but there is also the *party in government* and the *party in the electorate* (voters) as well (e.g., see Key 1964, Beck 1997).

It is the party *organizations* at all levels (national, state, and local) that help to select and elect candidates. They do this by first nominating candidates as their choices for the general election. The process of nominating usually consists of either a *primary*, where voters select a nominee, a *caucus*, where party members gather to agree upon a nominee, a *convention*, where party members gather in one location to formally choose a nominee, or some combination of these methods.

Presidential Nominations

We can see all three of these methods in presidential party nominations. In the late summer of presidential election years, the national party organizations (the Democratic National Committee and the Republican National Committee) each hold a national *convention* to formally select their presidential nominees. At the convention, delegates representing all 50 states and many territories vote to select the nominees. Most all delegates are bound by state and/or party rules to vote for particular candidates, so the outcome is rarely in doubt (leading some to talk more of coronations than conventions). So, how are the delegates chosen, and why are they bound to one candidate? This is where the other methods come into play.

All states and territories hold either a primary or caucus[4] to choose their delegates to the national conventions. A *primary* can be either open to all voters or closed to all but registered party members (there are some other variations as well). Voting takes place at polling places around the state, much like any election. A *caucus* involves only party members meeting around the state. They involve more effort as participants must gather in one spot (an auditorium or gymnasium) to openly debate the choices (e.g. see: http://www.c-span.org/Events/C-SPAN39s-Iowa-Presidential-Caucus-Pre-Show/9131/). Because of the effort involved, caucuses usually involve far less of the electorate than do primaries. The Democratic Party requires all of its primaries and caucuses to use **proportional representation** rules which allocate delegates favoring candidates in proportion to their support in the primary vote or the caucus. The Republican Party allows states to use **winner-take-all** rules, where the top finisher gets *all* the state's delegates, if they so choose.

To win elections, the party organizations help candidates appeal to the *electorate*. The focus of these "get-out-the-vote" (GOTV) efforts is two-fold. First, the organizations want to make sure their supporters – the *party in the electorate* (often called the "base") turn out to vote. Next,

---

4 Or in some cases, like the Texas Democratic Party's delegate selection, a combination of both.

they want to reach out to independent and uncommitted voters to win their support. Particularly strong or popular candidates may even reach out to supporters of other parties. Today, these are high-tech efforts to target and appeal to the public using mailing and email lists, consumer and demographic data, and social networking media (e.g., YouTube, Twitter, Facebook) in addition to traditional speeches, fliers, rallies, and TV/radio advertisements.

Candidates who win the general election will take their seats in office to become their party's *party in government*. In legislating or administering policy, they will attempt to represent their party and to get its agenda enacted into law.

Modern Regional Bases

The Democratic and Republican parties have competed head-to-head as our only major parties for over 150 years. Currently, the Democratic Party's regional bases are in the Northeast, the Great Lakes region, and the West. The Republican Party's regional bases are in the South, the Upper Midwest, and in the Great Plains. This distribution is evident in the 2008 presidential Electoral College results (e.g., see http://www.realclearpolitics. com/epolls/maps/obama_vs_mccain/). While this distribution is accurate, it is also misleading.

It should also be noted that both parties are *competitive* in many areas nationally. Instead of a divided red and blue America (with red representing Republican and blue representing Democrat), some argue that a more accurate portrayal of party competition today is of a "purple America" (e.g., see Ansolabehere, Rodden, and Snyder 2006)[5].

Realignment

The current alignment of political parties has not always been the case. We have seen many different partisan alignments. At any given time, there is a set of parties competing over the issues of the day. This set of parties competing over these issues comprises a **party system**. New events and new generations with new issues will alter the composition of—and competition between—the parties, leading to a new party system. This change is often referred to as **realignment** (Burnham 1970). Through much of our history, realignments occur with surprising regularity –

---

5 For a graphic representation of this notion, see http://www.princeton.edu/~rvdb/JAVA/lection2008/

approximately every 30 years. Perhaps it is a result of generational change. In any case, most electoral scholars identify five or six realignments in our history (e.g., see Sundquist 1983), usually resulting in a dominant party. They are identified here by approximate year:

- *1800*: In a sense, 1800 saw an *alignment* rather than a *re*alignment since this was the point at which political parties were developing. Indeed, the very development of parties was the issue. Recall the differing views on organizing between the Federalists and Anti-Federalists. The Federalists disliked factions, believing them detrimental to the public good, while the Anti-Federalists saw organizing as the key to success. The Anti-Federalists' organization into Jefferson's Republicans paid off as they became the dominant party in American politics for many years (and, indeed, the only party for a few years).

- *1828*: A new generation of Americans saw the rapid disappearance of property requirements for voting. This change meant voting and politics were no longer limited to the wealthy elite. In a more practical sense, it made public campaigning a viable option for election. Andrew Jackson was the first person to run for president by openly campaigning for votes among the public. It was the new issue of the political age – political participation, and Andrew Jackson's Democrats capitalized on the expansion of the vote to ordinary (white, male) citizens to become the dominant party for the next 30 years.

- *1860*: An old issue, slavery, became the issue of the age as the nation debated its expansion into the west. The industrial North – less dependent upon slavery – was the locus of a growing movement to abolish the practice, while the agricultural South was still dependent upon it. The issue fractured both the Whigs and Democrats, destroying the former, and leaving the Democrats as a largely Southern, pro-slavery party. In 1854, the abolitionists united to form a new party, the Republicans. The growing anti-slavery movement rapidly catapulted the party to majority status (aided by the secession of largely Democratic Southern states from the union in the 1860s). They would remain the majority party nationally until well into the 20th century.

- *1896*: The late 19th century saw the United States emerge as a major industrial, economic power in what we might today call the *first* age of globalization. The major issue was how far to pursue industrialization and globalization. The Democrats, still located largely in the more agricultural South, resisted the trend while the Republicans embraced it. The nation sided with the Republicans, re-energizing their majority at the dawn of the 20th century.

- *1932*: Perhaps the most iconic realignment occurred in the 1930s as a result of the Great Depression – the greatest period of economic distress the country has experienced. The issue for the age was the extent to which the federal government should actively combat it. While both parties embraced at least some activism (it may be argued that Herbert Hoover, the Republican president at the time the Depression hit in 1929, made greater use of the federal government to address the nation's troubles than any previous president[6]), it was the Democratic Party under Franklin Delano Roosevelt that eventually advocated extensive use of the federal government to actively combat the effects of the Depression (the **New Deal**). An increasingly distressed public flocked to Roosevelt and the Democrats, who won unprecedented majorities in the 1930s.

- *1960s*? If the 30-year cycle held, we would expect to see another realignment in the 1960s. However, there is scant evidence of any traditional realignment. The Democratic Party maintained a relatively strong majority through the 1970s and weaker majority into the early 1990s. While there were new issues – most notably the **civil rights movement**, and more recently the rise of economic and social issues – they led neither to a new majority, nor to radically reformed parties. To this day, while Democratic support has weakened notably, there is little corresponding increase in support for Republicans. Instead, beginning in the 1970s, people began to leave both parties and identify as independents (e.g., see the American National Election Studies data on party identification: http://www.electionstudies.org/nesguide/toptable/tab2a_1.htm). This change leaves us with a more competitive two-party system, but not with a "50-50" division of Democrats and

---

6 See for example the Reconstruction Finance Corporation, created in 1929 (http://www.archives.gov/research/guide-fed-records/groups/234.html).

Republican. More accurately we now have a "33-33-33" division that includes independents – leading some to say there has not been a *re*alignment, but rather a *de*alignment, or a movement away from political parties (Nie, Verba, & Petrocik 1976, Rosenof 2003).

In the mid-1990s, many proclaimed a Republican realignment. There were similar claims of a Democratic realignment after the 2006 and 2008 elections, and again by Republicans after the 2010 elections. All are wrong. The key to realignments is their establishment of a stable, long-term party system, which means you can never proclaim one after only one or two elections. They may only be designated in retrospect after a decade or more.

Minor Parties

That only two major parties have dominated our politics for over 150 years does not mean no other parties exist. There are dozens and possibly even hundreds of smaller parties[7], which raises a few questions.

<u>Why are there only two major parties?</u>

There are several contributing reasons. First, as noted earlier, we divided into two major factions very early on, leading almost inevitably to our two major parties. Second, though, is that our divisions have never been so vast as to sustain many major parties. We share several universal values (see chapter 4) that do not leave much support for additional parties. Third is our self-fulfilling skepticism of third parties. Most all of us are not so issue driven that we will back parties with little chance of winning, even if we agree with their issue positions. In fact, there is evidence to the contrary – we often adjust our own issue positions to conform to the party we support (Campbell et al 1960, Fiorina 1981, Green et al 2002, Karol 2009). We like to back winners, essentially because the rather reasonable logic is that parties do us no good unless they can actually win elections. Of course, if we do not support them, they will not win. It is a vicious cycle for third parties.

Last, and least appreciated, are rules. Rules matter. While we like to think that elections are simply "The candidate with the most votes wins,"

7 The site Politics1.com lists 44 others at the time of this printing (see: http://politics1.com/parties. htm)

it is more complicated. Different rules may lead to different outcomes even with the same set of votes. All American elections are state-run; it is a delegated power (see chapter 3). There are federal regulations and constitutional requirements imposed on the states, but the bottom line is that they actually run the contests. This in itself is a "rule" that matters! It means 50 states have 50 sets of differing electoral rules. Since all contemporary state legislatures and governors, who write the rules, are under the control of one major party or the other, those rules are generally favorable to the major parties. The first hurdle third parties must clear is negotiating 50 different sets of rules – none of which were written by (or for!) them.

There are two sets of rules that have the greatest effect: voting rules and ballot access rules.

- *Voting Rules*: The most common American voting rules are Single-Member District, Plurality rules – known as **SMDP**. Not all U.S. elections are SMDP, but most are.
  - o As the name implies, **Single-Member Districts** have only one representative. It is how we elect representatives to Congress and state legislatures. For example, the state of Georgia is currently apportioned 13 U.S. representatives based on its population (see chapter 2). The state does not, however, simply elect 13 people state-wide. Federal law requires states to create one electoral district per representative – so Georgia must elect one representative each in 13 separate districts. It is this winner-take-all nature (often referred to as "first-past-the-post") that advantages major parties. You must have enough support to finish first. As such, it may be better to think of *single-winner elections*. Contrast this with **Multi-Member District** systems (or *multi-winner elections*), where each district elects several representatives. If states were allowed to use multi-member systems for Congress, Georgia might hold a single, state-wide election where the top 13 finishers won office. Another possibility might be a handful of districts electing several representatives each. In either case, candidates can finish second, third,

or lower and still win office. This procedure gives minor parties a much better chance.

- o In **Plurality** elections, the threshold for victory is simply getting more votes than anyone else. Contrast this to **Majority** elections where the threshold is higher: more than half of the votes cast (or alternatively, more votes than everyone else combined). The advantage of plurality rules to major parties may seem counter-intuitive at first. Since winning requires a lower threshold, it is tempting to think minor parties have a better chance at meeting the lower standard – and they do. However, major parties do, too—and they get, by definition, more votes than minor parties (the very meaning of plurality, right?). In addition, they do so without needing help from anyone else. This situation leaves little hope for smaller parties. In contrast, even major parties will not always meet the higher standard of a majority election without help (see the case studies at the end of this chapter). That help may come in the form of coalitions with smaller parties to build the necessary majority—giving those smaller parties at least some influence (and a reason to stick around!).

- *State Ballot Rules*: As noted above, states control elections, and each sets its own rules. This power includes deciding which parties get access to limited ballot space. All states award space to parties who won a significant portion of the vote in previous elections—usually 20-25%. Major parties easily meet that standard, so their candidates appear on virtually all ballots. However, minor parties rarely do that well, so they generally do not get automatic access. They must seek it each time. To get access, states have all manner of requirements: fees (ranging from a few to thousands of dollars), petition signatures (again, ranging from a handful to thousands), paperwork, and legal action. Minor parties have to spend precious resources meeting these requirements, while the major parties are already out campaigning. This structure means the major parties can devote all of their time and money to campaigning while minor parties have to devote a significant portion just to get on ballots.

Chapter Six: Political Parties, Voting, and Elections   121

So why do they bother?

Minor parties bother because they have a message. That message usually involves individuals, issues, or just a better way (or any combination of those things).

Some minor parties are vehicles for a single candidate. The Reform Party of the 1990s was the classic example of a single-person, or cult-of-personality party (see http://reformparty.org/ and http://www.rpusa.info/). Its life blood was two-time presidential candidate Ross Perot, a billionaire who practically bankrolled the entire party from his own pocket. While he was a candidate in 1992 (when the entity was the more loosely-organized "United we Stand America"), and 1996, the Reform Party was born and rose to become the most formidable third party in decades. In 1992, Perot captured almost 20 million votes – the best showing for a third party presidential candidate in 80 years. In 1996, he ran for the Reform Party's nomination at a convention that he paid for. In the general election, he captured over 8 million votes – a significant drop, but still one of the best third party showings in years. After that, Perot began to withdraw from active participation in the party, and in 2000, he declined another bid for president. The effect on the party was dramatic. Public support dropped, and the party fractured among internal fighting. The official party nominated conservative columnist Patrick Buchanan for president, and a splinter group nominated Dr. John Hagelin. Combined, they managed to win fewer than 600,000 votes. The Reform Party (though it still exists today) was effectively dead.

Some minor parties are, in a sense, super-interest groups. Much like a traditional interest group, they will focus on a single issue (or a small range of related issues). However, they will go beyond merely trying to influence government; they will actively run candidates for office. Perhaps the best known national single-issue party is the Green Party (technically, a collection of parties with international roots). While generally a liberal party, their focus is on environmental issues (see http://www.greenparty. org, and http://www.gp.org). Green Parties originated in Germany in the 1980s, and came to the United States in the 1990s. They reached the height of their prominence in 2000 when their presidential candidate, long time consumer activist Ralph Nader received over 2 million votes for president. The party continues to function nationally, claiming over

140 elected officials nation-wide as of November, 2010 (see http://www.gp.org/elections/officeholders/).

Still other minor parties are organized and function just like the major parties with a range of issue positions and fielding candidates throughout the country. They are simply smaller. One of the more prominent better-way parties is the Libertarian Party (http://www.lp.org). The Libertarians ran over 800 candidates nation-wide in 2010 (see http://www.lp.org/2010-candidate-list). While Libertarian philosophy supports minimal government, the party neither focuses on a narrow range of issues (like a single issue party), nor does it revolve around a single person. In a very real sense, the Libertarian Party functions just like the Democratic and Republican parties; it is just a smaller version.

Minor parties are most successful when their message has two components: 1) it resonates with the general public, and 2) it has been ignored by the major parties. The rise of Ross Perot and the Reform Party in the 1990s best exemplifies these components. His 1992 candidacy revolved around concern about growing annual national budget deficits (and their cumulative impact on the national debt). In the 1970s and 1980s, both major parties had campaigned on balancing the federal budget, yet the publicly-held portion of the national debt more than tripled between 1976 and 1985 (Office of Management and Budget 2010). This lack of action by both parties over many years (in spite of their rhetoric) led many people to listen closely to Perot when he chided the major parties and focused on reducing the deficit. The Reform Party's success shocked the major parties into action. In 1997, a Democratic president and a Republican-led Congress negotiated a balanced budget that quickly led to budget surpluses into the start of the next decade. This action removed deficits as an issue, leaving little reason for continued public support for the Reform Party.

Basics: Voting and Elections

The basics of voting and elections largely encompass four questions: Who votes? How do we decide? What do the results mean? and What can our vote affect?

Who votes, part 1: the history of suffrage

At our founding, the answer to "Who votes?" was, "Not many!" While the original Constitution did not set voting requirements, most of the states restricted voting to propertied white males (often with additional restrictions based on religion, wealth, and other factors). In some states, free blacks and women could vote, though by the early 1800s no states allowed female suffrage. Since that time–with some notable and unfortunate exceptions–the trend has been toward expanding suffrage:

- In the first third of the 19th century, states dropped most all of their property and wealth requirements, opening participation far beyond just the elites in society.
- Following the Civil War and the abolition of slavery, the first constitutional voting requirement was enacted when the 15th Amendment extended suffrage to otherwise qualified African American males.
- A long-developing women's rights movement produced the next constitutional requirement when the 19th Amendment extended suffrage to otherwise qualified females.
- By the mid-1960s, many "baby-boomers" had reached their late teens. At the time, voting in all states was restricted to those 21 and older. With the Vietnam War raging, many called for increased political rights for the young, arguing that if the government can draft 18-year-olds into the military, then they should be guaranteed the right to vote. In 1971, the 26th Amendment guaranteed just such voting rights to 18-year-olds nation-wide.

By the 1970s, the vote was guaranteed (in *theory* – more on that below) to most everyone over 18. The remaining exceptions were (and still are) for convicted felons and those deemed mentally incompetent. Yet all was not well. Turnout rates were dropping significantly. In the 19th century, voter turnout often exceeded 80% of those eligible. As late as the 1960s, 60% of those eligible were voting in presidential elections. By the 1970s, though, that percentage had dropped to around 50% and remained around there through the rest of the 20th century. In recent years, the focus has been more on encouraging voter turnout than on expanding suffrage.

<u>Added Barriers: Some Intended, Some Not</u>
While the trend generally is toward expanding suffrage, that expansion has not been uniform and includes both regulations depressing turnout (often

unintentionally), and deliberate attempts to deny the vote to some – most notably African Americans.

Voting rights extended to former slaves by the 15th Amendment were originally enforced by federal troops during the Reconstruction era in the 1870s. When those troops were removed in the late 1870s, southern states enacted laws known as **Jim Crow laws**[8] to strip African Americans of social and political rights. These laws included barriers to voting. Among these barriers were:

- *Literacy Tests*: Many states required these tests of potential voters who could not prove their education. They were often administered in an unfair manner, with long, difficult tests given to African Americans (e.g., see examples from Louisiana: http://www.crmvet.org/info/la-littest.pdf and Alabama: http://www.crmvet.org/info/litques.pdf) while similarly educated whites were simply given short words to spell. Some illiterate whites could not pass even the simplified tests. However, these tests affected African Americans to a far greater degree since the literacy rates for newly freed slaves (who, as slaves, were legally prohibited from being educated) and their descendants well into the 20th century (who were limited to inferior, segregated schools) were much higher than the rates for whites.

- *Grandfather Clauses*: Even illiterate whites were often allowed to vote if their ancestors had that right prior to Reconstruction. Since most white ancestors had the right while slaves were denied it, African Americans were forced to prove their literacy while whites were often exempted from any required proof.

- *Poll Taxes*: State laws required potential voters to pay an annual tax in order to vote. The sums were small but still out of reach for many African Americans and poor whites. They were cumulative – if you could not pay the first time, you likely could never pay since you had to pay all back taxes as well. While these taxes affected poor whites, enforcement was lax, and the taxes were also subject to grandfather clauses that exempted whites.

- *White Primaries*: Because the Democratic Party dominated the south, almost literally to the exclusion of any Republican

8 For more information on Jim Crow laws, see the 2002 PBS documentary, *The Rise and Fall of Jim Crow* at http://www.pbs.org/wnet/jimcrow/voting_start.html

participation (e.g., see presidential election maps, especially from 1880 to 1940: http://cstl-cla.semo.edu/renka/ui320-75/renka_papers/party_system_maps.asp), winning the Democratic Party nomination for office was effectively the same as winning the general election. Democrats declared their organizations to be private and claimed the right to control their membership. They prohibited African American participation in party primaries, which as noted above, effectively disenfranchised them.

- *Difficult Registration and Voting Requirements*: In addition to formal restrictions, there were all manner of methods used to discourage African American participation. Michael J. Klarman (2004) describes some discriminatory registration methods:

> *Some registration boards...registered voters at undisclosed times in secret locations... Whites discovered through word of mouth where and when to show up to register, while blacks were kept in the dark... Registrars required blacks to fill out their own forms and flunked them for trivial errors, while they filled out whites' forms for them. Blacks but not whites were asked to recite the entire U.S Constitution or to answer impossible and insulting questions, such as "How many bubbles are in a bar of soap?"... Some registrars did not even bother to indulge in the pretense of legality and informed blacks that they would not be registered regardless of their qualifications.* (p.244)

There were similarly discriminatory voting practices. Polls were often located in segregated white neighborhoods, meaning the few registered African Americans would have to travel great distances into hostile locations. There were complex procedures developed to facilitate disenfranchisement of African Americans. One notorious example was South Carolina's "eight box" law, "which operated as a literacy test by requiring voters to deposit ballots in the correct boxes" (Klarman 2004, p. 31). Any mistake would invalidate all ballots. As with the registration procedures described above, whites were usually given assistance as needed while African Americans were not.

- *Intimidation and Violence*: Threats to the livelihood, safety, health, and even lives of potential African American voters turned voting procedures and requirements that might sound innocuous into very dangerous and discouraging hurdles. For example, some states required the names and addresses of registered voters be published in local papers. While this caused little concern for whites, African Americans knew that being publicly identified as voters often cost them their jobs, and even worse, subjected them and their families to beatings and killings (and their homes to burnings) from local Ku Klux Klan members.
- *Registration and Identification Requirements*: Not all barriers involve deliberate suppression. Early in our history, when only a few prominent citizens could vote, no system of tracking voters was needed. As suffrage expanded and the ranks of eligible voters swelled, states began requiring eligible voters to register with the state to help track who voted (Fischer & Coleman 2006). The purpose was to curb fraud (e.g., in the 19th century, some states recorded more votes cast than there were eligible voters!). A major effect however, is a significant decline in turnout. That is, registration is a hurdle to overcome that is especially problematic among:
    - o The Less Educated – because it requires awareness and knowledge of elections well before they are held. If we know anything about elections, we are much more likely to know approximately when Election Day is than to be aware of registration deadlines.
    - o Lower **Socioeconomic** Classes – because voter registration is likely to be a very low priority for someone struggling to maintain food and shelter for their family. Upper classes are much more likely to have the time, ability, and awareness to be involved.

There have been recent attempts to make registration easier (see below). In recent years, several states enacted strict photo identification requirements for voting (e.g., see Georgia's requirements: http://www.sos.ga.gov/gaphotoid/). These laws generally require people to produce a valid photo ID (usually a driver's license, passport, state employee or student card, or something similar) before they can vote. Proponents claim the laws are needed to help prevent voting fraud, while opponents claim the requirements place an undue burden on those—like the elderly, minorities, and the poor—who are otherwise qualified to vote, but are less likely to either possess such ID or to be able to obtain them. There are many challenges to these laws. As of 2011, the Supreme Court has upheld Indiana's version.

By the mid-1960s, most of the deliberate attempts to suppress African American voting had been removed. In *Smith v. Allwright* (1944), the Supreme Court declared that white primaries were unconstitutional. In 1964, the U.S. Constitution was amended to outlaw all poll taxes. In 1965, the federal Voting Rights Act outlawed many of the remaining discriminatory practices and provided for federal enforcement of voting rights.

Who votes, part 2: making it easier

Originally, registration meant taking time off to physically travel to a specific location to fill out paperwork. This fact added to the hurdles faced by the less educated and the lower classes, who were not aware of the locations and/or not able to take the time or travel the distance to register. In recent decades, attempts have been made to ease the burdens of registration. Most notably, the **Motor Voter Act of 1993** requires all states to offer mail-in registration forms, and also requires them to offer the forms at most state government facilities like schools and many state services locations like motor vehicle bureaus (hence the name "Motor Voter"). In addition, many states have made greater efforts to promote voter registration in high schools, colleges, and among the public in recent years.

Many states have also attempted to make voting itself easier by liberalizing their absentee ballot rules (which were traditionally used for voters who certified that they could not get to their local voting location to vote) and by lengthening the time allotted for voting – in some cases by many weeks. For example, Georgia now allows voting up to 45 days prior to traditional election days, and allows voters to cast absentee ballots with no explanation required (effectively creating a mail-in voting system). Also, in the wake of the controversial **2000 presidential election** (which was held up for over a month by voting controversies in Florida), Congress passed the Help America Vote Act. Among other things, it provided money to help states upgrade their voting equipment and required states to allow people to cast provisional votes if their eligibility is in question[9].

How we decide: Voting Cues

When we cast votes, we are choosing among alternatives. How do we decide? The answer is that we use **voting cues**, or indicators. Historically, the most important of these is *party identification* (i.e., which candidate belongs to the party we favor?). As information has become easier to obtain in recent decades (at first with the immediacy of radio and television, and now with the information explosion on the internet), *issue positions* (i.e., which candidate's issues do we most like?) have become an increasingly prominent indicator as well. Beware of issues, though (more on that below)! While these are the most prominent cues, there are others. Here's a brief discussion:

- *Party Identification*: Very few Americans are formal (i.e., "card-carrying") party members. That does not mean we lack strong attachments. Americans have very strong personal attachments. Most of us identify with a party. Recent polls say about 60% of the public identifies with a major party – and the number reaches 90% if "leaners" (self-described independents who, when pressed, express some support for a party) are included (see: http://www.gallup.com/poll/15370/Party-Affiliation.aspx). This party attachment begins early in life as part of our political socialization (see chapter 4).

    Prior to the age of mass media (especially before radio and television), parties were *the* source of political information. Well into the 19th century, most major newspapers were run by one of the major parties and made no pretense of objectivity. Political rallies and speeches were considered social events. With little

---

9 Such votes would be counted later, if the voter's eligibility was certified.

independent information, party labels served as our primary (and often *only*) cue.

Modern commercial media displaced parties as a prime source of political information. With other sources increasingly available, Americans drifted away from political parties, with independents becoming as common as partisans. By the late 20th century, most observers said parties were "in decline." Even as they have revitalized in the last couple of decades (first as fund-raisers, and now as ideological competitors), this decline allowed other cues to rise in prominence.

- *Incumbency*: As parties declined in influence, more candidates appealed directly to the public through radio and television. With little help from the parties, voters searched for other cues, with **incumbency** (who currently holds office?) filling the gap (Mayhew 1974). The thinking is that, with less party information, voters began to notice who was currently in office (the incumbent), and began voting for them. Incumbents had the finances and organization to take advantage of new media to out-campaign obscure and underfunded challengers. Though parties re-emerged as major players, incumbents still enjoy greater support than their challengers. For example, at a time of seemingly great dissatisfaction with the federal government, incumbents running for re-election to the U.S. House of Representatives in 2010 won 87% of the time (and that success rate was actually a 20-year low!).

- *Issues*: The mass media age (radio, television, internet) has made information easier for us to obtain. As such, voters focus increasingly on candidate issue positions. It is laudable to say, "I don't vote just for a party label, I want to know where the candidates stand on the issues!"–however, one must beware that issues can be manipulated.

  o **Valence (one-sided) issues** are campaign favorites. Many candidates will carefully emphasize issues they know you will agree with. "Criminals should be punished!" or "I believe in America!" are examples. You might find yourself saying, "I agree with that statement!," but has the candidate actually said anything substantial?

Next time you hear an issue statement from a candidate, try applying the "stupidity test." Imagine the opposite of the statement. If the opposite is debatable, then the statement is probably reasonable ("Social Security should be reformed," vs. "Social Security should be preserved"). If the opposite sounds stupid ("Criminals should be punished" vs. "Criminals should go free"), then the statement is absurd

o   Another favorite is attempting to appease all sides on an issue particularly on divisive issues. For example, about abortion a candidate might say, "I am personally opposed to it, but I don't believe government should get involved." There is nothing intrinsically wrong with this kind of issue position, but be aware that it may be designed to appeal to both sides. It says to pro-life supporters that the candidate is on their side, but it also says to pro-choice supporters that they have nothing to fear from the candidate.

- *Candidate Characteristics*: In addition to the major cues, we use any number of others to help us decide. Most common among the remainder are candidate characteristics. We like to think candidates will understand us and help us. *Demographics* like race, gender, and ethnicity help us understand who candidates are and whether they can relate to our concerns. Other *background* characteristics like occupation, education, religion, ideology, childhood, and residence help us understand their experiences and whether they can empathize with our life. Lastly, basic *personality* traits like honesty, competence, friendliness, and intelligence help us understand how approachable they are and how they might handle the responsibilities of office.

What votes mean: Rules (again!)

This consideration may be decisive, yet it is little appreciated. Rules matter. They affect outcomes. In other words, how we translate votes into outcomes is how we know who wins. We tend to take words like "vote" and "election" for granted. However, it is not that easy.

First, different votes do different things. *Party primaries* select nominees to represent the party in a general election. If you vote in a primary, you have exercised an important civic function, but you have not elected anyone to office. *General elections* fill government offices for fixed terms, while *special elections* are used to fill vacancies temporarily. Some states allow *recall elections* that can actually remove someone from office. Most unusual is the *presidential election* where you do not actually vote for president at all! It is an indirect system where you, in fact, vote for electors for your state who in turn vote for president.

Second, rules vary from election to election and from state to state. The same set of votes might lead to different winners using different rules. Again, rules matter! Single-Member District, Plurality (SMDP) rules discussed earlier are one example. Elections using SMDP rules can produce different outcomes from Multi-Member District and Majority rules. We discussed earlier how these rules affect political parties. Let us now see how they affect elections.

The following example (based on Robert Ross 1988) demonstrates the effect of rules on outcomes, even with the exact same set of voter preferences. We start with four candidates: A, B, C, and D. A is supported by 40% of the population, B is supported by 30%, C is supported by 20%, and D is supported by 10%. In a straight, SMDP election, where there is one winner needing only more votes than anyone else, A wins (see Table 6-1, Plurality column). However, if the rule is changed to a multi-member one, with say three winners, then A, B, and C would win. The votes have not changed, only the rules.

In a single-member (or "single-winner") election with a *majority* rule, the same set of votes produces yet another result. Since the initial result, where A leads with 40%, does not produce a majority for anyone, we need a way to force one, which is done with a second, *run-off* election between the top two finishers, A and B. Since the supporters of C and D can no longer vote for them, they must decide between A or B. Table 6-1 lays out the distribution of preferences among all voters. Looking at C's supporters, we see that their second choice is D, their third is B, and their last is A. Thus, we deduce that they prefer B over A. From the table, we also see that D's supporters also prefer B over A. So, the result of the runoff is that A gets the 40% of their own supporters, and B gets the 30% of their supporters *plus* the 20% of C's supporters, *and* the 10% of D's supporters for a 60% majority. Again, no votes have changed, only the rules. A plurality rule favors A, but a majority rule favors B.

Yet another possibility is **approval voting**, where voters may cast votes for *each* candidate they like. Proponents argue this is a more accurate representation of our preferences as it allows us to cast votes for two or more candidates if we cannot make up our mind or if we like two or more equally. The winner of such a vote would be the most widely approved candidate among the voters. In Table 6-1, we can determine voter approval by observing the vertical bars ("|") among the voter preferences. Voters approve of choices to the left of the bar, and they disapprove of choices to the right. For example, the 40% whose first choice is A also approve of D, but not of C or B. Using this rule, we find that the first 40% cast votes for both A and D. The next 30% vote for both B and C. The next 20% vote only for C (which shows you can still cast a traditional single vote under this rule). The last 10% vote for everyone *except* A. Tallying these votes, we now find that C is the most widely approved candidate. Again, there are no changes in voters or their preferences, only in the rules.

Table 6-1: Distribution of Voter Preferences and Results Using Different Voting Rules

Votes	1st Choice	2nd	3rd	4th	Plurality	Majority	Approval
40%	A >	D > |	C >	B	A = 40✓	A = 40	A = 40
30%	B >	C > |	D >	A	B = 30	B = 60✓	B = 40
20%	C > |	D >	B >	A	C = 20		C = 60✓
10%	D >	B >	C > |	A	D = 10		D = 50

Notes: ">" = "is preferred to"; "|" = approval threshold (approve | disapprove); "✓" = rule winner
Source: Ross, Robert S. 1988. *American National Government: Institutions, Policy, and Participation.* Guilford, CT: Dushkin Publishing Group, Inc. p. 222.

The bottom line: Again, rules matter. The same voters with the same preferences produced different results using different rules!

What voting affects:

The quick answer to this question is not everything. In other words, we do have some ability to shape our government, but we cannot shape everything. Our reach is limited.

How is it limited? The most obvious answer is that not everything or everyone in government is subject to election. We cannot vote on:

- presidential advisers or other executive branch officials.
- congressional staff members.
- federal judges or Supreme Court justices.
- many state and local administrative and judicial officials.
- federal laws or regulations.
- many state and local laws or regulations.

Even when we can vote, it is often in a limited fashion. For example, since U.S. Senate elections are staggered (see chapter 7), with only one-third of the Senate up for election every two years, we can only change that much in any single election. In other words, two-thirds of the Senate is insulated from us in every election. In addition, the reach of our vote is limited by geography; we can only vote for U.S. Senators in our state and U.S. Representatives in our local congressional district (and state and local geography is usually even *more* limited). Those geographic districts also limit our ability to act collectively, since many groups among the public (i.e., racial, ethnic, gender, occupational, ideological, religious, and others) are fragmented among many districts and states[10].

<u>Too Many Votes?</u>
There are more than a half-million elected officials in the United States (e.g., see Shelley 1996). Add to that party primaries, run-off elections, recall elections, special elections, judicial elections, sheriff and school board elections among other local offices, and even policy proposals on ballot measures and state constitutional amendments, and it becomes quite clear that Americans have a lot of voting to do! This amount contributes to a phenomenon known as "voter fatigue," which helps account for why turnout rates in the United States are far lower than in similar democracies. Consider this example:

There were five elections conducted in 2010 to determine who Georgia's 9th Congressional District representative to the U.S. House would be. Why five? First, the incumbent – Republican Nathan Deal – resigned his House seat in March 2010 to run for Governor of Georgia (spoiler alert: he won). This situation required a special election to fill the seat until the term expired in January of 2011. The special election

---

10 Sometimes deliberately so. See "gerrymandering" in chapter 7.

was held in May. Second, since Georgia's election laws require a majority vote to win, a run-off election was needed because none of the candidates received a majority. The run-off was held in June. So, it took two votes just to fill out the term. Tom Graves was elected to fill the seat.

It does not end there. The regular vote to fill the next term was still scheduled for November 2nd, and the party primary votes for this election were scheduled for July 20th. The Republican primary (there were no Democratic candidates) required a runoff vote which was held in August. The incumbent, Tom Graves, won the runoff. So, there was a special election in May, a run-off for that special election in June, a party primary in July, a primary run-off in August, *and* the election in November (Graves won) – five elections for one seat in one year! There could even have been a sixth, a November run-off, had any significant opposition kept Graves from getting a majority.

It gets even more interesting. Like many states, Georgia has attempted to make voting easier by allowing people to vote up to 45 days before an election. This early voting meant people could vote in the July 20th primary as early as June 7th. It is noteworthy because the special election run-off date was June *8th*, meaning it was possible for voters to vote in the regular election primary at the same time or even before they voted in the special election run-off (Fielding 2010). Of course, this situation created some confusion. Some voters in the 9th District, who intended to vote in the special election run-off accidentally voted early in the primary vote instead (Redmon 2010)!

Money

In the past, political parties and election campaigns revolved primarily around organizing and energizing people in order to win elections. The focus was on face-to-face gatherings like campaign rallies. Today, things are far more complex. Make no mistake, people are still important. Our votes are, after all, the bottom line. However, as communications technologies (radio, television, internet) and campaign techniques (polling, phone-calling, direct mail marketing, and other public relations methods) develop, parties and campaigns have changed. In addition to the traditional armies of staffers and volunteers spreading out to win over our votes, there are now groups of more elite technology and marketing experts working behind the scenes to win us over as well.

These new experts and their technologies and techniques are far more expensive than the hoards of staffers and volunteers. This in turn pushes money and fund-raising to the forefront, requiring parties and campaigns to seek out ever-greater amounts of cash. Candidates and parties naturally turned to wealthy supporters for large donations to meet the demands. By the 1970s, an increasingly uneasy public grew concerned that politicians were being "bought" by these wealthy contributors (that is, that politicians were ignoring the public and focusing on keeping their few, wealthy contributors happy). This situation led to federal regulations (see below) that limited the amount of money individuals could contribute in any election to $1000 per candidate. Oddly enough, these regulations make fund-raising more important because far more contributors were now required to pay for increasingly expensive campaigns[11].

Campaign Finance Reform
Some campaign finance regulations date back more than a century. The Tillman Act of 1907 prohibited the direct contribution of corporate funds to campaigns. The Taft-Hartley Act of 1947 similarly prohibited direct contributions from labor unions. However, there have been two major waves of reforms in recent decades. The first was in the 1970s. Spurred on by perceived loopholes in the first wave, the second was in the late 1990s and early 2000s[12].

<u>The Federal Election Campaign Acts of the 1970s (FECA)</u>
In 1971, 1972, and 1974, Congress enacted laws that:

- limited contributions to federal campaigns from individuals ($1000 per candidate, per election) and from groups ($5000 per candidate, per election);
- required groups representing various interests (known as Political Action Committees) to register with the federal government before they could contribute to federal campaigns;
- limited both candidate and independent (individuals and groups not connected with any candidate) spending in federal elections

---

11 Where a candidate could once raise $100,000 from a single wealthy donor, they now had to seek out 100 people to get the same amount.
12 A good description and history of campaign finance may be found on the Federal Election Commission website at http://www.fec.gov/pages/brochures/fecfeca.shtml

(House, Senate, Presidency);
- created the Federal Election Commission (FEC) to oversee federal campaign regulations; and
- set up a system of public funding for presidential nominations and elections.

Opponents of these regulations claimed they violated the First Amendment speech rights of both candidates and potential contributors, and they challenged the laws in court. In the case of *Buckley v. Valeo* (1976), the Supreme Court upheld many of the regulations. However, they struck down the spending limits as unconstitutional, saying that candidate and independent spending amount to protected speech. In addition, they said contribution limits only apply to activities involving "express advocacy"– meaning words that clearly advocate the election or defeat of a candidate. Contribution limits and public funding of presidential campaigns set the tone for federal elections for the next two decades. However, things were changing.

<u>Soft Money and Issues Ads</u>

In 1979, one change in FEC interpretations led to what is called **soft money**. This money is used for non-campaign, "party-building" activities like get-out-the-vote drives or issue advertisements (as opposed to express campaign advertisements). Based on the Supreme Court's "express advocacy" restriction in *Buckley*, soft money contributions are not subject to limitations. Little-noticed at the time, this change, combined with federal court rulings in the 1990s that said candidate images and names used in ads do not amount to express advocacy, had profound consequences as the political parties re-invented themselves as soft money machines. Wealthy supporters were no longer able to donate more than $1000 to candidates or groups that run ads saying something like "Vote for Smith," but they now could pour unlimited contributions into political parties and groups that run **issue ads** saying "Smith is good for America" or "Smith supports legislation X while Jones opposes it." (for examples of issue ads in the 2000 presidential campaign, see: http://www.gwu.edu/~action/ads2/partyadlist.html).

The Bipartisan Campaign Reform Act of 2002 (BCRA)

By the late 1990s, as issue ads saturated the airwaves before every election, many saw them as a loophole rendering contribution limits meaningless. The argument was that the average television viewer, in weeks before an election, would not distinguish between ads that say "Bob Dole will cut our taxes" and ones that say "Vote for Bob Dole." Calls for new legislation to close the perceived soft money loophole were lead by U.S. senators John McCain (R-AZ) and Russell Feingold (D-WI). Their proposals were debated for several years and finally enacted into law in 2002 as the Bipartisan Campaign Reform Act. This law banned political parties from using soft money in federal elections (and restricted state parties' soft money) so that contributions from wealthy contributors to political parties were once again limited. However, to compensate for 30 years of inflation, the individual contribution limit was doubled to $2000 and subsequently indexed to the inflation rate (as of 2010, the limit was $2400). In addition, issue ads featuring candidate names and faces were limited. Ads could not show or mention a candidate 30 days before a party primary or 60 days before a general election.

The new laws were soon challenged, but the Supreme Court in 2003 upheld all but a few minor provisions.

"527" Groups, *Citizens United,* and beyond

BCRA did little to stem the flow of money in elections. For one thing, the national parties subsequently became very adept at raising record sums of money through good old-fashioned limited contributions. For another, while parties were restricted from using soft money and running issue ads, many types of outside groups were not. Tax-exempt "527" groups (named for Section 527 of the federal tax code) could exploit a difference between tax law and campaign law. Tax law prohibits these groups from engaging in campaign activity, but remember *Buckley* and the FEC said issue ads are *not* campaign ads. Therefore, 527s could run all the issue ads, using all the unlimited money, they wanted![13] Traditional interest groups formed 527s. More importantly though, members of political parties that could *not* spend soft money simply went out and formed 527s which could.

---

13 Other types of tax-exempt groups, known as 501(c)(3) and 501(c)(4) groups could run these ads as well.

In the 2004 elections and beyond, the airwaves were still saturated with issues ads. But they were no longer party ads, they were 527 ads. Then came *Citizens United.*

In addition to the long-standing bans on corporate and union campaign contributions, BCRA also restricted them from using their own funds to engage in "electioneering" (though their members could form political action committees to raise funds and make limited contributions. See chapter 5). In 2008, a little-known, non-profit corporation known as Citizens United wanted to broadcast and advertise a documentary titled "Hillary: The Movie," which was critical of presidential candidate Hillary Clinton. A federal court held that doing so would violate the BCRA restrictions on issue ads and on corporate electioneering. The case reached the Supreme Court in 2009, originally simply to determine whether or not the film and its ads amounted to issue ads or "electioneering." However, the Court ordered the case to be reheard a year later, this time to determine the far more consequential question of whether or not the BCRA restrictions on corporations and unions use of their own funds is constitutional. In a 5-4 vote, the Court struck down the restrictions as unconstitutional violations of the First Amendment's speech protection (*Citizens United v Federal Election Commission*, 130 S.Ct. 876). This ruling opens the door for corporations and unions to use their own money for any political activity they desire (except for direct contributions, which are still prohibited).

Where will this lead? Will we see multi-million dollar product marketing campaigns that endorse candidates ("Vote for Smith for president because she uses our product!")? It is trite to say that only time will tell, but surely the issue is not yet resolved. The question remains: What place does money have in our elections?

Majority versus Plurality in the real world – Some Case Studies

While most states use SMDP rules, Georgia does not. It requires a majority for election. In fact, a 1966 law made it the only state to require majority votes for all nominations and elections[14]. If no candidate receives a majority, the state requires a later run-off election between the top two vote-getters. This situation has had real-world consequences for the people of Georgia.

---

14 However, it exempted local municipalities using other rules prior to the law's adoption.

Case Study #1: 1992 Georgia Senate Race

"Wyche Fowler Jr....would defeat Paul Coverdell" said the *New York Times* on November 4th, 1992 as it analyzed exit polls from the previous day's election ("1992 Elections..." 1992). They were right, sort of. Incumbent Democratic Senator Wyche Fowler was up for re-election. He was challenged by Paul Coverdell, former state Republican Party Chair who most recently served as President George H. W. Bush's Peace Corps Director.

Republicans were making inroads into the traditionally Democratic state. George H. W. Bush won the state easily in the 1988 presidential election. However, Democrats were still the majority. In 1992, Arkansas Democrat Bill Clinton won the state over Bush in the presidential race, and Senator Fowler hoped to win re-election. According to the *Times* article, "Democrats tried hard to insure Mr. Fowler's re-election, seeing that he campaigned with Georgia's senior Senator, Sam Nunn, an enormously popular figure" ("1992 Elections..." 1992). The article reported that with 65% of the vote counted, Sen. Fowler led Mr. Coverdell, 51% to 46%. A third candidate, Libertarian Jim Hudson, was getting most of the remaining 3%.

Most observers expected Sen. Fowler to finish ahead of Mr. Coverdell. If the state used a simple plurality rule, that would be the end of it – Sen. Fowler would win. However, because of Georgia's majority rule, the numbers were crucial. If Sen. Fowler's total fell below 50%, he would have to face Mr. Coverdell several weeks later in a run-off election. When the final numbers were tallied, Sen. Fowler finished with 49.2% of the vote to Mr. Coverdell's 47.7%. It was not over.

The run-off drew national attention, big names, and big money. Senate leader Bob Dole (R-KS) and (soon to be former) First Lady Barbara Bush campaigned for Mr. Coverdell while President-elect Clinton, Vice President-elect Al Gore, and actress Kim Basinger, a Georgia native, campaigned for Sen. Fowler. Libertarian Jim Hudson, who was no longer in the race, endorsed Coverdell and urged his supporters to vote for the candidate. These factors sealed the fate of the run-off. When the votes of the November 24th run-off were totaled, Sen. Fowler finished with 49.4% of the vote – virtually identical to his general election percentage. But with the help of Hudson's supporters, Mr. Coverdell finished with 50.6% to become Georgia's new senator.

If Georgia had a plurality rule, Fowler would have been re-elected. But with majority rule in place, Libertarian support delivered the election to Coverdell. This was not inconsequential. In 1990, Americans for Democratic Action gave Fowler a 72% liberal rating while the American Conservative Union gave him a 35% conservative rating (Barone & Ujifusa 1991). In 1994, the same groups rated Coverdell at 5% liberal and 100% conservative (Barone & Ujifusa 1995). A moderate-to-liberal Democrat was replaced by a conservative Republican. Majority rule made a difference.

Case Study #2: 2009 Atlanta Mayoral Race

Seventeen years to the day after the 1992 election, Atlanta held their municipal elections, including elections for mayor, city council, and other offices. The incumbent mayor, Shirley Franklin, was term-limited and could not seek re-election, which left a wide open field racing to succeed her. The rule was again majority, but Atlanta elections are technically non-partisan, meaning party labels do not appear on the ballot. So, it would not be a typical Democrat-versus-Republican election. Any number of Democrats, Republicans, and others, might wind up on the ballot. In the heavily Democratic city, six candidates, no self-identified Republicans, qualified for the ballot. Three quickly emerged as front-runners: City Council President Lisa Borders, State Senator Kasim Reed (both Democrats), and City Council member and business owner Mary Norwood (an independent). Norwood lead the race throughout the summer and fall because of support from the business community and from northern, more Republican and white, districts. Reed and Borders trailed, with most of their support coming from the southern, overwhelmingly Democratic and black, areas (e.g., see Atlanta Mayor's Race District Map: http://www.ajc. com/news/atlanta-mayor-race-2009-185261.html).

The issue of race came to the fore in August as the Black Leadership Forum released a memo publicly that urged African American voters to support Borders, an African American (Galloway 2009a). Reed is also African American. Norwood is white. If elected, Norwood would become the first white mayor in over three decades. In the fall, it appeared that Norwood was getting half or more of the white vote while black voters were divided between all three. In addition to the racial overtones, partisan politics also emerged with claims that Norwood, who had voted in both

Democratic and Republican primaries in the past, was a Republican (a claim Norwood denied; see Galloway 2009b).

On election day, Norwood did indeed finish first. However with a majority election rule, her 45.8% of the vote was not enough to avoid a run-off against second-place finisher Kasim Reed, who received 36.3%. Borders was the odd one out with 14.5%. She subsequently endorsed Reed. Run-offs are very low turnout events, as voters are often worn down by multiple votes throughout the year (see "Too Many Votes?" above). The November election drew about 30% turnout, and local officials expected about half that amount in the run-off. However, the controversies over race and partisanship made this a high-profile election. Borders's endorsement plus support from the Democratic establishment benefited Reed, who was virtually tied with Norwood as the run-off approached. Both candidates saturated the airwaves with ads. The close contest plus all the interest produced an almost unheard-of 8% *increase* in turnout. Much like the November election, and true to the racially polarized atmosphere, votes were cast largely along racial lines, with Norwood leading in the largely white northern districts and Reed ahead in the largely black southern districts (McWhirter 2009).

Reed's momentum carried him to victory in the run-off. He finished with 50.4% to Norwood's 49.6%, a margin of fewer than 700 votes. A recount confirmed Reed's victory.

Unlike the 1992 Senate race, it is harder to say what policy differences might have arisen had Norwood been elected, but it is clear that neither candidate had the full support of the entire city. With plurality rule, Norwood would now be Mayor of Atlanta. However the run-off produced by a majority rule lead to Reed's ultimate election. Again, rules matter!

Discussion Questions

1. Why did political parties become such a central part of our political environment if the founders derided them as "factions"? In other words, what do they do that might make them so central?
2. Compare "third" or "minor" parties to the major parties. A list can be found here: http://www.politics1.com/parties.htm. Peruse their web sites and compare their goals, organization, and success to that of the two major parties.
3. Compare our largely two-party system to other systems (e.g.,

Great Britain's three-party system or Israel's multiple-party system). How do their party systems affect their politics?

4. As noted earlier, our history is full of attempts to disenfranchise African Americans (see chapter section: "Added Barriers: Some Intended, Some Not"). Some were obvious (white primaries), but some seemed more innocuous to whites (publishing names and addresses of registered voters). Today, there are still provisions that might not concern whites while they seriously concern blacks. For instance, many states have toughened their identification requirements in the name of combating voter fraud. Why might this concern African Americans? Contact or visit a nearby chapter of the NAACP (http://www.naacp.org) and investigate their concerns with these tougher restrictions.

5. Many campaign finance regulations were enacted in the name of preventing the appearance of elections being "bought" by wealthy contributors. Is there any validity to this concern? Explore campaign contribution data on these sites to investigate the role of money in election campaigns: http://www.cfinst.org/, http://www.fec.gov.

References

Ansolabehere, S., Rodden, J., & Snyder, J. M. (2006). Purple America. *The journal of economic perspectives, 20*(2), 97-118.

Barone, M. & Ujifusa, G. (1991). *The almanac of American politics 1992*. Washington, DC: National Journal Inc.

Barone, M. & Ujifusa G. (1995). *The almanac of American politics 1996*. Washington DC: National Journal Inc.

Beck, P. A. (1997). *Party politics in America.* (8th ed.). New York, NY: Longman.

Burnham, W. D. (1970). *Critical elections and the mainsprings of American politics.* New York, NY: W.W. Norton.

Campbell, A., Converse, P., Miller, W., & Stokes, D. (1960). *The American voter*. Hoboken, NJ: John Wiley & Sons.

Fielding, A. (2010, May 16th). Runoff, primary overlap may cause confusion for voters. *The Gainesville Times*. Retrieved from http://www.gainesvilletimes.com/archives/33258/.

Fiorina, M. P. (1981). *Retrospective voting in American national elections*. New Haven, CT: Yale University Press.

Fischer, E. A. & Coleman, K. J. (2006, March 22). Voter registration systems. Retrieved from http://www.american.edu/spa/cdem/upload/2-Fischer_Coleman-Voter_Registration_Systems-AU.pdf

Galloway, B. (2009a, August 27). The memo that's about to shake the Atlanta mayor's race [Web log message]. Retrieved from http://blogs.ajc.com/political-insider-jim-galloway/2009/08/27/the-memo-about-to-shake-the-atlanta-mayors-race/

Galloway, B.(2009b, November 1). Dems gamble against Norwood: State party claims she's a closet Republican. *The Atlanta Journal-Constitution*, p.B4.

Green, D., Palmquist, B., & Schickler, E. (2002). *Partisan hearts and minds*. New Haven, CT: Yale University Press.

Karol, D. (2009). *Party position change in American politics*. New York, NY: Cambridge University Press.

Key, V.O., Jr. (1964). *Politics, parties, and pressure groups*. New York, NY: Crowell.

Klarman, M. J. (2004). *From Jim Crow to civil rights: The Supreme Court and the struggle for racial equality*. New York, NY: Oxford University Press.

Madison, J. (1787, November 23/2011). Federalist #10: The Same Subject Continued: The Union as a Safeguard Against Domestic Faction and Insurrection. *The New York Packet*. Retrieved from http://thomas.loc.gov/home/histdox/fed_10.html.

Main, J. T. (2006). *The Anti-Federalists: Critics of the Constitution, 1781-1788*. Chapel Hill, NC: University of North Carolina Press.

Mayhew, D. R. (1974). Congressional elections: The case of the vanishing marginals. *Polity, 6*(3), 295-317.

McWhirter, C. (2009, December 3). Mayoral votes cast along racial lines: Atlanta's voting pattern crosses class lines, AJC analysis shows. *The Atlanta Journal–Constitution*, p.A1.

Nie, N. H.,Verba, S., & Petrocik, J. R. (1976). *The changing American voter*. Cambridge, MA: Harvard University Press.

Office of Management and Budget. (2010). *Table 7.1—Federal debt at the end of year: 1940-2015*. Historical Tables. Retrieved from http://www.whitehouse.gov/sites/default/files/omb/budget/fy2011/assets/hist07z1.xls.

Office of the Clerk of the U.S. House of Representatives. (2010). *Party divisions of the House of Representatives (1789 to Present)*. Retrieved from http://clerk.house.gov/art_history/house_history/partyDiv.html.

Purdum, T. S. (1992, November 4). The 1992 elections: State by state. *The New York Times*. Retrieved from http://select.nytimes.com/gst/abstract.htmlres=F10614F939590C778CDDA80994DA494D81.

Redmon, J. (2010, July 21). Congressional election redos costly, confusing. *The Atlanta Journal-Constitution*. Retrieved from http://www.ajc.com/news/georgia-politics-elections/congressional-election-redos-costly-575715.html.

Rosenof, T. (2003). *Realignment: The theory that changed the way we think about american politics.* Lanham, MD: Rowman & Littlefield.

Ross, R. S. (1988). *American national government: Institutions, policy, and participation.* Guilford, CT: Dushkin Publishing Group, Inc.

Senate Historical Office. (2010). Party Division in the Senate, 1789-Present. Retrieved from http://www.senate.gov/pagelayout/history/one_item_and_teasers/partydiv.htm.

Shelley, F. M. (1996). *The political geography of the United States.* New York, NY: The Guilford Press.

Sundquist, J. L. (1983). *The dynamics of the party system.* (Revised Ed.) Washington, DC: The Brookings Institution.

Wood, G. S. (1998). *The creation of the American republic, 1776-1787.* Chapel Hill, NC: University of North Carolina Press.

Table of Cases
Buckley v. Valeo, 424 U.S. 1 (1976).

Citizens United v Federal Election Commission, 130 S.Ct. 876 (2010).

Smith v. Allwright, 321 U.S. 649 (1944).

Chapter Seven
Congress
Carl D. Cavalli

Learning Objectives
After covering the topic of Congress, students should understand:

1. The origins and representative nature of Congress and the roles of individual members.
2. The organization of Congress, including the leadership and the committee system.
3. The functional processes, including legislating and annual budgeting.
4. Influences on the decision-making of members of Congress.

Abstract[1]

The framers created a bicameral congress out of their concern that the legislature is the most powerful branch. Beyond simple division into two houses, they deliberately created differences: different terms, and different methods of apportionment. They allowed each house to create its own rules and organization. This separation results in a complex parallel structure of rules and behavior that produces significantly differing views on policy from representatives and senators—even though both are attempting to represent their constituents. The resulting legislative and budgetary processes are difficult, complicated, and more likely to lead to failure than success for any given proposal. In recent decades, the Congress has evolved to meet public demands for greater democracy and openness, and has attempted to adapt to increasing polarization between the political parties. This evolution results in even greater complexity and a focus on responsiveness (to constituency) over responsibility.

Introduction
The First Branch

The first branch of government described in the Constitution is the Congress. This choice was deliberate of the framers. If politics is about "who gets what, when, how" (Lasswell, 1936), then it is important to first consider those who *decide* these things—the Congress.

---

1 Portions of this chapter were originally included in Cavalli, Carl. D. 2000. Congress. Lesson 9 in POLS 1101: American Government. University System of Georgia eCore™

Congress does its work in the Capitol building in Washington, DC. Not surprisingly, the structure of the Capitol itself lends clues to the operation of Congress. The building is divided into three connected segments: two large columned wings on either side, connected in the center by a towering dome. The center dome is vast, decorative, and largely empty (except, of course, for the hordes of gawking tourists). All the action occurs in the two intricate and busy wings. The architecture of the building is a close metaphor for the Congress itself: two complicated, active houses forever linked to one another and to the public (those gawking tourists). Why two? Why linked? And above all, why so busy?

Basics

Bicameralism

Bicameralism is the division of legislative body into two chambers. In our case, Congress is divided into two houses: the House of Representatives (or simply, ''The House'') and the Senate. What is the purpose of bicameralism? James Madison had this to say in Federalist #51, "In republican government, the legislative authority necessarily predominates. The remedy for this inconveniency is to divide the legislature into different branches; and to render them, by different modes of election and different principles of action, as little connected with each other as the nature of their common functions and their common dependence on the society will admit."

The framers feared Congress might become the most powerful, and thus dangerous, branch. Their solution to the problem of power was division. With the *legislative* branch, this meant division into two houses. Notice Madison's quote above, though. The focus is not on simply dividing the Congress into two *twin* houses. Rather, it is "to divide the legislature into *different* branches. . . as little connected with each other" as possible. Here are some examples of these differences:

Two Different Branches

- The House is larger, with 435 members apportioned according to the population of each state (states with larger populations have more representatives), while the smaller Senate has 100 members apportioned two per state regardless of population.

Because of this system, representatives in the House generally have fewer constituents than do senators. There are from 1 to 53 representatives per state whereas both senators in each state represent its entire population.

- The previous point means each representative has about the same number of constituents whereas senators represent vastly different numbers of constituents. It also means a representative's constituents are usually more homogeneous than a senator's.
- Representatives' terms of office are a short two years, while senators serve for six years.
- Representatives are generally younger than senators: first, because the Constitution requires them be at least 25 while it requires senators be at least 30, and second, because the House is often informally considered a stepping-stone to the Senate.
- The Constitution designates that all revenue bills originate in the House (but the Senate must still concur), while the Senate has exclusive powers to confirm executive and judicial appointments and ratify treaties negotiated between the United States and other nations.

Why the differences? The answer may come from examining the *effects* of these differences.

With generally smaller constituencies and a shorter term of office, the connection between House members and the public is both closer and more direct. The short two-year term also means representatives are consistently in campaign mode (think about it: They are forever either running for re-election this year, or next year). There is often a got-to-get-it-done-now-because-I'm-up-for-re-election mentality. In addition, the generally smaller, more homogeneous constituency also means representatives are less likely to deal with diverse opinions on any issue.

With larger and more varied constituencies, a longer term of office, and generally older members, the Senate is more "elite"—less directly connected to the public. The mentality in the Senate is often one of going slow and of considering a wide array of views on any issue. George Washington is supposed to have said that "we pour legislation into the senatorial saucer to cool it" (Thomas Jefferson Encyclopedia 2009).

The differences between the houses produce different *perspectives*. The views of senators will *differ* from the views of representatives. They will argue. There is an often-repeated tale that suggests a junior House Democrat once referred to House Republicans as "the enemy." This junior representative was quickly corrected by a more senior member who intoned that the Republicans are simply rivals—"the *Senate* is the enemy!" (e.g., see Ornstein 2008). What we today refer to as "gridlock" is something to which the framers would not object. They feared quick action far more than they feared delay.

Lawmaker, Representative

What is the role of a legislator? Most people would answer that the basic job is to create laws. This description is correct, but incomplete. Equally important is a focus on representing the public. But what does "representation" mean? There are several ways of defining the term.

Representation

Does Congress truly represent the public? One way to assess representativeness is to see if it shares the same *demographic* characteristics as the public. In other words, does Congress *look* like the public? The answer is clearly no! A 2010 study found that the average age in Congress is 58.2—more than 20 years older than the average American (Manning 2010). Most members are lawyers or political professionals.[2] Also, while there are more women and minorities in Congress than ever, they are still vastly underrepresented compared to the general public. For example, in 2010, 17.2% of Congress was female compared to over 50% of the general public, and just under 8% of Congress was African American compared to around 13% of the general public. In addition, there are far more military veterans and far more Protestants than are found in the general public. So, from a demographic standpoint, Congress does not represent the public at all.

However, demography is not the only type of representation. Another type is known as *agency* representation. Do members of Congress speak for their constituents (in the same way that "agents" in the entertainment and

---

2 A "political professional" is someone who has worked most of their lives in political offices, either as legislative or administrative assistants, or as elected officials in local or state offices before their election to Congress.

sports professions speak for their clients)? This assessment method yields a far more positive answer. One way to measure agency representation is to see if constituents express their satisfaction with their incumbent representatives by voting to re-elect them. Over the last 25 years, re-election rates in the House average over 90% and have not dropped lower than 87%. Over the same period, rates in the Senate average over 80% and have not dropped lower than 75% (The 2010 rates were 87% in the House and 84% in the Senate). These consistently high re-election rates are particularly interesting given the relatively low levels of public support shown for the Congress as a whole in recent decades—currently in the teens, and rarely above 50% over the last 25 years (Gallup 2010). In total, this data suggests that while the public does not often approve of the collective actions of Congress as an institution, they are more than satisfied with their own members of Congress.

Indeed, researchers like David Mayhew (1974) find that it is this "electoral connection"—regularly facing the voters—that largely promotes agency representation. It appears to be a conscious design of lawmakers. Their desire for re-election produces a palpable focus on what Richard Fenno (2003) calls "home style." That is, legislators are concerned about how they are perceived by their constituents. As Fenno says,

> *there is no way the act of representing can be separated from the act of getting elected. If the congressman cannot win and hold the votes of some people, he cannot represent any people. . . [T]he knowledge that they will later be held accountable at the polls will tend to make [representatives'] behavior more responsive to the desires of their constituents.* (p.233)

To build support, "[M]embers of Congress go home to present themselves as a person and to win accolade: 'he's a good man,' 'she's a good woman'... And their object is to present themselves as a person in such a way that the inferences drawn by those watching will be supportive (p.55). Beyond simply appearing "good," leadership and helpfulness are also part of the presentation: "[T]he core activity is providing help to individuals, groups, and localities in coping with the federal government.

. . . it is a highly valued form of activity. Not only is constituent service universally recognized as an important part of the job in its own right. It is also universally recognized as powerful reelection medicine (p.101).

DISTRICTING: WHO IS YOUR "AGENT?" Rules matter. They affect outcomes. Congressional representation is affected by rules for creating congressional districts[3]. As noted earlier, representatives in the House are apportioned by state population (so the most populous state, California, currently has 53 representatives while the seven least populous states each have only one representative). Federal law requires states with more than one representative to draw individual districts for each. Constitutionally, those districts must be as equal in population as possible. Federal law also requires the creation of districts where minority groups comprise the majority of the district population where possible[4]. Population shifts and demographic changes are measured by the decennial United States Census. These requirements mean district boundaries must be redrawn at least every decade as indicated by population and demographic shifts detected by the census. How the boundaries are redrawn—"redistricting"—can have a decisive effect on who we elect to represent us.

For example, a state with a population large enough to be apportioned three representatives must create three districts. However, state legislatures are free to draw the boundaries as they please, keeping in mind the population and minority requirements. Yet, how those boundaries are drawn can strongly affect who gets elected as the districts' representatives.

Figure 7.1: Districting Possibilities in a Hypothetical State

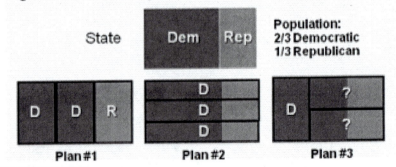

3 This is not a concern in the Senate, where both senators in a state represent the *entire* state–an effectively fixed "district."
4 This provision has been challenged in federal court.

Figure 7.1 provides an example of possible district boundaries in a state with three districts and an evenly-distributed population. Assuming people vote for the candidate of their party, the plans produce a state represented by anywhere from a solidly Democratic delegation (Plan #1) to a potentially majority Republican delegation (Plan #3). In other words, the state's population may be represented by notably different representatives depending upon how the districts are drawn. When you consider not only partisan, but also ideological, racial, ethnic, and other demographic differences within most states, it is easy to see why redistricting often results in heated battles.[5]

These battles frequently involve **gerrymandering**[6]. The term "gerrymander" has its roots in the districting process used in Massachusetts in the early 19th century under the direction of Governor Elbridge Gerry (where one unusually-shaped district was said to look like a salamander). Today, the term is used to describe districts deliberately drawn to advantage one group of people over another. Most battles have been fought over racial, ethnic, and partisan gerrymandering. Historically, this was one method of disenfranchising African Americans. Concentrations of African Americans were divided between districts to prevent any district majorities. This method of dividing a population is known as "cracking" (see Plan #2 in Figure 7.1) and was used to prevent the election of blacks (or sympathetic whites) to Congress. The method in part explains the lack of *any* black representatives elected from southern states in Congress from 1901 to 1965 despite black populations often 25-50% of the total state population (Gibson & Jung 2002). As noted above, federal law now prohibits racial/ethnic "cracking" and requires the creation of "majority-minority" districts where possible, though the law has been challenged in court.

Another method of gerrymandering is known as "packing" (see Plan #1 in Figure 7.1). This involves concentrating a group into as few districts as possible. This often guarantees electing someone from (or sympathetic to) that group in those districts, but leaves surrounding districts lacking in that group. Critics of majority-minority districts see them as "packing"

5 For example, see this article on Florida redistricting: "Florida congressional redistricting battle turns heated." February 11, 2010. News-Press.com, Fort Myers, Florida. Reposted by the Collins Center for Public Policy. February 12 2010. Retrieved December 21, 2010 from http://www.news-press.com/article/20100211/NEWS0107/100211052/1075/Florida-congressional-redistrict-group-head-challenged-to-draw-own-fair-map.

6 Pronounced *with a soft "g", as in "jerry"*

and note that while they lead to the election of some minority members, they ultimately lead to more racially or ethnically polarized politics while diluting minority influence in more numerous surrounding districts (defeating the very rationale for requiring them).

As the nation has become more politically polarized, partisan gerrymandering has become increasingly common (e.g., see Cooper 2010). States controlled by one party will draw districts to advantage their party. States under divided control (between state legislative houses and/ or the governor) will battle it out. Some states (most recently California) have turned to independent districting commissions. These range in power from mere fig leaves for the legislatures to truly independent bodies.

Delegate v. Trustee

A final point about representation: What exactly does the word mean? Some say the legislator's role as a "representative" is to simply reflect the wishes of their constituents. This definition is known as the *delegate* theory of representation. Rep. Ron Paul (R-TX) seemed to invoke the delegate theory to defend changing his stance on the policy forbidding homosexuals to serve openly in the military (often called "Don't Ask, Don't Tell"). A long-time supporter of the policy, he recently voted to repeal it, saying, "I have received several calls and visits from constituents who, in spite of the heavy investment in their training, have been forced out of the military simply because they were discovered to be homosexual... To me, this seems like an awful waste" (Weigel 2010).

Others say their role is to use their knowledge to do what is best for their constituents, regardless of what the constituents say. This idea is known as the *trustee* theory of representation. Rep. Eric Massa (D-NY) invoked the trustee theory in voicing his opinion regarding health care legislation to a gathering of liberal activists by saying, "I will vote adamantly against the interests of my district if I actually think what I am doing is going to be helpful" (Pickett 2009).

Yet, others note that the roles are not necessarily distinct. Consider the words of Rep. Gary Peters (D-MI):

My philosophy is that my sole responsibility is to represent and fight for the people who elected me to serve them. That means

> *seeking out opinions and listening to local residents constantly. I try to listen to as many views and collect as much information as possible, thoroughly read legislation and then vote my conscience based on the answer to this question: Does the proposal improve the lives of people in our community? Representing the people you serve and voting your conscience are not mutually exclusive if your primary goal is to help solve problems people are facing.* (Gilbert 2010)

Philosophers from Edmund Burke in the 18th century to today argue over which role for a representative is proper. At least one entire book has been devoted to the subject (see Pitkin 1967).

There are additional factors to consider regarding this debate. For many members of Congress, "representation" applies to more than simply their constituents. They will also represent, among other things, their political party, ideology, region, religion, race, ethnicity, and gender. Given some of these considerations, sometimes demographic representation *is*, in fact, agency representation!

Organization
The Leadership

There are two types of congressional leadership: institutional and partisan. The institutional leaders are the presiding officers. That is, they preside over the floor of each chamber. With more rules, this means more in the House than it does in the Senate. The partisan leaders are in charge of their respective parties in each house. They develop their party's legislative agenda, and co-ordinate their positions on issues of the day.

Institutional Leadership

The institutional leader of the House is the Speaker. The Speaker is elected by a majority vote of the entire House. The vote is traditionally a party-line vote, so the Speaker is always a member of the majority party. The institutional leaders of the Senate are the Senate president and president pro-tempore. Constitutionally, the Senate president is automatically the vice president of the United States. This rule means the Senate president may or may not be a member of the Senate's partisan majority. The president pro-tempore traditionally is the senior-most member of the majority party[7].

House rules empower the Speaker, who has the authority to decide to which committee(s) bills are referred. Also, as the officer presiding over floor debate, the Speaker has the power to enforce formal limits on floor activity—debating and amending bills—that are set by the House Rules Committee. To add to these powers, the Speaker also has the ability to appoint the majority party members of that committee. Together, these powers mean the Speaker controls the legislative process, almost literally, coming and going! The House legislative process begins with the Speaker, the Speaker significantly shapes the committee that sets the rules for legislative consideration, and the Speaker has the authority to enforce those very rules on the floor.

Here are a couple of views from past Speakers on what it is like to be Speaker (note the similarity):

- "The power of the Speaker of the House is the power of scheduling" — Thomas P. "Tip" O'Neill (D-MA), Speaker 1977-1987. November 15, 1983. Congressional Record, daily ed., 98th Congress, 1st sess.

- "When you are Speaker you get to set the agenda" — Newt Gingrich (R-GA), Speaker 1995-1998, in Rosensteil, Thomas B., and Edith Stanley. November 9, 1994. For Gingrich, It's 'Mr. Speaker'. Los Angeles Times. p. A2.

In the Senate, with very few rules, the president (of the Senate) and president pro-tempore have little to do in those roles. In addition, they both have other formal roles to play—the president is the vice president of the United States, and they play increasingly important roles as advisors to modern presidents. The president pro-tempore, by virtue of traditionally being the senior-most member of the majority party, is almost always chair of an important Senate committee. The *real* leadership in the Senate falls to the majority party leader (see below).

Partisan Leadership

---

7 The Speaker and the President Pro-Tempore are second and third in the line of succession to the presidency, respectively, behind the Vice President.

Each party in each house has its own leadership. They coordinate party policy positions and manage their party's voting. The majority party leader (the leader of the party with the most seats) in each house is also in charge of scheduling floor activity (mainly, when bills come to the entire house for debate and passage). The minority party leaders serve mainly to organize and coordinate their party in opposition to the majority. These leaders are assisted by party "whips" (formally, "assistant floor leaders"). Whips act as the eyes and ears of their party. They link the leadership to everyone else. Mostly, they are vote-counters and negotiators. It is their job to keep everyone informed of the legislative schedule and to round up votes in support of their party.

In the House, the majority leader effectively serves *under* the Speaker (who, recall, is always a member of the majority party) as part of a leadership team. In the Senate, however, without a strong institutional leader it is the majority leader that runs the show. With few formal rules in the Senate, power is exercised informally and strategically.

What follows is an exploration of one past Senate majority leader's method of running the Senate.

THE "JOHNSON TREATMENT" Before he served as vice president of the United States in the 1960s, Lyndon B. Johnson was a United States representative (1937-1949) and senator (1949-1961) representing the state of Texas. He rose quickly to serve in the position of Senate majority (Democratic) leader (1955-1961).

Because of the lack of formal Senate rules, there was never much use for any kind of leadership—institutional or partisan. Johnson, however, transformed the position of majority leader into a powerful one.

He was always interested in acquiring and using power. He wanted to use the position of majority leader to advance the legislative agenda of the Democratic Party during the Republican presidency of Dwight D. Eisenhower (1953-1961). He managed to transform the position on the sheer force of his will and personality—through something that became known as "the Johnson Treatment." The effectiveness of the treatment began with Johnson's thorough and breathtaking knowledge of those with whom he would interact. He knew the likes, dislikes, predilections, and indiscretions of every senator. He then would put this knowledge to use when he needed to build support for legislation. Here is a description of "The Treatment" by journalists Rowland Evans and Robert Novak:

> *Its tone could be supplication, accusation, cajolery, exuberance, scorn, tears, complaints, the hint of threat. It was all of these together. It ran the gamut of human emotions. Its velocity was breathtaking, and it was all in one direction. Interjections from the target were rare. Johnson anticipated them before they could be spoken. He moved in close, his face a scant millimeter from the target, his eyes widening and narrowing, his eyebrows rising and falling. From his pockets poured clippings, memos, and statistics. Mimicry, humor and the genius of analogy made the treatment an almost hypnotic experience and rendered the target stunned helpless.* (Evans and Novak 1966)

No future Senate leaders possessed Johnson's talents, so "The Treatment" was not seen again after Johnson. However, the expectation of an active, involved majority leader subsequently became the norm.

The Rank and File

By "rank and file" we mean everyone else—those members not in leadership positions. As noted earlier (see "Representation" above), Congress is more demographically diverse than ever. Its ranks since the 1950s are increasingly filled with political professionals. This change has consequences for the functioning of Congress.

Political professionals often see Congress as a career, making continual re-election important. These careerists will act as "policy entrepreneurs" or "professional legislators"—deliberately seeking issues on which to legislate to demonstrate their value to their constituents. Their growing ranks have transformed Congress into a sort of legislating machine with specialized subcommittees (see "The Committee System" below) and increasing numbers of staff and support agencies (e.g., see the Congressional Budget Office [http://www.cbo.gov] and the Congressional Research Service [http://www.loc.gov/crsinfo]), all geared toward developing legislation on issues of interest to their constituents.

Much of this activity involves *pork barrel legislation*—usually defined as legislation or funding for projects of little to no benefit beyond a single district (the term is loosely related to the idea of "bringing home the bacon" to please local voters). Pork barrel projects take the form of things like research grants for local institutions, and funding for highways, bridges, museums, and parks. The process generally involves inserting amendments—or "earmarks"—into vital "must-pass" legislation like the annual federal budget. Mutual support among legislators (or "logrolling") virtually assures their passage.

While the public and many legislators decry earmarks as wasteful spending, often calling for limiting and/or banning the practice (United Press International 2010), actually restricting them can be difficult at best. "Pork barrel" is often in the eye of the beholder. That is, one person's wasteful pork barrel spending is another's vital jobs program (an especially likely view within the benefitting district).

The increasing diversity of Congress has led to the growth of another type of organization: *congressional caucuses*. These caucuses are groups of legislators promoting particular interests within Congress[8]. While there have been groups promoting ideological and commercial interests for a long time, recent decades have seen a growing number of caucuses representing demographic interests. Most prominent among these is the Congressional Black Caucus see http://www.thecongressionalblackcaucus.com/).

Taken together, policy entrepreneurism among the rank and file and its attendant effects on staff, structure, and legislating produce tremendous advantages for incumbent legislators. As noted earlier (see "Representation" above), re-election rates for incumbents have remained consistently high in recent decades. The developments discussed here play a large part in those high rates.

However, below the leadership level, the most prominent organizations in Congress are committees.

The Committee System

Long before he was elected president, Woodrow Wilson wrote extensively about our government. Of the congress, he said, "Congress in session is Congress on exhibition, whilst Congress in its committee rooms is Congress at work" (Congressional Government, 1885). Wilson's quote still holds true over 125 years later! In it, Wilson conveys some important

8 For a list of caucuses (formally known as Congressional Membership Organizations) in the 111th House of Representatives, see: http://cha.house.gov/member_orgs111th.aspx

points. One is that most of the speechifying, arguing, and blustery debate you may see or hear takes place on the floor of each House. Second, and more important, is that the real work of writing, shaping—some say "crafting"—legislation takes place in the smaller, behind-the-scenes groups we call committees and sub-committees.

Why Committees?

The Constitution allows each house to organize itself in any way it sees fit. Why, then, would both houses choose to organize into committees? It may have something to do with workload and expertise. Consider the alternative of each house working on legislation as one large group as opposed to several smaller groups. There have been about 14,000 pieces of legislation proposed in recent two-year congressional sessions. Without committees, it would be impossible to address anywhere near this number of proposals. In addition, committees are not undifferentiated groups. Each committee focuses on a specific topic. This focus helps to promote expertise within the Congress that further "greases" the process.

Types

If you are familiar with any committees in Congress, they are probably one of the "standing" committees, which are permanent, legislative committees. However, they are not the only committees in Congress. Here are brief descriptions of the four basic committee types:

- Standing: They are permanent and focus on legislating. They contain only members of one chamber.
- Select (or Special, or Ad Hoc): They are temporary and generally used to investigate issues that do not fit neatly into any standing committees. They, too, contain only members of one chamber.
- Joint: They may be permanent or temporary and are generally advisory. They exist to coordinate policy between the House and Senate. As such, they contain members from both chambers.
- Conference: The most temporary and specific of all committees. They are created as needed, solely to resolve differences between House and Senate versions of a single bill. They contain members from both chambers (usually members from the standing committees that developed the bill).

Committee Assignments
Members inform their party's selection committee of their preference for assignments. These preferences are usually based on their own interests, expertise, or on improving their re-election prospects. While the selection committees consider these factors, committee assignments are based mainly on seniority.

Seniority System
Seniority is defined as the length of continuous service. This definition applies to both chamber and committee service. Chamber seniority is a factor in committee assignments, while committee seniority is a factor in determining the committee's leadership. Members with greater chamber seniority may request committee assignments before members with less chamber seniority. Within each committee, a chair is determined largely on the basis of committee seniority. Majority party committee members with the greatest committee seniority have first choice at chairing the committee.

Using chamber seniority to determine committee assignments is not unlike the registration process used at most colleges and universities (that is, seniors get to register for a class first, while freshmen must settle for whatever classes are still available after everyone else has registered).

Why seniority? While not a formal rule in either chamber, seniority is a strong tradition in both. It is clear that both chambers feel the benefits outweigh the drawbacks. What are the benefits? Chamber seniority tends to promote continuity and legislative expertise by rewarding members for remaining in Congress. Committee seniority also promotes expertise by putting in charge those who have spent the most time on a particular committee. In addition, one of the less-appreciated benefits of committee seniority is that it helps avoid leadership fights—no confusion, no campaigning, no battles, no power struggles; If you are the senior member of the majority party on a committee, you get the chair if you so desire. Case closed!

There are drawbacks. Consider the following questions. Are people necessarily better suited for a committee or for a chair just because they have been around a long time? If someone keeps their chair mainly by seniority, are they more or less likely to listen to anything other committee members may have to contribute?

Seniority has been, and continues to be, the primary basis for selecting chairs. However, not everyone has always considered it to be the wisest of methods for committee assignment and chair selection. Here is the story of some that questioned the value of seniority.

<u>Once Upon A Time, In A Congress Far, Far Away…</u>

In the 1950s, Congress was under the control of a few conservative, southern Democrats. They got their power through seniority. With no Republican opposition in the South, they constantly won re-election (racking up far more seniority than their eastern, northern, or western colleagues). As conservatives, they were resistant to change and opposed most legislation brought before them.

However, society was changing. The Civil Rights Movement was in full swing by the late 1950s. There were many calls for legislation to end racial segregation and promote civil rights and integration. In addition, the Cold War between us and the Soviet Union had evolved into an arms and space race—with many feeling that the Soviets were ahead of us in science and technology. This fear led to many calls for legislation to promote education and develop technology. By 1958, there were so many calls for action that a huge number of Democrats were elected to Congress because of their support for new programs. Because of their proposals for change, they were labeled "programmatic liberal" Democrats. In 1964, another wave of these Democrats was elected. By the mid-1970s, these liberals were gaining seniority, which finally gave them the numbers they needed to challenge the old southern conservatives.

The stage for confrontation was set: The southern conservatives wanted nothing to do with these new proposals—and as committee chairs, they were able to thwart many (though not all) attempts at change. These refusals left the growing ranks of liberals frustrated and vowing to change the way Congress did business.

In 1975, four senior members of the House were denied their committee chairs by the rest of the House Democrats. One was forced out because of a scandal (involving him and someone known as "Fanne Fox, The Argentine Firecracker"). The other three were forced out because they had not been responsive to other members of their committees. In other words, they were *not* forced out because of specific *wrongdoing*, they were forced out for doing *precisely* what chairs had done all along—running their committees in a dictatorial fashion. This action was the warning shot by the liberals that seniority would no longer be the sole determinant for committee chairs.

The liberals formalized their control through the Subcommittee Bill of Rights, a new set of House rules that steered power away from committee chairs. It stated that committees must follow set rules. They must have subcommittees, and committee chairs could not control what the subcommittees did. The bill also limited the number of chairs anyone could hold, forcing the southern conservatives to give up several chairs to the less senior liberals. It also said that all legislation must be referred to the subcommittees—so there was less chance that a committee chair could kill a proposal by refusing to act on it. Subcommittees, who were often chaired by the younger programmatic liberal Democrats, became the locus of power and activity in the House.

The less formal Senate did not pass any similar changes. However, the influx of programmatic liberals changed the way they did business as well. The result was that, by the late 1970s, power was spread out among many more people than it was just a decade earlier.

When Republicans finally gained control over Congress in 1995, they attempted to reverse the decentralization trend. One of their first acts was to repeal the Subcommittee Bill of Rights. Because the new Republican Speaker, Newt Gingrich of Georgia, had enough support from his party to hand-pick some chairs, he—and not the chairs—was really the beneficiary of this change. By this time, though, the die of decentralization had been cast. Congress operated under "subcommittee government" for a generation by the late 1990s, and was becoming used to it.

While seniority was attacked from the left in the 1970s and from the right in the 1990s, it still survives as a formidable tradition in Congress.

Operation

Once again, Woodrow Wilson is on target (and in a rather poetic fashion!) with the following passage from his book: "Once begin the dance of legislation, and you must struggle through its mazes as best you can to the breathless end—if any end there be" (*Congressional Governemnt*, 1885).

The process of creating laws is often referred to as labyrinthine—having lots of twists and turns where proposals can (and do) disappear. To understand the method for this madness, let us explore the process.

The Dance

Proposals may come from anywhere: constituents, interest groups, the president, and yes, even members of Congress come up with ideas now and then! Most proposals come from the president. Why? The Executive Branch is charged with carrying out the laws, so they are in the best position to make suggestions.

Proposals go round and round through the legislative path. They may or may not emerge at the end. Of the 14,000 proposals introduced in typical recent congresses, only 400-500 become law—and often over 100 of these are ceremonial in nature (Singer 2008).

Proposals must pass both houses in identical form before being sent to the president to consider. They may begin in either house (or both simultaneously), with one exception: constitutionally, all bills for raising revenue must begin in the House.

In the House, bills are first submitted to the Speaker's office. The Speaker determines which committee(s) to send the bill. One of the changes made in the mid-1970s was to give the Speaker the power of "multiple referral," which allows the Speaker to send a bill to several committees at once or to divide pieces of a bill among several committees. Once in committee, bills are first referred to a specialized subcommittee, which is where the action begins. The subcommittee holds hearings to gather information on the bill. They then "mark up"—make changes to, or "amend"—the bill based on information from the hearings. They then vote on whether or not to send the bill to the full committee. If the majority of the subcommittee fails to support the bill, it is dead. If they do support the bill, it then goes back up to the full committee for further consideration.

Action in the full committee is the same as in the subcommittee: hearings, mark-up, vote. In a sense, it is a second chance to affect the bill—this time by a somewhat wider circle of actors. If the full committee fails to support the bill, it is dead. If they do support it, it will eventually go before the entire chamber.

In the Senate, bills are first submitted to the office of the majority leader who will, in consultation with the minority leader, refer the bill to one or more committees. The committee and subcommittee process in the Senate is identical to the House process (see above). If the full Senate committee supports the bill, it will also go before the entire chamber. However, at this point the House and Senate paths differ.

In the House, because it is such a large body, there are strict limits on debating and amending legislation on the floor. In the smaller Senate, there are no such limits. Debate and amendments are unlimited and need not be *germane* (related to the issue).

In the House, each and every bill gets a rule from the Rules Committee before it is scheduled for floor action by the entire chamber. The rule may place limits on floor debate and amendments. House rules specify that the *maximum* allowable debate on any bill is one hour per member. In addition, the rules require all debate and all offered amendments to be germane. The Rules Committee may enact stricter limits on debate (all the way down to no debate at all), and may place limits on amending (all the way down to no amendments at all) as well. These abilities make the Rules Committee a very powerful force in the House. Keep in mind—the Speaker exercises control over it (see the earlier discussion of the Speaker's powers).

With no similar rules in the Senate, there is no similar referral to any rules committee. They consider legislation using *unanimous consent agreements* (UCAs). These are agreements (negotiated between proponents and opponents) on debate and amendment limits that—as the term implies—require the consent of everyone in the chamber. There are no standard rules to enforce UCAs. This lack of enforcement power is often used strategically in the form of a **filibuster**—an attempt to talk a bill to death—or a *hold* (which is basically a *threat* to filibuster). It works this way: to debate legislation, senators seek recognition to speak. When granted, they may engage in discussion and debate. As long as they are recognized, no other action takes place on the Senate floor. Under UCAs they voluntarily give up that recognition after a while so others may speak. However, a senator wishing to disrupt the process may continue to speak. At this point, the senator is said to be filibustering.

Remember, there are no standard limits on a filibuster—including the content of the discussion. Some filibustering senators have sung songs. Some have read recipes. Some have even read from phone books! All is fair during a filibuster. It is not a tactic used lightly, though. Consider this: If you filibuster my bill today, I just might come back tomorrow and filibuster your bill.

The one way to end a filibuster is through a cloture vote. *Cloture* is essentially a petition among senators to formally limit debate on a bill. However, it is very difficult to invoke cloture because the vote is not determined by a simple majority. Invoking cloture currently requires 60 votes, which is a very high standard.

Modern Filibusters: Sanitized For Your Protection?

In earlier times, filibusters were tiresome and physically difficult—as depicted in the classic film *Mr. Smith Goes to Washington*. In the past, senators wishing to filibuster had to talk continuously—hour after hour. The record for an individual filibuster was set in 1957 by Senator Strom Thurmond (D—SC), who spoke continuously for just over 24 hours in opposition to civil rights legislation. For one person, that may be a long time, but for the entire process, it is really not very long. Some began to realize that one way to elongate a filibuster is to work in concert with others. Teams of senators may filibuster for days, weeks, or longer. When one Speaker tires, a sympathizer rises to ask a question—which may take several hours—giving the original Speaker a much—needed break (the rules allow a senator to maintain recognition while others are asking questions). Thus, a typical filibuster involves several senators taking turns speaking and asking questions of each other. A classic example of this was the 57 days that several senators held control of the floor during debate over the Civil Rights Act of 1964.

In recent decades, though, the way the Senate handles debate has changed in ways that has lead to an explosion of filibustering. First, majority leaders of both parties began the practice of scheduling two or more bills for floor action at the same time. They will then bring up one of the bills for debate—but they will seek to invoke cloture *first*—*before* any debate occurs. If the cloture vote fails, the bill is pulled off the floor in favor of one of the others scheduled at the same time. Consequently, bills may now be kept off the floor with simply the *threat* of a filibuster—often called a "hold." A senator will essentially say to the majority leader, "If you bring up this bill, I will filibuster."

In addition, when a traditional filibuster *does* occur, the Senate now acts in a "genteel" manner. Instead of forcing around—the—clock sessions, the Senate will adjourn each evening. When it reconvenes in the morning, the previous Speaker is recognized first—to continue their debate (filibuster).

Together, these changes make filibuster/cloture activity the focus of the contemporary Senate. If we use cloture petitions as indicators of the filibuster or hold, we can see a truly massive increase in this activity. In the fifty years before the process changed—from the 1920s through the 1960s—there were a total of 56 cloture petitions. In 2007—2008 *alone*, there were 139 petitions (United States Senate 2010).

The End Game

In order for a bill to become law, it must pass both houses in identical form and be submitted to the president. Given the ability of both houses to amend legislation, *if* bills pass both houses, they are almost always different from one another. These differences must be resolved if the legislation is to be presented to the president. One way to resolve any differences is to have one house simply adopt the other's version. Sometimes it happens, but given the different perspectives of the two houses, it is not likely (see "Bicameralism"). Often, both houses will call for a *conference committee* consisting of members of each house (usually from the committees that worked on the bills). As noted earlier, conference committees exist solely for the purpose of resolving the differences between the House and Senate versions of a bill. Once those differences are reconciled, the committee disbands.

The reconciled version is presented to both houses for an up—or—down vote (conference reports may not be amended). If it passes both houses, it is presented to the president, who may sign it into law (or allow it to become law without signing it), or veto it. If it is vetoed, it is returned to the Congress, where both houses may try to override the veto with a two—thirds vote in favor from each house[9]. If such a vote is successful, the bill becomes a law without the support of the president.

The dance must begin anew with each new Congress. If a bill has not become law by the time Congress adjourns before the next congressional elections, it must begin the process all over again at the start of the new Congress the following January.

---

9 Except for "pocket vetoes," which are vetoes occurring while Congress is not in session. Pocket vetoes may not be overridden.

The Budget

In addition to legislating, Congress also keeps the federal government running by passing an annual budget. The rules governing this process have a profound effect on both the functioning of Congress and the distribution of power within it.

The process is relatively simple. Early every year, the president submits a budget proposal to the Congress. It consists of requests from all federal agencies and organizations for operating funds, as well as requests from the president for funding new programs and policies. Congress then molds these proposals into a budget for the following year.

From February through mid—April, the Congress works on *authorizing* legislation. This step is the typical legislative process described above. While there are many exceptions, in general, for laws to take effect the following year, they must be authorized by mid—April of the current year. This legislation includes a budget for the program/policy (the maximum funding it may legally withdraw from the U.S. Treasury). Authorization must be completed by April 15th, when Congress must approve a preliminary budget resolution.

While budgets have now been authorized, not a single penny has been allocated yet. The process of actually doling out money to each policy/program is known as the *appropriations* process. Appropriations are the next step. From May through mid—June, two huge committees— the Appropriations Committees in each house—do this work. They decide how much funding each policy/program actually gets. Appropriations must be completed by June 15th, at which point Congress must approve another—binding—budget resolution.

Not every policy/program gets everything it wanted. Difficult economic times or less than expected revenue may mean some items get appropriations that fall short of their authorized maximum. In many instances, this shortfall may require rewriting the authorizing legislation to accommodate the newer budget realities. Orders from the Appropriations Committees to rewrite are known as *reconciliation* orders. These orders mean standing committees must return to work legislating. They must complete their work by the end of September. The new budget ("fiscal") year begins on October 1st.

This relatively straightforward process—authorization, appropriation, reconciliation—sounds as though it can be carried out simply and completely every year. Is it? No. Modern budget realities mean frequent funding shortfalls, and that means fights over every last penny. The process is *rarely* completed in time for the new fiscal year. The government cannot operate without a budget (even if the money exists, it cannot be withdrawn from the Treasury without the proper legislation). To avoid a shutdown, Congress will pass a *continuing resolution*, which is a joint resolution (which must be presented to the president, just like regular legislation) that allows the government to continue spending at current levels. Continuing resolutions may last anywhere from a few hours to several months or longer.

Continuing All Year

The budget for 2007 was never completed. This year marked the first time since the budget process was adopted in 1974 that the government failed to finish the process. By the end of 2006, the outgoing Congress had completed work on funding for only two areas: defense and homeland security.

After losing seats in the 2006 elections, the outgoing Republican majority passed a continuing resolution that left the remaining work to the new Democratic majority taking office in 2007. Once the Democratic majority assumed control of both houses in January 2007, they quickly realized that they could not complete work on the 2007 budget while simultaneously working on the 2008 budget. They simply passed another continuing resolution to fund the remainder of the government through the end of the fiscal year (September 2007) at the 2006 levels.

2008? You guessed it! Congress did not complete the budget in time for the start of fiscal year 2008 (in October 2007), so they had to pass yet another continuing resolution. This lasted through December of 2007— marking the first time the government operated for more than an entire year under these continuing resolutions.

Congressional Evolution[10]

While the 1960s may have been a time of great social change in the United States, the 1970s and beyond were a time of great change in the Congress. Changes in the membership and operating rules were discussed

---

10 Much of this section is based on Sinclair, Barbara. 2007. *Unorthodox Lawmaking.* 3rd ed. Washington DC: CQ Press.

earlier. Those changes went hand-in-hand with changes in the legislative process and the functioning of Congress. What has emerged is a far more complicated institution using far more "unorthodox" processes (Sinclair 2007).

The "Traditional" Process

Prior to the institutional reforms of the mid—1970s, when committee chairs still ruled the show, the legislative process was relatively simple and open. Bills were referred to a single committee in each house. In the House, the rules for debate and amendments were generally open—allowing members the maximum amount of debate and relatively unrestricted ability to propose amendments. The amendments were often supportive and they usually passed. In the Senate, the process was similarly open. Unanimous consent agreements were relatively simple and filibusters were rare. House—Senate differences in legislation were often minor and were resolved in small (often single—digits) conference committees.

The Modern Process

Beginning in the 1970s as congressional power became more dispersed, but especially in the 1980s and later as the parties became increasingly polarized, the process grew far more complex. To allow the growing ranks of policy entrepreneurs many avenues to tend to their constituents, bills were often referred to several committees in each house, which led not just to action within each committee, but also to negotiations *between* committees as well. To keep fragile coalitions together in the House, floor rules became more restrictive. These rules left no time for most members to speak. Complex rules limiting amendments became the norm. In the Senate, unanimous consent agreements became more complex and more limiting. Protracted negotiations among senators to avoid potential filibusters became commonplace. Yet, even with these negotiations, the amount of filibustering increased significantly. Prior to the 1970s the number of filibusters (as measured by cloture votes) in each two—year Congress usually numbered in the low single digits. From the 92nd Congress (1971-72) through the 99th Congress (1985-86) the number fell below 20 only twice. From the 100th Congress (1986-87) to the present, the number has fallen below 40 only once, and topped 100 for the first time in the 110th Congress (2007-08) (United States Senate 2010).

Negotiation rules the day not only within the Senate, but between the houses as well as ever—larger conference committees (often containing over 100 representatives and dozens of senators) discuss major changes in legislation—often, in effect, rewriting bills. Furthermore, negotiations occur not only within Congress itself, but between Congress and the president too, as presidents try to secure votes for passage of their programs and as Congress tries to avoid presidential vetoes.

What Happened, and Why?

The changes in membership and operating rules discussed earlier (see "ONCE UPON A TIME...") had a profound effect on the behavior of the institution and its members. Barbara Sinclair (2007) notes three factors involved in the increasingly complex legislative environment:

- Internal reforms: Changes in the composition of the Congress in the 1960s and beyond (especially the influx of "programmatic liberals" discussed earlier) and changes in the media landscape (especially the increased imagery of television) led to a greater focus on individuals in Congress. In the Senate, this meant extended debate and a greater number of amendments to legislation. Passing legislation increasingly required 60 votes to stop the growing number of filibusters. In the House, there were shifts in power to accommodate these changes—downward to increasing numbers of subcommittees and upward to the Speaker—reducing the power and autonomy of the standing committees. This made legislating more difficult for the majority party.
- The budget process: As part of the reforms in the 1970s, a formal, annual budget process was created by the 1974 Budget and Impoundment Act. This new process provided Congress with a mechanism for comprehensive policy change. In other words, policies must now "fit" into a single annual budget. Congress can no longer simply pass laws and worry about the budgetary consequences later (as it could before the 1974 law was passed).
- The political environment: From the 1960s onward, three things became more common in the political environment—adding to the complexity of the legislative process: divided government, partisan polarization, and budget deficits. From 1911 to 1961 there were

only 14 years of divided government (where the majority party in one or both houses of Congress is not the president's party). From 1961 to 2011 that number more than doubled to 30 years[11]. At the same time, the two parties have become more polarized as conservative southern Democrats defected to the Republican party and liberal northeastern and western Republicans defected to the Democrats. This left Democrats largely moderate to liberal and Republicans largely moderate to conservative by the 1990s (e.g., see Kohut et al 2010)[12]. At the same time, increasingly common budget deficits create a "zero—sum game" where new policies become more difficult to fund. All of this makes the widespread cooperation needed to work the legislative process more and more elusive.

"Other Stuff"
How Members Decide

Just as voters use cues (see Chapter 6) in elections, so do members of Congress use them to decide whether or not to vote for legislation. Though written 30—plus years ago, John Kingdon's (1977, 1981) research on congressional voting is still considered the standard. According to Kingdon, there are several "actors" that influence congressional voting: constituents, fellow legislators, party and committee leadership, interest groups, the Executive Branch, congressional staff, and media.

As Kingdon says, the obvious place to start is with *constitutents*—the voters. It is all too easy to say legislators should simply represent their constituents. Reality is far more complicated. For one thing, most votes cast by members of Congress involve regulatory, budgetary, or arcane procedural issues about which, as one representative bluntly said, "[m]ost of my constituents don't care" (Kingdon 1981, p.32). When voters *do* care, though, even the most homogeneous constituencies may not possess a single, obvious opinion. A related complication is the intensity of voter

---

11 Including the unprecedented year of 2001, where the government went from divided to unified and back to divided (because of a single party defector) in the space of six months.

12 For a *literally* graphic representation of this increasing polarization in Congress, see Keith Poole's NOMINATE data at http://voteview.com. To view the changes from the 1960s, start at http://voteview.com/hs87.htm and repeatedly click on the "Forward" button. The House is represented on the left and the Senate on the right. The red "D"s are Democrats and the blue "R"s are Republicans. Notice how they move further and further apart as you forward into the 1980s and especially the 1990s.

preferences. Many voters may hold an opinion on an issue, but they may not feel strongly about it. Should a legislator vote with an apathetic majority, or with an intense minority? Because constituents are not always the best source, legislators also look to other actors.

- *Fellow legislators*, including *party and committee leaders,* can sometimes provide direction. Fellow legislators provide a trusted and convenient source whereas the leadership is often a strategic source—especially to the ambitious legislator.
- Despite our jaundiced view of *interest groups*, they are often a valuable source of information regarding an issue. This makes them valuable at times when there is no constituency consensus and/or when legislators lack detailed knowledge of the issue at hand.
- While *presidents* often possess "a store of credit" with their *own* party members, Kingdon finds remarkably little reliance on the Executive Branch as a source of direction (Kingdon 1981, p.186), which is most likely because of both partisan and institutional competition. That is, at any given time, a large portion of Congress is not from the president's party (often a majority—see the discussion of "the political environment," above). In addition, Congress is fiercely protective of its constitutional power and position. This interinstitutional rivalry sometimes keeps even fellow party members from relying on the president. Also, local constituencies are often at odds with the president's national concerns. What appears to be executive influence can better be explained by partisanship.
- While rarely credited by members of Congress as a source, their own staff commonly provide significant direction:

> *Adequate staff, the argument runes, could considerably ease the information burdens and the claims on the congressman's time. In the process the staff could be expected to be an influence on congressmen's decisions of considerable importance, since they work with the legislators day in and day out, presumably have their*

> *confidence, and supposedly are in a position to furnish*
> *and withhold information, suggestions, and advice.*
> (Kingdon 1981, p. 201)

- The *media* and *other sources of information* also provide direction to members of Congress. Traditional media and ever—expanding Internet sources may affect members both directly and through their influence on many of the other cues noted above. Members of Congress also have access to information not available to the outside public. This extra information would include committee and staff reports, Executive Branch reports, and in some cases, classified information.

Other Activities

Lastly, while the basic job of Congress is legislating, and the main focus of that job is representation, there are other tasks Congress performs.

- Perhaps the most important is **oversight**. Oversight can take two related forms. First, it is the review of existing laws and programs to see if they are functioning as Congress intended, which is often closely connected to the budget process to see if existing laws and programs require budgetary adjustments. The second form involves investigations into businesses, industries, or other aspects of society—often in the wake of crimes, scandals, natural disasters, or economic distress—to see if government action is warranted.
- As noted at the start of this chapter, the Senate has exclusive powers to confirm executive and judicial appointments and ratify treaties negotiated between the United States and other nations. This authority gives the Senate an increasingly important source of input into the other two branches of government as it acts as a check on presidential power. In addition, the 25th Amendment requires the House join the Senate in confirming appointments to fill vice presidential vacancies.
- In extreme instances, Congress also has the ability to discipline and even remove its own members and to impeach and remove members of the other two branches. Each house may *expel* a

member upon a two-thirds vote of that house. **Impeachment** and removal from office of an executive or judicial official is similar to indictment and conviction in the court system. Constitutionally, the House has the sole power of impeachment. When impeached, an official is then tried by the Senate (with the chief justice of the Supreme Court presiding), which requires a two-thirds vote to convict and remove from office.

Discussion Questions

1. Do the nature of Congress and the roles of its members make it a truly representative body?
2. Explore how parliamentary systems function and compare them to our congressional system.
3. Attend a state legislative or city council meeting or visit the local office of a U.S. representative or senator. After doing so, consider: Do legislatures actually function as textbooks suggest they do?
4. Are interest groups *vital* to democracy, or do they *distort* democracy? You can research one of the largest and most controversial influences on Congress at these and other sites:
   -About.com: *Issues, Organizations, and Interest Groups* (http://usgovinfo.about.com/blorgs.htm)
   -Twyman & Whitney: T*he American Citizen and Interest Groups in American Politics*: (http://www.twyman—whitney.com/americancitizen/links/lobbies.htm)
   -The Center for Public Integrity: *LobbyWatch Project* (http://projects.publicintegrity.org/lobby/)

References

Cooper, M. (2010, September 5). How to tilt an election through redistricting. *The New York Times*. Retrieved from http://www.nytimes.com/2010/09/26/weekinreview/26cooper.html.

Evans, R., & Novak, R. (1966). *Lyndon B. Johnson: The exercise of power*. New York, NY: The New American Press.

Fenno, R. F., Jr. (2003). *Home style: House members in their districts.* (Longman Classics ed.) New York, NY: Longman.

Gallup. (2010). [Graphs and charts representing a poll on Congressional approval ratings]. Congress and the Public. Retrieved from http://www.gallup.com/poll/1600/Congress-Public.aspx.

Gibson, C., & Jung, K. (2002). Historical census statistics on population totals by race, 1790 to 1990, and by Hispanic origin, 1970 to 1990, for the United States, regions, divisions, and states. Retrieved from http://www.census.gov/population/www/ documentation/twps0056/twps0056.html.

Gilbert, G. (2010, March 27). Trustee or delegate? Congress' role up for debate. *The Oakland Press.* Retrieved from http:// www.theoaklandpress.com/articles/2010/03/27/opinion/ doc4baad223e460d306155519.txt?viewmode=fullstory.

Kingdon, J. W. (1977). Models of legislative voting. *The Journal of Politics.* 39(3), 563—595.

Kingdon, J. W. (1981). *Congressmen's voting decisions,* (2nd ed.). New York, NY: Harper & Row.

Kohut, A., et al. (2010). Voters rate the parties' ideologies. *Pew Research Center for the People & the Press.* Retrieved from http:// people—press.org/report/636/.

Lasswell, H. D. (1936). *Politics: Who gets what, when, how.* New York, NY: Whittlesey House.

Manning, J. E. (2010). Membership of the 111th congress: A profile. *Congressional Research Service Report R40086.* Retrieved from http://www.fas.org/sgp/crs/misc/R40086.pdf.

Mayhew, D. R. (1974). Congress: The electoral connection. New Haven, CT: Yale University Press.

Ornstein, N. (2008). Our broken senate. *The American: The Journal of the American Enterprise Institute.* 2(2).

Pickett, K. (2010, August 16). Rep. Massa: I will vote against the interests of my district. *The Washington Times*. Retrieved from http://www.washingtontimes.com/weblogs/watercooler/2009/aug/16/video-rep-massa-i-will-vote-against-interests-my-d/.

Pitkin, H. F. (1967). *The concept of representation*. Berkeley, CA: University of California Press.

Sinclair, B. (2007). *Unorthodox lawmaking*. (3rd ed.). Washington, DC: CQ Press.

Singer, P. (2008, December 1). Members offered many bills but passed few. *Roll Call*. Retrieved from http://www.rollcall.com/issues/54_61/news/30466-1.html.

Thomas Jefferson Encyclopedia. (2009). Senatorial saucer. Retrieved from http://wiki.monticello.org/mediawiki/index.php/Senatorial_Saucer.

United Press International. (2010). McConnell switches, back earmark ban. Retrieved from http://www.upi.com/Top_News/US/2010/11/15/McConnell-switches-backs-earmark-ban/UPI-21901289846681/.

United States Senate. (2010). Senate action on cloture motions. Retrieved from http://www.senate.gov/pagelayout/reference/cloture_motions/clotureCounts.htm.

Weigel, D. (2010, May 28). Ron Paul: Constituents changed my mind on 'don't ask, don't tell'. *The Washington Post*. Retrieved from http://voices.washingtonpost.com/right-now/2010/05/ron_paul_constituents_changed.html.

Chapter Eight
The Presidency
Carl D. Cavalli

Learning Objectives
After covering the topic the presidency, students should understand:

1. The origins and executive nature of the presidency and the roles played by presidents.
2. The sources of presidential power.
3. The organization of both the White House and the larger Executive Branch.
4. The growth of presidential power and how that power has changed over the past century.

Abstract[1]

The framers envisioned a presidency that left them concerned about what they termed "energy in the executive." In other words, they thought the presidency would not be powerful enough. Contemporary politicians and scholars present a very different view. They often debate whether or not the presidency has in fact become too powerful. Related to this shift in the views about power is a shift in what is perceived to be the main sources of presidential power. The framers created an office empowered by, and limited by, the Constitution. However, modern analysts see the office empowered by a very different—and extra-constitutional—source: the public.

Introduction
The Second Branch?

The president is the head of the Executive Branch. By executive, we mean that it is the branch designed to carry out (or *execute*) policy. The framers clearly treated the executive as a secondary branch. It is discussed in Article II of the Constitution. Article I covers the Legislative Branch largely because they felt it would be the most powerful branch. It seems more the opposite today. How can this be so?

---

1 Portions of this chapter were originally included in Cavalli, Carl D. 2000. The Presidency. Lesson 10 in POLS 1101: American Government. University System of Georgia eCore™

Basics

Presidential Roles

It is best to begin exploring this question by reviewing the expectations placed on presidents. That is, what roles do they play in our system? Generally, they play two roles: Chief of State and the head of government.

<u>Chief of State</u>

One role the president plays is that of national symbol or national representative. The presidency is the only office in this country elected by the entire nation. Presidents have come to embody their symbolic role in many ways.

Presidents often claim to be a voice for the American people (e.g., see Barger 1978, Teten 2007). Whether this is true or not, their priorities do become our priorities—when a president suggests the nation focus on an issue (like civil rights or health care), we do engage in debate. We may not always agree with the president, but we do wind up discussing these issues as a nation.

In addition, presidential involvement in international affairs is the equivalent of American involvement. When the president signs an international agreement, America is committed to that agreement. When the president receives another nation's ambassador, it is *America* recognizing the existence of that country.

Consider the following private presidential conversations that were recorded on Dictabelts in the White House. Is it just the president talking, or is it *America* talking?

- Following the space flight of Major Gordon Cooper on May 16, 1963, President John Kennedy called him and said, *"We're* very proud of you, Major" (Miller Center 2010a, emphasis added).
- On the birthday of famed poet Carl Sandburg, January 6, 1964, President Lyndon Johnson called Sandburg and said he wanted "to tell you how fortunate *America* was to have you with *us"* (Miller Center 2010b, emphasis added).

These conversations were not intended for public consumption, and so they provide us with good evidence that presidents often speak for all of America even in private moments. Of course, a glance at most public presidential addresses reveals the same character. You can see this by perusing the White House video (http://www.whitehouse.gov/video) and briefing (http://www.whitehouse.gov/briefing-room) websites.

Head of Government

The other role of the president is that of chief executive or "chief operating officer" of the United States. In this role, the president is recognized as the person atop the federal government's policy-making team.

In a sense, the president as the head of government is in charge of the day-to-day operations of the United States government. The president is, of course, the person charged with carrying out the laws of the land (as noted earlier). The president is also charged with evaluating the laws and recommending changes.

Most of the legislative proposals that Congress works on actually originate in the Executive Branch. The executive departments and agencies charged with carrying out the laws will also evaluate those laws: Are the laws having their intended effect? Are any changes needed? If so, what? All of this information eventually flows back up to the president, who will in a very real sense act as chief *legislator* in addition to being the chief executive.

Shortly after speaking to Carl Sandburg, President Johnson also called Minnesota Senator Eugene McCarthy regarding civil rights legislation in the Senate. He said, "I want you to pull together those other Democrats and make them attend the meetings, make them keep their mouths shut, make them vote down the amendments, and get me a bill out on that floor!" (Miller Center 2010c). Though seated in the White House, Johnson is clearly acting as a legislator during this phone call.

Chief Legislator entails more than just evaluating and recommending laws. The president also has the constitutional power to veto legislation. Congressional legislation must be submitted to the president for approval. The president can either sign it into law or veto it. If the president vetoes a bill, it is dead unless two-thirds of each house of Congress votes to override the veto (see Chapter 7). This action would enact the bill into law without presidential approval. It is hard enough to get sufficient votes to pass a bill in the first place, so you can imagine the difficulty of trying to get two-thirds of each house to override a veto. The consequence is that, generally, nothing becomes law without the president's approval[2]!

These roles are a lot to invite in one person. How does this compare to other nations? Who plays these roles in other countries? Compare the United States to the United Kingdom. In the United Kingdom, these roles are separated. The Queen acts as the ceremonial Chief of State, and the Prime Minister acts as the day-to-day head of government. In the United States, we combine them into one person, which would seem to make our presidents very powerful people. This statement is true, but the framers designed a system where one powerful executive does not go unchecked. We tether our presidents (that is, we limit their independence). They are tied to the Congress and the courts through checks and balances (see Chapter 2), and they are tethered to the public through elections. In the United Kingdom, the Prime Minister is tethered only to the majority party in the House of Commons, and the Queen is not tethered to anyone.

In some instances, we can actually see a combination of these two roles. Our recognition of the president as a national leader has led us to allow them substantive powers.

Executive Orders

As the head of government, the president supervises the Executive Branch. This responsibility includes deciding how to execute the laws of the land.

Bolstered by the role of Chief of State, the president has a lot of authority. That authority is exercised through the issuance of executive orders. If, for example, the Executive Branch is charged with carrying out various programs called for by legislation, the president may issue executive orders directing whom to hire and how to disburse the appropriate funding. While divorced from any congressional authorization, these orders carry the same official weight as laws and at times may be used by presidents in place of legislation in the face of an uncooperative Congress.

The effects of this kind of order may have profound consequences, not only for the Executive Branch, not only for the program involved, but also for the individuals hired and for the society at large.

---

2 There is a third possibility—the president may let a bill become law without signing it by letting it sit for 10 days. This option essentially says, "I don't like this bill, but I don't want to fight it." It is not a commonly exercised option.

The situation was true for one of the most famous executive orders in the post-World War II era: EXECUTIVE ORDER #10952. With Executive Order #10952, President John F. Kennedy created the Equal Employment Opportunity Commission in 1961. It was charged with insuring that, in all contracts using federal funds, the contractors must take affirmative action to ensure that applicants are employed, and employees are treated fairly during employment, without regard to race, creed, color or national origin.

This order marked the first time the term "affirmative action" was used by the federal government. It put the weight of the federal government behind the cause of civil rights with consequences (and controversy) still felt today.

Executive Agreements

An executive agreement is an agreement between the President of the United States and the head of another country. While the president has the constitutional power to negotiate treaties with other countries, such treaties require the approval of two-thirds of the Senate. Executive agreements, on the other hand, do not require any congressional approval (although any money or changes in the law that may be required to fulfill an agreement must be approved by Congress through the normal legislative process), yet they are recognized as having the same force of law as treaties. This recognition has been granted—and upheld by the courts—precisely because of the president's standing as Chief of State. In other words, it is recognized that the president has the power to speak for the country and to commit its resources in an agreement with other nations. For example, despite an official policy of neutrality, President Franklin Roosevelt took it upon himself to reach an agreement with the United Kingdom to exchange U.S. warships for British bases during the opening months of World War II. At the time, there was no specific provision, either legal or constitutional, empowering the president to do this sort of thing. He justified his actions on the commander-in-chief and executive powers found in the Constitution, as well as a minor law permitting the president to dispose of obsolete military equipment. Congress eventually acquiesced to this by passing the Lend Lease Act of 1941, which permitted the president to lend "defense articles" to any government "whose defense the president judges vital to the defense of the United States."

Executive Privilege

Executive privilege is the claim by presidents of their right to refuse to hand over information requested by Congress. It is invoked by presidents under the logic that the constitutional provision for separation of powers means that the Congress has no right to force the president to turn over information to them. It is most often used with the rationale of maintaining secrecy for purposes of national security.

In his battle with Congress over materials related to the Watergate scandal, President Richard Nixon tried to exert an absolute claim of executive privilege. In the case of *United States v. Nixon* (1974), the Supreme Court ruled that, while presidents do have a right under the separation of powers to claim executive privilege, the right is not absolute.

In 1998, Federal Judge Norma Holloway Johnson ruled that executive privilege does not cover presidential conversations with White House aides absent any national security claims. In so ruling, she compelled reluctant presidential advisers to testify in the investigation into President Clinton's affair with Monica Lewinsky.

More recently, the administration of President George W. Bush invoked claims of executive privilege on a number of occasions, including its refusal to disclose documents relating Vice President Dick Cheney's meetings with energy company executives during the administration's development of energy policy proposals and its refusal to allow White House personnel to testify before Congress during the investigation into the firing of U.S. attorneys (e.g., see Holding 2007).

What Makes a President Powerful?

In one of the most famous explorations of presidential power, political scientist Richard Neustadt (1990) claims that the constitutional powers of the president amount to no more than the powers of a clerk.

Remember, the framers designed the presidency as an office which merely carries out the laws passed by Congress. Yet, modern presidents are often referred to as the most powerful person on Earth. During the Cold War, presidents were referred to as "the leaders of the free world." This description sounds like a lot more than just a clerk. How can it be?

If Neustadt is correct, most presidential power does not come directly from the Constitution. It must come from somewhere else. An exploration of presidents' constitutional and other formal sources of power, along with their more political and informal sources, may help clarify this confusion.

Constitutional and Other Formal Sources of Power
These sources of power stem from either the Constitution itself or from federal law.

The Vice President
The vice presidency is established in both Articles I and II of the Constitution. Our first vice president, John Adams, said, "I am nothing. I may be everything." The first part of Adam's lament is based on the lack of formal duties for vice presidents. This case was especially true in Adams's day, because vice presidents were then the second-place finishers in the presidential elections—which meant they were the opposition as far as the new president was concerned. So, vice presidents were then largely isolated from their presidents. The 12th Amendment changed this situation by providing for the separate election of vice presidents, which grew into a system where vice presidents are largely elected with their own party's presidential nominee.

The second part of Adams's quote, "I may be everything" is based on the vice president's position as first in the line of presidential succession. Should a president die, resign, or become incapacitated, it is the vice president who takes over as president. It has happened eight times in our nation's history (eleven times, if you count the six hours that Ronald Reagan's vice president, George H.W. Bush took over while Reagan was undergoing an operation and the two times that George W. Bush's vice president, Dick Cheney, took over while Bush was undergoing colonoscopies).

Today, vice presidents are on much friendlier terms with their presidents. They often play the part of trusted presidential advisers. More and more, vice presidents are charged with leading various presidential initiatives. For example, President Clinton's vice president, Al Gore, was put in charge of the president's "reinventing government" initiative, which explored ways to reduce the size and complexity of the executive branch. Vice president Dick Cheney has been described by many as the most powerful vice president ever (Walsh 2003, Kuttner 2004). Cheney acted not only as a trusted advisor, but also led many of the administration's policy initiatives, including those regarding energy policy and anti-terrorism policy.

As noted in Chapter 7, vice presidents are also formally charged with presiding over Senate floor debate, but since that debate is essentially unregulated, this duty is without true power. Oftentimes, the vice president is mainly an electoral resource—someone to help a presidential candidate pull in votes in an area of the country where that person might be weak.

The White House Staff and The Executive Office of the Presidency

Positions and organizations in these two entities may be based on direct presidential creation or on congressional statutes (or some combination thereof). They act as personal/political and policy advisers to the president, respectively.

- The White House Staff are the people who most immediately surround the president. They act as personal advisers. These people advise the president on what to say, when to say it, what to do, who to meet, and when. The president's Chief of Staff coordinates this group, which includes people like speech writers, press and appointment secretaries, and political advisers.
- Members of Executive Office of the Presidency (or E.O.P.) act as policy advisers to the president. They advise the president on what policies to pursue and propose and assist with management of the federal bureaucracy. This group includes economic advisers, legislative advisers, and domestic and foreign policy advisers, among others.

The president appoints members of the White House Staff and E.O.P. They do not require Senate confirmation because they are advisers without any true operational responsibility. In addition, they serve "at the president's pleasure." This phrase means they serve only as long as the president wants them. The president may fire them at any time without cause.

Because of their advisory role, presidents often place some of their closest acquaintances in these positions. New presidents generally replace all of the previous occupants with people they want and trust. Information on White House offices and agencies may be found on the White House website (see: http://www.whitehouse.gov/adminstration).

Cabinet Departments and Executive Agencies
These are the organizations created by congressional statutes. They actually carry out policy. In this capacity, they both assist the president in fulfilling the roles of the chief executive, and they are also in a position to provide the president with advice on future policies to pursue. These departments and agencies are grouped according to substantive topics, much like the committee system in Congress. Examples include the departments of Agriculture, Commerce, Defense, and Homeland Security, The Small Business Administration, and NASA.

The president nominates the heads of these organizations, but unlike the advisers, they require Senate confirmation. The reason for this distinction is that, unlike the advisers, these organizations have operational responsibilities (in other words, unlike advisers, they actually do something). They carry out the will of Congress (in the form of laws), so Congress has a say as to who heads these departments and agencies.

Like the advisers, department and agency heads serve at the president's pleasure. Generally, incoming presidents will replace most or all department and agency heads with their own people. Everyone below the few top levels in these organizations are neither appointed nor fired by the president. They are hired under provisions of the Civil Service (see Chapter 9) based on merit and cannot be fired except for cause. As such, lower level department and agency employees often serve in their positions as careers which cross two or more administrations. Information on cabinet departments and executive agencies may be found at the USA. gov website (see: http://www.usa.gov/Agencies/Federal/Executive.shtml).

It is clear from all this information that cabinet departments and executive agencies are more independent and removed from the president than are the White House Staff and E.O.P.

WHO DO YOU TRUST?
Presidents have many sources of advice. Members of the White House Staff and the E.O.P. are hired as advisors, but cabinet secretaries and agency heads are also in a good position to provide advice—especially since they are the ones actually out there carrying out laws and policies.

Since members of the White House Staff and the E.O.P. depend on the president for their jobs, they sometimes become "yes people" and shield the president from bad news. Understandably, this characteristic makes them potentially poor advisors[3]. The cabinet may actually be in a better position to give advice. After all, they know if policies are working or not because they are running them! But will presidents listen to them? Cabinet departments and executive agencies are less dependent on the president for their jobs (since the heads of these organizations require congressional confirmation and everyone else is a civil service hire). As such, they are much more likely to say no to the president when needed. Is there potential here for a president to become isolated in a "White House Fortress" favoring those White House aides who are least likely to be honest over the cabinet and executive officers who have real-world experience? Is there any evidence that recent presidents have favored their White House and E.O.P. advisors over their department and agency heads?

Appointment Power

The Constitution empowers the president to appoint all federal judges and Supreme court justices, and top-level cabinet and executive agency personnel (including the ambassadors who represent the United States around the world), who are subject to Senate confirmation (see Chapter 7). In addition, presidents may hire White House staff as they see fit. These appointments amount to over 6,000 people by recent estimates. This ability is considered a source of power, because it gives the president the ability to shape the Executive Branch. The president has the power to appoint area and issue experts and/or to reward loyal supporters with jobs ("patronage"). Also, while judicial appointments serve for life, Executive Branch appointments (except for those in regulatory agencies) serve "at the president's pleasure." As mentioned earlier, this power is best illustrated at the start of each new administration, especially if the new president is not from the same party as the outgoing one. At that time, most, if not all, incumbent department and agency heads resign to allow the incoming president to nominate more "friendly" replacements[4].

3 When she was President Reagan's Assistant for Public Liaison, Elizabeth dole once ironically remarked, "The president doesn't want any yes-men and yes-women around him. When he says no, we all say no"

4 Though rarely admitted, there is evidence that most presidents ask new appointees to submit a standing letter of resignation. Presidents will pull out these letters when they want to replace someone but wish to avoid the distasteful act of firing them (which sometimes leaves the impression

Legislative Power

Though not part of the Legislative Branch, many consider the president our "chief legislator" (Rossiter 1956, p. 14; see also Cavalli 2006). The president is an important actor throughout the legislative process. The presidency is actually the primary source of legislative proposals. In fact, in some instances, such as with the federal budget, the president is actually required by federal law to submit proposals[5]. The Constitution even requires the president to recommend legislation "from time to time" (Article II, Section 3). This process has become institutionalized as the president's annual "State of the Union Address." The agenda-setting function gives the president a lot of influence over Congress's legislative work (e.g., see Light 1999).

Modern presidents tend to live or die by the success of their campaign proposals (Cavalli 2006), which almost always involve legislative proposals. So, once proposals are submitted to Congress, presidents have a natural interest in taking steps to ensure their passage. Much of their time is spent building support for their proposals both publicly and with members of Congress.

The constitutional veto power (Article I, Section 7) also gives presidents influence at the end of the process. All legislation must be presented to the president who may sign it into law (or allow it to become law without signature after ten days) or reject it with a veto, which the Congress may try to override and enact into law on its own[6] (see Chapter 7).

So, the head of the Executive Branch is actually one of the most influential players in the legislative process at all stages: The beginning (recommends legislation), the middle (builds support), and the end (signs or vetoes).

Chief Diplomat and Commander-in-Chief

The president is also our chief diplomat and commander-in-chief of our armed forces. The president effectively manages our relationship with the rest of the world. As chief diplomat, the president meets with foreign

that the president erred in their hiring).

5 The Budget Act of 1921 requires the president to submit a budget to Congress every year. A related example is the Employment Act of 1946 which requires the president to submit an annual economic report to Congress that includes direction on how to achieve future economic goals.

6 Except for "pocket vetoes," which are vetoes occurring while Congress is not in session. Pocket vetoes may not be overridden.

heads of state, negotiates treaties, and enters into executive agreements with them, and receives foreign ambassadors in recognition of their government. As commander-in-chief, the president oversees the nation's military establishment:

> *In times of peace he raises, trains, supervises, and deploys the forces that Congress is willing to maintain. With the aid of the Secretary of Defense, the Joint Chiefs of Staff, and the National Security Council—all of whom are his personal choices—he looks constantly to the state of the nation's defenses.* (Rossiter 1957, p. 11)

> *In [times of war] the President's power to command the forces swells out of all proportion to his other powers. All major decisions of strategy, and many of tactics as well, are his alone to make or to approve.* (Rossiter 1956, p. 12)

WHO LET THE DOGS OUT?

Though the Constitution makes the president the commander-in-chief of our armed forces (Article II, Section 2), it gives the power to declare war to the Congress (Article I, Section 8). The power to, as Shakespeare put it, "Cry 'Havoc,' and let slip the dogs of war" (*Julius Caesar*, Act III, Scene I) is actually divided between the two branches. This division has generated a long-lasting tension between them that particularly flared up during the Vietnam War. As with all post-World War II military actions, this "war" was never declared by Congress. Presidents simply began committing troops into military action without seeking a formal declaration from Congress. The escalation of the Vietnam War by presidents Lyndon Johnson and Richard Nixon in the face of drastically declining public and congressional support led Congress to pass the War Powers Resolution in 1973. The act limits the president's ability to commit troops into hostile action without the express consent of Congress. Though never challenged in court for fear of losing, all presidents since its passage have considered the act an unconstitutional infringement on their power as commander-in-chief. Congress, also fearing that they would lose a court challenge, has never fully insisted on the act's enforcement. Instead, the two sides seem to have reached a mutual understanding where presidents will continue to commit troops to action without any formal war declaration by Congress. In place of a formal declaration, though, presidents will seek some sort of consent (e.g, see CNN politics 2002), and Congress, not eager to appear unpatriotic or unsupportive of the military, will most always grant that consent.

These constitutional and formal sources of power are available to all presidents. As such, they would not explain variations in presidential power. In addition, in and of themselves, they have changed little over time. The size of the executive branch has grown tremendously, especially during the 20th century. However, the appointment power has actually been curtailed—largely through the Civil Service Act. As noted earlier, Richard Neustadt claims all these resources make the president nothing more than a clerk (with a really top-notch support staff!). They do not, according to Neustadt, explain the modern transformation of the presidency into something often regarded as the most powerful position on earth. To explain that, we must move beyond the formal sources.

Political and Other Informal Sources of Power

These sources of power are not formally specified either in the Constitution of in federal law. However, Neustadt and others say they are responsible for much of the power of the modern presidency.

Support: Election and Approval

Whether through election or through ever-present public opinion polls, a president with the support of the public can accomplish a lot. For example, presidents often suggest legislation to Congress. Congress is more likely to act on those suggestions if the president can claim that the American people support such legislation. After all, the American people collectively comprise the voter who put members of Congress in office (and can take them out as well!). A president who claims a popular mandate because of a landslide electoral victory and/or high public approval ratings can claim such support. One without such a mandate cannot.

Support: Party and Interest

Political party is a source of loyalty and cooperation that can bridge the separation of power built into our system. This was the original intent of the Anti-Federalists as they organized themselves into the party that evolved into today's Democratic Party (see Chapter 6). Presidents can often count on their fellow partisans to support their initiatives and proposals. In Congress, this support translates into votes. There, it helps even more if the president's party is the majority—more able to control the process and to deliver a victory for the president. Obviously, a Congress controlled by the other party can severely constrain a president's influence over policy.

Groups can work to build public support for presidents. This support in turn, can bolster a president's influence over Congress when seeking legislation. Democratic presidents will often seek to work with labor unions like the AFL-CIO, while Republican presidents will often seek to work with business groups like the Chamber of Commerce.

Leadership

When the president raises an issue, it becomes the topic of discussion for many, if not most, Americans. For example, if the president says we should debate the issues of reforming Social Security or access to affordable health care, the country debates those issues. We may or may not agree with the president's position, but if it is an issue to the president, then it is an issue to us. In fact, we expect presidents to do this.

Think about what you look for in a presidential candidate. Do you look for one who says "I promise to do the best I can to execute the laws of the land" or one who says "I want to change this and that?" Most Americans clearly prefer the latter. It gives the president the opportunity to set the agenda for the nation. That is, to lead the way on the issue upon which we will focus our energies.

Media

When the president says it, it is news. It is as simple as that. The White House is simply required coverage for any major news organization. This fact means that the presidents can rely on the media to convey their ideas to the public through speeches and press conferences among other possibilities. In fact, with the development of the Internet, presidents have far more avenues to advance their ideas than ever before. Ironically, many presidents often distrust the media, seeing them as the enemy rather than as an ally (Nelson 2000). However, presidents who see the benefits can use the media as a conduit to exercise the leadership discussed earlier. In the television—and now, Internet—age, presidents are increasingly "going public" to sell their policies directly to the people (Kernall 1986). The Internet especially allows presidents to communicate directly with the public, avoiding the scrutiny and punditry of news media.

Presidential Power Redux

The contention among presidential scholars like Richard Neustadt is that presidents' constitutional and formal powers add up to no more than that of a servant to Congress. Yet, we know that the president is thought of oftentimes as the most powerful person on earth. Neustadt and many others claim that presidential power stems from persuasive abilities backed up by public support and skillful use of other informal resources (Neustadt 1990, Tulis 1987, Jacobs 2010, Tichenor 2010).

THE "JOHNSON TREATMENT" COMES TO THE WHITE HOUSE. Shortly after the assassination of President John F. Kennedy in November 1963, the new president, Lyndon Johnson, formed a commission to investigate the murder. One person he asked to serve on the commission was Senator Richard Russell of Georgia, one of the most senior and powerful members of Congress at the time.

Sen. Russell tried to decline the appointment. Yet, President Johnson took the audacious step of simply announcing that Russell, among others, had been appointed to the commission. In a conversation recorded on a Dictabelt on the evening of November 29, 1963, President Johnson tells Sen. Russell that the announcement has already been made (Miller 2010d). Russell protests, "I just *can't* serve on that commission!"

Over the course of many minutes, Johnson simply wears Russell down. Russell is relentlessly bombarded with a mixture of flattery ("I've got one man that's smarter than the rest..."), patriotism ("You're going to serve your country and do what is right!"), loyalty ("I'm begging you!", "...your president's asking you to do these things...because I can't run this country by myself!"), and conspiracy theories ("The Secretary of State... [is] deeply concerned...about this idea that [Soviet Premier] Kruschev killed Kennedy.").

Eventually, a resigned Russell says, "We won't discuss it any further, Mr. President, I'll serve."

The Growth of Presidential Power

As noted earlier, the Executive Branch was not first on the minds of the framers, the Legislative Branch was. They clearly felt that Congress would be the dominant of the two branches. Their vision held true through the 19th century and into the 20th, but then, things began to change.

The Legislative Branch is designed to discuss and debate, which are essential abilities for law-making in a democratic society. The Executive Branch is designed to execute, in other words, to do things. It is designed for action. In the 20th century, a series of major—indeed international—crises touching several generations of Americans began to permanently shift our main expectation of the federal government from one of democratic deliberation to one of action.

The Great Depression of the 1930s, The Second World War in the early 1940s, and the Cold War of the late 1940s through the late 80s all required action—in many instances immediate action—on an often massive scale. We began to expect the federal government to secure our well-being from threat after threat. The government responded by taking unprecedented action to manage the economy during the Great Depression, and to beef up our military capabilities and international involvement throughout the Second World War and the Cold War. These responses are now permanent areas of government activity. Concerns over domestic and international terrorism in the early 21st century have perpetuated this activity.

So how do these things empower the presidency? Quite simply, all this activity required legislation and each new law and program required another executive agency and more presidential advisors.

"The President Needs Help"

So said the Brownlow Committee on Administrative Management in its 1937 report following President Roosevelt's attempts to cope with expanded government in the face of the Great Depression. The committee recommended a formal structure to help manage the growing number of agencies and the laws and programs they administer. Over time, most of their recommendations were adopted as the Executive Office of the Presidency. This management assistance in turn allows the pursuit of a broader array of policies, further empowering the Executive Branch.

Congressional Accomplices

In some instances, the Congress actually ordered the president to take action. For example, in the last several decades, presidents have been required to monitor and manage levels of national inflation and unemployment. They have also been required to certify which foreign countries are worth of our highest levels of trade.

The more laws, the larger the Executive Branch. The larger the Executive Branch, the greater the effect of presidents and presidential decision on our lives. By the late 1920s, the Executive Branch grew to and has remained at over 1.5 million civilian personnel. There are yet another 2 million military personnel under the Department of Defense. These numbers make the Executive Branch the largest single employer in world history!

The President in Action as Chief Legislator—A Case Study of Lyndon Johnson and Medicare[7]

Several decades ago, leading presidential scholar Richard Neustadt said, "Laws and customs now reflect acceptance of [the president] as the great initiator, an acceptance quite as widespread at the Capitol as at his end of Pennsylvania Avenue" (Neustadt 1990, p. 7). This statement is as true now as it was when he first wrote those words in 1959. Modern presidents are elected and judged "not by their ability to implement laws…, but by their ability to get their proposals enacted into law" (Cavalli 2006, p. 1).

As president during much of the late 1960s, Lyndon Johnson was deeply involved in the legislative process. Doris Kearns (1976) says that "[o]ther presidents had paid close attention to the Congress, but the scope and intensity of Lyndon Johnson's participation in the legislative process were unprecedented" (p225). Of Johnson, she also says,

> *he had to know how much to involve which members of Congress in what bill, selecting for each member the kind of participation that promised him the greatest reward, deciding where to draw the line in order to avoid the kind of over involvement that might expose his program to crippling opposition in advance. And he had to know*

---

7 This case study is borrowed in large part from Chapter 8 in Cavalli, Carl D. 2006. *Presidential Legislative Activity*. Landham, MD: University Press of America.

> *these things himself, directly, from face-to-face talks,*
> *because only Johnson was in contact with all the*
> *varied groups and subgroups in both Congress and the*
> *administration.* (Kerns 1976, p.225)

She quotes Johnson as saying

> *There is but one way for a President to deal with the*
> *Congress, and that is continuously, incessantly, and*
> *without interruption. If it's really going to work, the*
> *relationship between the President and the Congress has*
> *got to be almost incestuous. He's got to know them even*
> *better than they know themselves. And then, on the basis*
> *of his knowledge, he's got to build a system that stretches*
> *from the cradle to the grave, from the moment a bill is*
> *introduced to the moment it is officially enrolled as the law*
> *of the land.* (Kearns 1976, p.226)

It is clear that Johnson believed contact with Congress was the key to influence in the legislative arena. There is merit to his thinking; there is at least some correlation between contact and legislative success on the aggregate level (Cavalli 2006).

Does this hold true in individual instances? In other words, is there evidence that presidential contact with members of Congress plays a part in getting individual pieces of legislation passed? Using data on presidential activity, including contact with members of Congress, we can take tentative steps to explore these questions surrounding Johnson's and Kearn's statements.

The first step is to select a bill. It is best to select a prominent bill, one that dominated the political landscape during its existence. This helps provide some confidence that a large amount of the presidential-congressional interaction is connected to the legislation being considered.

Contemporary examples of proposals fitting these criteria would be President George W. Bush's 2008 Wall Street aid package, and President Barack Obama's 2009 economic stimulus package and 2010 health care legislation. At the times, these plans were virtually the sole focus of both ends of Pennsylvania Avenue.

One bill during the Johnson Administration that meets the criteria was the Medicare Act of 1965. It passed the House on April 8th, 1965 and the Senate later that summer. In addition it was a high priority item. Lyndon Johnson repeatedly emphasized the importance of Medicare:

> *Throughout the 1964 Presidential campaign I repeatedly promised that medical care for the elderly would be "at the top of my list" of proposals to the new Congress. . . .In my State of the Union message on January 4 [1965], I asked the Eighty-ninth Congress to make Medicare its first order of business. . . . To dramatize the importance we attached to it, we asked the leadership to designate it "S-1" in the Senate. . . and "HR-1" in the House* (Johnson 1971, pp 213-215).

It is clear from Johnson's own words that he felt Medicare was of primary importance. According to *Congressional Quarterly*, the Medicare bill was the administration's top concern in 1965 ("Ways and Means...", 1965). Biographer Robert Dallek (1998) notes that Johnson believed Medicare to be the centerpiece of his Great Society program, and thought it essential that the policy pass the 89th Congress.

It appears that the Medicare bill is an appropriate one to use. The question is whether or not there is a relationship between the amount of presidential contact with members of Congress and their vote on the bill. A high degree of support among those most in contact with the president is not a perfect measure of presidential influence (there is a notable "chicken-and-egg" problem here: support may foster contact in some instances— the president may work most closely with those who are most supportive). However, some relationship is necessary to demonstrate and benefit to contact (i.e., while a relationship is no guarantee of influence, the lack of a relationship clearly challenges any notion of influence).

To address Johnson's potential influence, we need to restrict our data in certain ways:

- Senators voted later in the year and may have been influenced by the House vote, so they are excluded from this study.
- The further back in time before the House vote, the less relevant the data, so the examination of Johnson's contact with House

members is restricted to approximately one month before Medicare's passage on April 8th, 1965.

- The data will be limited to only those members of Congress with who Johnson had had any contact during this period. The reason for this is that, quite simply, even with all the talk about the importance of interaction, Johnson only had *direct* contact with a relatively few members (amounting to approximately 10% of the House), leaving the rest to interact with liaison staff. Given this limited overall contact, no analysis would return any meaningful results. And given the focus on what is essentially the *value* of contact, a focus on only those with whom he *did* contact can help tell us whether or not contact with others would boost his support if needed.
- Finally, only contact with rank and file House members is included (i.e., contact with the leadership is excluded). While choosing a prominent issue like Medicare does not boost the likelihood that any given contact will concern that topic, the leadership are much more likely than the rank and file to be contacted on any number of matters at any given time period. It is more probable that the rank and file will be contacted solely concerning legislation of the moment.

Limiting our study to those House rank and file with who the president had had some contact in the month before the vote leaves us with 49 members. Among those members, there is a mild but statistically significant relationship between the amount of contact a House member received from the president in the month before the Medicare vote and that member's vote on the Medicare bill[8]. While it again must be noted that there is "noise" in this data (it is virtually certain that Medicare, while prominent, was not the sole topic of all contacts), there does appear to be some relationship between contact and vote. While the "chicken and egg" problem, among others, remains, it is apparent that the ability to predict the Medicare vote of the rank and file House members is enhanced by knowing how much contact they had with Johnson.

Although this inquiry appears to support Johnson's beliefs, too much should not be read into these results. The temporal sequence is good. All

---

8 The correlation coefficient is .29 (p<.05).

contact does indeed precede the vote on Medicare. However, we have not eliminated potential outside causes.

For example, while there is a mild correlation between contact and vote, there are strong and statistically significant correlations between both political party and ideology and the Medicare vote (with Democrats and liberals more likely to support the legislation)[9]. This information suggests that many members of Congress may be predisposed to support Medicare, regardless of contact. These three variables do explain the bulk of the variance in Medicare vote among those contacted by Johnson, but only ideology holds up as a statistically significant variable when all three are considered.

So we expect presidents to be active in the legislative arena, but should they be? Does it do any good? Our case study provides but one example. While it is technically less than conclusive, it is surely okay to say that old adage applies here: "It couldn't hurt!"

Discussion Questions

1. Discuss the nature of executive power and the framers' intentions for the presidency.

2. From where do other nations' leaders derive their power? For example, compare the source of power in both the British monarch and Prime Minister to our presidents.

3. Visit or contact either your state governor's office or a state executive agency, or if possible, the White House or a federal agency or cabinet department and explore the "every-day" meaning of executive power.

4. Perhaps the most famous modern study of the presidency is Richard Neustadt's *Presidential Power*. Contrary to earlier views, Neustadt suggested the main power source is *not* the Constitution (as the best known work at the time–Edward S. Corwin's *The President: Office and Powers*–suggested), but rather presidents' persuasive abilities, as affected by their situation relative to others ("status and authority"). His work is still celebrated today (e.g., see Michael Nelson's tribute in *The Chronicle of Higher Education*: "Neustadt's 'Presidential Power' at 50," http://chronicle.com/

---

9 The correlation coefficient between party and Medicare vote among those contacted by Johnson is .42 (p<.01), and the correlation coefficient between ideology (as measured by ADA scores) and Medicare vote among those contacted by Johnson is .74 (p<.01).

article/Neustadts-Presidential/64816/). Later research built on his ideas:

- o Aaron Wildavsky's 1966 "The Two Presidencies" (*Trans-Action*, vol. 4, iss. 2, pp 7-14)
- o Graham Allison's 1971 The Essence of Decision (Boston: Little, Brown, and Co.)
- o James David Barber's 1972 Presidential Character (Englewood Cliffs, NJ: Prentice-Hall)
- o Samuel Kernell's 1986 Going Public (Washington, DC: CQ Press)

Use these classic works as a starting point to research changing views on the nature of presidential power.

References

Barger, H. M. (1978). The prominence of the chief of state role in the American presidency. *Presidential Studies Quarterly, 8*(2), 127-139.

Cavalli, C. D. (2006). *Presidential legislative activity.* Lanham, MD: University Press of America.

CNN Politics. (2002, September 4). Bush to 'seek approval' from Congress on Iraq. *CNN.* Retrieved from http://articles.cnn.com/2002-09-04/politics/congress.iraq_1_military-action-camp-david-congressional-leaders?_s=PM:ALLPOLITICS.

Dallek, R. (1998). *Flawed giant: Lyndon Johnson and his times, 1961-1973.* New York, NY: Oxford University Press.

Holding, R. (2007). Privileged positions. *Time, 170*(4), 57-8.

Jacobs, L. R. (2010). The presidency and the press: The paradox of the White House communications war. In Nelson, Michael (Ed.), *The presidency and the political system* (9th ed.). Washington, DC: CQ Press.

Johnson, L. B. (1971). *The vantage point: Perspectives of the presidency, 1963-1969.* New York, NY: Holt, Reinhart & Winston.

Kearns, D. (1976). *Lyndon Johnson and the American dream.* New York, NY: Harper & Row.

Kernell, S. (1986). *Going public: New strategies of presidential leadership.* Washington, DC: CQ Press.

Kuttner, R. (2004, February 25). Cheney's unprecedented power. *The Boston Globe.* Retrieved from <http://www.boston.com/news/globe/editorial_opinion/oped/articles/2004/02/25/cheneys_unprecedented_power/>.

Light, P. C. (1999). *The president's agenda: Domestic policy choice from Kennedy to Clinton.* Baltimore, MD: The Johns Hopkins University Press.

Miller Center of Public Affairs. (2010a). John F. Kennedy - Dictabelt Recordings 19A.3-Kennedy and Gordon Cooper (May 16, 1963). Audio retrieved from http://web2.millercenter.org/jfk/audiovisual/whrecordings/dictabelts/conversations/jfk_dict_19a3.mp3.

Miller Center of Public Affairs. (2010b). Lyndon B. Johnson - January 1964 Tape #6401.06, Citation #1198, Carl Sandburg. Audio retrieved from http://web2.millercenter.org/lbj/audiovisual/whrecordings/telephone/conversations/1964/lbj_wh6401_06_1198_sandburg.mp3.

Miller Center of Public Affairs. (2010c). Lyndon B. Johnson - January 1964 Tape #6401.06, Citation #1204, Eugene McCarthy. Audio retrieved from http://web2.millercenter.org/lbj/audiovisual/whrecordings/telephone/conversations/1964/lbj_wh6401_06_1204_mccarthy.mp3.

Miller Center of Public Affairs. (2010d). Lyndon B. Johnson - November 1963 Tape #K6311.06, Citation #14, Richard Russell. Audio retrieved from http://web2.millercenter.org/lbj/audiovisual/ whrecordings/telephone/conversations/1963/lbj_k6311_06_14_ russell.mp3

Nelson, M. (2000). Why the media love presidents and presidents hate the media. *The Virginia Quarterly Review*. 76(2), 255-68.

Neustadt, R. E. (1990). *Presidential power and the modern presidents*. New York, NY: Free Press.

Rossiter, C. (1956). *The American Presidency*. New York, NY: Harcourt, Brace, and Company.

Teten, .R. L. (2007). "We the people": The "modern" rhetorical popular address of the presidents during the founding period. *Political Research Quarterly*. 60(4), 669-682.

Tichenor, D. J. (2010). The presidency and interest groups: Allies, adversaries, and policy leadership. In Michael Nelson (Ed.), *The presidency and the political system*, (9th ed.). Washington, DC: CQ Press.

Tulis, J. K. (1987). *The rhetorical presidency*. Princeton, NJ: Princeton University Press.

Walsh, K. T., et al. (2003). The man behind the curtain. *U.S. News & World Report*. 135(12), 26-32.

Ways and means approves broad welfare measure. (1965). *Congressional Quarterly Weekly Report*. 23(1), 562.

Wertheimer, M. M., & Gutgold, N. D. (2004). *Elizabeth Hanford Dole: Speaking from the heart*. Westport, CT: Praeger.

Chapter Nine
Executive Agencies
Barry D. Friedman

Learning Objectives
After reading this chapter students will be able to:

1. Explain why the assortment of executive institutions is necessary to administer the laws that Congress enacts.
2. Describe the various structural forms of executive institutions.
3. Understand the various ways in which executive officials obtain their jobs.
4. Evaluate the relationships that the executive institutions conduct with the president, Congress, the judiciary, and the institutions' respective clientele groups.

Abstract

Article II, Section 3, of the Constitution empowers the president to "take Care that the Laws be faithfully executed." Executing the thousands of laws that Congress has enacted requires the work of more than one official, so an enormous administrative apparatus (commonly referred to as the "bureaucracy") is in place to execute the laws under the president's supervision. During the 222 years since the Constitution went into effect, the administrative establishment has grown piecemeal, with a wide variety of institutional forms (such as departments, multi-member commissions, government corporations, and other types) that have been installed for sound or arbitrary reasons. The officials who are appointed to serve in the Executive Branch obtain their jobs in a variety of ways, sometimes based on rewarding loyalty to the president and sometimes based on installing the most qualified individual. While the president struggles to cause his subordinates to take direction from him, he discovers to his chagrin that bureaucrats—to serve their own interests or to hold on to their jobs—routinely act, instead, to indulge members of Congress, clientele groups, and others who are just as adamant as the president about their own interests that, they are convinced, ought to be served by the administration.

Introduction

In Article II, the U. S. Constitution presents a pithy description of what the president's job will be. Perhaps the principal duty assigned to the president is the one that is inherent in the job of being the chief executive. The **executive power** is the power to execute the laws (or, synonymously, to administer the laws). Thus, Article II, Section 3, states, ". . . [H]e shall take Care that the Laws be faithfully executed. . ." And while the Constitution is laconic in its discussion of the presidency, it is virtually silent about the organizational structure that will help the president execute (administer) the laws. Article II refers off-handedly to "the principal officer in each of the executive **departments**" and "the heads of departments." Otherwise, the Constitution left the first Congress to figure out how to structure the Executive Branch and the first president to figure out how to manage it.

In 1789, the year in which the Constitution went into effect, the first Congress enacted laws establishing the Department of Foreign Affairs (renamed, within months, as the Department of State), the Department of the Treasury, and the Department of War (known since 1949 as the Department of Defense). Meanwhile, President George Washington and his principal advisor, Alexander Hamilton, designed the format by which the president would interact with his top-ranking subordinates. He began to conference regularly with **Secretary** of State Thomas Jefferson, Secretary of the Treasury Alexander Hamilton, Secretary of War Henry Knox, and **Attorney General** Edmund Randolph. At some point, James Madison referred to this group as the president's **cabinet**, and the term had come into accepted use by 1793.

The Structure of the Administrative Establishment

In order to explain the structure of the national government's administrative establishment, this section of the chapter will classify the components of the administrative establishment into four components. This classification system is a simplification of the countless forms of administrative entities, but it will serve as a helpful introduction to the structure of the Executive Branch.

DEPARTMENTS AND BUREAUS

As the introduction observed, Article II of the Constitution refers to "departments," and the first Congress established three of them. The department is, therefore, the oldest form of administrative apparatus in the Executive Branch. A department houses some number of **agencies**. An agency may house some number of **bureaus**. Generally speaking, a bureau is the smallest unit of administration. Accordingly, the Executive Branch is popularly referred to as the **bureaucracy**. The traditional term for the head of a department is "secretary" (i.e, an assistant in whom an executive can confide), for the head of an agency is "director," and for the head of a bureau is "chief." But this general hierarchy of department–agency–bureau is very much a generality; not a single department of the national government adheres consistently to this nomenclature. Over time, departmental components have arisen haphazardly with titles such as administration, center, institute, office, and service.

Today, the national government has 15 departments. The departments are listed here in order of their department heads' cabinet seniority. Cabinet seniority determines the order of presidential succession, after the vice president, speaker of the House, and president pro-tempore of the Senate.

- Department of State (1789)
- Department of the Treasury (1789)
- Department of Defense (1789)
- Department of Justice (1870; expansion of attorney general's office, established in 1789)
- Department of the Interior (1849)
- Department of Agriculture (1862)
- Department of Commerce (1903)
- Department of Labor (1913)
- Department of Health and Human Services (1953)
- Department of Housing and Urban Development (1965)
- Department of Transportation (1967)
- Department of Energy (1977)
- Department of Education (1979)
- Department of Veterans Affairs (1989)
- Department of Homeland Security (2003)

As an example of how a department is structured, here is a guide to the components of the Department of Commerce.

Department of Commerce
| *Bureau of Industry and Security*
| *Economic Development Administration*

| *Economics and Statistics Administration*
|--| Bureau of Economic Analysis
|--| Census Bureau
| *International Trade Administration*
| *Minority Business Development Agency*
| *National Oceanic and Atmospheric Administration*
|--| National Environmental Satellite, Data, and Information Service
|--| National Marine Fisheries Service
|--| National Ocean Service
|--| National Weather Service
|--| Office of Oceanic and Atmospheric Research
|--| Office of Program Planning and Integration
| *National Telecommunications and Information Administration*
|--| Office of Spectrum Management
|--| Office of International Affairs
|--| Office of Policy Analysis and Development
|--| Office of Telecommunications and Information Applications
|--| Institute for Telecommunications Sciences
| *National Institute of Standards and Technology*
|--| Building and Fire Research Laboratory
|--| Center for Nanoscale Science and Technology
|--| Chemical Science and Technology Laboratory
|--| Electronics and Electrical Engineering Laboratory
|--| Information Technology Laboratory
|--| Manufacturing Engineering Laboratory
|--| Materials Science and Engineering Laboratory
|--| Center for Neutron Research
|--| Physics Laboratory
|--| Technology Services
| *National Technical Information Service*
| *Patent and Trademark Office*
|--| Patent Office
|--| Trademark Office

This chart shows how the department houses a number of agencies (whose names are italicized), and some of the agencies house a number of bureaus. However, the titles of these entities are rarely referred to as "agency" or "bureau," in so far as Congress tends to disregard such conventions when naming new executive institutions.

The departments that the first Congress established arose for the purpose of accomplishing inevitable functions of a national government: the Department of State, diplomacy; the Department of the Treasury, finance; and the Department of War, military operations. The Department of Justice, an elaboration of the Office of Attorney General, was established in 1870 to represent the national government in legal matters. The theme of most departments established in and since 1862 has been very different. Those departments, such as the Department of Agriculture, were established not to carry out a function of the government but, rather, to provide services to certain people or businesses, known as their **clientele**. The secretaries of these **clientele-oriented departments** are known to be committed to the well-being of their respective clientele groups, rather than to the health and prosperity of the nation as a whole. The creation of the Department of Homeland Security (2003) brought about a department that, like the earliest departments, is responsible for a government function–in this case, preparing for and responding to natural disasters and turmoil caused by humans (especially terrorists).

Today, the president rarely convenes a meeting of the cabinet. He is well aware that most of the department heads are committed to the well-being of their respective clientele groups, and so their advice would tend to be directed toward those interests. When the president does bring the cabinet together, the purpose is likely to be the creation of a "photo opportunity" for the sake of attracting publicity. However, as Thomas E. Cronin (1975) observed, the president will usually confine his solicitation of advice from department heads to the secretaries of defense, homeland security, state, and treasury, and the attorney general–i.e., heads of the functional departments because they are most likely to share his more generalized concern about the general condition of the nation. Cronin refers to those department heads as the president's **inner cabinet**, and to the heads of the clientele-oriented departments as the president's **outer cabinet**, to indicate the president's perception of the former as being a source of more useful advice to him.

EXECUTIVE OFFICE OF THE PRESIDENT

The U. S. Constitution is designed to put the three branches of the government in competition with each other for power. From 1789 to the early twentieth century, Congress's clear motivation was to limit the power of the president by limiting the personnel resources available to him. President Washington and his successors had so little help assigned to them that they sometimes hired assistants and paid them out of their own pockets. One of the ways in which Congress limited the president's scope of authority was to control the process of compiling the national government's annual budget. Congress clearly intended to freeze the president out of this exceptionally important government function.

In 1921, Congress threw in the towel, admitting that the time-consuming budgeting process had grown to the point that the legislature could no longer handle it. Very reluctantly, Congress enacted the Budget and Accounting Act of 1921. The law's creation of the president's Bureau of the Budget significantly expanded the size of the White House workforce. Otherwise, the president's personal staff remained modest.

President Franklin D. Roosevelt's New Deal programs, designed to respond to the challenges of the Great Depression, were predicated to some degree on the need for more presidential leadership and, therefore, more staff. In 1937, he appointed a Committee on Administrative Management (popularly known as the **Brownlow Committee**) to recommend improvements in the organization of the Executive Branch. The most famous sentence of the committee's report said, simply, "The president needs help."

Congress was mostly antagonized by the report's recommendations, in so far as it is loath to give the president more resources that he can use to expand his base of power. But, again reluctantly, it gave Roosevelt authority to augment his White House staff in 1939. In accordance with this temporary authority, Roosevelt created the **Executive Office of the President** (EOP). The Bureau of the Budget (which is now known as the **Office of Management and Budget**) became the first component of the EOP.

One might wonder why the president, who has the assistance of the workforce of the 15 departments at the ready, would need a separate establishment, the EOP, to help him. The answer is that each of the 15 departments has a specific mission to carry out programs in its respective area of function or constituency. The EOP, on the other hand, has, as its purpose, the job of helping the president in his *general management* of the entire Executive Branch. The Office of Management and Budget (OMB), for example, helps the president to ensure that Executive-Branch agencies are properly funded and that the agencies spend the money responsibly and lawfully.

Today, the EOP houses the following institutions:

- Council of Economic Advisers
- Council on Environmental Quality
- National Security Council and Homeland Security Council
- Office of Administration
- Office of Management and Budget
- Office of National Drug Control Policy
- Office of Science and Technology Policy
- Office of the U. S. Trade Representative
- Office of the Vice President
- Executive Residence
- White House Office

REGULATORY INSTITUTIONS

Whenever a government makes prescriptions about what we may or may not do (such as outlawing murder), we can literally say that the government is regulating our behavior. But, in modern times, when people say something about government **regulation**, they are probably referring to rules made by government officials that direct *business owners and managers* about how they should run their companies. For example, the Environmental Protection Agency directs owners of industrial facilities to limit the quantity of pollutants that they emit into the air and waterways.

While all governments impose regulation in one way or another, Congress broke new ground in 1887 when it enacted the Interstate Commerce Act. On this occasion, the members of Congress believed that it had become necessary to extensively regulate the behavior of the owners and managers of the nation's railroad lines. Agriculture interests were complaining about the prices that the railroads were charging to haul agricultural products. But, in the Interstate Commerce Act, Congress did not simply prescribe standards for future railroad-company actions.

Instead, Congress established a new multi-member decision-making body, which it called the Interstate Commerce Commission (ICC). And it gave the ICC the power to regulate the railroads by *delegating legislative power* to it. Specifically, the ICC could study actions of the railroad industry and then promulgate (i.e., issue) **rules and regulations** *having the force of law*. Without further action by Congress, therefore, the ICC could make policies backed by the threat of penalties that could include fines and imprisonment.

The ICC and similar regulatory institutions are very worthy of note, if for no other reason than that they extraordinarily possess *all three of the major powers of government*, the separation of powers notwithstanding.

- They have the power to make rules and regulations that have the force of law. Therefore, we say that they have **quasi-legislative** ("kind of legislative") power.
- They have the power to issue notices and summonses in order to administer their rules and regulations. Therefore, they have *executive* power.
- If a regulated party objects to the way in which the regulatory institution has administered the rules, the institution has the power to hold a hearing in order to adjudicate the matter. Therefore, we say that these institutions have **quasi-judicial** ("kind of judicial") power.

Most (but not all) of the regulatory establishments that Congress created from 1887 until the 1950s had these characteristics:

- Each one was created to regulate *one* industry. For example, the ICC was established to regulate the railroad industry. The Federal Communications Commission was established to regulate the broadcast-communication industry.
- The focus of the regulation to be developed by these establishments was **economic regulation**–especially prices charged by the industry and how companies would report their financial status to the government and to investors.
- Although the ICC was originally established as a component of the Department of the Interior, in 1889 Congress decided

to insulate the commission from control by the president by lifting it out of the Department of the Interior and making it independent. Thus, it was Congress's common practice for several decades to create **independent regulatory commissions** (IRCs)–multi-member bodies that would be independent of day-to-day presidential supervision. Since 1935, when the U. S. Supreme Court handed down its decision in the case of *Rathbun* *("Humphrey's Executor") v. United States*, 205 U.S. 602 (1935), members of these commissions have been immune from dismissal by the president during the commissioners' terms of office. The court invalidated President Franklin D. Roosevelt's dismissal of Federal Trade Commission member William E. Humphrey because of the possession by FTC members of quasi-judicial power. The court disliked the idea that a president could influence a commission member who might be involved in adjudicating a case to find in a certain way by threatening the member's job.

Here are examples of the IRCs that have been established to regulate single industries:

- Interstate Commerce Commission (railroads, and later trucking), 1887, terminated 1995.
- Federal Power Commission (electric utilities), 1920, succeeded by the Federal Energy Regulatory Commission in 1977.
- Federal Communications Commission (radio and television), 1934.
- Civil Aeronautics Board (airline fares), 1938, terminated 1985.
- Federal Maritime Commission (ocean-borne transportation), 1961.
- Nuclear Regulatory Commission (nuclear energy), 1975.

During the 1950s, a body of literature in economics and political science arose that revealed the IRCs' propensity to eventually do the bidding of the regulated industry rather than to serve the public interest. For this reason, the reputation of the IRCs deteriorated. In addition, the theme of Congress's and the public's interest in regulation changed; instead of being principally concerned about prices, Congress and the public showed more concern about human issues such as worker safety and the condition of the environment. Therefore, since 1960, when Congress has established regulatory institutions, it has done so in these ways:

- Instead of creating an independent multi-member commission, Congress will create (a) a regulatory agency that is housed within one of the 15 departments and headed by one administrator who reports to the secretary or (b) an **independent executive agency** that is *not* housed in a department and is headed by one administrator who reports directly to the president.
- The focus of the regulation to be developed by these agencies is **social regulation**–i.e., pertaining to the safety of consumers, workers, etc., to the condition of the environment, or some other noneconomic value.
- Instead of regulating *one* industry, the social-regulatory agency regulates a function of *all* industries. For example, the Occupational Health and Safety Administration (OSHA), a component of the Department of Labor, regulates the function of protecting worker safety in all industries. Similarly, the EPA, an independent executive agency whose administrator reports to the president, regulates the function of controlling pollution emissions in all industries.

Here are examples of social regulatory agencies that regulate functions of all industries:

Name	What It Regulates	Type, Location	Date Est.
Federal Trade Commission	Truth in advertising and labeling; anti-competitive behavior	Independent regulatory commission	1914
Equal Employment Opportunity Commission	Fairness in employment	Independent regulatory commission	1965
National Highway Traffic Safety Administration	Automobile safety	Agency in the Department of Transportation	1970

Environmental Protection Agency	Pollution emissions	Independent executive agency	1970
Occupational Safety and Health Administration	Worker safety	Agency in the Department of Labor	1971
Consumer Product Safety Commission	Product safety	Independent regulatory commission	1972
Office of Surface Mining Reclamation and Enforcement	Environmental effects of coal mines	Agency in the Department of the Interior	1977

In so far as some of these agencies are housed in the departments, this category of Executive-Branch entities overlaps the first category (departments and bureaus), preventing these categories from being genuinely mutually exclusive.

PUBLIC ENTERPRISES (GOVERNMENT CORPORATIONS)

The Executive Branch contains a number of institutions that are known as **public enterprises** and as **government corporations**. These institutions have a different purpose and a different structure than those described above. The purpose of these institutions is to sell products and services to people and businesses that want to purchase them. In this regard, the intention is that the users of the products and services will pay for the institutions' operating costs, rather than all of the taxpayers paying for them. Thus, in the operation of these corporations, the government relates to members of the public as a businessman would, rather than as the sovereign customarily does. The structure is somewhat different as well. The **red tape** to which government departments are subjected tends to be relaxed for the corporations in order to avoid strangling them. For example, while a government department has a fiscal-year budget whose remaining balance becomes inaccessible at the end of the fiscal year, a corporation does not forfeit the balance of its operating treasury just because the fiscal year expires.

Here are some active public enterprises of the U. S. government:

- Tennessee Valley Authority (sells electricity in the Tennessee Valley area, 1933).
- Federal Deposit Insurance Corporation (sells bank-deposit insurance to banks, 1933).
- U. S. Postal Service (sells postage stamps for mail delivery, 1970).
- National Railroad Passenger Corporation (popularly known as Amtrak, sells tickets for travel on railroads, 1971).

How Executive-Branch Employees Obtain Their Jobs

While elections in the United States tend to be frequent and complicated, there are only two officials of the national government's Executive Branch whose names on the ballot result in their selection: the president and the vice president. All of the other employees have obtained their jobs through some kind of appointment process, such as these:

- *Partisan appointment.* Officials whose jobs involve advising the president and helping to make public policy obtain their jobs through **partisan appointment**. That means that the president or one of his top subordinates appoints such individuals based on arbitrary preference. The reason for the arbitrary preference can be any criterion that the president values. In the case of President Washington and his several successors, the major qualification for appointment tended to be membership in the landed gentry. Upon the 1828 election of Andrew Jackson, loyalty to Jackson and the Democratic Party became the major criterion. When party loyalty is the criterion, we refer to appointments as being **patronage** or **spoils** appointments. Today, the president's appointments to cabinet-level positions tend to be based on a blend of apparent loyalty, experience, and ability. The president is loath to appoint an unqualified individual to head a department for fear that the incompetence will throw the department into disarray. Loyalty may be increasingly more important for sub-cabinet policymaking positions as the risk posed by ineptitude becomes less severe. In the case of ambassadorships, a president will award any number of them to his most generous supporters who not only made contributions to his campaign but also raised funds from many other affluent individuals. It has been settled law since the U. S. Supreme Court handed down its opinion in the case of *Myers v. United States*, 272 U.S. 52 (1926), that the president may dismiss all of his partisan appointees in the Executive Branch, not including the members of independent regulatory commissions, who may not be removed during their terms of office.

Presidential appointments to the most prominent positions in the Executive Branch–notably cabinet-level and top sub-cabinet-level positions, seats on independent regulatory commissions, and ambassadorships–require a vote of **confirmation** by the Senate if they are to be effective. His appointments to less prominent positions do not require Senate approval. The jobs of the president's appointees have an "Executive Schedule" (EX) rating that determines the appointees' salary.

Pursuant to the Civil Service Act of 1883, partisan appointment to positions below the policymaking level is now illegal.

- *Professional and clerical positions.* For professional and clerical jobs whose incumbents are relatively uninvolved in policymaking, appointees obtain their jobs through merit appointment to positions listed in the "General Schedule (GS) Classification System." A person may obtain a job as a file clerk and be at the GS-1 level. A physician working as an experienced medical officer may be at the top, GS-15 level. On occasion, an outstanding experienced civil servant may be promoted beyond the GS-15 rank: A civil-service executive may be appointed to "Senior Executive Service" rank, a non-executive may be appointed to "Senior Level" (SL) rank, and a research scientist may be promoted into the "Scientific or Professional" (ST) rank. In the national government, professionals and clerical employees are appointed on the basis of **merit** to the **federal civil service**. All decisions about appointment and promotion are based on merit. A candidate's merit may be assessed through an examination, evaluation of his educational transcripts, evaluation of his résumé, and observation of his performance in an employment interview. In theory, the most qualified individual obtains the job. In order to eliminate patronage and spoils considerations in decisions about retaining and promoting employees, the civil-service system awards job security to appointees after a 1-year probationary period and then a 2-year "career-conditional" period. The job security protects civil-service employees from dismissal as long as they do their jobs competently and obey laws and rules. An employee threatened with dismissal is entitled to impressive due process, including numerous hearings in which his appeal is heard. So complicated and lengthy is this process that executives rarely make the effort to dismiss an employee who is determined to hold on to his job.

- *Uniformed appointment.* Enlisted personnel and officers in the armed services obtain their jobs through uniformed appointment. The ranks of enlisted personnel, including noncommissioned officers, are specified by "Enlisted" (E) codes. For example, in the Army, a private has an E-1 or E-2 rank and a sergeant major has an E-9 rank. The ranks of officers are specified by "Officer" (O) codes. For example, in the Navy, an ensign has an O-1 rank and an admiral has an O-10 rank. Appointment as an officer is based on merit. No particular merit is required to enlist as a private. Once a person is a member of the armed services, subsequent personnel decisions, such as promotions, are based on merit. One's adherence to a political party is not a basis for appointment or promotion; on the other hand, one's political activity can be deemed to interfere with her duty to serve the commander-in-chief (i.e., the president), the secretary of defense, and so forth, and can stop a soldier or officer's career in its tracks.

- *Impartial appointment.* Jobs involving trades, crafts, and unskilled labor (such as groundskeeper and janitor) are filled by impartial appointment of applicants to positions in the "Federal Wage System," in which the employees have "Wage Grade" (WG) ranks. The managers who hire these employees do a relatively cursory review of the candidates' applications, on which the applicants describe their training and experience. While the requirement of merit varies with some jobs requiring no particular merit for appointment, it is impermissible for the administration to take candidates' political beliefs or activity into account.

The Principles of Bureaucracy

Max Weber (pronounced vā' bûr) was one of the legendary founders of the modern discipline of sociology. In 1922, he published a description of the characteristics of bureaucracies. Generally speaking, the institutions of the U. S. national government's Executive Branch conform to Weber's descriptions. He offered these observations about the way in which bureaucracies operate.

- *Hierarchy.* Weber explained that a bureaucracy is arranged as a **hierarchy**. That means that those whose positions are located atop the bureaucracy have more authority than those whose positions are located at the bottom. The arrangement of power based on this "scalar principle" is known as the **chain of command**. That means that those at the top of the bureaucracy issue commands, and commands are communicated vertically from the top to the bottom as lower-level employees are expected to implement the orders.
- *Unity of command.* The principle of **unity of command** means that each member of the bureaucracy reports to one and only one supervisor.
- *Division of labor.* The organization of a bureaucracy is also based on the existence of a **division of labor**. This term means that work is distributed such that certain tasks are assigned persistently to the same individuals day after day, so that employees specialize in their regularly assigned tasks. Employees do not discover, upon their arrival at work on a given day, *what kind* of function they will carry out on that day.
- *Merit.* Weber said that decisions about appointments, promotions, and so on in the bureaucracy are based on qualifications rather than arbitrary criteria.
- *Adherence to rules.* A bureaucratic organization has a set of rules that determine how it will operate and what standards apply to employees. Some of these rules may be called **standard operating procedures** (or SOPs). Managers and employees are expected to be knowledgeable about these rules and to obey them; disobedience may attract a penalty.
- *Impersonality of policies.* In a bureaucracy, any kind of reward

or disciplinary penalty directed toward an employee is expected to have resulted exclusively from the job-related performance or behavior of the employee, *not* on favoritism or prejudice. Therefore, if a supervisor fires an employee, the supervisor might point out to the employee that "it's nothing personal."

Defiance of Hierarchical Authority

The Constitution directs the president to "take Care that the Laws be faithfully executed." Therefore, the expectation must be that the officials and employees who staff the Executive Branch are responsible for helping the president ensure that the laws enacted by Congress are administered. Unfortunately for presidents, compliance with their directives is hard to come by. Presidents Thomas Jefferson and William Howard Taft are both quoted as having said, "Every time I made an appointment, I ended up with nine enemies and one ingrate." Many research studies have been conducted to determine why the president's subordinates exhibit recalcitrance. This section of the chapter will describe what those studies have revealed.

OVERSIMPLICITY OF THE HIERARCHICAL MODEL

As we mentioned above, Weber identified hierarchy, in which a chain of command is inherent, as a characteristic of bureaucracy. In the national government's Executive Branch, the president would, presumably, take note of laws enacted by Congress, notify the bureaucracy about them, and instruct his subordinates about the manner in which he wants the laws administered; then, the Executive Branch's workforce would administer the laws as the president has instructed them to do. However, while the Executive Branch is working to administer laws, other institutions in and out of government are operating simultaneously and attempting to exert influence in the execution of the laws. In the case of the other two branches of the government–the legislature and the judiciary–they arguably have a legitimate basis for monitoring how the laws are being executed and making generally inescapable demands that Executive-Branch officials act in ways that are contrary to the president's preferences.

A list of institutions and other influences that may persuade the bureaucracy to act in such a contrary manner follows:

<u>Congress</u>. The president competes for influence over the bureaucracy with Congress, but Congress tends to be more persuasive to Executive-Branch officials. As explained in Chapter 7, one of the routine functions of congressional committees is **oversight** of Executive-Branch agencies. After Congress has enacted a law and the Executive Branch proceeds to administer the law, congressional committees exhibit ongoing interest in whether the Executive Branch is administering the laws in the manner in which Congress intended. In order to carry out their oversight function, committees may summon Executive-Branch officials to testify. If an official resists, the committee may issue a subpoena commanding the official's appearance. In the case of high-ranking officials, such as the president, vice president, or department heads, the White House may fight the subpoena on the basis that such officials have busy schedules and should not be at Congress's beck and call. On rare occasions, a federal court may consider whether the subpoena should be enforced and backed up with the threat of a penalty for contempt of Congress. Another compelling reason for agencies' attentiveness to Congress and its committees is Congress's exclusive power to appropriate money to Executive-Branch agencies. Agencies are reluctant to antagonize members of Congress, knowing that Congress is the source of financial resources. Harold Seidman (1980, p. 54) reported that a cabinet member is more likely to lose his job because of a breakdown in his relationship with a congressional committee rather than because of a disagreement with the president.

<u>Judiciary</u>. The nation's 222 years of experience with the U. S. Constitution has resulted in general acceptance of the federal courts as the conclusive decision-makers about the constitutionality of laws, the acceptability of executive agencies' administration of laws, and the disposition of federal criminal cases. An order from a federal court to Executive-Branch officials is something that no official wants to defy, even if the president wants them to defy it. The officials know that defiance of a court order can expose them to fines or imprisonment. Just the threat of having to hire one or more lawyers and pay legal fees in order to deal with an altercation with the judiciary can be a very expensive proposition for an official.

<u>Clientele groups</u>. Many institutions in the Executive Branch have connections with **clientele groups**. For example, each of the clientele-

oriented departments–such as Agriculture, Commerce, Education, Labor, and Veterans' Affairs–has, as its principal purpose, the delivery of services that will gratify its clientele group. Therefore, the secretary of Veterans' Affairs cannot afford to alienate the leadership of such groups as the American Legion and the Veterans of Foreign Wars. Given the choice between angering the president or angering the department's clientele groups, a department official will usually focus on trying to appease the clientele groups. The president may forget about the argument, but the clientele groups are likely to carry a grudge against the official whose job, as they understand it, is to serve them every day.

As another example, many of the independent regulatory commissions (IRCs) were established to regulate a single industry (e.g., the Interstate Commerce Commission that was established to regulate the railroad industry). A body of economics and political-science literature arose in the 1950s and exposed the fact that the IRCs were susceptible to the phenomenon of **clientele capture**. This term refers to the tendency of IRCs to promote the industries that they are supposed to regulate, instead of promoting the public interest. Economists George J. Stigler and Claire Friedland (1962) reported that prices charged by regulated electric companies were no more than they would be *without* regulation. The Civil Aeronautics Board, whose purpose was to regulate air fares, was shut down in 1985; after the CAB's elimination, air fares dropped precipitously.

The behavior of Executive-Branch institutions that shows more concern for pleasing clientele groups than for pleasing the president is described by a sociological term: **going native** (Katz and Kahn, 1966, p. 51). In literature of sociology, a member of an organization is said to "go native" when he identifies with the people on the wrong side of his organization's boundary. Accordingly, when President Richard Nixon's assistant for domestic policy, John Ehrlichman, became exasperated with the uncooperativeness of clientele-oriented department appointees whom the president appoints "and then the next time you see them is at the Christmas party. They go off and marry the natives" (quoted in *Los Angeles Times–Washington Post News Service*, 1973, p.79).

Others. Agencies may also be influenced to make decisions unwanted by the president by such other entities as labor unions, employees' professional associations, civil servants protected by job security, and the news media.

The result of all of these relationships is that presidents are left with frustration as many of their orders to the bureaucracy are disregarded. In fact, Howard Ball (1984, p. 6) reported that, in 1969-1970, "there was noncompliance with more than half of the president's orders, commands, requests, and directives to the Executive Branch." Defiance of the president's orders does not usually result in attempts by the president to dismiss the recalcitrants. Presidents are fully aware of the pressures that the officials of clientele-oriented departments experience from their clientele groups, and know that replacement of such officials will simply result in more officials who go native. Frequent dismissals would simply make the president look inept, because, as the public is aware, he appointed the officials in the first place and the public would tend to wonder about the president's judgment.

THE FORCE FIELD DIAGRAM
    The organization chart of the Executive Branch of the national government is conventionally presented this way:

President

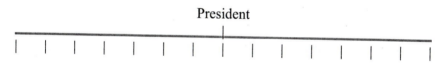

C A B I N E T M E M B E R S

    The chart continues and expands downward by identifying sub-cabinet appointees, agency heads, bureau chiefs, and civil servants.
    However, the multiple points of access and influence into the bureaucracy that are available to all sorts of political actors, as described in the preceding paragraphs, result in a reality that is far more complicated than that hierarchical chart. Grover Starling (2010/2011, p. 63) counters with a chart called the "force-field diagram," which reflects the multitude of influences that affect an agency's decision-making process.
    The heads of agencies, far from being responsible solely to the political appointee to whom they report, finds themselves on the receiving end of countless demands, orders, and pieces of advice that they can ill afford to disregard as they make rules, regulations, and other policies and decisions. This causes them to routinely give less weight to what they

know are the president's policy preferences and to try to appease all of these other entities that may be applying pressure on them day in and day out. The simple chain-of-command principle may not stand up to this more complicated fact of life for executive officials.

Discussion Questions
1. What factors complicate the president's effort to manage the Executive Branch?
2. Why do executive officials frequently disobey presidential directives? What does this behavior reveal about the motivations and incentives that executive officials sense and that influence how they do their jobs?
3. How much power do executive agencies, their executives, and their civil-service employees exercise? What are the sources of their power?

References
Ball, H. (1984). *Controlling regulatory sprawl: Presidential strategies from nixon to reagan.* Westport, CT: Greenwood Press.

Cronin, T. E. (1975). *The state of the presidency.* Boston, MA: Little, Brown.

Katz, D., & Kahn, R. L. (1966). *The social psychology of organizations.* New York, NY: John Wiley and Sons.

Seidman, H. (1980). *Politics, position, and power: The dynamics of federal organization.* New York, NY: Oxford University Press.

Starling, G. (2010/2011) *Managing the public sector.* (9th ed.), Boston, MA: Wadsworth/Cengage Learning.

Stigler, G. J., & Friedland, C. (1962, October). What Can Regulators Regulate? The Case of Electricity. *Journal of Law and Economics, 5,* 1-16.

Weber, M. (1922). *Wirtschaft und gesellschaft: Grundriss der verstehenden soziologie.* Tübingen, Germany: J. C. B. Mohr.

Chapter Ten
The Federal Judiciary
Brian M. Murphy

Learning Objectives
After covering the topic of the federal judiciary, students should understand:

1. The relationship of state courts to the federal judiciary.
2. The jurisdiction of federal courts.
3. The structure of the federal judicial system.
4. The procedures of the U.S. Supreme Court.
5. The powers of the federal judiciary.

Abstract

The judicial system in the United States is based on the doctrine of federalism. Two court systems exist side-by-side, national and state, and each has a distinct set of powers. State courts, for the most part, are responsible for handling the legal issues that arise under their own laws. It is primarily when a federal question is presented that the federal judicial system can become involved in a state court. Otherwise, state judiciaries are autonomous even from one another. The Constitution precisely outlines the types of cases that can be heard by federal courts, yet it is almost impossible to force a federal court to hear a case that falls under its jurisdiction if the judge(s) wants to avoid it. The authority of the U.S. Supreme Court has slowly grown over time, largely through the power of judicial review. Nonetheless, federalism has managed to remain a significant barrier against federal courts becoming too powerful. The judicial system designed by the founding fathers continues to survive after 200 years.

Introduction

The federal judicial system is the least commonly known and least understood branch of American government. In 2007, 78% could not name the current Chief Justice of the U.S. Supreme Court but 66% were able to identify at least one of the judges on the TV show *American Idol* (Jamison, 2007). Much of judicial work is conducted out of the limelight and courts are not considered an important influence in the daily lives of people. It is clear the founding fathers believed that the federal judicial system would be the weakest of the three branches because, as Alexander

Hamilton wrote, it "has no influence over either the sword or the purse" (Hamilton, 1961:465). In other words, courts cannot command an army (or even police) to ensure that decisions are enforced or allocate money to implement one of their rulings. Judges must depend on the other branches in order to get anything done. According to an oft-repeated story, President Andrew Jackson supposedly mocked a decision by Chief Justice John Marshall with the words, "John Marshall has made his decision, now let him enforce it" (Schwartz, 1993:94).

But times and the role of the federal judiciary have changed. One scholar even concluded that the United States is now operating under a "government by judiciary" because the U.S. Supreme Court can revise the Constitution by how it interprets the wording (Berger, 1997). As Chief Justice Charles Evans Hughes once quipped, "We are under a Constitution, but the Constitution is what the judges say it is" (Hughes, 1916:185).

The actual power of federal courts lies between these two extreme viewpoints. While the federal judiciary remains dependent on Congress and the president to enforce judicial rulings, the courts are not powerless in the tussle over checks and balances. This chapter shall carefully examine judicial power and define the powers and limitations of federal courts. What must be kept in mind, however, is that relatively few cases ever end up in federal courts. Most judicial decision-making takes place at the state level. The old adage that "I'll fight all the way to the U.S. Supreme Court" is legally impossible in the overwhelming majority of cases. State courts handle most of the legal action in the United States, so that is where we will start our discussion of the judicial system. Federalism applies to the judicial system as well.

State Court Systems

In the United States, two court systems exist—federal and state—and there is remarkably little overlap between the two. In most situations, decisions on matters of state law are resolved by state courts, and no federal court, not even the U.S. Supreme Court, can overrule, which means that state courts usually render the final judgment on most cases involving state law. The principal way a case from state court can end up in the federal judiciary is when a **federal question** is involved in a dispute. A federal question is defined as a legal issue that concerns a federal law, federal treaty, or federal Constitution.

Let us look at an example. An African American walks into a restaurant in a small town and is forcibly thrown out by the owner, breaking the visitor's arm. This scenario presents several potential legal claims, including aggravated assault and the violation of federal civil rights laws. The first issue, aggravated assault, constitutes a question of state law, while the civil rights claims are federal in nature. Where will this case be heard? Since state law is at stake, the case will go to a state trial court. What about the federal questions? Contrary to what some believe, state courts have the authority to decide federal questions when they are mixed with state law.

Judges in state courts are bound by two legal constraints in deciding cases that combine state and federal issues. First, Article VI, Section 2 of the U.S. Constitution, called the **Supremacy Clause**, declares the following:

> *This Constitution, and the Laws of the United States ...*
> *and all Treaties ... shall be the supreme Law of the Land;*
> *and the Judges in every State shall be bound thereby,*
> *any thing in the constitution or Laws of any State to the*
> *contrary notwithstanding.*

As such, judges at the state level must swear to obey the federal Constitution, laws, and treaties regardless of state law. If there is a conflict between the two, the Supremacy Clause requires a state judge to enforce federal law over state law. The second legal constraint on state judges involves the interpretation of federal law. Does the state's supreme court, for example, have the authority to instruct lower courts in its state how to interpret a federal law? In 1816, the U.S. Supreme Court ruled that state courts are bound by its holdings on federal questions (*Martin v. Hunter's Lessee*, 1816) no matter what the state's highest court has decided on the issue. In short, state judges must apply the rulings of the U.S. Supreme Court in deciding federal questions and should ignore any state law or state court ruling that is in contradiction.

Now, let us take another look at the restaurant dispute. At trial, the state court can rule on both the aggravated assault and civil rights issues. However, the judgment on aggravated assault will be based on state law while the civil rights controversy should follow the rulings of the U.S.

Supreme Court. In a state case, the right to a jury trial varies depending whether a criminal or civil case is involved. A jury trial in a criminal case is available under the Sixth Amendment when a jail term of six months or more is a possible outcome of a trial (*Duncan v. Louisiana*, 1968). A civil case differs from a criminal case in several ways: (1) a criminal case involves either jail time or a fine as an outcome while a civil case is seeking either monetary damages (e.g., to cover injuries suffered in an auto accident) or a declaration of rights (e.g., to decide who owns a piece of property or who has custody of a child); (2) the government is always a party in a criminal case while a civil case is a lawsuit between private parties; (3) the government's **burden of proof** in a criminal case requires establishing guilt beyond a reasonable doubt while the burden of proof in a civil case is the **preponderance of evidence** (i.e., the winning side is the one with the majority of evidence in its favor); and (4) states are under no constitutional mandate to provide juries in any civil case, although states are not forbidden from allowing them (*Minneapolis & St. Louis R.R. v. Bombolis*, 1916).

The O.J. Simpson murder case illustrates the differences between criminal and civil trials. Simpson was charged criminally with the murder of his ex-wife (Nicole Brown) and Ronald Goldman. Simpson was famously acquitted of both murders in 1995. A few years later in 1997, however, Simpson lost a civil suit to the families of Brown and Goldman for battery (touching without consent) and for wrongful death (causing death without legal justification)—the latter a civil parallel to murder. Legally, the outcome of a criminal case has no bearing on a civil case for the same act because the burdens of proof are not the same. Consequently, Simpson was found *liable* (the term guilty does not apply in a civil case) for $33.5 million for the wrongful death of Goldman, battery against Goldman, and battery against ex-wife Brown. In other words, O.J. Simpson was not guilty of murder but liable for causing the wrongful death of the same person!

Since all states guarantee the right to one appeal, a higher court can review the trial court's decision. It should be noted that the U.S. Constitution has no specific provision that requires the right to appeal a trial court's decision, even in cases heard in federal courts. The right to appeal is possible solely because every state as well as the federal government has enacted this right into law and, at least in theory, it can be taken away. An appeal is not possible merely because the loser is unsatisfied with the outcome of a trial. Nor can a person appeal claiming innocence. Rather, appeals can only be based on a **question of law** that alleges an error(s) in procedure or law occurred at the trial (e.g., evidence that should have been excluded was allowed or a juror was biased and should not have been permitted to serve). In practical terms, an appeal is arguing the judge made a mistake during the trial that could have impacted the outcome. Since an error in legal procedure or law is the basis of the claim, no juries exist in appellate cases because the average person lacks a legal education to know whether the judge committed a legal error. Juries are only found in trial courts and are used to determine questions of fact, such as guilt or innocence. Judges decide all questions of law during a trial. If a person declines a jury trial, the judge acts as both judge and jury (known as a **bench trial**).

In a criminal case, only the defendant can appeal if convicted. The government cannot appeal an acquittal. However, either party can appeal after the verdict in a civil case. Why would the winning party want to appeal? Consider Ward Churchill, a tenured professor at the University of Colorado. On the day after the destruction of the World Trade Centers on September 11, 2001, he wrote an essay comparing some of the workers in the buildings to Adolf Eichmann, who coordinated the Holocaust for Nazi Germany. Outrage emerged on a national level as the essay slowly worked its way across the Internet. Churchill was eventually investigated by the university for this writing as well as on allegations of plagiarism. He was fired in 2007 by University of Colorado Board of Regents for repeated and intentional academic misconduct. In 2009, a jury decided that he had been fired in retaliation for his article but only awarded $1 in damages. Although Churchill won the civil case, he might contemplate appealing in an effort to collect a higher settlement.

Another popular misconception is that a person can be found innocent on appeal. It cannot happen, of course, because an appeal can be based only on questions of law, not questions of fact. If a person wins on appeal, the usual result is that a new trial is conducted before a different judge and jury and the legal error from the first trial will be corrected. Take the famous case of Ernesto Miranda, who was convicted at trial for sexual assault. Miranda appealed to the U.S. Supreme Court, which held that Miranda's confession could not be used as evidence because he was never warned about his right to refuse to answer police questions. Miranda was not set free but was given a new trial in which he was again convicted because enough evidence of guilt existed without his confession. Thus, a person on re-trial after a successful appeal can lose again and even receive a harsher sentence than the original penalty. Appeals are clearly not without risk.

Once the trial is over, a decision must be made on whether to appeal. All states allow only a certain number of days to make this decision or forfeit the right. In the restaurant case, let us assume the **plaintiff** (the person bringing the case) lost on both issues at the trial court. Specifically, the jury decided that no aggravated assault took place because the restaurant owner (the **defendant**, or the person being sued) was defending himself and no civil rights violation occurred since the plaintiff was kicked out for being unruly. Where will the appeal be heard?

Most states and the federal government have three levels of courts in their judicial system:

- Trial courts that determine questions of fact
- Intermediate appellate courts (found in most, but not all, states) where decisions on questions of law are made by judges sitting without juries
- State supreme courts (although the highest court is not always called "supreme" in all states) that—for the most part—hear appeals from intermediate appellate courts. If no intermediate appellate court exists in a state (http://www.appellatecourtclerks. org/links.html), an appeal from a trial court's decision is taken directly to the state's highest court

In our example, let us assume that the intermediate and state supreme courts both upheld the decision of the trial court. Now what?

The decision on state law (aggravated assault) is over and no further appeal is possible. The decision of the state's highest court will be the final word on a matter of state law. With respect to the federal question (a possible civil rights violation), the losing party can appeal directly to the U.S. Supreme Court. No other federal court, in fact, is allowed to take the case.

Aside from an appeal from a state's highest court to the U.S. Supreme Court, there are two other ways in which federal courts can become entangled with state courts. Upon conviction in a criminal case and an unsuccessful appeal to the state's highest court, a prisoner can file a ***habeas corpus*** petition to a federal trial court (called a U.S. District Court) claiming that a violation of a federal constitutional right took place (such as not being allowed to cross-exam a key witness). If granted, the federal judge will issue a writ of *habeas corpus* — which translates into "you have the body" — to the jailor requesting that the prisoner be brought before the U.S. District Court to determine the legality of detention. In this way, *habeas corpus* serves as "the fundamental instrument for safeguarding individual freedom against arbitrary and lawless state action" (*Harris v. Nelson*, 1969). Much like an appeal, a new trial at the state level will generally be ordered if the federal judge finds that a constitutional right was indeed denied. The new trial is designed to correct whatever error happened in the initial hearing.

The final way federal and state courts interact is through a **diversity suit**. These cases arise when citizens of different states (hence the word "diversity") are involved in a civil case. The founding fathers were concerned that an unbiased court would not exist in a diversity suit because state judges might favor citizens from their own state. Consequently, the Constitution (Article III, Section 2) empowered Congress to grant federal courts the authority to handle such cases, and in the Judiciary Act of 1789, this jurisdiction was assigned initially to federal circuit courts. Certain cases are exempt from diversity jurisdiction since it would be inappropriate for federal courts to become involved. These cases include divorce, alimony, custody, wills, and the administration of estates. In deciding a diversity case, a federal judge will actually apply the appropriate state—not federal—law that governs the situation.

Over time, the number of diversity cases exploded to the point where the federal judiciary became overwhelmed. Congress responded by shifting less important diversity cases (currently defined as a lawsuit that has less than \$75,000 at stake) to state courts. If the amount in controversy exceeds \$75,000, the defendant (the person being sued by the plaintiff) has a choice between taking the case to state court or to a U.S. District Court.

The relationship between state and federal courts can be summarized as follows:

- State judges must apply federal law over state law if the two are in conflict.

- Appeals from a state's judicial system are submitted from the state's highest court directly to the U.S. Supreme but only the parts of the case that concern federal questions.
- *Habeas corpus* petitions from prisoners convicted of a state crime can be reviewed by U.S. District Courts if the breach of a federal constitutional right is alleged.
- U.S. District Courts may hear a civil suit between citizens of different states if $75,000 or more is at stake and the defendant elects federal over state court.

While separate, state and federal courts do interact on a narrow but important range of issues.

State court systems are entirely independent from each other. The decision of a state court rarely has an impact outside its own borders. The lone exception—mandated by Article VI, Section1 of the U.S. Constitution—requires each state to give **full faith and credit** to the judicial decisions in other states. This clause means that a decision issued in one state will be respected by all other states (*Mills v. Duryee,* 1813). The Full Faith and Credit Clause is intended to prevent a person who loses a case to avoid compliance by moving elsewhere. Thus, if a defendant loses a civil case in Pennsylvania and is ordered to pay $15,000, the defendant cannot escape the decision by changing residence to Georgia. The plaintiff merely has to file suit in Georgia to have the judgment enforced against the defendant. There is no need for a new trial since a valid and final decision was already rendered. The clause is frequently used in marriage and divorce situations. People, for example, will sometimes marry in a state with lower age requirements, return to their home state, and the marriage must be honored—even though it would be illegal if performed in that state. The Full Faith and Credit Clause, in short, protects the integrity of each state's judicial system to make its own judicial decisions.

Federal Jurisdiction

Two conditions must be met in order for a case to be heard before a federal court: jurisdiction and justiciability. **Jurisdiction** simply means that a court has the authority to decide a case. Article III of the U.S. Constitution outlines the kinds of cases federal courts are eligible to handle, but leaves it up to Congress to actually assign each potential area of jurisdiction. Congress, however, can only provide federal courts with the powers allowed in the Constitution; it cannot expand federal judicial jurisdiction to cases beyond what is specifically authorized in the Constitution. Moreover, Congress can change federal jurisdiction at any time by removing authority it had previously awarded to federal courts (*Ex Parte McCardle*, 1869). An effort to remove an area of federal jurisdiction is typically intended to deny federal judges the power to decide controversial issues. For example, members of Congress have introduced bills to deny federal courts the jurisdiction to hear cases involving abortion, prayer in the school, and busing to desegregate public schools. Such efforts almost always fail in Congress because they are driven by politics rather than legitimate legal concerns. The independence of the judiciary is too deeply a part of the American political culture to allow the politics of emotional causes to interfere.

The jurisdiction of federal courts can be established in one of two ways. First, the Constitution identifies certain topics (**subject matter jurisdiction**) as appropriate for federal courts: federal questions (issues arising under federal laws, treaties, and Constitution) as well as **admiralty and maritime** law (disputes involving navigation and shipping on navigable waters). Second, the Constitution delineates certain parties (**party jurisdiction**) as suitable to bring cases to federal court: (1) the U.S. government, (2) one of the states, (3) citizens of different states (diversity cases), and (4) foreign ambassadors and counsels. If a case involves either a subject matter or party that falls under federal jurisdiction, a judge will next examine whether the issue is justiciable.

Justiciable means that a dispute is a matter appropriate for a court to resolve. In other words, courts should not be bothered with problems where a judicial decision is not necessary. Why waste a court's time? Judges look at five factors in making this determination, any one of which could render a case not relevant for judicial consideration.

- *Case or controversy:* The dispute must involve parties with a genuine conflict. Federal courts will not answer hypothetical questions. When George Washington sought advice about American neutrality during the European wars of the 1790s, the Supreme Court in a letter (not in a judicial ruling) declined to give an advisory opinion. Until an actual controversy arose about

Washington's policy on neutrality, the justices believed that federal courts would not know what was to be decided.

- *Finality:* A federal court's decision must be final. The concept of separation of powers would be violated if someone other than a higher court should have the authority to review and modify a judicial decision. Judges alone can make judicial rulings. When a congressional statute allowed the Secretary of War to review pension decisions made by federal courts, the Supreme Court held that the federal judiciary should not become involved because the Secretary of War could overturn anything a judge decides (*Hayburn's Case*, 1792).

- *Standing*: The plaintiff must suffer personal damage to a right protected under federal law or the U.S. Constitution. When Congress enacted a law requiring mandatory drug testing to get a job at the U.S. Postal Service, the union representing postal employees sued on the grounds that the statute violated privacy rights. A U.S. Appellate Court ruled that the union lacked standing because the drug testing policy applied only to job applicants who were not yet members of the union (*American Postal Workers Union v. Frank*, 1992). The union itself, therefore, had not suffered any damage and thus had no standing.

- *Political Questions:* A federal court will not hear an issue that can be better handled by another branch of government. Consequently, the U.S. Supreme Court refused to rule on the constitutionality of the Vietnam War by claiming that foreign policy decisions should be made by Congress and the president (*Massachusetts v. Laird*, 1970). A majority of justices argued that judges have no expertise that qualifies them to be experts on international relations. The Vietnam War was not a legal question but a political one.

- *Timeliness*: Cases must reach federal courts at a time when the outcome of a decision can make a difference. Judges will not take cases that arrive too early (**ripe**) or too late (**moot**). When a white male applicant was denied admission into the University of Washington Law School even though minority applicants with lower test scores had been admitted, a court ordered the white applicant to be enrolled pending resolution of the lawsuit. By the time the issue reached the U.S. Supreme Court, the white applicant was in his final quarter of school and would graduate no matter what happened in the case. For this reason, the lawsuit was declared moot and no ruling was made (*DeFunis v. Odegaard*, 1974). Ripeness is the reverse of moot in the sense that a case is considered unprepared for decision. When a federal law prohibited federal civil service employees from taking part in political campaigns, a complaint by employees was thrown out because no one had yet been arrested (*United Public Workers v. Mitchell*, 1947). According to the Supreme Court, the threat of arrest does not mean anyone would actually be arrested under the law, so that there was nothing yet to decide.

Only the requirement of a "case or controversy" is mentioned in the Constitution (Article II, Section 2); the remaining four factors have been created by the U.S. Supreme Court as elements of the Case or Controversy clause and are frequently used by federal courts as an excuse to dodge controversial cases. Take the Vietnam War lawsuit that was evaded for being a "political question." Justice William Douglas challenged the majority opinion in a dissent complaining the case did indeed present a justiciable issue—whether the president had the constitutional power to engage in a military action without congressional approval. Was the legality of the Vietnam War truly a "political question" or was the Supreme Court merely dodging a problem on purpose because it was too controversial? In short, justiciability is an ambiguous concept that can be interpreted quite freely by federal judges. The bottom line is that justiciability enables a federal court to avoid a case it does not want to decide.

Once jurisdiction is established and a judge rules an issue justiciable, a case is eligible for a federal court to hear.

The Structure of Federal Courts

Article III of the U.S. Constitution directly mentions only the U.S. Supreme Court, but it empowers Congress to create additional federal courts as needed. Like most state systems, the federal judiciary today is divided into three levels: trial court, intermediate appellate court, and Supreme Court. The first step in bringing a case to federal court is identifying the correct trial court in which to file suit. Congress has created a host of options, with the selection of the specific trial court depending upon the issue at stake in the lawsuit. Here is a partial list of the complex alternatives: Contract claims against the federal government go to the U.S. Court of Federal Claims, international trade and customs issues are handled by the U.S. Court of International Trade, bankruptcy cases belong to U.S. Bankruptcy Courts, and federal income tax disputes are taken to the U.S. Tax Court. These courts are designed to handle narrow, highly technical issues and the judges are chosen on the basis of their background in these specialized areas of law.

An important distinction must be made between federal courts. Except for the U.S. Supreme Court, all other federal courts have been created by Congress but not under the same constitutional power. The most important federal courts were authorized under Article III, the section of the Constitution that deals with the judicial branch, and they are limited to exercising only judicial powers (i.e., deciding legal cases and controversies). These courts are the following: U.S. District Courts, U.S. Circuit Courts of Appeal, U.S. Supreme Court, U.S. Court of Claims, and U.S. Court of International Trade. The president nominates judges on these courts, and appointment depends upon approval by the U.S. Senate. Article III judges, who "hold their Offices during good Behaviour," meaning they cannot be removed except by death, resignation, or impeachment by the House of Representatives and conviction by the Senate. Even senility and incompetence are not grounds that can justify dismissal of an Article III judge. It is interesting to note that Article III does not spell out any specific qualifications that must be possessed to be a federal judge; not even a law degree is a necessity.

Congress also created a series of federal courts under Article I, the section of the Constitution that involves the legislative branch. This section enables Congress more flexibility in setting up courts because it is not restricted by the provisions of Article III in terms of powers and tenure. So-called Article I, or **legislative courts,** are typically assigned certain non-judicial duties, such as administrative roles, and the judges do not have a lifetime appointment. Most, but not all, Article I judges are nominated by the president and approved by the Senate to serve a specific term (8-15 years). The current list of legislative courts is the following: U.S. Magistrate Courts, U.S. Bankruptcy Courts, U.S. Court of Appeals for the Armed Forces, U.S. Tax Court, and U.S. Court of Appeals for

Veterans Claims. In the past, Congress has changed the status of an Article I court to an Article III court to give the judges more independence.

The workhorses at the federal level are the 94 U.S. District Courts. These trial courts (courts of original jurisdiction) hear all crimes against the U.S., most federal civil actions, and certain diversity cases. Each state has at least one U.S. District Court and, based roughly on population, a state may be allocated extra court(s). Georgia, for example, has three U.S. District Courts while California has four. The number of judges assigned to a district ranges from two to twenty-eight. Moreover, U.S. District Courts can be found in the District of Columbia, Puerto Rico, and in three U.S. territories: The Virgin Islands, Guam, and The Northern Mariana Islands. To relieve the heavy caseload (almost 400,000 cases are filed annually with U.S. District Courts), Congress in 1968 created magistrate judges to deal with minor matters such as preliminary hearings, warrants, bail, and lesser criminal offenses.

As a trial court, U.S. District Court judges decide cases either alone or with a jury. Federal law requires District Court judges to write an opinion explaining their decision when sitting without a jury. The Sixth Amendment awards the right to a jury trial in all federal criminal cases, but $20 must be involved under the Seventh Amendment for the right to a jury trail to apply in a federal civil case. Most federal cases are resolved at the District Court level. Only about 10% of decisions are appealed on the basis of a question of law.

Congress has created 12 U.S. Courts of Appeal that have jurisdiction over a set of U.S. District Courts and federal agencies within a defined geographic region (called a **circuit**). Each circuit, in turn, is numbered (see map below). Thus the U.S. Court of Appeals for the Eleventh Circuit takes all appeals from the U.S. District Courts located in Georgia, Florida, and Alabama (nine District Courts in total). As noted, federal agencies (like the Social Security Administration) can render decisions and these too are appealed to the appropriate U.S. appellate court. A thirteenth appellate court, the Court of Appeals for the Federal Circuit in Washington, D.C., was launched in 1982 to manage appeals involving patents from anywhere in the country as well as appeals from decisions by the Court of International Trade and the Court of Federal Claims.

Figure 10.1

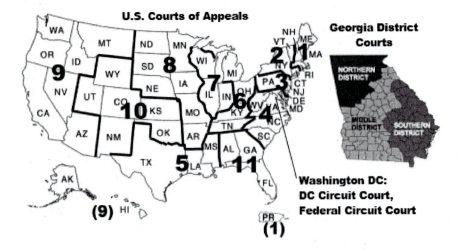

A federal appellate court has from six judges (First Circuit) to twenty-eight judges (Ninth Circuit). The appellate judge in the circuit with the most seniority serves as chief judge until the age of 70, although the person can continue as a regular member of the court. Individual cases are generally heard in three judge panels without juries, with judges normally assigned to a panel by the chief judge. The winning party is determined by a majority vote. In rare cases (less than 1% of the total), all judges in a circuit—a requirement relaxed by Congress for appellate courts with 15 or more members—will be present for a case in what is known as an *en banc* hearing. Such hearings tend to take place either to deal with a controversial case or to review a panel's ruling in the circuit. The fact that all, or almost all, appellate judges in the circuit are deciding the case is intended to give more weight to the eventual judgment. An *en banc* hearing may be requested by any member of the court and is convened when at least a majority of judges are in favor (some circuits require less than a majority vote).

The decision by a U.S. Court of Appeal is binding on all U.S. District Courts and federal agencies in the circuit. An appellate court, in other words, does not have the authority to issue compulsory orders outside its geographic jurisdiction. Thus it is possible that the interpretation of a federal law can vary across the nation when different U.S. Courts of

Appeals deliver conflicting rulings on a law. These contradictions can only be ironed out by the U.S. Supreme Court, if it chooses to do so. Only about 15% of decisions by U.S. Courts of Appeal are appealed to the Supreme Court.

U.S. Supreme Court

Congress determines the number of justices on the Supreme Court. Historically, the size of the Court has ranged from 6 to 10 members. The current size of nine justices was set in 1869, although President Franklin Roosevelt (FDR) in the 1930s famously threatened to increase the membership by "packing" the Court with a majority who would support his programs. FDR became frustrated when his New Deal legislation kept being declared unconstitutional by a 5-4 vote. Congress, however, was reluctant to support a proposal that would enable judicial decisions to be manipulated for political purposes, and it dropped the court-packing plan when one justice suddenly stopped opposing New Deal laws in a move sometimes called "a switch in time that saved nine."

One member of the Supreme Court is nominated by the president to serve as Chief Justice of the United States (not Chief Justice of the Supreme Court). The other eight members are known as associate justices. The chief justice has a few formal powers not possessed by the other justices. In particular, the chief justice votes first on cases, assigns the author of the court's opinion if voting with the majority (if the chief justice is in the minority, the writing assignment is doled out by the associate justice in the majority with the most seniority), and heads the Judicial Conference of the United States that administers all federal courts.

At least six justices are needed to decide a case. If a tie vote occurs (3-3 or 4-4), the ruling of the last court to decide the case—usually a U.S. Court of Appeals or a state's highest court—is allowed to stand. It does not mean, however, that the Supreme Court is agreeing with the ruling of the lower court. It merely means that the Supreme Court itself was unable to reach a decision.

While the U.S. Supreme Court is commonly considered to take cases solely on appeal, the U.S. Constitution (Article III, section 2) assigns a limited **original jurisdiction**. In these instances, a case goes directly to the Supreme Court, and the justices serve as the trial court. The decision by the justices is final and no further appeal is possible. Four types of cases constitute the Supreme Court's original jurisdiction:

- Cases between two or more states.
- Cases between a state and the United States.
- Cases involving ambassadors and foreign counsels.
- Cases in which a state is suing a citizen of another state or a foreign nation.

Since the Supreme Court has little time to devote to an actual trial, Congress (28 U.S.C. section 1251) awarded U.S. District Courts **concurrent jurisdiction** over the last three types of cases. Concurrent jurisdiction denotes that a particular type of case can be heard by more than one court. In practical terms, most of the Supreme Court's original jurisdiction is shared with U.S. District Courts to the point where it is a waste of time to request the justices to consider a case that falls in these categories (with an appeal through U.S. Courts of Appeal to the U.S. Supreme Court still feasible). Moreover, the last category of original jurisdiction was restricted by the Eleventh Amendment (1795) to prevent a state from being sued by a citizen of another state or a foreign country under the doctrine of **sovereign immunity** (i.e., the concept that a government cannot be sued without its consent).

Only cases between two or more states remain within the Supreme Court's exclusive original jurisdiction. These cases most often involve disputes over borders or water rights, such as a dispute between New York and New Jersey over ownership rights to Ellis Island (*New Jersey v. New York*, 1998). Even here, the tradition is to appoint a **master** (usually a retired federal judge) to examine the evidence and recommend an outcome to the Supreme Court. It is seldom that more than one or two cases annually will be heard under original jurisdiction.

By far, the caseload of the Supreme Court comes from its appellate jurisdiction—over 5,000 appeals annually. Remember that, under the Constitution (Article III, Section 2, Clause 2), federal appellate jurisdiction is assigned with "such exceptions and under such regulations, as the Congress shall make." Currently, appellate cases are derived from the 13 U.S. courts of appeals, from the U.S. Court of Appeals for the Armed Forces, from U.S. district courts (in exceptional circumstances), and from the highest state courts when a federal question exists. There are three avenues of appeal to the U.S. Supreme Court: (1) **writ of appeal** (when federal law gives the automatic right to have a certain type of case reviewed by the Supreme Court), (2) **writ of certification** (when a lower federal court requests instructions on a point of law never before decided), and (3) **writ of certiorari** (when a writ of appeal is not available). The first two avenues generate few cases, especially since Congress severely cut back on the availability of the writ of appeal in 1988.

Today, the writ of certiorari (or more commonly, writ of cert) is the primary means of appealing to the Supreme Court. According to the Supreme Court's Rule 10(9), "Review on writ of certiorari is not a matter of right, but a judicial discretion. A petition for writ of certiorari will be granted only for compelling reasons." The Supreme Court uses the *rule of four* to determine which appeals are granted; the Court considers an appeal if four justices vote to accept (only three votes are necessary if six or seven justices are present). Only about 100 cases are heard annually. Denial of a writ does not mean the justices agree with the previous ruling, only that not enough justices believe a substantial question was raised that is worthy of review. The justices simply do not have time to correct every error that occurred in lower courts. Moreover, the granting of the writ provides no indication of how the Supreme Court will ultimately rule on the case. The losing party in the lower court may still lose.

The Supreme Court begins its regular session on the first Monday in October and continues until late June or early July. When petitions are received, the chief justice creates the Supreme Court's agenda and places each either on the "discuss list" or "dead list." Petitions assigned to the dead list will routinely be denied unless any justice requests a particular petition to be shifted to the discuss list. The justices meet together in conference on Wednesdays and Fridays and, by tradition, begin with a handshake. Since 1910, only justices are allowed in the room. The associate justice with the least seniority must respond to knocks at the door and leave to collect books or papers for the other members. The chief justice is allowed to speak first on whether to accept or deny petitions on the discuss list and is followed by the associate justices in order of seniority, with voting taking place in the reverse sequence. Again, four votes are required to schedule a hearing on a case.

Oral arguments are conducted Mondays through Wednesdays beginning in early October and running through late spring. Two-week breaks are periodically arranged to enable the justices an opportunity to research and write. During oral arguments, each side is typically allocated a half-hour and justices can interrupt at any time—cutting into a lawyer's time. The **Solicitor General**, nominated by the president and confirmed by the Senate, argues cases in which the federal government is a party. Public access is permitted on a limited basis.

During conference, the justices discuss and vote on the cases heard at oral argument. A majority vote determines winning and losing parties. The chief justice assigns the opinion writer only if a member of the majority side (which happens over 80% of the time). When the chief justice is on the losing side, the associate justice in the majority with the most seniority has the duty of determining the author of the court's decision. Justices circulate drafts of their opinions and must take great care to ensure that their wording does not alienate members of the majority. It has happened that an opinion begins as the majority decision but, due to the way in which the decision is written, may end up the losing side. Justices are allowed to alter their votes on a case up to the very moment a decision is announced to the public.

Justices on the losing side have the option of writing a **dissenting opinion**. Since a dissenting member is speaking for no one else (although other justices can support the dissent), these opinions tend to be more candid and sometimes insulting. Even justices in the majority can write separate **concurring opinions,** and these must be read carefully. In a concurring opinion, a justice may merely want to elaborate on the reasons for agreeing with the majority but may also express concerns about aspects of the decision. A common situation is when a justice agrees as to the winning party but does not support the rationale behind the Court's opinion. For example, five justices could rule that a conviction should be overturned, with four believing that evidence was improperly admitted but the fifth that a juror was biased. It now becomes complicated.

If a majority (five justices) does not endorse both the outcome and the rationale for a decision, the Supreme Court issues what is called a **judgment** (Cross, 2009:323). Such opinions only identify the winning and losing parties and do not establish precedent that is binding on lower courts. A **precedent** requires judges to follow the ruling of a higher court in their jurisdiction when dealing with a case that presents similar facts. This doctrine (known as *stare decisis*) was created to ensure that people are treated the same in applying legal standards. An appellate court binds only the courts within its jurisdiction with its precedents. Thus, the U.S. Supreme Court binds all courts, state and federal, when it decides a federal question, while a U.S. Court of Appeals binds only the U.S. District Courts in its circuit.

Precedent is established only when a majority agrees on the outcome as well as the rationale behind a decision. Here, the Supreme Court issues an *opinion* that is binding on all federal courts. The relationship with state courts is more complex. State judges, of course, must obey the precedents of the U.S. Supreme Court on federal questions. When a case originating in state court is decided, the Supreme Court typically **remands**, or sends the case back, to the highest court in the state to enforce its ruling. At this point, state courts will sometimes evade obeying the U.S. Supreme Court in a completely legal way. The U.S. Constitution is not the only source of rights possessed by citizens. A state can always "impose higher standards … than required by the Federal Constitution" so long as they are not interfering with a federal interest (*Cooper v. California*, 1967). One study found that 12% of the cases remanded to state courts by the U.S. Supreme Court reversed winning and losing parties (Note, 1954).

Consider an example. In 1976, the U.S. Supreme Court held the search of an impounded car by the police was permissible under the Fourth Amendment even though no probable cause existed that contraband was to be found inside the vehicle (*South Dakota v. Opperman*, 1976). On remand, the state's supreme court ruled the search unconstitutional under the state's constitution (*State v. Opperman*, 1976). In other words, the state court refused to obey a direct ruling by the U.S. Supreme Court by giving the citizens of South Dakota more protection than allowed under the U.S. Constitution. Police need a warrant to search an impounded car in South Dakota—but nowhere else in the country—in the absence of probable cause. The Supreme Court of the United States may not be the last word after all!

Powers of the Federal Judiciary

Aside from deciding cases and controversies, the Constitution is silent on the powers to be exercised by federal courts. This lack of clarity differs from the careful attention devoted to enumerating the powers belonging to Congress and the president. Thus the exact authority of federal courts had to develop over time in response to issues as they arose. It is not surprising that service on the Supreme Court was not viewed initially as too significant a position. John Jay, the first chief justice, stepped down to become governor of New York, something that surely would not happen today.

The landscape began to change when John Marshall became chief justice in 1801, and he continued serving until 1835. His influence vastly expanded the power of all federal courts. The key decision was issued in *Marbury v. Madison*, 5 U.S. 137 (1803). The case would make a good soap opera. In the 1800 election, the Federalists lost control of the presidency and both houses of Congress. Before the new administration took office under Thomas Jefferson, the Federalists sought to move quickly to create a host of new judicial posts to which members of the party would be appointed. Federal courts, therefore, would be packed with Federalists who would seek to frustrate Jefferson in any way possible. As luck would have it for the Federalists, the Chief Justice of the Supreme Court resigned, and President John Adams immediately nominated John Marshall, his Secretary of State, to the position, and the Senate confirmed. Adams requested Marshall to continue as Secretary of State for the little time remaining in his term.

In its last days, the Federalist Congress enacted several laws signed by Adams; one of which established 42 new positions of Justice of the Peace for the District of Columbia. Adams nominated and the Senate confirmed all 42 appointments the day before Jefferson was to assume office. Adams signed the commissions, and it fell upon the Secretary of State to deliver them. Marshall worked throughout the night and managed to give out all but four of the commissions before midnight. The new Secretary of State, James Madison, walked into his office to discover the undelivered commissions. Since the papers had been signed and sealed, Marshall assumed Madison would complete the project. Jefferson, however, instructed Madison to ignore the commissions.

William Marbury, and the other promised recipients of a judgeship, filed suit directly before the U.S. Supreme Court under its original jurisdiction. A federal law enacted in 1789 had expanded the Supreme Court's original jurisdiction to allow suits against federal officials to perform their legal duties. Marshall, who was responsible for the mess, was now in position to decide the dispute as Chief Justice. The situation suddenly became more complicated. Jefferson asserted that he would not provide Marbury his commission no matter what the Supreme Court ruled. Several members of Congress additionally threatened Marshall with impeachment if Marbury won. As a result, a in box with no way out. He could decide for Marbury and be defied by Jefferson and even be impeached. Or he could decide against Marbury—who probably deserved to win—and be publicly humiliated for no backbone while also lowering the prestige of the court system. The drama was more compelling because Jefferson and Marshall were second cousins and were splitting apart the family. In a brilliant maneuver, Marshall managed not only to evade the dilemma but to enhance the power of the federal judiciary at the same time.

Marshall wrote the opinion in *Marbury v. Madison* for a unanimous Supreme Court. While acknowledging that Marbury deserved the commission and admonishing Madison for not performing his duty, Marshall lamented that the Supreme Court lacked authority to order Madison to comply. The reason is that the federal law enabling Marbury to file suit directly before the Supreme Court was not one of the four types of cases listed in Article III as part of its original jurisdiction. In other words, Congress added a fifth type of case to the Supreme Court's original jurisdiction. Could a law of Congress override the Constitution? Marshall answered in the negative because "all those who have framed written constitutions contemplate them as the fundamental and paramount law of the nation." In simple terms, the Constitution is superior to congressional statutes.

Only one important question remained: are courts required to follow a federal law that is inconsistent with the Constitution? In a famous sentence, Marshall concluded: "It is emphatically the province of the judicial department to say what the law is." If a federal law violates the Constitution, federal courts are empowered to strike down the law. Separation of powers entrusts courts with the authority to interpret laws, and the Constitution must be interpreted like any law. These reasons meant Marbury was in the wrong court and would have to file suit elsewhere, an option that would not be worth his time since his term as Justice of the Peace was soon to expire. Thus Marshall succeeded in publicly rebuking

Jefferson and in making the Supreme Court a feared institution that could nullify acts of Congress. As might be expected, the decision stirred a storm of controversy, and the Supreme Court waited 54 years before daring to strike down another congressional statute. Marshall, without using the term, claimed the power of **judicial review** for the court system. As it has evolved, the concept of judicial review has come to include the following elements:

- It is a power possessed by all courts, state and federal.
- It enables acts of Congress or of any public authority to be challenged.
- If found to be in violation of the federal Constitution, the law or action is voided and can be ignored.

Keep in mind that only the U.S. Supreme Court has national jurisdiction so that it alone can exercise judicial review that applies across the country. The use of judicial review by other courts is limited to the geographic area within its jurisdiction: a U.S. Court of Appeals controls the courts in its circuit; a state's highest court controls courts in the state, etc. Moreover, it is not only legislative bodies that can be challenged but executive officials as well. It was the U.S. Supreme Court, for example, that forced President Richard Nixon to turn over the recordings made in the Oval Office by rejecting Nixon's argument that a president—unlike other citizens—could withhold information demanded by a court (*United States v. Nixon*, 1974).

Judicial review is a hotly debated topic for several reasons. First, the power is not mentioned in the Constitution itself. Marshall found the power a logical extension of the judiciary's authority to interpret laws, but the Constitution's failure explicitly to collaborate renders the rationale open to questioning. If the founding fathers wanted the courts to utilize judicial review, critics contend the power would have been written into the Constitution since the issue was discussed at the Constitutional Convention. Second, opponents warn that the power is subject to abuse with little oversight. Woodrow Wilson once described the Supreme Court as a constitutional convention in continuous session. A majority on the Supreme Court can interpret the Constitution to say almost anything, and the only way to reverse is by the grueling process of amending the Constitution. A number of amendments (Eleventh, Fourteenth, Sixteenth,

Nineteenth, and Twenty-Sixth) have been adopted specifically to override decisions of the Supreme Court, while hundreds of proposals to do so have been introduced into Congress over the years. Finally, judicial review has been blamed for undermining the doctrine of separation of powers by enabling courts to write what amounts to legislation. Did the Supreme Court "legislate" when it required police to inform detained individuals of four rights before questioning them? The Fifth Amendment only declares that no person "shall be compelled in any criminal case to be a witness against himself," and the Supreme Court added the words about issuing warnings to detained individuals.

Judicial review is surely a potent weapon that will survive if for no other reason than its use is inevitable. The judiciary must have some way under checks and balances to protect its authority. The real debate should focus on when the exercise of judicial review is appropriate. **Judicial activists** consider the proper role of courts to include "filling in the holes" left by the Constitution's vague language. They believe it is the duty of judges to minimize potential social disruption caused by the lack of clear policy guidelines, such as when public schools were integrated. The Constitution should be considered a living document that changes with society. Judicial activists, however, have been accused of promoting ideological agendas. Controversial decisions on abortion (*Roe v. Wade*, 1973), contraception (*Griswold v. Connecticut*, 1965), and contracts (*Lochner v. New York*, 1925) have been faulted for imposing the personal values of judges on society without any direct support in the language of the Constitution.

Advocates of **judicial restraint** contend that judges should decide cases on the basis of precedent and overturn laws only when a conflict with the Constitution is unmistakable. This approach is best accomplished when judges try to remain within the original intent or meaning of the founding fathers and avoid merely making up policy, yet judicial restraint is almost impossible to practice consistently. Justice John Paul Stevens, for example, could not resist chiding Justice Antonin Scalia, the Supreme Court's most vocal champion of judicial restraint, for overturning long-standing precedent to achieve what many considered an ideological result on the Second Amendment: "It is, however, clear to me that adherence to a policy of judicial restraint would be far wiser than the bold decision announced today" (*District of Columbia v. Heller*, 2008). It would seem that the proper role of judicial review lies somewhere between the extremes of judicial activism and judicial restraint.

Aside from judicial review, federal courts are frequently called upon to engage in **statutory interpretation** where they attempt to understand the meaning of a law. Here, judges are not examining a law for its conformity with the Constitution but are merely trying to make sense of it (Cross, 2009). If Congress enacts a law requiring all "able bodied" males age 18 to be subject to the military draft, for example, is a male "able bodied" if he has flat feet? Typically, courts decide such cases by seeking to identify the legislature's intent when the law was enacted and applying this intent to the circumstances presented by the situation. Laws are hardly written with a great deal of precision, and the opportunity for courts to interpret statutes is quite frequent. Unlike judicial review, however, Congress is able to alter court interpretations of statutes more easily. Since the courts are not interpreting the Constitution, Congress can reverse the judicial interpretation of a statute simply by re-writing the law. One study found that Congress overturned 124 Supreme Court decisions based on interpretations of federal law in a 23-year period (Eskridge, 1991:335-341). The doctrine of checks and balances is alive and well!

Discussion Questions
1. Is the Supreme Court the "least dangerous branch," as once described by Alexander Hamilton? Justify your answer on the basis of the material in the chapter.
2. From the reading, what are the checks on the powers of the judiciary? Are the checks adequate to prevent the abuse of judicial power? Explain.
3. Which position makes the most sense to you, judicial activism or judicial restraint? Justify your position. Is a Republic or Democratic judge more likely to favor judicial restraint? Explain your answer.
4. The chapter makes a case that federalism is "alive and well" in the relationship between state and federal courts. What evidence is available to support this position?

Civic Exercise
    Interview a lawyer who has argued cases before both state and federal

courts and ask the following questions:

1. Do you prefer taking a case to state or federal court? Explain why.
2. Did any of your state cases involve federal questions? If so, to what extent was the state judge knowledgeable about federal law?
3. Do you prefer arguing cases before juries or judges alone? Explain why.
4. Discuss whether civil cases or criminal cases are more difficult to litigate.
5. Have you ever argued an appellate case? If so, how does the experience differ from a trial court? Explain the concept of "perfecting the record."
6. In your opinion, do federal courts have too much power? Cite examples.
7. Federal judges, for the most part, are appointed while state judges are elected. Is there a difference in the quality of judges in comparing the two selection methods?
8. In your experience, did a federal judge use the doctrine of "justiciability" to avoid hearing a case that should have legitimately been taken? Discuss the incident(s).
9. Does the option of taking a diversity case to a federal court still make sense since the original justification was the fear of not being able to find a fair forum in state court?
10. Do the decisions of the U.S. Supreme Court regularly impact your daily practice of law? Justify your response.

References

Berger, R.(1997). *Government by judiciary: The transformation of the Fourteenth Amendment.* (2nd ed.), Indianapolis, IN: Liberty Fund.

Cross, F. B. (2009). *The theory and practice of statutory interpretation.* Palo Alto, CA: Stanford University Press.

Eskridge, W. (1991). Overriding supreme court statutory interpretation decisions. *The Yale Law Journal,* 101(2), p 331-341.

Evasion of Supreme Court mandates in cases remanded to state courts since 1941. (1954, May 8). *Harvard Law Review,* p. 1251-1253.

George, J. J. (2006). *Judicial opinion writing handbook.* (5th ed.), Buffalo, NY: William S. Hein & Co., Inc.

Hamilton, A. (1788/1961). Federalist Paper 78. In Clinton Rossiter (Ed.), *The Federalist Papers* (352-357). New York, NY: The New American Library.

Hughes, C. E. (1916). *Addresses.* (2nd ed.), New York, NY: Putnam.

Jamison, K. H. (2007). Public understanding of and support for the courts: 2007 Annenberg Public Policy Center judicial survey results. Retrieved from http://www.law.georgetown.edu/ Judiciary/documents/finalversionJUDICIALFINDINGSoct1707. pdf.

Schwartz, B. (1993). *A history of the Supreme Court.* New York, NY: Oxford University Press.

Supreme Court of the United States. (2010). Rules of the Supreme Court of the United States. Retrieved from .http://www.supremecourt. gov/ctrules/2010RulesoftheCourt.pdf.

Court Cases

American Postal Workers Union v. Frank, 968 P.2d 1373 (1992)

Cooper v. California, 386 U.S. 58, 62 (1967)

DeFunis v. Odegaard, 416 U.S. 312 (1974)

District of Columbia v. Heller, 554 U.S. __ (2008)

Duncan v. Louisiana, 391 U.S. 145 (1968)

Ex Parte McCardle, 74 U.S. 506 (1869)

Griswold v. Connecticut, 381 U.S. 479 (1965)

Harris v. Nelson, 394 U.S. 286, 290-91 (1969)

Hayburn's Case, 2 U.S. 409 (1792)

Lochner v. New York, 198 U.S. 45 (1925)

Marbury v. Madison, 5 U.S. 137 (1803)

Martin v. Hunter's Lessee, 14 U.S. 304 (1816)

Massachusetts v. Laird, 400 U.S. 886 (1970)

Mills v. Duryee, 11 U.S. 7 (1813)

Minneapolis & St. Louis R.R. v. Bombolis, 241 U.S. 211 (1916)

New Jersey v. New York, 523 U.S. 767 (1998)

Roe v. Wade, 410 U.S. 113 (1973)

South Dakota v. Opperman, 428 U.S. 364 (1976)

State v. Opperman, 247 N.W.2d 673 (1976)

United Public Workers v. Mitchell, 330 U.S. 75(1947)

United States v. Nixon, 418 U.S. 683 (1974)

Chapter Eleven
Civil Liberties and Civil Rights
K. Michael Reese

Learning Objectives
After covering the topic of civil liberties and civil rights, students should understand:

1. The defining characteristics of civil liberties and civil rights.
2. The sources of civil liberties and civil rights.
3. The importance of civil liberties and civil rights in a functioning democracy.
4. The roles of the U.S. Supreme Court and the Congress in expanding, and limiting, the
5. scope of civil liberties and civil rights.
6. The process by which most provisions of the Bill of Rights were applied to the states.

Abstract
This republic does not exist in a vacuum. Nor does it exist only as a structural conceptualization of governmental operations and processes. The republic also exists, and perhaps most importantly so, because of its relationship with its people. No government can long endure, at least as a democracy, if this relationship is ignored, neglected, or abused. Our government has acknowledged this basic fact by promoting and protecting the fundamental freedoms that we now know as "civil liberties" and "civil rights." This chapter will examine the sources, scope, nature, and variety of American civil liberties and civil rights. Specific federal statutes and U.S. Supreme Court cases will be used to enhance this discussion.

Introduction
Civil Liberties and Civil Rights: Definitions and Distinctions
Despite the frequent references to civil liberties in our public discourse, there is no single universally-accepted definition of this concept. On occasion, the description seems to have been limited to the freedoms guaranteed by the First Amendment, such as freedom of speech, freedom of the press, and free exercise of religion (Wasserman, 2004, 152). Another position is that civil liberties are the freedoms guaranteed by the Bill of Rights–the first ten amendments to the Constitution (Rush, 2003, 59). For

purposes of this chapter, **civil liberties** include all of the freedoms and protections provided by the Constitution of the United States—those found in the Bill of Rights as well as other parts of the Constitution. With this definition in mind, it is important to understand that civil liberties protect individuals from governmental action, as opposed to private action. In this respect, it might be constructive to envision the concept of civil liberties as a shield against governmental abuse. It is also important to note that, while most of the civil liberties discussed in this chapter are expressed in specific Constitutional language, some, such as the right to privacy, are implied. For purposes of this chapter, the term **civil rights** means the rights of individuals to be free of discriminatory treatment, both public and private, based on such characteristics as race, national origin, or gender. In other words, civil rights focus on broader notions of fair treatment and equality rather than specific civil liberties (Stephens and Scheb, 2008, 3). Whereas civil liberties might be envisioned as a shield to protect specific freedoms, civil rights might well be viewed as a sword to promote equality. This chapter will now survey examples of civil liberties and civil rights.

Civil Liberties: Original Constitution
Selective Examples

Pursuant to the above-noted definition, one could identify a handful of civil liberties in the original Constitution. Two of these are found in Article I, Sections 9 and 10, which prohibit the federal and state governments from passing bills of attainder and *ex post facto* laws. A **bill of attainder** is a law that declares an individual or a group guilty of a crime and imposes punishment without benefit of a trial in a court. An *ex post facto* law is one which is "passed after the occurrence of a fact or commission of an act, which retrospectively changes the legal consequences or relations of such fact or deed" (Black's, 1968, 662). Some examples of *ex post facto* laws include the following retroactive government actions: criminalizing and punishing an act which was legal at the time of its occurrence, increasing the seriousness or punishment of a crime, and altering the rules of evidence to the detriment of a criminal defendant. Another of the civil liberties found in the original Constitution is the privilege of **habeas corpus**, found in Article I, Section 9, which allows an incarcerated person to challenge in court the legality of that incarceration. Finally, Article VI of the Constitution prohibits the federal government from requiring **religious tests** for public office.

The Bill of Rights and Civil Liberties
The Original Formulation

The Bill of Rights—those first ten amendments to the Constitution—were proposed and ratified practically in the shadow of the Constitutional Convention. During the debates over ratification of the Constitution itself, opposition focused largely on the omission of a list of individual rights (Kommers, Finn & Jacobsohn, 2010, 111). There was already widespread fear and suspicion of a strong and unfettered central government, and the Constitution's lack of expressed liberties exacerbated those concerns. The Bill of Rights represented a compromise, brokered by supporters of the new Constitution, designed to appease this opposition. The essence of this compromise was that, if the states would ratify the Constitution, the First Congress would then propose for consideration by the states' legislatures various amendments addressing specific fundamental rights (Epstein & Walker, 2010, 67). The compromise was successful. The Constitution was ratified in 1788; twelve proposed amendments were proposed and ratification of ten of them—the Bill of Rights—was completed by 1791. The original formulation that emerged from these events was that the Bill of Rights protected individual liberties from infringement by the federal government, but had no application to state governments. This view found support in the expressed language of the First Amendment, which begins with the admonition that "Congress shall make no law…" and prevailed in a couple of nineteenth century Supreme Court cases (*Barron v. Baltimore*, 1833; *Hurtado v. California*, 1884). The bottom line is that, from the outset of the republic and for over 100 years thereafter, none of the provisions of the Bill of Rights were applied to the states. States could, of course, provide similar freedoms and protections through their own constitutions and laws, but they were not required to do so by the Bill of Rights.

Selective Incorporation: Application of the Bill of Rights to the States

The original formulation changed in the late nineteenth century and early-to-mid twentieth century via the **due process clause** of the Fourteenth Amendment and a process known as **selective incorporation**. The Fourteenth Amendment, one of the Civil War Amendments designed to protect the rights of former slaves, was ratified in 1868. The amendment provides in pertinent part that no "State shall deprive any person of life, liberty, or property, without due process of law." Note that this clause was expressly directed at state action. In time, the debate focused on just what specific protections and freedoms were included in the basic principles of due process, requiring protection from infringement by all levels of government. With reference to the Constitution, the essential dilemma became one of deciding which of the provisions of the Bill of Rights were "incorporated" into due process of law and, thereby, made binding on the states. The U.S. Supreme Court became the ultimate arbiter of this debate. There were supporters of "total incorporation"—the position that all of the provisions of the Bill of Rights should, in one fell swoop as it were, be included in due process. For example, Supreme Court Justices Hugo Black and William O. Douglas were proponents of this position (Epstein and Walker, 2010, 81). However, a majority of the Court rejected this approach, opting instead for the doctrine of selective incorporation and its case-by-case analysis of the applicability of specific provisions of the Bill of Rights. History teaches us that the Court has incorporated most of the provisions of the Bill of Rights, but not all of them. The standard in this decision-making process seems to have been the Court's determination of whether, and to what extent, a particular provision was so essential to any reasonable understanding of ordered liberty and justice that it had to be part of due process (*Palko v. Connecticut*, 1937; *Duncan v. Louisiana*, 1968). Applying this standard, the Court has incorporated all but the following provisions of the first eight amendments: the Third Amendment prohibition against nonconsensual quartering of soldiers in peace time, the Fifth Amendment right to a grand jury hearing, the Fifth Amendment right to due process of law (because the due process clause of the Fourteenth Amendment makes this unnecessary), the Seventh Amendment right to a jury trial in civil cases, and the Eighth Amendment protections against the requirement of excessive bail and the imposition of excessive fines.

In cultivating an understanding of incorporation, there are some fundamental principles that must be remembered. First, the incorporation doctrine has primary application to the rights and liberties contained in the first eight amendments. The Ninth Amendment has significance for the implied right to privacy and will be discussed later in this chapter. The Tenth Amendment has primary relevance to the issue of inter-governmental powers and has never been a particularly fertile source of individual liberties. Second, once a provision has been incorporated, it applies to state action in every case thereafter. Third, it is the Supreme Court that ultimately decides which provisions of the Bill of Rights are incorporated. This decision is not optional with the states. In this process, the Court interprets the Constitution, the supreme law of the land under Article VI. The Constitution trumps any contrary state laws. Finally, states may, on the basis of their own laws and constitutions, extend greater freedoms and protections than the U.S. Constitution requires. In other words, states may do more than the required constitutional minimum, but not less.

Survey of Incorporated Civil Liberties
First Amendment
        The First Amendment protects freedom of speech, freedom of the press, the right to peaceably assemble, and the right to petition the government for redress of grievances. Collectively, these freedoms and rights might accurately be described as the **freedom of expression**. The Supreme Court has given a great deal of protection to freedom of expression, and that protection has on occasion been extended to **symbolic speech and symbolic actions**, often called speech plus. Examples include burning a flag (*Texas v. Johnson*, 1989), wearing a black armband to school (*Tinker v. Des Moines Independent Community School District, 1969*), and adorning one's clothing with offensive sentiments (*Cohen v. California*, 1971). One concept particularly associated with freedom of the press, including the broadcast medium, is **censorship**. Censorship, which requires government approval prior to publication, is rarely upheld by the courts. It is most likely to be tolerated, if it is tolerated at all, in a public school environment. Although intensely protected, freedom of expression is not absolute. At times, it must yield to a more compelling state need, and the Supreme Court has employed various tests in balancing these competing interests. One such test is the **clear and present danger test** articulated by Justice Oliver Wendell Holmes and forever and famously coupled with his pronunciation that no one has the right to falsely "shout fire" in a crowded theater (*Schenck v. U.S.*, 1919). Furthermore, three kinds of expression—**obscenity, defamation, and fighting words**—are not protected by the First Amendment. However, it is often difficult to ascertain whether expression is obscene or merely offensive, whether it is

defamatory or just unflattering, and whether it amounts to fighting words or simply unpopular opinions.

The First Amendment also contains two religious clauses—the free exercise clause and the establishment clause. The **free exercise clause** is essentially the freedom of religion—the freedom to worship as one sees fit, or not to worship at all. In this context, religious belief is absolute. On the other hand, religious conduct may be limited if the government can demonstrate a compelling need to do so. For example, the Supreme Court has upheld against free exercise challenges the government's prohibition of polygamy (*Reynolds v. United States*, 1878) and limitations on the use of controlled substances in religious rituals (*Employment Division v. Smith*, 1990). The **establishment clause** prohibits governments from endorsing a particular religion. Examples include such things as faculty orchestrated prayer in public schools or a government grant of public funds to a private organization to purchase bibles. On the other hand, there is often some involvement between a government entity and a religious oriented one, and reasonable government accommodation of religion is constitutional (Schultz, Vile, and Deardorff, 2011, 78). Indeed, failure to accommodate religion might result in a free exercise violation. In order to withstand an establishment clause challenge, the government's policy under review must have a secular purpose, must have a primary effect that neither advances nor inhibits religion, and must avoid excessive entanglement between the state and religion (*Lemon v. Kurtzman*, 1971). Of course, this ***Lemon* test** is easy to recite, but often very difficult to apply. A public school is an ideal laboratory in which to observe the interplay between these competing interests. Imagine yourself as a public school principal charged with the necessity of respecting the free exercise rights of students on the one hand, and of avoiding establishment problems on the other, all the while armed with the knowledge that a miscue in either direction could lead to a lawsuit.

Second Amendment

The Second Amendment gives the people the right to bear arms. It is noted in this chapter as an illustration that selective incorporation is not relegated to the distant past. The Supreme Court recently ruled that the right to bear arms—the right to defend oneself—was so fundamental that it had to be part of due process. Consequently, the Court incorporated the right to bear arms, making it applicable to federal and state governments (*McDonald v. City of Chicago*, 2010).

Fourth Amendment

The Fourth Amendment protects individuals from **unreasonable searches and seizures**. In this context, a search is a governmental intrusion into a person's **reasonable expectation of privacy** (*Katz v. United States*, 1967). A seizure might be described as governmental exercise of control over a person or thing. Note that, for Fourth Amendment purposes, both searches and seizures require governmental involvement. There is no Fourth Amendment protection against private searches and seizures. Many searches and seizures are unreasonable if not conducted with a valid warrant. However, the reality is that most searches and seizures are conducted without warrants. Examples include searches based on a valid consent or searches of a person after a lawful arrest. If **search warrants** are required, they must be supported by probable cause, must particularly describe the place to be searched and the persons or things to be seized, and must include the oath or affirmation by the government agent. **Probable cause to search** means sufficient information to lead a reasonable officer to conclude that the particularly described evidence is located on the particularly described premises. **Particularity** means enough detail to indicate what to search for and where to search it. The **oath or affirmation** is the officer's sworn statement that the information contained in the application for the warrant is, to the best of the officer's knowledge and understanding, truthful and correct. A judicial officer, such as a magistrate, will determine if these requirements are met and either issue or refuse to issue the warrant. Pursuant to the **exclusionary rule**, evidence seized in violation of the Fourth Amendment is inadmissible to prove the guilt of the individual whose rights were violated (*Weeks v. United States*, 1914; *Mapp v. Ohio*, 1961). There are some exceptions to this rule, the most notable of which is the **good faith exception**. Under this exception, the contested evidence is admissible if the officer exhibited objective good faith, such as reasonably relying on a properly issued warrant that is later determined by a higher court to be constitutionally deficient (*U.S. v. Leon*, 1984). Some states, such as Georgia, do not recognize a general good faith exception to the exclusionary rule (*Gary v. State*, 1992).

Fifth Amendment

Two of the most notable provisions of the Fifth Amendment are the privilege against self-incrimination and the protection against double jeopardy. The **privilege against self-incrimination** means that an individual may not be forced to provide testimonial evidence that could lead to his or her criminal prosecution. For example, a person could "exercise the fifth" when called as a witness in a trial or a hearing, or when subjected to **custodial interrogation** by government agents. Indeed, the famous *Miranda* warnings are based primarily on the privilege against self-incrimination (*Miranda v. Arizona*, 1966). These warnings are required if, and only if, the suspect is interrogated while in custody. The warnings are not required if there is custody without interrogation or interrogation without custody. If the warnings are not rendered when required, any incriminating statements made by the suspect will be inadmissible at a subsequent trial. Under the **public safety exception**, the requirement of the warnings may have to yield until the danger to the public is neutralized (*New York v. Quarles*, 1984).

The **double jeopardy** clause prohibits multiple prosecutions for the same offense. A state could not prosecute a criminal defendant over and over for the same crime in hopes of finally getting a conviction or of obtaining a harsher punishment than what was previously imposed. There are some exceptions to the double jeopardy prohibition. For example, the state may retry a case when the first trial ended in a mistrial, such as a hung jury—the inability of the jury to agree on a verdict. The state may also retry a case if the defendant was initially found guilty but had the conviction reversed on appeal. Note also that the Fifth Amendment prohibits multiple prosecutions for the **same offense**. Pursuant to a concept known as **dual sovereignty**, two separate offenses are committed, even if there is only one transaction, if the defendant violates the laws of two sovereigns. An example might be the robbery of a federally insured bank. This would be one robbery, but two offenses because there would be violations of federal and state law. In such a situation, both the federal and state governments could prosecute, convict, and punish the perpetrator. Dual sovereignty would also apply if, in one transaction, the laws of two different states were violated (*Heath v. Alabama*, 1985).

There are two other Fifth Amendment issues that are worthy of mention. One deals with **eminent domain**, an implied power that allows states to condemn private property and take it from unwilling sellers. However, the **takings clause** of the Fifth Amendment requires the taking to be for a **public use** and that **just compensation** be paid for the property. The other noteworthy Fifth Amendment issue is the right to a grand jury. A **grand jury** is a group of people summoned by the state to consider evidence against someone charged with a crime. The prosecution presents its case to the grand jury in a private hearing. If the grand jury agrees with the prosecution that the accused committed the crime in question, it will return an **indictment** or **true bill** against the accused. In other words, the prosecution must obtain the indictment before the case can be taken to trial. As noted above, the grand jury requirement has not been incorporated and, consequently, is not binding on the states. However, many states have chosen to include such a requirement in their own constitutions.

Sixth Amendment

Most of the rights associated with the trial of a criminal defendant can be found in the Sixth Amendment. These include the right to counsel, the right to a speedy trial, the right to a public trial, the right to a jury trial, the right to confront the accuser, and the right to compulsory process. Concerning the **right to counsel**, there is usually no issue when the defendant is financially able to pay for a private attorney. The problem arises when an **indigent defendant**—one unable to pay for a lawyer—is accused of a crime, and the rules vary, depending on whether the crime is a felony or a misdemeanor. Generally speaking, a **felony** is a crime punishable by a fine and/or a year or more in prison, and a **misdemeanor** is a crime punishable by a fine and/or up to twelve months in jail. The Supreme Court has ruled that states must appoint counsel for indigent defendants in all felony cases (*Gideon v. Wainwright*, 1963). However, the state must appoint counsel in misdemeanor cases only if the actual punishment, as opposed to potential punishment, is incarceration or something akin to incarceration, such as a suspended sentence or probation (*Argersinger v. Hamlin*, 1972; *Scott v. Illinois,* 1979; *Alabama v. Shelton*, 2002). It is important to note that the right to counsel will often extend beyond the parameters of the trial itself and attach in various pre-trial and post-trial procedures.

Although the Sixth Amendment makes provision for a **speedy trial**, it gives no indication as to just what "speedy" means. There is always some delay between an arrest and a trial. When, then, does such a delay violate the speedy trial provision? In addressing this issue, the Supreme Court has never articulated a bright-line rule as to when a constitutional violation occurs. Rather, the Court has concluded that several variables should be considered in this analysis. These variables include the length of the delay, the reason for the delay, the defendant's assertion of the right, and any prejudice or detriment to the accused because of the delay (*Barker v. Wingo*, 1972). It should be noted that, even though the constitutional speedy trial provision contains no specific time frame requirements, the federal government and most states have legislatively created such requirements. For example, the **Federal Speedy Trial Act of 1974** generally requires that a trial commences within 100 days of an arrest or receipt of a summons.

The insistence on a right to a **public trial** was unquestionably a response to the old practice of conducting trials behind closed doors out of sight of family, the community, and the media. It was possible that a defendant could be tried, convicted, and sentenced without anyone else knowing what happened. The idea is that a public trial assures fairness.

The **right to a jury trial** is one of America's most treasured legal traditions. That tradition is based on the belief that ordinary citizens are better able to judge innocence or guilt than are those who might have some stake in the outcome. Although the language of the Amendment provides for this right in "all criminal prosecutions," the Supreme Court has not adopted the position that the right attaches in every criminal case. Instead, the Court has ruled that the right attaches only when the defendant is charged with a "serious offense," one with a **potential punishment of more than six months imprisonment** (*Baldwin v. New York*, 1970). Another jury trial issue involves the size of the jury. At the time of the Revolutionary War and the subsequent founding of the Republic, it was customarily understood that a jury consisted of twelve people. Consequently, the minimum number of jurors in federal criminal cases has always been twelve. However, this issue remained open in regards to state criminal trials. The right to a jury trial itself was incorporated in 1968 (*Duncan v. Louisiana*). Two years later, however, the Supreme Court ruled that the required minimum number of jurors in state criminal trials is six (*Williams v. Florida*, 1970). In concluding this discussion, it is important to understand the distinction between the Sixth Amendment's requirement of a jury trial in criminal cases on the one hand, and the

Seventh Amendment's provision for a jury trial in **civil cases** on the other hand. As indicated earlier in this chapter, the Seventh Amendment has never been incorporated and is not, therefore, applicable to the states. The **confrontation clause** entitles a defendant to confront the accusers. Usually this clause means a physical, face-to-face confrontation in court, but this is not always required. For example, it is possible to use a one-way closed circuit television procedure in child molestations cases, whereby the child and the attorneys are in one room while the defendant, judge, and jury observe from the courtroom (*Maryland v. Craig*, 1990). The **right to compulsory process** gives the defendant the power to subpoena witnesses to testify. This power is essentially the same one the state has to subpoena prosecution witnesses. A **subpoena** is a summons by a court to appear and testify.

Eighth Amendment

The Eighth Amendment includes protections against excessive bail, excessive fines, and cruel and unusual punishment. As indicated earlier, the first two have never been incorporated and are not, therefore, binding on the states. In fact, there is no constitutional right to bail at all. The purpose of bail, if it is allowed, is to insure the appearance of a defendant at the trial. In determining whether bail is excessive, the courts would consider such things as the seriousness of the crime, the risk of flight, and the community ties of the defendant.

The protection against **cruel and unusual punishment** has generated substantial case law. Punishments can be cruel and unusual in two different ways. One possibility would be a punishment that is inherently barbaric or inhumane. Examples might be cutting the hand off of a convicted thief or poking the eyes out of a convicted "peeping Tom." These would be unconstitutional punishments in this country. Punishments can also be cruel and unusual, even if they are not barbaric, if they are excessive for the crime. In many situations, the death penalty falls into this category. The Supreme Court has never ruled that the death penalty is inherently cruel and unusual, but this punishment is excessive for most crimes. For example, the Court has held that the imposition of the death penalty for the crime of rape would violate the Eighth Amendment (*Coker v. Georgia*, 1977; *Kennedy v. Louisiana*, 2008). Clearly, it would be unconstitutional to impose the death penalty for less serious crimes, such as theft or forgery.

Today, there seems to be a narrow range of crimes for which the death penalty could be imposed. These include certain criminal homicides, treason, air piracy, and a handful of other crimes. The debate over the propriety of imposing the death penalty has been longstanding and will no doubt continue unabated for the foreseeable future.

Civil Liberties: Beyond the Bill of Rights
Fourteenth Amendment

Recall that the Fourteenth Amendment was one of the Civil War amendments designed primarily to promote and protect the rights of former slaves. It provides for national and state citizenship for all persons born or naturalized in the United States. It also contains three distinct clauses: the privileges and immunities clause, the due process clause, and the equal protection clause. The **privileges and immunities clause** prohibits states from abridging the rights of U.S. citizens. It was originally believed that this clause would be at the forefront of advancing change and equality. However, this prospect failed to materialize because the Supreme Court, in an early case, articulated a very narrow interpretation of the clause (*Slaughterhouse Cases*, 1873).

As previously discussed, the **due process clause** prohibits the states from depriving any person of life, liberty, or property without due process of law. There are two dimensions of due process. **Substantive due process** protects individuals from arbitrary, unreasonable, and capricious state actions. An example of such a state action would be a law that requires parents to send their children to public schools with no options for private schools or other educational possibilities. Another example would be a state law limiting welfare eligibility to individuals who were born in that state. The point is that a state must have a very good reason—and sometimes a compelling need—to deprive a person of life, liberty, or property. **Procedural due process** relates to steps or procedures required to protect an individual's substantive due process rights. An example would be the requirement of notice and an opportunity to be heard before suspending a student from college. The greater the potential deprivation, the more elaborate the protective procedures must be. If a state proposes to send a person to prison or the death chamber, it will be required to provide a wide range of procedural protections, most of which have previously been discussed in this chapter.

A simplistic but perhaps useful thing to take from this discussion is that substantive due process focuses on what the state intends to do to a person, and procedural due process focuses on how the state intends to do it. The overriding concern in all of this is fundamental fairness. In each situation, ask yourself whether it is fundamentally fair for the state to deprive this person of this liberty or property interest. If so, then ask yourself if the state's procedures for implementing that deprivation are fundamentally fair.

One final due process issue concerns the **right to privacy**. There is no language in the Constitution that expressly provides for a general right to privacy. Nevertheless, the Supreme Court has ruled that you do have such a right. It has been variously suggested that this implied constitutional right has its roots in provisions of the First, Third, Fourth, and Fifth Amendments (Kommers, Finn & Jocobsohn, 2010, 239).

These approaches, coupled as they were with very specific rights associated with the aforementioned amendments, were somewhat limited in scope. They were simply not conducive to a recognition of a general right to privacy. Another, more promising approach, was found in the **Ninth Amendment**, which provides as follows: "The enumeration in the Constitution of certain rights shall not be construed to deny or disparage others retained by the people." The Supreme Court eventually relied on this language as a basis for the existence of a broad, general right to privacy (*Griswold v. Connecticut*, 1965). More recently, the liberty component of the due process clause has been viewed as the primary constitutional basis for the right to privacy. This view is especially true in cases involving intimate familial issues, such as marriage, rearing children, sexual orientation, and abortion (*Roe v. Wade*, 1973).

The Fourteenth Amendment also prohibits states from denying any person the equal protection of the laws. The **equal protection clause** has been the constitutional basis for a variety of challenges to alleged discriminatory state actions. In much of the twentieth century, there were numerous court cases alleging equal protection violations due to racial discrimination. For example, the equal protection clause was the basis for challenges to segregated public schools systems (*Brown v. Board of Education*, 1954). Violations could also be based on gender, age, marital status, or a variety of other factors. Equal protection challenges are apt to arise when **similarly situated groups** are treated differently. The reality is that states do discriminate, but not all cases of discrimination constitute violations of equal protection. In evaluating claims of violations, the Supreme Court has employed various tests, or levels of judicial scrutiny. The two primary tests are the rational basis test and the strict scrutiny test. The test used depends on the nature of the alleged discrimination.

The Court uses the **rational basis test**, sometimes called the traditional test, in cases involving alleged discrimination pursuant to various social and economic policies. An example of such a policy would be a state's cap on the total welfare grant to families, resulting in larger families receiving less, per capita, than smaller families (*Dandridge v. Williams*, 1970). Under this test, the law, although discriminatory, would be constitutional if the state could demonstrate a rational connection between a legitimate government interest and the means chosen to achieve that interest. The means chosen by the state need not be the only way, or even the best way, to achieve the legitimate state interest. It just needs to be a rational way to do so. In addition, the law is presumptively constitutional and entitled to a great deal of judicial deference or benefit of the doubt.

The Court uses the **strict scrutiny test** in cases involving **suspect classifications** and **fundamental rights**. In this context, a classification simply means the grouping of people. If that grouping is based on race or national origin, it is inherently suspect and the Court will "scrutinize" it very closely. Under this test, the law is presumptively unconstitutional, no judicial deference is forthcoming, and the state has the burden of demonstrating that the classification is necessary to achieve a compelling government interest. In other words, there are no least restrictive means to accomplish an interest so strong that it simply has to be done. The same standards of review are used when the alleged discrimination abridges fundamental rights—those rights expressly or implicitly granted by the Constitution. Obviously, a state has a much better chance of winning a lawsuit under the rational basis test than it does under the strict scrutiny test. In other words, the higher the level of judicial scrutiny, the greater the difficulty the state has in winning a case.

The Court has more recently crafted an intermediate or heightened level of scrutiny in cases involving **quasi-suspect classifications,** such as gender and illegitimacy. Under this test, the level of judicial scrutiny and the corresponding degree of difficulty for the state falls somewhere between rational basis and strict scrutiny.

The Constitution and Voting Issues

Voting rights are civil liberties that are sometimes overlooked or ignored, even by potential voters. There are three constitutional amendments that relate specifically to the right to vote, and they deserve at least some mention. The **Fifteenth** and **Nineteenth Amendments** prohibit states from abridging the right to vote on the basis of race and gender, respectively. The **Twenty-Sixth Amendment** prohibits states from abridging the right to vote of citizens who are eighteen years of age or older.

Civil Rights

Over the years, Congress has enacted innumerable pieces of civil rights legislation. In fact, this occurrence has been ongoing since as early as 1868. Recall our characterization of civil rights legislation as a sword designed to promote widespread equality. In many instances, these statutes have application in public and private settings. The following discussion focuses on some selected examples of this kind of legislation. Please be aware that there are many others available for your consumption.

Selective Examples of Civil Rights Legislation

Compliance with several civil rights statutes is activated when an institution or organization receives federal financial assistance. For instance, **Title VI of the Civil Rights Act of 1964** bans racial discrimination in any program or activity receiving federal funding. As an example, assume that a private college received a federal grant to support scientific research. That college must comply with Title VI. If the college rejects a prospective student's application for admission on the basis of race, there would be a violation of Title VI. **Title IX of the Education Amendments of 1972** prohibits sex discrimination by educational programs or activities that receive federal financial assistance. One prominent example where Title IX was used occurred in collegiate sports to create and enhance opportunities for women athletes. Similarly, **Section 504 of the Rehabilitation Act of 1973** bars federally funded programs from discriminating against an individual solely on the basis of that individual's handicap.

Other civil rights statutes are not conditioned on the receipt of federal funding. One is the **Equal Pay Act of 1963**, which prohibits gender discrimination in the form of unequal pay for comparable work. This Act addresses the problem of women employees being paid far less than their male counterparts in similar working conditions. In a related vein, **Title VII of the Civil Rights Act of 1964** forbids employment discrimination, such as refusal to hire and discharge, on the basis of race, sex, religion, or national origin. Similarly, the **Age Discrimination in Employment Act of 1967** protects workers forty and older from discriminatory actions. The **Civil Rights Act of 1968** prohibits discrimination in housing and other public accommodations on the basis of race, sex, national origin, religion, and other considerations. For signs of Title VII's impact, check the newspaper's classified ads regarding homes for sale. The **Americans with Disabilities Act of 1990** was designed to eliminate barriers to persons with disabilities in such areas as employment, education, transportation, and other public services. As you stroll across campus, look for designations that a building or a restroom or some other facility is handicapped accessible. If you see such designations, they represent the institution's efforts to comply with this Act. The **Voting Rights Act of 1965** attacked racial discrimination in voting in a variety of ways. For instance, the Act voided artificial barriers to voting, such as the baffling and unfathomable literacy tests that many southern states required potential voters to pass. It also contained provisions for monitoring voter registration processes and election-day practices.

These are but a few of the plethora of civil rights acts that are operative in this society. One issue related to civil rights statutes and the equal protection clause and quite controversial at times is **affirmative action**. Affirmative action is essentially a public policy originally designed to eliminate employment barriers for minorities and women. It evolved into a more aggressive attempt to eradicate the vestiges of past discrimination, often involving hiring preferences, minority set-asides, and quotas. Its heyday extended from the 1960s into the early 1980s. Since then, the results have been uneven and seemingly inconsistent. For example, when confronted with challenges of **reverse discrimination** in college admissions, the Supreme Court has sometimes approved and sometimes disapproved efforts to assure admission of disadvantage students (*Gratz v. Bollinger*, 2003; *Grutter v. Bollinger*, 2003).

Case Study—Civil Liberties for Native Americans

As previously discussed, the Bill of Rights recognizes and protects civil liberties by limiting the powers of the federal government. The

Supreme Court, in interpreting the due process clause of the Fourteenth Amendment, selectively incorporated most of the provisions in the Bill of Rights, thereby protecting civil liberties against state infringement. In their relationships with the federal and state governments, Native Americans enjoy the same freedoms, protections, and rights as anyone else. However, many Native Americans are confronted by another tier of authority—their tribal governments. Tribal governments are not considered to be part of the federal government. Consequently, the Bill of Rights had no application to the tribes. Similarly, the Fourteenth Amendment expressly provides that no state shall deprive people of life, liberty, or property without due process of law. Tribal governments are not states. They are not limited by the due process clause or the results of the selective incorporation. The civil liberties defined and described elsewhere in this chapter have no application to tribal governments. The cumulative effect of all of this is that individual Native Americans, *vis-à-vis* their own tribal governments, had little or no protection for basic rights and freedoms. Congress addressed this shortcoming with the passage of the **Indian Civil Rights Act of 1968**, which grants individuals many of the freedoms and protections found in the Bill of Rights and the Fourteenth Amendment and discussed earlier in this chapter. However, there are at least two noteworthy exceptions. Recall that the First Amendment contains two religion clauses—the free exercise clause and the establishment clause. The Indian Civil Rights Act includes a free exercise clause but has no establishment clause. This omission means that individual Native Americans are free to worship as they choose, but it also means that tribal governments can endorse a religion. In other words, there can be a tribal religion, but the tribe cannot coerce anyone into accepting that religion. The other major exception involves the right to counsel in criminal cases. Remember that the Sixth Amendment requires appointed counsel for indigent defendants in all felony cases and many misdemeanor cases. The Indian Civil Rights Act provides a right to counsel, but only at the defendant's own expense (Reese, 1992, 37).

Conclusion

Our sojourn into the world of civil liberties and civil rights is done. You are now acquainted with many basic constitutional freedoms and at least a sampling of civil rights legislation. You have had occasion to consider the intersections of the Congress and the Supreme Court and their respective roles in the development of these rights and freedoms in this republic. You have had the opportunity to evaluate the ebb and flow of civil liberties and civil rights as they are refined by time and circumstance. Similarly, you are now in a position to weigh the propriety from a contemporary perspective of the policies, the purposes, and the processes associated with many of these rights and liberties. To be sure, all of these observations are important, but there are two remaining observations that are even more compelling. First, please be aware that this chapter is not meant to be exhaustive. It is a survey, a mere summary, of some critical freedoms and rights. There is so much more to learn. Second, and perhaps most importantly, the liberties and rights discussed in this chapter belong to you. These are your freedoms, your rights, your choices. Use them. Take care of them. Keep them safe.

Discussion Questions
1. Distinguish between civil liberties and civil rights.
2. Identify the constitutional right that you most treasure, and discuss why you feel so passionately about that particular right.
3. Concerning civil liberties, how would you change the Constitution? What would you add to it, or take from it, to make it more relevant and meaningful for you?
4. Discuss how a state might constitutionally take a criminal defendant to trial without first providing that defendant with a grand jury hearing.
5. How is it possible that a defendant in a state criminal trial could have rights that are not required by the U.S. Constitution?
6. Concerning the civil rights statutes explored in this chapter, identify and discuss any that you would modify or eliminate.

References
American with Disabilities Act of 1990 § 42 U.S.C. § 12101-12213 (2006).

Black, H. C. (1968). *Black's law dictionary*. St. Paul, MN: West Publishing Company.

Epstein, L., & Walker, T. G. (2010). *Constitutional law for a changing America,* (7th Ed.). Washington, DC: CQ Press.

Equal Pay Act of 1963 § 29 U.S.C. § 206 (d) (2006).

Indian Civil Rights Act of 1968 § 25 U.S.C. § 1301-1303 (2006).

Kommers, D.P., Finn, J.E., & Jacobson, G.J. (2010). *American constitutional law: Liberty, community and the Bill of Rights,* (3rd Ed.). New York, NY: Rowan & Littlefield.

Schultz, D., Vile, J. R., & Deardorff, M.D. (2011). *Constitutional law in contemporary America: Civil rights and liberties.* New York, NY: Oxford University Press.

Section 504 of the Rehabilitation Act of 1973 § 29 U.S.C. § 701-796 (2006).

Stephens, O.H., Jr., and Scheb, J.M. II. (2008). *American constitutional law: Civil rights and liberties* (4th Ed.). Belmont, CA: Thomson Wadsworth.

Title VI of the Civil Rights Act of 1964 § 42 U.S.C. §2000d-2000d-7 (2006).

Title VII of the Civil Rights Act of 1964 § 42 U.S.C. §2000e-2000e-17 (2006).

Title VIII of the Civil Rights Act of 1968 § 42 U.S.C. § 3601-3631 (2006).

Title IX of the Education Amendments of 1972 § 20 U.S.C. § 1681-1688 (2006).

Voting Rights Act of 1965 § 42 U.S.C. § 1973-1973gg-10 (2006).

Wasserman, G. (2004). *The basics of American politics,* (11ᵗʰ Ed.). New York, NY: Pearson Longman.

Table of Cases

Alabama v. Shelton, 535 U.S. 654 (2002).

Argersinger v. Hamlin, 407 U.S. 25 (1972).

Baldwin v. New York, 399 U.S. 66 (1970).

Barker v. Wingo, 407 U.S. 514 (1972).

Barron v. Baltimore, 7 Pet. 243 (1833).

Brown v. Board of Education, 347 U.S. 483 (1954).

Cohen v. California, 403 U.S. 15 (1971).

Coker v. Georgia, 433 U.S. 584 (1977).

Dandridge v. Williams, 397 U.S. 471 (1970).

Duncan v. Louisiana, 391 U.S. 145 (1968).

Employment Division v. Smith, 494 U.S. 872 (1990).

Gary v. State, 262 GA. 573 (1992).

Gideon v. Wainwright, 372 U.S. 335 (1963).

Gratz v. Bollinger, 539 U.S. 244 (2003).

Griswold v. Connecticut, 381 U.S. 479 (1965).

Grutter v. Bollinger, 539 U.S. 306 (2003).

Heath v. Alabama, 474 U.S. 82 (1985).

Hurtado v. California, 110 U.S. 516 (1884).

Katz v. United States, 389 U.S. 347 (1967).

Kennedy v. Louisiana, 554 U.S. ___ (2008).

Lemon v. Kurtzman, 403 U.S. 602 (1971).

Mapp v. Ohio, 367 U.S. 643 (1961).

Maryland v. Craig, 497 U.S. 836 (1990).

McDonald v. City of Chicago, 561 U.S. ___ (2010).

Miranda v. Arizona, 384 U.S. 436 (1966).

New York v. Quarles, 467 U.S. 649 (1984).

Palko v. Connecticut, 302 U.S. 319 (1937).

Reynolds v. United States, 98 U.S. 145 (1878).

Roe v. Wade, 410 U.S. 113 (1973).

Schenck v. United States, 249 U.S. 47 (1919).

Scott v. Illinois, 440 U.S. 367 (1(79).

Slaughterhouse Cases, 83 U.S. 36 (1873).

Texas v. Johnson, 491 U.S. 397 (1989).

Tinker v. Des Moines Independent Community School District, 393 U.S. 503 (1969).

United States v. Leon, 468 U.S. 897 (1984).

Williams v. Florida, 399 U.S. 78 (1970).

Weeks v. United States, 232 U.S. 383 (1914).

Chapter Twelve
Public Policy
Barry D. Friedman

Learning Objectives

After covering the topic of theories of democracy, students should understand:

1. Identify who has influence in the making of American public policy.
2. Explain the various "models" of public policy that political scientists have formulated to describe how public policy is developed in the United States.
3. Identify the assortment of instruments and devices available to the government for enforcing policies.
4. Describe the origin and implications of the national government's chronic deficit spending.

Abstract

The significant decisions that government policymakers—most prominently legislators but also executives and judges—make are described as public policies. While most of the contents of this textbook focus on the U. S. government's institutions and their political intrigue, this chapter examines the outputs of these institutions and political activities. Public policy comes about in a plethora of ways, but political scientists have developed "models" to describe the most common processes that give birth to policies. The policy-process model describes how a problem is identified, how it comes to the attention of policymakers, and how a policy to address the problem is formulated and legitimated. Other models state that policies come about through incremental change, rational analysis, pursuit of individuals' selfish interests, interest groups' competition with one another, cooperative efforts of those who specialize in a policy area, or direction by the elite class. The government possesses a range of instruments to accomplish policy execution—such as imprisonment, taxation, subsidies, and propaganda. The persistent demand from the public for services and benefits has outpaced the national government's ability to raise tax revenue to pay for their costs, resulting in annual budget deficits. These deficits have accumulated to a staggering total of

$14 trillion, which threatens to incapacitate the governmental system of the United States.

The Things that Government Does

At any given time, many people have a lot of ideas about what they want government to do. Sometimes, they want the government to do certain things that are necessary to promote the public interest; for example, they may have observed a lot of accidents at certain intersections in a small town, and believe that it is time for the local government to install traffic lights. Sometimes, they want government to do certain things that will make themselves, specifically, better off. A legislator might want a new state highway, featuring a shiny new bridge that will cross a river, because he expects that his constituents will appreciate his effort and vote for his reelection. In fact, he may arrange for the bridge to be named after him. A lobbyist for an interest group may ask friendly legislators to arrange for a tax credit that benefits the businesses that are affiliated with his organization. All of this activity of demands, accommodations, and votes results in official government decisions. We often refer to such a decision or a set of decisions as a **public policy**.

The ingredients of public policies of the U. S. national government are found in documents and instruments such as these: the Constitution, the statutes, the appropriations laws that constitute the government's budget, executive orders promulgated by the president, rules and regulations promulgated by regulatory agencies, and opinions of the Supreme Court. As a result of the decisions that all of these documents and instruments reflect, the national government can be said to have public policies in such policy areas as agriculture, consumer protection, crime suppression, the economy, education, energy, environmental protection, fairness in employment, foreign affairs, forest and park preservation, illicit drugs, housing, military operations and readiness, public health, relief for poor families, taxation, trade, transportation, and unemployment.

How Public Policy Comes About

Public policies come about in numerous ways. Policy experts have described a typical manner in which a policy comes about. The **model** presents a six-step **policy process**, and these steps occur in sequence as shown in the flow chart in Figure 12.1 (Dye, 2010/2011, p. 29).

Figure 12.1: Six-Step Policy Process Model

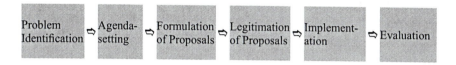

Problem Identification ⇨ Agenda-setting ⇨ Formulation of Proposals ⇨ Legitimation of Proposals ⇨ Implement-ation ⇨ Evaluation

Here is an explanation of each of the steps to which the policy-process model refers:

- *Problem identification.* The process begins when someone or some group identifies a problem that some segment of the population is experiencing. For example, a member of Congress may be receiving letters from constituents that express complaints about a particular situation. Or the news media may notice some kind of difficulty being experienced by some number of people, and report the problem to their viewers, listeners, and readers.
- *Agenda-setting.* Public policy scholars have conceived of an **agenda of public policy.** On this agenda are supposedly listed policy problems that have come to the attention of public policymakers, such as the president or members of Congress, such that they now recognize the need to take some sort of actions to remedy the problems. According to this model, public policymakers are generally reluctant to acknowledge that they have to take action on some problem, because remedies cost money and money is scarce. So, the model says, it is only when the demands for action become numerous and adamant that policymakers conclude that they can no longer ignore the demands. At that point, the problem becomes an entry on the agenda of public policy. There really is no document that is entitled "The Agenda of Public Policy." However, there are certain places to which you may direct your attention for clues about what problems are on this metaphorical agenda. If you would like to know what is on the president's agenda, you might examine the content of his State of the Union message. If you would like to know what is on Congress's agenda, you might examine the legislative calendars of the Senate and the House of Representatives, respectively.

- *Formulation of proposals.* The decision by policymakers to address a problem will prompt some kind of activity to formulate specific proposals. Here are the kinds of people and institutions who, from time to time, formulate proposals:
  - Employees of the Executive Branch (bureaucrats) are known to be active in the formulation of proposals. Some of the most extensive pieces of legislation that have made their way through the legislative process are known to have originated in the bureaucracy.
  - Congressional staff members—those who work for senators and representatives in their own offices or who work for congressional committees—are known to be prolific authors of legislation.
  - Interest groups may employ individuals, such as lawyers, who understand the legislative process and will deliver proposed bills to members of Congress and congressional committees.
  - **Think tanks** often develop policy ideas. A think tank is an institution that employs scholars who develop policy proposals based on their knowledge in their respective fields of study. The think tank will make the policy proposals available to policymakers who are looking for solutions to problems on the agenda of public policy.
- *Legitimation of proposals.* In a democratic system like that of the United States, policies must be made legitimate before they can be put into effect. Here are some ways in which policies are legitimated:
  - When Congress enacts a bill, it provides legitimacy to the bill's purpose and content. The public understands Congress to be the legitimate representative of the public, which elected the legislators, pursuant to Article I of the Constitution.
  - When the president signs an act of Congress into law, he adds to the perception of the enactment's legitimacy. The public acknowledges the president's unique position as the only nationally elected official (along with the vice

president), and respects his signature on the newly minted law.

o On occasion, a lawsuit that challenges the constitutionality of a law will be considered by the Supreme Court. When the court declares the law to be constitutional, the declaration causes the law to take on a virtually impenetrable aura of legitimacy.

o Policymakers depend on the Executive Branch officials who administer a law to do so in a way that supports the appearance of legitimacy. For example, when an agent of the Federal Bureau of Investigation explains to a suspect that the suspect has been arrested because of his disobedience of a specific law enacted by Congress and signed by the president, the agent is indicating that the arrest is occurring in accordance with the law and is not an arbitrary and capricious action by the bureau and other officials of the criminal-justice system.

- *Implementation.* Once a policy has been enacted and signed into law, the executive branch is responsible for administering the law.
- *Evaluation.* At some point, and, policy specialists hope, at regular intervals, the execution and results of a policy will be evaluated to determine whether the policy is beneficial and the execution is effective. If not, the policy should be reconsidered and either redesigned or abandoned.

More Specific Models of How and Why the Participants Make Public Policy

Supplementing the policy process model that the previous section of the chapter described are a number of other models that explain more specifically who are influential in making policy and what their motivations are when they participate in the policymaking process. The following list presents some of the most well-known models to which modern literature about American government often refers.

Incrementalism Model

In 1959, Charles E. Lindblom published the first description of the **incrementalism model of public policy**. Lindblom explained that most policy that the national government implements in a given year is simply the previous year's policy with small (incremental) modifications made to it. The logic is difficult to challenge. Such an approach to policymaking saves time as well as the arduous effort to innovate new policy technologies. This approach also allows the full use of existing organization, equipment, and other infrastructure, without having to acquire new kinds of resources to support a radically different policy approach. The government's—particularly the bureaucracy's—familiarity with the ongoing policy approach allows for the development of experience that contributes to efficiency and gradual refinement of implementation methods. Few political scientists argue with the conventional wisdom that the incrementalism model is the best single explanation of policymaking in the national government.

Rationalism Model

If incrementalism is the preferred method of policymaking, then the **rationalism model of public policy** is its theoretical antithesis. The rationalism model contends that the fundamental criterion for sound policy is the realization of the greatest possible net benefit (i.e., difference between benefit and cost) to society. The rationalism model proposes that policymakers who are trying to design a policy should consider the principles that society values, develop an assortment of policy alternatives that would satisfy society based on those principles, evaluate the policy alternatives, and then compare the alternatives and select the one best alternative (i.e., the optimal choice).

If there is one evaluation method that the largest number of proponents of the rationalism model advocates, it is the method of "cost-benefit analysis." In evaluating a policy alternative, one would utilize cost-benefit analysis by listing and quantifying the costs associated with the alternative and then listing and quantifying the benefits associated with the alternative. A value of net benefit can be computed by subtracting the sum of the costs from the sum of the benefits. An alternative whose net benefit is less than zero could be eliminated without further thought. A value of benefit-cost ratio can be computed by dividing the sum of the benefits by the sum of the costs. An alternative whose benefit-cost ratio is less than one could be eliminated without further thought.

We know that incrementalism comes naturally to public policymakers.

In so far as rationalism does *not* come naturally, the model has to have advocates who try to persuade policymakers to actually try to utilize it. This effort by the advocates is an uphill battle, because of the complications associated with the rationalism model. Some of the complications are as follows:

- The analytical process is exceptionally time consuming. Some of this time inevitably involves the acrimonious policy arguments (e.g., in the legislature) that deliberations about newly conceived policy proposals provoke.
- Because of the model's methodological requirements that call on policy designers to list the possible policy alternatives, these policy designers are challenged to conceive of a number of currently nonexistent policy technologies. This process strains the human imagination.
- The radical redesign of policy may require existing organization, equipment, and other infrastructure to have to be replaced with new organization, equipment, and other infrastructure, at significant cost.
- Replacing policy approaches with which we have years of experience with newly designed approaches with which we have *no* experience introduces the significant threat that we will encounter unwelcome surprises when the new approaches are implemented. Such unanticipated consequences can be very costly and can agitate the general public, clients of agencies, and the government officials who have to try to appease those who have suffered from the problems that were not foreseen.

Public-Choice Model

Credit for the **public-choice model of public policy** is given to James M. Buchanan, Jr., who won the 1986 Nobel Prize in Economic Science for developing it. Buchanan explained that decisions about public policymaking are made by a wide range of individuals, all of whose actions are oriented toward the realization of their self-interests. The model traces these self-interest-oriented actions all the way back to each voter, who, as Anthony Downs (1957) explained, makes decisions about which candidates to vote for based on whose policy platforms will result in the most gratification (especially wealth) for that individual. Downs similarly explained that political-party leaders in the United States prefer the development of party platforms that will appeal to the largest number of voters, so that their political parties can win the upcoming elections. As chapter 7 of this book explains, members of Congress decide how to vote on bills based on whether the bills establish policies that will appeal to their constituents (e.g., policies that offer entitlement programs to the entire public or groups within the population and policies that supply "pork" to the senators' states and the representatives' congressional districts).

In summary, the public-choice model conceives of the arena of public policymaking as a giant marketplace of ideas, including policy proposals, in which government officials and individual citizens "shop" for policies that will benefit them and then support them. The question of whether such self-interest-oriented decisions in the public policy arena can be aggregated to create any kind of coherent, productive result for society resembles the question of whether the self-interest-oriented decisions of business owners, employees, and shoppers can be aggregated to create any kind of coherent, productive result in the commercial and industrial marketplace. The capitalist economist Adam Smith (1776) argued that "the invisible hand" guides participants in the commercial and industrial marketplace to make self-interest-oriented decisions that, in the final analysis, benefit society. The same logic can be applied, by analogy, to argue that self-interest-oriented decisions by individuals in the policy arena can similarly benefit all.

Group-Theory Model of Public Policy

Based on David B. Truman's classic monograph, *The Governmental Process: Political Interests and Public Opinion* (1951), in which he describes the influential role of interest groups in the American political system, policy scholars such as Dye (2010/2011, pp. 19-20) have conceived of a **group-theory model of public policy**. Dye presents a diagram that illustrates, for a theoretical policy matter, a scale of alternative policy options on which the existence of competing special-interest groups is noted. On this diagram (see Figure 12.2), the existence of two such groups is indicated by circles that are drawn (1) at the groups' respective positions on the scale of alternative policy options and (2) in relative proportion to the groups' influence (in terms of number of members, wealth, connection to influential decision-makers, and so on).

Figure 12.2: Scale of Alternative Policy Options for Competing Groups

The triangle (analogous to a fulcrum that balances a see-saw or other lever) is placed under the scale at a location that "balances" Group A and Group B's respective interests. Note, on this theoretical example, that the fulcrum is located closer to the larger Group A's position in deference to A's size, but not completely at A's extreme position in deference to Group B's existence.

Accordingly, this model states that policymakers determine where to set policy based on the competition of the interest groups that are active in the particular task environment for the policy area.

As an example, consider the policy area related to abortion. In 1973, the U. S. Supreme Court handed down its opinion in the case of *Roe v. Wade*, 410 U.S. 113 (1973). Confronted with a heated policy debate involving the pro-life and pro-choice groups, the court handed neither group a conclusive victory. Instead, it split the difference, prohibiting state legislatures from outlawing abortion during the first trimester of a pregnancy and allowing state legislatures to outlaw abortion (with certain specific exceptions) in the third trimester. Of course, the court, in its opinion written by Associate Justice Harry A. Blackmun, did not explain its rationale in these pragmatic terms, in accordance with its practice of citing provisions of the Constitution and the laws. But the effort to provide some sort of satisfaction to both sides is unmistakably identifiable.

Subgovernment Model of Public Policy

The **subgovernment model of public policy** states that, in any particular policy area, there is an "iron triangle" partnership involving the congressional committees, executive department or agency, and interest groups active in that policy area that dominates policy in that policy area. This influential model of public policymaking has already been described in chapter 5.

Elitism Model of Public Policy

In 1956, the sociologist C. Wright Mills published a memorable work entitled *The Power Elite*. Mills states the disconcerting fact that wealthy Americans have a disproportionate amount of influence in the determination of what public policy will be. In interpreting Mills's theory, Dye (2010/2011, p. 21) produces this diagram (Figure 12.3):

Figure 12.3: Elitism Model of Public Policy

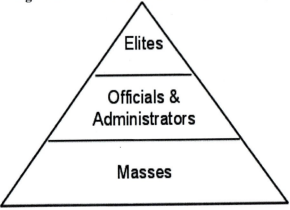

According to this **elitism model of public policy**, the elites provide policy direction to the officials and administrators. The population of officials and administrators includes elected and appointed government officials, such as the employees of the bureaucracy. The officials and administrators impose policy execution upon the masses. Mills dismisses the question of whether elections allow the masses to control the policy decisions of officials and administrators by characterizing American elections as a sham. In the final analysis, Mills insists, the officials and administrators will do what the elites require. The possession of enormous wealth seems to guarantee the aristocrat a position of influence. Really, what does any ordinary person do when he meets a wealthy person:

challenge him or try to charm him?

Other Models of Public Policy

The list of models that appears above includes some of the most popular models. This chapter does not list and describe the other models. Policy scholars believe that the incrementalism model is the best explanation for policy decisions, but others may very well be useful in describing how policy develops in certain circumstances. Being aware of these models can help an observer of politics and government to explain how some of the most visible policies arise in the American system.

Instruments of Public Policy

Max Weber (1918) wrote that government has "a monopoly of the legitimate use of physical force." While private-sector organizations have no mechanisms for compelling the public to act in accordance with their preferences, obviously the range of instruments available to the government to influence citizens' behavior is much wider than the range of those available to other entities. A list of the instruments of public policy that government can use follows.

Imprisonment and Capital Punishment

The government has the unique capacity to punish disobedience to government policy by an individual through taking away his liberty by imprisoning him or through taking his life by executing him. In a liberal society like the United States, the government exercises restraint in taking such action. For example, the Bill of Rights requires that an accused individual be accorded due process before a prison sentence or capital punishment can be inflicted on him, and limits, to some degree, the kinds of actions for which a person may be punished. Nobody may be punished for exercising civil liberties; the First Amendment, for example, guarantees that nobody will be imprisoned solely on account of making unpopular political statements.

Fines

While not quite so severe as the penalties of imprisonment and execution, fines may be imposed by the government as the consequence of disobedience to public policies. Speeding tickets and parking tickets are examples of misdemeanor offenses that may result in fines. The punishment for many felonies involves imprisonment or fines or a combination of the two.

Conscription

When it needs personnel for such purposes as to staff the Army to prepare for or wage military conflict, the government has the power to conscript (draft) individuals for certain periods of time, taking them from their homes and relocating them to a place—in the United States or elsewhere—that the government finds convenient.

Taking of Property

The government has the impressive power to condemn an individual's property and to convert the property to the government's use. This power is known as **eminent domain**. The Fifth Amendment requires that the government pay for the property, but, in the final analysis, the amount of the payment will ultimately be determined by the government's judiciary if the individual and the government do not reach a mutually agreeable settlement. A common reason for the government to take somebody's property would be to obtain the land necessary to build a new interstate highway.

Taxation

Another government power—one that citizens dislike but tolerate—is the government's power to tax a variety of items and activities. The national, state, and local governments tax earned income (payroll tax), total amounts of earned and unearned income (income tax), profits resulting from the appreciation of value of property and investments (capital-gains tax), property such as real estate and automobiles (property tax), retail purchases according to price (sales tax), retail purchases according to quantity of an item (excise tax), gifts (gift tax), and inheritances (estate tax). Although an income tax will tend to discourage some people from earning income, in so far as a tax is a penalty on the thing being taxed, the national government has greatly complicated the income-tax law (the Internal Revenue Code) to encourage certain behaviors. The mechanisms of the income-tax law that encourage behaviors are known as loopholes, deductions, and credits. An example is the government's desire to encourage home ownership. In order to persuade more people to buy a home, Congress inserted a provision in the Internal Revenue Code to allow taxpayers to deduct the mortgage tax that they pay from their individual amount of income when they calculate how much tax they must pay on that income. Another example is the government's desire to encourage people to donate to charities. A person's donations to charities are deductible, just as mortgage tax is deductible.

User Fees

The government may charge individuals who use certain government services for the use of those services. Such charges are called **user fees**. An example is a toll that might be charged for operating a motor vehicle on a highway. Government corporations such as Amtrak and the Postal Service support themselves mostly through the collection of user fees.

Subsidies

The government may endeavor to influence individuals' behavior by offering a subsidy. For example, Congress has offered subsidies to farmers who plant certain crops or who refrain from planning certain crops, depending on how the national government has wanted to affect the supply of such crops. The farmer simply receives a check from the U. S. Treasury to pay him for his cooperation.

Benefits, Including "Entitlements"

For the purpose of helping a disadvantaged group, or for the purpose of helping some constituency whose favor legislators would like to curry, the government may bestow a benefit. Medicaid—health care paid for by the government—is offered to poor people so that they do not find medical assistance to be inaccessible. Veterans receive an array of benefits, many of which are administered by the Department of Veterans Affairs; these benefits include health care and college tuition assistance. There are some benefits that are awarded selectively to applicants in accordance with the discretion of government officials. For example, the secretary of the Department of Housing and Urban Development may have the discretion to decide whether to provide funding to a community for a proposed housing project. On the other hand, some benefits are known as

entitlement programs. In the case of these programs, the law describes the qualifications for obtaining the benefit, and every individual who qualifies is entitled to the benefit; program officials do not have the discretion to deny the individual's application for the benefit to which he is legally entitled. Therefore, the entitlement benefit is, under the law, the qualified individual's property. He is entitled to the benefit as long as he continues to satisfy the criteria of the program.

Adjusting Monetary Variables

The Federal Reserve Board affects the economy by adjusting the nation's monetary arrangements. For example, the board may adjust the discount interest rate—the rate at which it loans money to banks—or adjust the money supply, for the purpose of causing interest rates on loans to rise or fall.

Propaganda and Persuasion

The government may attempt to affect the public's behavior through propaganda—rhetoric designed to influence how people think about politics, government, and society. Government agencies generate colossal amounts of written and oral communication to try to obtain support and influence behavior. This and other efforts at persuasion are designed to cause the public to act in a certain way without using policy instruments that involve the use of more forceful government power. Governments have sometimes used persuasion to try to influence people to carpool to work, refrain from littering, join the volunteer Army, and mail Christmas gifts weeks before the holiday.

Laissez Faire Inaction

Lastly, the government may decide to do nothing about a problem along the lines of the approach of ***laissez faire***. This is still considered a public policy. There are many public health activists who encourage the national government to provide free needles to drug addicts because such a program could arguably suppress the spread of the HIV virus. Congress has received this advice and made a conscious decision to do nothing about it. This, too, is a policy.

Public Policy and Money

Obviously, there is a close association between public policy and money. Hardly any public policy to accomplish something can be implemented without money. It is the duty of the legislature to arrange for the Executive Branch to have funds so that the laws can be administered. Congress enacts laws for such purposes as to impose taxes so that revenue can be raised. Then, Congress enacts **appropriation** laws to appropriate money for the use of the Executive Branch. The U. S. Constitution states, in Article I, Section 9, "No money shall be drawn from the treasury, but in consequence of appropriations made by law. . ."

Each January, the president presents to Congress the proposed budget of the national government, which the Office of Management and Budget has developed under the president's supervision, for the fiscal year that will begin later that year on October 1. Much of Congress's attention for the nine months that follow is directed toward considering the president's proposed budget, deciding on Congress's own preferences for how money should be spent, and enacting a set of appropriation laws. Once Congress has enacted, and the president has signed, these laws, the national government has a budget for the upcoming fiscal year.

The national government's budgeting process is guided by the incrementalism model of public policy that is discussed above. That is to say, the most important determinant of the budget of a particular bureau is how much the bureau was awarded for the preceding fiscal year. Routinely, the president and Congress will provide for a bureau the appropriation amount that it received for the previous year plus a modest increase. Only a specific change in policy would tend to significantly change the size of a bureau's budget either upward or downward.

A government bureau must exercise discipline in ensuring that it will not overspend its appropriation. If OMB officials determine that a bureau is failing to "live within its means," the officials may proceed to intervene in the bureau's managerial processes. There is, however, one glaring exception, which involves the entitlement programs discussed above. An entitlement program cannot "run out" of money. The president is obligated to ensure that funds are made available for entitlement programs, without limit, even as new applicants come forward and demonstrate their eligibility. For example, if a veteran is qualified for a tuition benefit that is an entitlement under the law, no government official can tell the veteran that a quota has been reached. The official must award the benefit, and the president and his subordinates must ensure that the money is available to fund it.

Entitlement programs grow, but they never go away. As James Q. Wilson explains, "An entitlement, once bestowed, cannot easily be withdrawn" (1975, p. 89). The beneficiaries of an entitlement program will fight like lions if their entitlement is threatened. The late House Speaker Thomas P. "Tip" O'Neill Jr. observed ruefully that Social Security is "the 'third rail' of American politics," so dangerous is it for elected officials to even speak about decreasing the program's benefits. (O'Neill's "third rail" metaphor refers to the high-voltage rail that powers electrified railroad trains, such as most subway trains.)

You have probably heard the news that the national government has been spending more for programs than it is collecting in revenue. Every year, the national government operates "in the red"—with a deficit. The national government's deficit in a given fiscal year adds to the accumulated amount of the government's debt. In 2011, the debt has surpassed the astronomical sum of $14 trillion. Comparing this amount to the gross domestic product of the United States in 2009—$14.1 trillion—should make the problem clear to any astute observer. The national government's debt is now approximately equal to the size of the nation's entire economy!

In Chapter 7, there is a discussion of the strategies that members of Congress use to get reelected. These strategies include insertions in laws of provisions for "pork" projects for members' states and congressional districts. They also include the creation of entitlement programs, and assortments of other kinds of benefits. Members of Congress—regardless of their political-party affiliation—have been so determined to ensure their reelection that they have been indiscriminate in creating and expanding these programs. The national government reached the point that no more programs could be funded with current-year tax revenues. Undeterred, members of Congress proceeded to fund new programs and program expansions with **deficit spending**, as a way of life. By now, the debt that has accumulated is beyond the nation's ability to repay. Much of this debt is owed to foreign investors, who will—sooner or later—want to be repaid with interest.

Aggravating the problem of deficit spending has been the nation's continuing involvement in extraordinarily expensive military operations in such places as Afghanistan and Iraq. During previous military operations, such as World Wars I and II, the United States undertook two or four years worth of warfare, financed by debt. The Global War on Terrorism—a real war with sprawling and active U. S. military involvement—is in its 10ᵗʰ very expensive year. Any official who might have fantasized about balancing the national government's budget would have thrown in the towel upon realizing that these expenditures are an apparently permanent component of the budget.

At this point, no reputable economist will deny that there will be consequences for this decades long, reckless spending spree. Economists do argue about what the consequences will actually be. One consequence is already recognizable: The hands of national-government policymakers are clearly tied by the monstrous debt. Many proposed programs that might really be needed today to respond to real problems are being set aside because the national government is broke. Many Americans who voted for President Barack Obama in 2008 are wondering aloud why he is is not "doing more," but where is the president going to find money to fund more programs? How the national government will finance the Patient Protection and Affordable Care Act, which the president signed into law on March 23, 2010, remains an intriguing mystery. One of the sad facts of the government's indebtedness is that our college-age population, younger children, and children not even born yet will not be able to escape the consequences of our presidents' and Congress's lamentable irresponsibility. For years, critics warned policymakers that they were "mortgaging our children's future." Presidents and members of Congress ignored these critics. But, without a doubt, the bill will come due.

Discussion Questions

1. Is the process of public policymaking in the United States one that is dominated by a few influential decision-makers or that results from widely dispersed opportunities to participate? Explain.
2. Which model of public policymaking do you consider to be most persuasive?
3. What factors lead Congress to use the threat of imprisonment as an instrument of policy in some cases, and persuasion in other cases?
4. If you were president, what would you do about the national government's $14-trillion debt? What implications of your

approach might you anticipate?

References

Downs, A. (1957). *An economic theory of democracy.* New York, NY: Harper and Row.

Dye, T. R. (2010/2011). *Understanding public policy,* (13th Ed.). Boston, MA: Longman/Pearson Education.

Lindblom, C. E. (1959). The science of 'muddling through'. *Public Administration Review,* 19, 79-88.

Mills, C.W. (1956). *The power elite.* New York, NY: Oxford University Press.

Smith, A. (1776). *An inquiry into the nature and causes of the wealth of nations.* London, England: W. Strahan and T. Cadell.

Truman, D. B. (1951). *The governmental process: Political interests and public opinion.* New York, NY: Albert A. Knopf.

Weber, M. (1918, January). *Politics as a vocation.* Speech presented at Munich University, Munich, Germany.

Wilson, J. Q. (1975). The rise of the bureaucratic state. *Public Interest,* 41, 77-103.

Chapter Thirteen
State and Local Government
Ross C. Alexander

Learning Objectives

After covering the topic of state and local government, students should understand:

1. The structure, functioning, and common components of state governments in the U.S.
2. The structure and functioning of the various types of local governments in the U.S.
3. The degree to which state and local government affects the lives of citizens on a daily basis.
4. How states and local governments have had to increasingly rely on alternative funding strategies to generate operating revenue and address budget deficits.

Abstract

There are over 87,000 (U.S. Census Bureau) governments in the United States—one federal government, 50 state governments, and tens of thousands of local governments (cities, townships, counties, special districts, etc.), yet we often overlook these vital governmental entities that impact our lives on a daily basis. In addition to exploring the basic composition, administration, and functioning of state and local government, this chapter will explain how individuals can become more involved and engaged in the public policy decisions of their communities. Then, this chapter will address the various funding strategies that states, counties, and cities have had to devise and employ to deliver services in the current economic crisis, many of which are innovative, non-traditional, and driven by necessity.

Introduction

Former Speaker of the U.S. House of Representatives Thomas "Tip" O'Neill once famously quipped that "All politics is local." Whether or not this statement is entirely accurate is open to debate, but the notion that state and local government has an effect on the daily lives of citizens is undisputable. Most government exchanges and interactions are with agents of state and local government and include such offices and officials as: public school teachers, police officers, social workers, county commissioners, city councilors, city and county managers, building inspectors, city planners, parks and recreation directors, firefighters, tax assessors, code enforcers, economic developers, city engineers, city and county clerks, state regulators, park rangers, bus drivers, and more. Elected and appointed officials at the state and local level make policy decisions in the areas of education, transportation, taxation, land use, growth and development, health care, emergency management, social services, immigration, and environmental protection, among others. They shape and control budgets and expenditures ranging from the small (tens of thousands of dollars) to the large (tens of billions of dollars).

Increasingly, as citizens clamor for more government services delivered more efficiently and effectively (without tax increases), state and local governments must devise strategies to generate revenue and meet citizen demands. Voter turnout for state and local elections is less than turnout in national level, especially presidential, elections. Traditionally, the lower the level of government, the lower the rate of voter turnout, which is unfortunate considering that these "lower" levels of government are closest to the people. It is not uncommon for voter turnout for primary elections at the local level to be in the single digits (Hajnal and Lewis, 2003).

State Governments
Constitutional Authority

The Tenth Amendment to the United States Constitution reads, "The powers not delegated to the United States by the Constitution, nor prohibited by it to the States, are reserved to the States respectively, or to the people." This so-called **Reserved Powers Clause**, although simply-written, is the constitutional basis for federalism and has resulted in a great deal of controversy and strained relations between the federal government and the states (as described in detail in earlier chapters). Nevertheless, state governments were created as co-equal entities by the framers of the Constitution and are therefore constitutionally-legitimate. Article I, Section Eight of the U.S. Constitution explains in detail powers given to the federal government (specifically Congress), powers shared by the federal government and state governments (called **concurrent powers**), and powers given exclusively to the states. Examples of powers given to the federal government and Congress solely include regulating interstate commerce, coining money, declaring war, raising an army, and making laws "necessary and proper." Examples of concurrent powers that the federal government shares with the states include collecting taxes, establishing courts, borrowing money, making and enforcing laws, and chartering banks and corporations. Finally, powers that states possess exclusively include establishing local governments, regulating intrastate commerce, conducting elections, and ratifying amendments to the U.S. Constitution. As society has become more complex and as citizens have demanded more services, government has expanded exponentially at all levels. Today, states make policy decisions affecting millions of people, concerning millions and billions of dollars.

State Constitutions

Because of federalism, states are constitutionally-legitimate entities and each state, therefore, has its own constitution. Many **state constitutions** (such as those of Virginia, South Carolina, and New Hampshire) existed prior to the writing of the U.S. Constitution in 1787 and were models and guides for the founding fathers at the Constitutional Convention. James Madison, in fact, utilized the Virginia constitution of 1776, written by Thomas Jefferson, as a template for the Virginia Plan which greatly influenced the U.S. Constitution. The U.S. Constitution is brief (roughly 7,400 words including the Bill of Rights) in comparison to most state constitutions, which are longer and more detailed, averaging roughly 26,000 words, and therefore less flexible. For example, Alabama's constitution adopted in 1901 is over 300,000 words. Even Vermont's constitution, which is the shortest, is over 8,300 words–longer than the U.S. Constitution (Hammons, 1999, 840). While the hallmark of the U.S. Constitution is its flexibility and endurance, having only been amended 17 times since 1791, state constitutions are amended much more frequently (115 times on average), or as is the case with many states, re-crafted altogether.

Most states have had several constitutions since 1776. An exception is the Massachusetts constitution, ratified in 1780, which is the longest-enduring written constitution in the world (Kincaid, 1988, 13). The current Georgia constitution was ratified in 1983, is the "newest" state constitution, and, in fact, is the 10th constitution in the state's history. The original U.S. Constitution has endured since it was ratified in 1789. On the contrary, there have been 145 different state constitutions since 1776 (Hammons, 1999, 838). Louisiana has had 11 constitutions; Georgia 10; South Carolina 7; Florida, Alabama, and Virginia 6; and Arkansas, Texas, and Pennsylvania 5 (Hammons, 1999, 841). Another primary difference between the U.S. Constitution and state constitutions is the location of the Bills of Rights. In the national version, the Bill of Rights is not a formal component of the document itself, but rather the first 10 amendments. In most state versions, the Bill of Rights is found in the beginning and often in the very first section (which is true for the Georgia Constitution). Because state constitutions are longer, more detailed, amended more frequently, and less flexible, they can provide additional protections for citizens, something which has led to judicial evolution at the state level, influencing the actions of lawmakers and the decisions of judges (Kincaid, 1988).

How Institutions Function in the States

Like the federal government and the U.S. Constitution, state governments and constitutions outline separate branches of government with checks and balances that share power. In every state, the chief executive is the governor. The lawmaking body is the state legislature, often called the General Assembly. 49 states utilize a bicameral legislature. Nebraska's unicameral legislature is the only exception. The highest courts in the states are referred to collectively as "courts of last resort" because not every state refers to its highest court as the "supreme" court (the Georgia Supreme Court is the highest court in the state). Just as the founding fathers intended that Congress be the strongest branch of government, state legislatures, as described by most state constitutions, are intended to be the strongest entity in state governments. However, just as has been the case with the evolution of presidential power, governors in the states have gained a tremendous amount of power at the expense of state legislatures over time. As a result, governors today are probably much stronger than intended in many cases.

The traditional powers of **governors**, those usually listed explicitly in state constitutions, are similar to the powers of the president (Beyle, 1968). Governors traditionally possess the power to appoint officials in the Executive Branch, oversee state agencies, veto legislation, call the state legislature into general session, dispatch the national guard in times of crisis and emergency, and craft the budget, among others. In an informal sense, governors also serve as chief of their respective parties, spokespersons and ambassadors for their states, and chief lobbyists with their state legislatures, putting pressure on members to enact their agendas and policies. In terms of length of gubernatorial terms and re-eligibility, states vary tremendously. Most governors serve four-year terms, but a few serve two-year terms, as is the case in New Hampshire and Vermont. Governors in 38 states are limited to two terms of office, the Governor of Virginia is limited to one term of office, and the remaining are not term-limited (National Governors Association, 2010). The Governor of the State of Georgia is limited to two four-year terms.

As the federal government has devolved power back to the states since 1980 or so, governors have become more powerful, many even possessing name recognition on a national and international scale. Governors today are proactive policy entrepreneurs (Beyle, 1995), aided in no small part by the power of the **line-item veto**, whereby they can veto parts of legislation, but not the entire bill (43 governors possess this power). The president does not possess the line-item veto. In generations previous, the path to the U.S. presidency was through the Senate (John F. Kennedy, Harry Truman, Lyndon Johnson), but many recent presidents and presidential candidates previously served as governor (Jimmy Carter, Ronald Reagan, Bill Clinton, George W. Bush), demonstrating their ability to oversee state agencies, manage budgets, handle crises, and win elections on a smaller scale, yet fulfilling duties similar to that of the president. Not surprisingly, gubernatorial elections can cost tens of millions of dollars, looking very much like presidential elections and are marked by extensive television advertising, usage of professional campaign advisers, and negative campaign ads.

The composition, functioning, and especially size of **state legislatures** vary tremendously across the states. Nebraska's unicameral legislature has 49 members. The smallest bicameral legislature is Alaska's with 60 members. The Georgia legislature has 236 members with 180 in the lower house and 56 in the Senate. Oddly enough, the largest state legislature is found in one of the smallest states—New Hampshire—which has a 424 seat body with 400 members serving in the lower house and has one representative per approximately 3,000 citizens. Contrast that with

California, which has 80 members in its lower house, each representing roughly 423,000 people (National Conference of State Legislatures, 2010). Most states utilize four-year **terms of office** for both the lower and upper houses of their legislatures, although 12 states utilize two-year terms. All members of the General Assembly in Georgia serve two-year terms. Since 1990, many states have enacted **term limits** for state legislators; 15 states currently do so. Legislators in these states are limited from 6 to 12 years in office, depending on the state. State legislators in Georgia are not term-limited (National Conference of State Legislatures, 2010).

There is also a tremendous amount of variation among the states with regard to full-time v. part-time legislatures, which is determined by both compensation and number of days in session. Many states pay legislators well over $60,000 per legislative session, with California providing the highest pay at over $95,000. Conversely, many states pay their legislators less than $20,000 per legislative session, including Georgia, where legislators are paid $17,342 for the forty-day session. Not surprisingly, those states with longer legislative sessions (several months) provide greater compensation and more staff to its members. (National Conference of State Legislators, 2010). All states except Texas meet in yearly sessions. Women are better represented in state legislatures than in the U.S. Congress, where women traditionally comprise roughly 10-12% of the 535 member body. In 2009, there were 1,788 women serving in state legislatures (24.4%), including a low of 10% in South Carolina and 11% in Oklahoma, to a high of 37% in New Hampshire and Colorado (in Georgia, women comprise 18.7% of the legislature). This 24.4% number has increased only five percent in the last 15 years (National Conference of State Legislatures, 2010).

The financing of state legislator campaigns does not reflect the campaign finance model at the national level, where members of Congress are restricted by the Federal Election Campaign Act of 1974 and the Bipartisan Campaign Reform Act of 2002 which limit direct contributions to members of Congress by individuals and groups. Campaign contribution limits vary greatly across the states; seven states enact no limits on campaign contributions whatsoever. In Georgia, candidates for state legislature can receive $2,400 for the primary election and another $2,400 for the general election. Limits on **campaign contributions** (or lack thereof) can have implications, most notably the degree to which special interests have access to lawmakers and the extent to which they influence public policy. Furthermore, states with low campaign contribution limits tend to have more competitive elections with challengers winning at a higher rate (Hamm and Hogan, 2008).

In terms of daily functioning and policymaking, state legislatures function very similarly to the U.S. Congress, working primarily in **committees**. Legislators will serve on several permanent or standing committees and perhaps other ad hoc or temporary committees as well. Traditionally, seniority rules with longer-serving members holding positions on the more prestigious committees. These long-held legislative traditions and folkways may erode as state legislators are subjected to term limits.

The operation of the **judicial system** (the courts) differs somewhat throughout the states. As mentioned previously, not all states refer to their highest court as the supreme court. In some states, judges are elected on partisan ballots, in others on non-partisan ballots. Other states appoint their judges to all levels of courts, while others still utilize the Missouri Plan, which involves a combination of appointments and elections. The primary difference is that judges who must run for election, especially those on partisan ballots, must concern themselves with political issues and variables like those governors and legislators face, most notably fundraising. Today, competition for judicial seats is fierce and can cost candidates hundreds of thousands of dollars per election cycle (Bonneau, 2007). What is common among all the states is the amount of judicial business or cases heard by state courts in comparison with the federal court system. State courts are busier, including the state courts of last resort, which hear many more cases than the U.S. Supreme Court.

Local Governments
Authority

Local governments (counties, townships, cities, school districts, etc.) are not mentioned in the U.S. Constitution and, therefore, their power and authority is not constitutionally-based. Rather, as the U.S. Supreme Court decision that came to be known as **Dillon's Rule** clarified in 1868, local governments are creations of the state, subject to the authority and oversight of individual states, not the federal government. However, as counties, townships, cities, and other units of local government have expanded, they have become responsible for delivering more services to more people. As a result, they function almost as a third level or layer in the system of American federalism, even if they lack authority from the U.S. Constitution. It should be remembered that almost all units of government are local units of government.

Counties
   Counties are subdivisions of states delivering state services at the local level including, but not limited to record-keeping, licensing, transportation, economic development, law enforcement, water management, elections, planning and zoning, child protection, education, and parks and recreation. Counties exist in 48 states, with county-like entities called boroughs found in Alaska and parishes found in Louisiana. Texas boasts the most counties with 254. There are only three counties found in both Hawaii and Delaware. There are 159 counties in Georgia, the second-most of any state (National Association of Counties, 2010). Counties vary tremendously in size, from less than 100 square miles to over 10,000 square miles. Arlington County, Virginia, the smallest county in the United States, is only 26 square miles. Conversely, San Bernadino County, California, the nation's largest, is over 26,000 square miles. In terms of population, many rural counties throughout the United States have less than 5,000 residents while many urban counties have over a million people, including over five million in Cook County, Illinois and over nine million in Los Angeles County, California (National Association of Counties, 2010). This urban/rural distinction is important for counties because people living in rural areas rely more so on county government and the services it provides because those services are not provided or duplicated by other governments, most notably cities. Many people live in rural, unincorporated areas where government services are provided solely by the county.
   Historically, counties have been governed by an elected **commission**, which served as the legislative, policymaking entity for the county as well as the executive entity. In effect, each elected commissioner was responsible for overseeing a particular policy area. Relatively few counties still utilize this arrangement today due to the complex nature of modern county government and the potential for corruption that occurred before the era of professionalization spurred by the institution of the merit system at the

county level in the early 20th century. Rather, the commission system of government has evolved over the years and today, counties are governed most often by the **commissioner-administrator** or **commission-manager** system whereby the elected commission chooses a professional manager or administrator to oversee the day-to-day operations of the county. In this system, the commission fulfills its traditional legislative, policymaking function, but the manager or administrator is responsible for budget oversight, personnel administration, strategic planning, and other daily government functions. The commissioner-administrator/commissioner-manager system is the most commonly-used system of county governance today because of its relative efficiency and professionalism (Svara, 1993).

Yet other counties employ a **commission-executive** whereby the county executive is a separately-elected official functioning similarly to a county manager or administrator. The advantage to the commission-executive system is true separation of powers (National Association of Counties, 2010).

The least-utilized system of county governance is the **sole commissioner** model, found only in a few counties in Georgia and nowhere else. In these rural Georgia counties, the commissioner is a single person who functions as both the legislative and executive body for the county. As counties have grown, this system of government has become less appropriate and therefore rarely used. County commissioners and executives run on partisan ballots in most cases.

Finally, over 30 cities and counties in several U.S. states have consolidated into one governmental entity. **Consolidated governments** deliver services as one government, rather than duplicating city and county services, theoretically increasing efficiency of service delivery and saving money. New York City, Philadelphia, Indianapolis, Louisville, Nashville, and Jacksonville all operate as consolidated governments. Three consolidated governments are found in Georgia—Columbus-Muscogee, Athens-Clarke, and Augusta-Richmond (U.S. Census Bureau).

Townships

Just as counties are subdivisions of states, **townships** are subdivisions of counties, providing similar services to people living in mostly rural, unincorporated areas. Townships are found in 20 states primarily in the eastern United States and throughout the Midwest. Many states in the

South and West do not utilize townships as a separate government entity (there are no townships in Georgia). Townships are traditionally governed by a Board of Trustees or Board of Supervisors serving as the legislative body and may utilize a town manager or administrator to oversee the daily operation of the township (National Association of Towns and Townships, 2010). Townships, like other units of government, function most effectively when their actions and delivery of services is well-coordinated with other levels of government in the region, including counties and cities. Otherwise, their mere existence can be viewed by groups and citizens alike as duplicitous in nature, providing services that are already administered by counties, cities, or states (Visser, 2004).

Cities

There are over 19,000 municipal governments in the United States (U.S. Census Bureau), referred to here as **cities**. Cities vary tremendously in size and population, from a few dozen people (literally) to several million. Over 60% of all Americans live in cities (National League of Cities, 2010). Cities are "incorporated" or established by receiving a **charter** from the state legislature.

"A city charter is the basic document that defines the organization, powers, functions and essential procedures of the city government. It is comparable to the State Constitution and to the Constitution of the United States. The charter is, therefore, the most important single legal document of any city" (National League of Cities, 2010). Charters differ somewhat from state to state, depending on individual state constitutions, but traditionally, there are three different types of municipal charters: **special or specific charters**, **general or classified charters**, and **home rule charters**. Cities are granted a charter depending on population, proposed government structure, and other variables (National League of Cities, 2010). Those cities with **home rule** can make minor changes to their charters without receiving approval from the state legislature, most notably adjusting the local income tax rate. All cities in Georgia possess home rule.

Like counties, cities are governed by various systems, depending on tradition, era of incorporation, and state and regional political climate. The oldest form of city government is the **mayor-council** form of government whereby the mayor functions as the chief executive and the city council functions as the legislative body. A distinction in the mayor-council form of government is the "strong mayor" versus "weak mayor" classification. In those cities possessing "strong" mayors, the executive possesses greater authority with regard to budgetary and personnel decisions. Atlanta functions as a "strong" mayor system. Candidates for mayor and city council in mayoral systems tend to run on partisan ballots with candidates declaring a party affiliation. Other cities, albeit very few, utilize a **commission system** that looks similar to the county commission system, where the commission functions as both the legislative and executive entity. The most common form of city government is the **council-manager** or **council-administrator** system where the elected city council functions as the legislative policymaking body but selects a professional manager or administrator to oversee the day-to-day operation of the city (similar to the county commission-manager or administrator system described above). Candidates for city council in council-manager systems tend to run on non-partisan ballots, which usually results in lower voter turnout. Finally, the **town meeting** form of government exists only in New England and is not pervasive throughout the region. In a municipality utilizing the town meeting form of government, the entire electorate is allowed to participate in an annual meeting, the primary purpose of which is to pass the budget for the upcoming fiscal year. Policy administration is undertaken by select men, chosen by the electorate (DeSantis and Renner, 2002). The town meeting form of government is hampered by very low voter turnout.

Arguments exist on both sides for **partisan** and **non-partisan** elections. Advocates for partisan elections contend that party labels guide or aid voters in making candidate decisions and voter turnout is usually higher in partisan elections. Advocates for non-partisan elections contend that party labels are antiquated and do not aid professionals in providing city services to the public. The trend is towards non-partisan elections as the council-manager system of government becomes more pervasive, even in large cities that have traditionally possessed the mayoral form of government (Svara, 1999). With regard to term length and term limits of office-holders serving in city government, the overwhelming majority serve four-year terms of office and are not term-limited; less than 10% of cities limit the terms of office-holders (Svara, 2003, 14). It should also be noted that minority representation on city councils is higher for communities utilizing the council-manager form of government—21%—compared to the mayoral form of government—15% (Svara, 2003, 7).

Other Local Governments

Myriad other local governments exist in the United States and are too numerous to address in detail, although a few merit further investigation. **Councils of Governments** (COGs) are voluntary associations communities in metropolitan areas and exist to address issues and concerns that may affect several jurisdictions in a given region, such as land use, traffic and congestion, transportation, water use, and emergency management. COGs have little formal power but can be effective for strategic, long-term planning. The most successful COG is the one in the Minneapolis-St. Paul area (National League of Cities, 2010). **School districts** are an important unit of local government that make policy for schools in a given jurisdiction, such as a county, township, or city. School districts are governed by the school board, which functions as the legislative, policy-making body. The school board chooses a superintendent to oversee the daily operation of the district. School board members usually run on non-partisan ballots and serve four-year terms. School board politics can become contentious at times because boards oversee the curriculum for school children, making decisions about what children will learn, who will teach it to them, and which subjects should be emphasized (Land, 2002). There are over 13,000 school districts in the United States. The largest is the New York City district, which has nearly a million students (Selected statistics on enrollment, teachers, dropouts, and graduates in public school districts enrolling more than 15,000 students, by state: 1990, 2000, and 2006).

Finally, about one-third of all local governments are **special districts**. Special districts are created to regulate and manage specific services such as water and resources, fire prevention, emergency services, transportation, and even stadiums. These special districts encompass a defined geographic area and have significant taxing and regulating authority, their primary purpose being raising funds (America.gov). For example, if a city desires to build a new professional sports franchise, a special stadium district will be created and businesses and individuals owning property or buying goods in that geographic area will pay "tax" to fund that endeavor.

State and Local Government Financing—A Case Study
Unlike the federal government, states cannot pass a yearly budget with a deficit and incur debt over many years or even generations. 49 states have some type of **balanced budget** requirement in their state constitutions (National Conference of State Legislatures, 2010). During times of business and economic prosperity and boom, states often produce a surplus, allowing them to increase funding for existing programs and creating new programs, even refunding taxpayers some of their contributions in rare occassions. Conversely, during economic recessions, depressions, and crises, states are often faced with a budgetary shortfall, resulting in deep, dramatic, and permanent cuts to state programs; the result is less money for such things as education, transportation, public health services, and law enforcement. This situation has been the case nationwide since the most recent economic recession began in 2007. While states have undergone difficult economic times previously, the most recent crisis is unmatched since the Great Depression of the 1930s. In previous downswings in the economy, states began to devise non-traditional methods of raising revenue to fund government services. Beginning in the 1980s and 1990s, several states instituted first a state-sanctioned lottery and later state-sanctioned, legalized casino gambling as a means of generating much needed revenue. To help deal with current and future economic recessions, states may increasingly turn to legalized gambling to fund state programs. What follows is a case-study for the State of Georgia, which legalized the lottery in the early 1990s and may potentially turn to legalized casino gambling in the future.

Legalized Casino Gambling In Georgia: A Potential Plan[1]
Voters in Georgia approved the lottery in a referendum in 1992 and the Georgia Lottery Corporation began selling tickets in 1993. The effort to adopt a lottery in the state was spearheaded by Governor Zell Miller, who based his 1990 campaign largely on the platform of creating a lottery to subsidize college tuition for the state's college-bound students in addition to funding pre-kindergarten programs. This merit-based tuition assistance program eventually became the HOPE Scholarship program. Miller correctly assumed that the lottery would be more palatable to voters

---

1 This information is borrowed in large part from "The Feasibility of Legalized Casino Gambling in Georgia" by Alexander.

if the funds were tied to educational programs in the state. As Nelson and Mason (2004) chronicle, the lottery was also supported because Georgians had been gambling in illegal lotteries for decades. They were used to gambling; therefore, the adoption of a state-run lottery would not prove to be a significant divergence from existing social norms. In addition, citizens in south Georgia were frequent players of the Florida lottery: "Seven of the top ten sales points for the Florida lottery were along the Georgia border" (Nelson and Mason 2004, 661). Furthermore, the state was amid a financial crisis in the early 1990s and the lottery was viewed as a feasible means of generating much-needed revenue (Nelson and Mason 2004).

Today, lottery funds are appropriated specifically for certain educational programs, most notably the HOPE (Helping Outstanding Pupils Educationally) Scholarship which provides tuition assistance for students meeting eligibility criteria in post-secondary institutions throughout the state. HOPE also provides funds for pre-kindergarten programs. According to the Georgia Lottery Corporation (www.galottery. com), the HOPE program has provided over $9.3 billion for educational programs since 1993, including $853 million in FY 2007. HOPE has sent over one million students to college and provided funding for 790,000 4-year-olds in pre-kindergarten programs since 1993 (www.galottery. com). The Georgia lottery is considered by experts to be one of the best run in the nation (McCrary and Condrey 2003).

Unlike many states that do not tie lottery funds to specific programs, educational or otherwise, Georgia mandates that lottery-generated revenues be allocated for specific programs, such as the HOPE Scholarship. As Lauth and Robbins (2002) contend, many states have used lottery funds as a substitute for educational funds, not as an additional source. Georgia, however, has not succumbed to this scheme. Rather, lottery funds in the state continue to be allocated for the intended educational purposes. McCrary and Condrey (2003) further explain that the lottery in Georgia is among the best administered in the nation, enjoys a high degree of public support, and continues to fund the programs it was intended to fund upon its inception. However, Georgia is not alone in earmarking lottery funds for education. According to Evans and Zhang (2007), 37 states possess lotteries and 16 earmark funds for education. As a result, according to McCrary and Condrey (2003), "...the Georgia Lottery's success has also spread the seeds of its potential demise" (709). The solvency for this program may erode in the future as other states adopt similar lotteries, resulting in competition for gambling dollars, and as more students participate in programs funded by the lottery. These scenarios could result in a shortfall in funding for these educational programs.

In Georgia, the lottery receives a relatively high degree of public support in a socially and morally conservative region where gambling traditionally does not enjoy widespread public support for several reasons, most notably that its profits are used primarily to fund educational initiatives and that it is well-administered (von Herrmann 2002, 57). However, as von Herrmann (2002) further explains, support for gaming initiatives (especially the lottery) can diminish as profits diminish. While it is difficult to predict the breaking-point for the solvency of the Georgia lottery, policymakers should understand that publicly supported gambling and profits may fluctuate or diminish in the future, and they should therefore plan accordingly by either reconfiguring funding strategies or perhaps expanding gambling operations. So, the challenge to the State of Georgia is to ensure the solvency of these lottery-supported educational programs at a time when more and more students are eligible to receive aid. However, state budgets remain tight and fewer and fewer federal dollars are available to supplement educational programs. While the Georgia lottery and the HOPE Scholarship program have been a model of success for several years, new funding strategies and sources may need to be found for it to remain financially solvent for future generations. One revenue generation vehicle that may ensure the solvency of the HOPE Scholarship program for the foreseeable future is legalized casino gambling. This study examines the feasibility of expanding gambling in Georgia to include legalized casino gambling to supplement the funding of the HOPE Scholarship program, to aid in the redevelopment efforts of selected cities throughout the state, and to provide much-needed budget relief for the State of Georgia.

In Georgia, the lottery has been integral in funding many educational programs, such as the HOPE Scholarship. One could theorize that the success of the lottery in the state would result in voters being more supportive to the expansion of legalized gambling activities, especially legalized casino gambling. Nelson and Mason (2004) explain that one of the reasons Mississippi legalized casino gambling in the 1990s was to begin reaping gambling revenue before Louisiana and other states could adopt the measure.

States have adopted gambling for many reasons, mostly economic, but in many cases gambling adoption is about competition—"we'd better adopt it before our neighbors do," as Alexander and Paterline (2005) explain. This pressure to adopt gambling in Georgia existed prior to lottery adoption and even exists today surrounding the adoption of legalized casino gambling as other states in the region have already welcomed casinos (including Mississippi, Louisiana, Florida, and North Carolina). In fact, the Georgia Assembly passed House Resolution 618, the House Study Committee on Gaming, to explore the feasibility of casino gambling in the state, due in large part because other states had already adopted it or were considering adoption; Mississippi and North Carolina are mentioned specifically. So, while many in the state would be resistant to legalized casino gambling for reasons explained previously, others may perhaps be more accommodating. The resolution advocates the exploration and consideration of legalized casino gambling in Georgia primarily for the following reasons: the need to augment the budget of the City of Atlanta; as a vehicle by which the shopping center dubbed "Underground Atlanta" could be re-developed; as a means of increasing tourism in Augusta, Columbus, Dalton, Macon, Savannah, and Valdosta specifically; and finally, as a method of funding additional public safety initiatives in Atlanta. As proposed, the measure would require the cooperation of state and local officials including mayors of the aforementioned cities as well as representatives from each city's chamber of commerce. If gaming were to be adopted, which model should the state use? Riverboat gaming? Indian gaming? What? Furthermore, exactly how much money can be gained from legalizing casino gambling?

Commercial casinos operate in eleven states (Colorado, Illinois, Indiana, Iowa, Louisiana, Michigan, Mississippi, Missouri, Nevada, New Jersey, and South Dakota). Nevada, New Jersey, and coastal Mississippi tend to be considered in a different "class" than the other gambling states because they operate large, land-based casino operations on a much larger scale than the others. The riverboat gambling operations of Illinois, Indiana, Iowa, Missouri, and Louisiana possess many similarities in operation, revenue generation, and number of casinos. Before wide-scale expansion in the coastal region of the state, Mississippi operated on the Illinois/Iowa riverboat gambling model (Nelson and Mason 2004). In all riverboat states, the state controls the number of licenses available for casino operations. Individual casinos almost operate as pseudo-monopolies in a given region or market to minimize competition and maximize profits. Illinois has 9 casinos, Indiana has 10, Iowa has 13, Louisiana has 18, and Missouri has eleven (www.americangaming.org).

When riverboat gambling was adopted in the late 1980s and early 1990s throughout the Midwest, the intent was to spur economic redevelopment of riverfronts and downtowns and to generate much-needed revenue for host cities and states. As Alexander (2003) and Alexander and Paterline (2005) note, most host communities have reaped much-needed revenue from gambling. In many cases, gambling offers dollars that would not be available if the casinos did not operate. Gambling dollars are generally allocated for specific purposes, usually infrastructure improvement, community enrichment projects, education, and capital improvements in the host community in addition to tax dollars being allocated to the state. According to the American Gaming Association these states received the following casino tax revenues in 2009: Indiana ($878 million), Louisiana ($598 million), Illinois ($496 million), Missouri ($469 million), Michigan ($320 million), Iowa ($306 million), and Mississippi ($296 million).

The intent of riverboat gaming throughout the Midwest was to spur redevelopment of host communities and to generate revenue for host cities and states. 28 states allow Indian gaming, including some of those that also allow casino gaming. However, the intent of casino gambling on Indian reservations is different. The purpose of gambling for Native Americans is to generate revenue for host tribes, not host cities or states. Any economic impact the community or state receives is secondary, as Alexander and Paterline (2005) explain. That is not to say, however, that some host communities do not receive significant financial contributions from host tribes, but that financial reward is not contractually based or state controlled. Therefore, if a state were considering adopting legalized casino gambling, the greatest financial rewards would be reaped not through Indian gaming, but through riverboat gaming.

If Georgia were to adopt the riverboat model employed by states like Illinois, Indiana, Iowa, Missouri, and Louisiana, the financial gain could be significant. Georgia, like the states mentioned above (except Mississippi), possesses a lottery. Therefore, it would be relatively safe to assume that casino gambling profits reaped in addition to established lottery revenues would be similar to these states if Georgia were to adopt the Midwestern riverboat model of casino gambling. Demographically and geographically, Georgia is similar to several of these states that possess one major metropolitan area, several smaller metropolitan areas, and many rural cities and regions. Illinois, for example, allows several casinos in the Chicago metropolitan area (Joliet, Aurora, Elgin) with others geographically dispersed throughout the state, primarily along the Illinois, Mississippi, and Ohio rivers. Some of the Illinois casinos generate revenue and economic development to a more significant extent than others, but the economic impact is profound for host municipalities.

In most cases, host cities are receiving tens of millions of dollars per year in tax revenue from casino gambling. Elgin, IL receives almost 25 million dollars and Joliet, IL nearly 35 million dollars. When surveyed, government officials explain that without this revenue, many projects and services could not be provided in host cities (Alexander 2003; Alexander and Paterline 2005). It should also be noted that in some cases riverboat casinos do not necessarily require a river. Rather, artificial bodies of water created exclusively for the purpose of supporting a casino meet the requirements of the initial enabling legislation authorizing gambling. Furthermore, the "riverboat model" refers not necessarily to the existence of any body of water, but rather to the license and revenue allocation strategies of states that utilize this mode of gambling.

Using the riverboat model, where would Georgia choose to allocate licenses? Which communities would benefit most from casino gambling? Some have been calling for a casino to be placed in Underground Atlanta as a means of restoring it to its previous economic vitality in addition to providing budget relief for the City of Atlanta. Surely, cities like Augusta, Savannah, Columbus, Albany, Dalton, Rome, Macon, and Atlanta (among others) would at least investigate the possibility of hosting a casino as a means of generating revenue and economic development as well as increasing tourism. As traditional industries and economic anchors transition, downsize, or leave, cities must turn to other revenue sources to fund programs and services, spur development, and purchase necessary equipment. Gambling can also serve as a boon for tourism, perhaps developing additional sectors of municipal economies that have been untapped or under-developed in the aforementioned cities and regions.

There are a number of political factors to consider prior to gambling adoption in the state, but perhaps the state is at least ready to investigate seriously the expansion of legalized gambling to include casinos. As Lindaman (2007) indicates, however, morality politics remains a factor in the adoption of pro-gambling ordinances and policies, especially at the local level. If casino gambling generated anywhere near as much revenue as it does in other states that possess it, the educational programs supported by gambling in the state would be viable for the foreseeable future. Furthermore, many cities that desperately need supplemental revenue streams and redevelopment could benefit from casino gambling.

Another factor is market saturation. North Carolina possesses Indian gaming, but not casino gambling based on the "riverboat model." The nearest states that employ this type of gaming are Louisiana and Mississippi. However, as gambling diffuses (Nelson and Mason 2004) and proliferates throughout the nation as it becomes more economically viable and socially acceptable (Christiansen 1998), states throughout the South may begin to consider adopting the measure. The domino effect that occurred with lottery adoption 10 to 15 years ago may occur with casino gambling. As a result, it may be beneficial for the State of Georgia to consider casino gambling sooner rather than later—before the market becomes saturated, and it has to compete with neighboring states for gambling dollars. Even when adjacent states possess gambling, as in the cases of Indiana, Illinois, Iowa, and Missouri, there seems to be enough gambling revenue to sustain all enterprises, but revenues are perhaps highest when a state possesses a monopoly of sorts on gambling activities in a given region, an economic tenet that holds true with many businesses, not just casino gambling.

The state already possesses a model administrative infrastructure (McCrary and Condrey 2003) to oversee the allocation of gambling profits, which would make for a smoother transition from lottery-only gambling to casino gambling. Furthermore, in those states that utilize the riverboat model, the casinos are owned by private corporations that allocate tax revenues and money on a contractual basis. Therefore, the state would not have to be as involved as it is in the administration of the lottery. Of course, allowing casino gambling would probably have to be facilitated by a legislative proposal to the voters of the state, and would require a great deal of effort by pro-gaming policy entrepreneurs in the state legislature, the bureaucracy, and perhaps even the governor's office, similar to efforts required when the lottery was adopted in the early 1990s. However, due to the success of the lottery in Georgia, its tradition of participation in illegal lotteries and other forms of gambling, and the necessity of securing additional revenue streams on a large-scale basis, perhaps the political conditions may exist for passage of casino gambling legislation and subsequent approval from the voters.

In sum, the arguments in favor of adopting legalized casino gambling in Georgia include the sustainability of the HOPE Scholarship program as additional students become eligible for the program in the future, revenue generation for host municipalities in addition to potential economic development and tourism expansion, budget relief for the State of Georgia and host municipalities, most notably the City of Atlanta, and the establishment of a reliable revenue stream for the state and host cities at a time when the market is not yet saturated with casino gambling alternatives in the region.

A Civic Engagement Challenge—Becoming Involved in Local Government

One of the basic themes of this chapter has been that it is easier for citizens to get involved in "lower" levels of government, which is true for students as well. Students often have difficulty applying theories, themes, and lessons of government to their daily lives. One way in which they can better understand how government affects them is to become more involved. The civic engagement challenge for this chapter is for students to get involved with a local campaign in one of two ways: either by volunteering for a candidate for city council, county commission, school board, or another local office, or by running themselves. While the first option may be less difficult, the second option is certainly realistic. In many college towns, students have gained election to the city council or county commission. Students underestimate their political power. In a small or mid-sized college community, students comprise an overwhelming portion of the electorate. In most states, including Georgia, students can register to vote in the cities where they go to school. As a result, a candidate for office who is able to harness the political power of the campus and motivate students to vote would have a very good chance of winning an election. City council elections tend to have low voter turnout, and a few dozen votes could very well determine the outcome. A successful student-candidate would have to make sure he or she filed for the election on time, established his or her residency in the community, and drummed up support on campus. So, get going!

Discussion Questions

1. How do state constitutions differ from the U.S. Constitution? Which format is better? Why?
2. How does the composition and functioning of state legislatures differ across the states? In terms of size, term length, and structure, which model is best? Why?
3. Compare and contrast the various forms of local government structure. Which offers the best service delivery to citizens? Why?
4. Should cash-strapped states turn to alternative forms of revenue generation such as legalized casino gambling? Why or why not?

References

Alexander, R. C. (2008). The feasibility of legalized casino gambling in georgia. *Proceedings of the Georgia Political Science Association.* (2007 ed.).

Alexander, R. C., & Paterline, B. A. (2005). Boom or bust: Casino gaming and host municipalities. *International Social Science Review* 80(1,2), 20-28.

Alexander, R. C. (2003). *The effects of casino gambling on selected midwestern municipalities: Gauging the attitudes of local government officials, local business officials, and civic leaders.* Bloomington, IN: Authorhouse.

American Gaming Association. (2003). American Gaming Association. Retrieved from http://www.americangaming.org/.

Beyle, T. (1995). Enhancing executive leadership in the states. *State and Local Government Review,* 27(1), 18-35.

Beyle, T. (1968). The governor's formal powers: A view from the governor's chair. *Public Administration Review,* 540-545.

Bonneau, C. W. (2007). The effects of campaign spending in state Supreme Court elections. *Political Research Quarterly,* 60(3), 489-499.

Bureau of the Census. (2002). Census of government, government organization. *U.S. Department of Commerce,* 1(1). Retrieved from http://www.census.gov/prod/2003pubs/gc021x1.pdf.

Christiansen, E. M. (1998). Gambling and the American economy. *Annals of the American Academy of Political and Social Science,* 556, 36-52.

DeSantis, V. S., & Renner, T. (2002). City government structures: An attempt at clarification. *State and Local Government Review,* 34(2), 95-104.

Evans, W. N., & Zhang, P. (2007). The impact of earmarked lottery revenue on state educational expenditures. *Education Finance and Policy,* 2(1), 40-73.

Georgia Lottery Corporation. (2011). Georgia Lottery. Retrieved from http://www.galottery.com/.

Hajnal, Z. L. & Lewis, P. G. (2003). Municipal institutions and voter turnout in local elections. *Urban Affairs Review,* 35(3), 645-668.

Hamm, K. E. & Hogan, R. E. (2008). Campaign finance laws and candidacy decisions in state legislative elections. *Political Research Quarterly,* 61(3), 458-467.

Hammons, C. W. (1999). Was James Madison wrong? Rethinking the American preference for short, framework-oriented constitutions. *American Political Science Review,* 93(4), 837-849.

Kincaid, J. (1988). State constitutions in the federal system. *Annals of the American Academy of Political and Social Science,* 496, 12-22.

Land, D. (2002). Local school boards under review: Their role and effectiveness in relation to students' academic achievement. *Review of Educational Research,* 72(2), 229-278.

Lauth, T. P. & Robbins, M. D. (2002). The Georgia lottery and state appropriations for education: Substitution or additional funding? *Public Budgeting and Finance,* 22(3), 89-100.

Lindaman, K. L. (2007). Place your bet on politics: Local governments roll the dice. *Politics and Policy,* 35(2), 274-297.

McCrary, J. & Condrey, S. E. (2003). The Georgia lottery: Assessing its administrative, economic, and political effects. *Review of Policy Research,* 20(4), 691-711.

National Association of Counties. (2011). NACo: The voice of America's counties. Retrieved from http://www.naco.org/Pages/default. aspx.

National Association of Towns and Townships. (2011). NATaT: The National Association of Towns and Townships. Retrieved from http://www.natat.org/index.aspx.

National Conference of State Legislatures. (2011). NCSL home. Retrieved from http://www.ncsl.org/.

National Governors Association. (2011). National Governors Association: The collective voice of the nation's governors. Retrieved from http://www.nga.org/portal/site/nga/menuitem.b14 a675ba7f89cf9e8ebb856a11010a0.

Nelson, Michael and John Lyman Mason. 2004. The Politics of Gambling in the South. *Political Science Quarterly* 118(4): 645-669.

Snyder, T.D., Dillow, S.A., & Hoffman, C.M. (2009). Digest of
    Education Statistics 2008 (NCES 2009-020). National Center
    for Education Statistics, Institute of Education Sciences, U.S.
    Department of Education.Washington, DC.

Svara, J. H. (2003). *Two decades of continuity and change in american
    city councils.* Study Commissioned by the National League of
    Cities.

Svara, J, H. (1999). The shifting boundary between elected officials
    and city managers in large council-manager cities. *Public
    Administration Review,* 59(1), 44-53.

Svara, J. H. (1993). The possibility of professionalism in county
    government. *International Journal of Public Administration,*
    16(12), 2051-2080.

Visser, J. A. (2004). Townships and nested governance: Spoilers
    or collaborators in metropolitan services delivery? *Public
    Performance & Management Review,* 27(3), 80-101.

Chapter Fourteen
U.S. Foreign Policy
Jonathan S. Miner and Craig B. Greathouse

Learning Objectives

After covering the topic of U.S. foreign policy, students should understand:

1. The general elements of a foreign policy, and why every country has a specific policy that serves their best interests.
2. The important political and social actors who make U.S. foreign policy.
3. How history and current domestic and international issues shape U.S. foreign policy.
4. How current involvement in Iraq is a result of U.S. foreign policy.

Abstract

One of the most important areas of public policy in which the American government must engage is relations with other countries in the international system. U.S. foreign policy entails developing and advancing American national interests abroad by using all the tools and abilities of government and society. This chapter fits well toward the end of this volume as many of the subjects studied so far (the president, Congress, judiciary, bureaucracy, state and local governments, political parties, mass media and general public) have a prominent role in the process of making U.S. foreign policy. In this chapter, a discussion of the nuts and bolts of foreign policy will be coupled with an analysis of the specific actors who make and implement U.S. foreign policy, a survey of its prominent historical themes, and a contemporary application of this process to the current crisis in Iraq.

Introduction

Every day, on broadcasts across this country, the media details explosions in Iraq and Afghanistan which kill United States military personnel and innocent civilians. As people watch these reports, many ask obvious questions, such as, why are we there? What does the United States have to gain that justifies fighting two wars in Iraq and Afghanistan that cost billions of dollars and the lives of Americans? The short answer is simple – September 11, 2001. Since the attacks on New York, Washington, and Pennsylvania, the United States has been in the Middle East fighting terrorism and protecting the homeland from those who wish to attack once again. As President Bush declared in his first address to the nation on September 20, 2001, "Tonight, we are a country awakened to danger and called to defend freedom. Our grief has turned to anger and anger to resolution. Whether we bring our enemies to justice or bring justice to our enemies, justice will be done" (Cable News Network).

While this short and definitive explanation may make logical sense, the long answer to why the United States is involved in the Middle East is much more complex. A more complete explanation involves answering some of the following questions, such as, how does a response to the 9/11 tragedy become a U.S. foreign policy? What reasons could the U.S. possibly have to send troops so far away to such an unstable place for ten years? Who actually makes these decisions, and why do I not feel involved in making them? Why is this important to me anyway? How can I have my thoughts and opinions known and noticed by policy makers? This chapter answers many of these questions by bringing together many of the concepts and ideas you have learned in this reader and applying them to events that happen outside the United States. It also helps answer them by explaining how issues important to Americans at home become U.S. foreign policy abroad, what foreign policy actually is, who makes it, what it tries to accomplish, and why it is extremely important to each and every American citizen.

The final part of the chapter helps illustrate the making of U.S. foreign policy by applying these ideas to U.S. involvement in Iraq, a conflict in which the country has been directly involved since 1990. And while Iraq surely is a complicated place, U.S. involvement in Iraq is based upon a number of long-standing core values and priorities American foreign policy makers have applied to events all over the world throughout our history: **security**, **democracy**, **freedom**, **military superiority**, **trade** and **international leadership** (Greathouse and Miner, 2008). By understanding the connection between these ideas and two decades of involvement with Iraq, students will be able to better understand how American political issues become U.S. foreign policy and will have the tools to understand any U.S. foreign policy implemented in any part of the world.

What is foreign policy?
     Foreign policy can be explained as "the scope of involvement abroad

and the collection of goals, strategies, and instruments that are selected by governmental policymakers" (Rosati and Scott, 2007, 4). In other words, foreign policy represents the different needs, interests, and reasons for United States involvement abroad and the ways and means chosen to achieve those goals. Foreign policy is based upon the best interests of a particular country, in this case the United States. Whether these interests involve the export of products made in the U.S. or the importation of oil, a worry about terrorism, global pollution, or the drug trade, the foreign policy of the United States is determined by the issues and concerns most important to our country as a whole. The foreign policy of the U.S. is therefore not the same as that of Mexico and Canada because not all of our needs are the same; while the three countries share borders and many common interests, they also have different people, economies, and security needs which result in different foreign policies (Greathouse and Miner, 2010).

U.S. foreign policy is made by the government, but not the government alone. The president often leads in foreign policy making, but he is influenced and supported by Congress, the military, the media, the State Department, intelligence community, interest groups, the bureaucracy, and the public, among others. It is a bargaining process in which every interested person and group participates in the making of a foreign policy on a particular issue, using all of the power and skills they possess to shape a policy that is in their best interest and in the interest of the United States as a whole (Allison and Zelikow, 1999). One might think of this process as a board meeting; the president sits at the head of a conference table, and all around him sit representatives of all the interested parties on a given issue, such as terrorism.

U.S. foreign policy is the result of all interested parties discussing a particular national goal or interest and bargaining over the best way to achieve it abroad. A policy is agreed upon, and then carried out by each of those parties at the table: the president announces it, the government as a whole oversees and carries it out, and American citizens in the media, military and business, interest groups, and voters participate in its implementation. Foreign policies in other countries are therefore also different; while Canada and Mexico are both democracies, each has different national interests and political systems with its power distributed differently than in the U.S. Therefore, their "board room meetings" and the foreign policies that result are not the same as those of the United States. While this chapter explores only the U.S. foreign policy making process, it is important for students to understand that each country has a unique way of making such policies, and part of the U.S. foreign policy process is to understand and respond to other countries' policies in their own foreign policy.

Why is it important?

Foreign policy is important because it has an impact on the ability of the United States to provide for its citizens. Businesses care about foreign policy because they want to sell their products abroad. Ordinary people wish to remain safe from outside threats, such as terrorism and disease, and all Americans wish to buy foreign goods, such as cars from Germany and TVs from Japan. Americans need to be able to buy gasoline to power their cars, and the U.S. government wants to maintain good relations with each of these countries so that each of these goals (and many others) can be achieved for the benefit of all. Lastly, U.S. foreign policy is important because each American citizen has an impact on how policy is made and carried out. While it appears that foreign policy is made solely by the government, this chapter will show that this is not nearly the truth; all Americans participate in the making and implementation of foreign policy.

Basic elements

U.S. foreign policy is the result of bargaining and cooperation regarding a particular issue or need in the United States. But whether that issue is oil, trade, or nuclear weapons, its components are more basic: **power**, **wealth**, and common **values**. The capabilities of a particular country determine what kind of foreign policy it can develop; a poor country with few resources or people, a weak economy, or small military finds it more difficult to develop a foreign policy similar to a country that possesses each of these qualities in abundance (Rourke, 2007).

As Americans, we are extremely fortunate to have many natural resources, a large middle class, well-educated citizens, an open and democratic society, and a strong degree of national pride. In fact, the United States has among the largest economies in the world at 14.1 trillion as of 2009 (CIA World Factbook), a large and powerful military at 1.425 million active duty personnel as of May 2010 (Department of Defense), and a set of national ideals and beliefs that guide our actions both at home and abroad. These characteristics separate the U.S. from its neighbors, Canada and Mexico, and become the basic elements for any foreign policy that is made and carried out by our society.

Who Makes U.S. Foreign Policy?

The President and Executive Branch

The president is the undisputed leader in U.S. foreign policy. Article II of the Constitution grants the president the powers of commander-in-chief, chief diplomat, chief administrator, chief of state, chief legislator, chief judicial officer, and voice of the people. These powers establish a constitutional basis for the president to lead in overseas matters such as fighting wars, negotiating treaties, trade agreements, and diplomatic relations. Presidents are the leaders in making foreign policy in the U.S. and the official representatives of America overseas.

In addition to a legal basis, the president also derives a great deal of this power from his professional prestige and ability to persuade others to his line of thinking. The president is only one individual, but he has the most power and influence of any member of the U.S. government, and the entire country will listen to him if he chooses to exercise those powers. By using his standing as the most recognized and influential American, the president's "bully pulpit" enables extensive influence over the nation. Foreign policy is often made during times of crisis such as war or natural disaster, and it is at these times where presidential power is at its maximum as everyone looks to their top elected official for leadership in trying times.

It is during situations of crisis that the Executive Branch has greatly expanded in the 20th century to grant the president additional powers in foreign policy making (Yergin). Because of U.S. involvement in two World Wars and the Cold War, and advancements in communications technology, weaponry, and globalization, the Executive Branch has developed additional organizations to aid the president in these tasks. The National Security Act of 1947 created the Central Intelligence Agency and led to the development of an additional fifteen intelligence agencies under the leadership of the president. The act also created the National Security Council, a cabinet of executives including the Secretaries of State, Defense, Homeland Security, and the Chairman of the Joint Chiefs of Staff (the top military officer), all of which work hand-in-hand with the President in making and carrying out foreign policy decisions (Rothkopf). It is at these boardroom meetings where the tough decisions are made during times of crisis. For example, in the lead-up to the Iraq War (2003), President Bush worked very closely with Secretary of Defense Donald Rumsfeld, Vice President Dick Cheney, and National Security Advisor Condoleezza Rice in formulating the decision to invade based upon U.S. foreign policy interests. During the Cuban Missile Crisis (1961), President John F. Kennedy spent two tense weeks in constant consultation with Secretary of State Dean Rusk, Secretary of Defense Robert McNamara, National Security Advisor McGeorge Bundy, and Attorney General Robert Kennedy regarding the proper way to handle the crisis (Allison and Zelikow). Each of these presidents relied on the powers of the Executive Branch and the organizations created by the Act of 1947 to analyze, debate, and develop U.S. foreign policy regarding the crisis at hand. In response to each and every crisis the current administration convenes a set of people, holds debates and negotiations, and eventually arrives at U.S. foreign policy decisions based upon the winning arguments (Woodward). Each crisis in U.S. history is a unique study in foreign policy making, the organizations of the Executive Branch, and the personalities and arguments involved in handling the crisis (Elovitz).

The Bureaucracy

Decision making is a crucial part of the U.S. foreign policy process, but implementation by the bureaucracy actually applies the presidential decision to the world. Without them, foreign policies remain words on presidential letterhead. Each senior American leader heads a specific body of the U.S. government, and whether it is the Department of Defense, State Department, Treasury, FBI, or Homeland Security, each has a bureaucratic staff which is in charge of carrying out the policies.

The implementation of leadership decisions sounds simple, but the reality is far from it (Allison and Zelikow, 143). The bureaucracy is immense, complex, and comprised of different organizations with their own work cultures and individuals with their own career goals. A fitting example of these difficulties is the lack of cooperation between the FBI and CIA prior to the attacks of September 11, 2001. The entire intelligence community had produced a great deal of information regarding possible attacks by Al-Qaeda and Osama bin Laden, but these two lead organizations failed to cooperate, share information, anticipate the attacks, and notify senior American leadership in advance. Their effectiveness in protecting the homeland was significantly reduced by the competition between the FBI and CIA, a competition based upon different interests, goals, and ways of operation. This failure was widely seen as the reason the attacks could not be stopped in advance and resulted in a full scale congressional investigation that culminated in the "9/11 Report: The National Commission on Terrorist Attacks upon the United States" (Kean and Hamilton). Bureaucracy consists of many layers necessary to carry out U.S. foreign policy decisions, but also provides the opportunity to modify or even change the original presidential decisions, and in the aftermath of 9/11, the U.S. foreign policy process changed significantly to better serve American interests.

Congress

It is true that in the 20th century, the power to make U.S. foreign policy was increasingly transferred into the hands of the President and Executive Branch. This does not mean, however, that the other institutions of government do not retain some power in the policy making process. Congress remains influential in the making of U.S. foreign policy because it retains the power of oversight and the power of the purse. These powers enable the House of Representatives to regulate foreign policy decisions by controlling the funding necessary to implement them. Whether sending troops or diplomatic missions overseas, funding projects, or granting aid, the House controls the purse strings and directly approves or disapproves of U.S. foreign policy made by the Executive Branch.

Oversight by Congress is another of its powers in U.S. foreign policy making, taking many forms including the aforementioned 9/11 Report. Article II of the Constitution gives Congress the right of oversight, a duty to investigate actions of the Executive Branch when they are seen to be contrary to the interests of the American public. As a result of the Vietnam War, the War Powers Resolution of 1973 placed a series of reporting limitations on actions of the president overseas, requiring him to report back to Congress every 90 days to receive authorization for a further dispersal of funds and political permission to continue its activities overseas. Congress can also investigate any action of the government, and it is during such hearings that attention to foreign policy decisions of the Executive Branch is subjected to public scrutiny and often changed.

Interest Groups, the Media, and Public Opinion
The American public also has a crucial role to play in U.S. foreign policy making as the national barometer for presidential decisions and the focal point for interest groups and the media to draw attention to the leaders in Washington, D.C. Congress and the public, media, and interest groups have an almost symbiotic relationship in that congressional leaders cannot get elected without constituents (voters), and the two groups cannot communicate without a third party, the media. *While Dangers Gather: Congressional Checks on Presidential War Powers* discusses the two-way relationship of the media and Congress and the effectiveness of each actor to influence foreign policy (Howell and Pevehouse).

Public media outlets, talk radio, and network and cable news programs are also influential in communicating U.S. foreign policy to the public at large. In today's world, Americans receive their news from countless online and written sources, and this information comes with every conceivable opinion and bias. From conservative to liberal, anti-war to pro-business, news media and interest groups seek to inform ordinary citizens using their own unique take on the issue and to motivate them to support or oppose the government policy. From voting, picketing, and protesting to letter-writing campaigns and petitions, Americans have a direct impact on the making of U.S. foreign policy and the ways the government implements them.

Traditional foreign policy themes / issues

American foreign policy has at its core four themes which influence how decisions are made and which issues are considered most important. These themes have developed since the founding of our country and continue to influence how and when American policy makers make choices. The four themes are: **security**, **trade/economic growth**, **morality/American exceptionalism**, and **isolationism versus internationalism**. What makes these four themes unique is that they can at times be contradictory and create difficult decisions for leaders as to how the United States should act in any particular situation.

Security through either Global Isolationism or Internationalism

Security is, first and foremost, the theme that underlies American foreign policy. A primary goal of every administration is to ensure the physical security of the American state, and this can be seen by examining important documents like the U.S. Constitution, Monroe Doctrine, and Gettysburg Address, which show that at every point in our history, there is a focus on security of the state (Greathouse and Miner 2008). An early approach to ensuring the security of the state was to remain outside of the alliance system of Europe – a policy called isolationism – which regularly drew states into conflict. George Washington in his farewell address argued "it is our true policy to steer clear of permanent alliances with any portion of the foreign world" (http://avalon.law.yale.edu/18th_century/washing. asp). According to Washington, the U.S. needed to maintain a defensive posture and only become linked to others in extraordinary circumstances. The Monroe Doctrine continued to advocate that an intentionally separate America would remain safe and secure outside of the wars of the Europeans. The Senate's rejection of the treaty bringing the U.S. into the League of Nations after World War I can be seen as a continuation of that policy. This approach of ensuring the security of the U.S. by remaining outside of European alliances carried through the end of World War II.

With the end of World War II, the need for security brought America fully into the international system by participating in the United Nations (UN) and the North Atlantic Treaty Organization (NATO). Given the technology of the time and the need to limit the expansion of the Soviet Union, remaining outside of permanent alliances was no longer a viable option to ensure American security. The United States had changed its approach from isolationism to internationalism, a conscious effort to achieve security through international cooperation. By joining NATO and engaging in the strategy of containment during the Cold War period, U.S. foreign policy adopted an outward and international stance to ensure that neither its physical safety nor that of its allies would be threatened by the Soviet Union.

One element built into this theme is the willingness of America to use force to achieve the goal of security (Dunn 2003 p. 286), and a key change after World War II is the conscious choice to employ that force abroad. During the Cold War, containment was the American foreign policy used to keep the Soviet Union and its allies limited to the areas of influence they gained at the end of World War II, and not to allow them to control or influence other states in the system. The changes in the international system forced the U.S. to be proactive as the physical barriers which had previously protected it from overseas threats were lessened. No longer could distance and water ensure American security, thanks to the development of airplanes and missiles. The attempts to contain the Soviet Union and its communist allies during the Cold War, forced the U.S. to take action in Korea, Vietnam, Nicaragua, Greece, Germany, and numerous other places around the globe to protect its security.

Inevitably, this internationalist U.S. foreign policy would have some negative consequences which would increase the public desire to retreat again to isolationism. The reaction to American casualties during the 1965-75 Vietnam War, the deaths of 242 Marines during a 1983 peace-keeping mission in Lebanon, and 18 American soldiers during 1994 deployments into Somalia resulted in significant pressure to bring most troops home and limit American military and political actions to a very clearly defined area of influence in the Western Hemisphere. The end of the Cold War saw the resurgence of a significant element within the United States that believes that the U.S. should withdraw from the world to protect itself from outside influences. Whether this approach is viable or practical within the scope of a globalizing world is questionable but the tradition of isolationism will continue to influence how and when America acts.

With the fall of the Berlin Wall in 1989, the Gulf War in 1990, and the break-up of the Soviet Union in late 1991, the U.S. was again forced to reconsider what it meant to be secure. As the sole remaining **superpower**, it faced widespread local and regional conflict brought on by the end of the contest between Americans and Russians in the Cold War. The countries of the world were free of the threat of nuclear annihilation which hung over them during the Cold War, and were exercising that freedom by fighting for their own rights. Civil wars and international conflicts proliferated worldwide, creating an entirely new security environment from that of the Cold War.

The Gulf War saw the first large-scale U.S. military involvement in the Middle East, an action which was as much to retain access to oil as to restore the sovereignty of Kuwait. In addition to the Persian Gulf, conflicts in the former Yugoslavia, and between Israel and Palestine indicated a return to an internationalist foreign policy in which the United States focused on cooperative action abroad to protect not only the physical but the economic security of the country and its allies. The attacks on 9/11 reinforced this internationalist foreign policy. For the first, time significant damage was done to the U.S. by an outside terrorist organization, which resulted in deployment of American troops into Afghanistan and Iraq in the early 2000s under the banner of preventing future terror attacks on the U.S. (Afghanistan) and to prevent weapons of mass destruction (WMDs) from being directed towards the U.S. (Iraq).

While security is most definitely a constant theme in U.S. foreign policy, the means by which it is achieved varies and is often contradictory. The isolationist streak in U.S. foreign policy routinely comes into conflict with international crises which push the United States into the international system (Papp Johnson and Endicott 2005). For most of its history, the U.S. has tried to segregate itself from linkages and interactions from those outside of the Western Hemisphere. Up to the attack on Pearl Harbor, there was an extremely strong sentiment towards isolationism within the country, and remnants of those feelings and policies still exist today. When the U.S. considers its relations with other states and decisions about possible actions in the international system, it always includes security concerns within its dealings, but a cyclical conflict continues to rise as to how to best accomplish this goal.

Trade/Economics

From its earliest history, the welfare and prosperity of the United States has been based on economic growth and trade with other countries. There is an underlying assumption that by trading with other countries, the U.S. will benefit and the productivity of the country and the wealth of its citizens will increase. The creation of the American colonies was driven by economic growth concerns, and many of the underlying reasons leading to the American Revolution were based on economic concerns. Once free of British economic control, the importance of trade and economic growth has continually been considered by American leaders.

From the beginning, American presidents have acted to ensure that U.S. businesses would have access to markets to help promote growth in the American economy. Thomas Jefferson's decision to deploy ships from the American Navy to address piracy in the Mediterranean and the consideration of conscripting American sailors into the British navy (which was one of the issues leading to the War of 1812) are examples of American foreign policy actions to protect trade and commerce. American actions to expand the country westward and wars fought against Native American tribes were based on the potential economic returns of growing American territory. The Monroe Doctrine, Mexican American War of 1846-1848, and Spanish American War of 1898 were all fought in part to keep Europeans out of the Western Hemisphere and to protect and control economic development within the region. Similarly, the entrance of the United States into World War I was in part because of threats to American trade by German U-boats.

Following World War II, the government focused on building strong economic linkages between countries to prevent a future economic collapse of the level of the Great Depression and future conflict between trading partners. American foreign policy leaders assumed that states who engaged in trade would not fight each other, so if Germany and Japan could be quickly rebuilt economically and linked to the world economic system of trade, the chances of a future conflict would diminish. Underlying this idea was the thought that the U.S. would dominate world trade. With the fall of the Communist Bloc between 1989 and 1991, the focus on economic growth became even more pronounced. States which previously had not been part of the capitalist trading block were now open to trade which would in turn lessen the chances of war.

Modern foreign policy continues to show the importance of protecting American economic interests. The Gulf War in 1990/91 was driven (at least in part) by concerns over an Iraqi threat to oil supplies, and its possible impact on economic growth. Current U.S. relations with China are driven by the economic interests; the American government does not want to limit access of American goods to the Chinese markets due to the potential for economic growth in the U.S. that China provides. In sum, American policymakers cannot take action within the system without considering the impact on economics. The demand for expanding the economy and creation of more wealth forces policy makers to allow other issues to fall away if the economic returns are high enough.

Morality/American Exceptionalism

Americans have always viewed their country as special (Talbott, 2003; Papp, Johnson, and Endicott 2005). While this idea is not unique within the international system, the level of belief that the American way of life is superior has and continues to influence how the U.S. acts within the system. It has resulted in an American foreign policy pressing other actors to abide by American morals and follow American leadership due to its exceptional nature.

An early manifestation of this idea was the concept of Manifest Destiny, that America was rightly entitled to the stretch from the Atlantic all the way to the Pacific and to introduce its way of life and system of government. This attitude is seen in how America deals with countries in Latin America such as Mexico, Panama, Colombia, and Venezuela, pushing those countries to adopt political and economic systems which are similar to ours. From the administration of Theodore Roosevelt to the 14 Points of Woodrow Wilson, American exceptionalism has advocated that other states adopt democracy and American style economic structures and frequently acted as the "world's policeman." It pushed states to adopt an American political and economic model following World War II to prevent the threat of communism. Official American Cold War strategy, as advocated by National Security Council Report 68 (NSC-68), argued that the U.S. and its values represented freedom and growth while Communism, as represented by the U.S.S.R., represented slavery and a lack of societal progress.

Since the creation of the United States, its foreign policy has continually cited security and the defense of values and ideals as the basis for action in the international system. Both a retreat from international politics manifested as isolationism and the internationalist deployment of peace keepers in Lebanon, the former Yugoslavia, and Somalia were all justified by references to domestic security and values of the nation. These themes can be seen in U.S. involvement abroad, from the failure to ratify the League of Nations and the reluctance to enter both World Wars, to efforts at containment of the Soviet Union in Korea, Vietnam, Latin America, Eastern Europe, and the current conflicts in the Middle East. American foreign policy is based on recurrent themes developed as the country grew. In the case study following, we will discuss an example of how these themes work in more detail: the Iraq War. It is intended to provide the student with a real world application of the themes presented thus far in this chapter.

Case Study—Iraq

History

The 2003 decision to invade Iraq is one of the most complex and hotly debated foreign policy decisions undertaken by the United States in its history. The outcome of this decision was to launch a preventative war (attacking another country before it can attack you) while at the same time fighting against Al-Qaeda and the Taliban in Afghanistan. Underlying the decision to invade Iraq was 13 years of history leading back to the Gulf War (1990/91). The decision to invade Iraq, like all foreign policy decisions, was not made in a vacuum; the history of the situation and the current domestic and international political environments created the context in which the American government had to operate. In this case study, we apply the ideas and themes of this chapter to the Iraq crisis in order to better illustrate how U.S. foreign policy decisions are made and implemented.

Before we look specifically at the decisions leading up to the 2003 war with Iraq it is necessary to look back to the history which helped shape the issues and decisions faced by President George W. Bush almost 15 years later. In 1990, the military of Iraq under Saddam Hussein invaded the country of Kuwait and quickly conquered it. The Iraqis claimed that Kuwait had been drilling into its oil reserves, and that Kuwait was actually a province of Iraq. The actions of Saddam Hussein were quickly met by President George H. W. Bush (the father of George W. Bush) deploying American troops to protect Saudi Arabia and demanding the removal of Iraqi forces from Kuwait. The elder President Bush created a significant coalition, pulling together forces from Europe as well as other states in the Middle East, including Egypt, Syria, and Saudi Arabia. Once the decision to use force was approved by United Nations Security Council (through Resolution 678), American forces and their allies engaged in a destructive air campaign, followed by a 100 hour ground war to remove Iraqi troops from Kuwait.

As a result of the aggressive actions taken by Iraq and Saddam Hussein, a number of sanctions were put into place. Two no-fly zones (forbidding Iraqi military aircraft to operate inside) were established in the northern and southern part of the country to protect minority populations and stop continuing violence against them by the Hussein regime. There were restrictions on the amount of oil that Iraq could sell on the world market, and Iraq was ordered to allow United Nations (U.N.) inspectors into the country to monitor and destroy its attempts to create nuclear and chemical weapons. These sanctions, among others, were applied to Iraq to force Saddam Hussein to comply with the mandates of the United Nations and the common views of the international community. At times during this period, American airstrikes were undertaken in limited amounts to punish the Iraqi government for non-compliance. Saddam Hussein finally expelled the U.N. weapons inspectors, which created significant tension between the U.S. / U.N. and Iraq and even caused the Iraqis to sponsor an attempt to assassinate President George H.W. Bush while on a visit to Saudi Arabia.

These events had an important influence on the decision making process and the foreign policy authorizing the invasion of Iraq in 2003. By examining the formation and development of this U.S. foreign policy, the reader should better understand the reasons behind the policy, as well as the actors who wrote and implemented it. An analysis of this crisis also helps highlight the themes and concerns inherent in every U.S. foreign policy decision since the founding of our nation more than 200 years ago.

The President and the Executive Branch

The final decision for the invasion of Iraq fell to President Bush, as with all significant foreign policy decisions. His choice, based on discussions with his primary advisors in the Executive Branch and information from the bureaucracy and intelligence community, began to turn the country towards war during 2002. The major theme developed by President Bush and presented to the American public was that the actions of Iraq to build and develop weapons of mass destruction were a direct threat to American security.

President Bush engaged in several major addresses and released the 2002 National Security Strategy (NSS), all of which advocated an internationalist American response towards threats to the U.S., such as Iraq. In his State of the Union speech in 2002, the president clearly identified Iraq as part of an "Axis of Evil" (which also included Iran and North Korea) that threatened the U.S. with its efforts to develop weapons of mass destruction in clear violation of United Nations Security Council resolutions and international public opinion dating back twenty years. The National Security Strategy clearly highlighted the need to make America secure and to take action when potential threats began to emerge rather than wait until they are imminent.

All of these events took place during a climate in which security concerns, a primary theme in U.S. foreign policy, were at unprecedented levels and on the mind of every American after the attacks of September 11, 2001. The Bush Doctrine, as this position became known, was clearly only possible because of the resonance of the theme of security after 9/11 and the near 80% public approval ratings (BBC Bush approval ratings http://news.bbc.co.uk/2/hi/6038436.stm) the president enjoyed at the time.

The Executive Branch worked in concert with the wishes of the president and enhanced his ability to establish the Bush Doctrine as the U.S. foreign policy towards Iraq. However, this process was not easy, as there were two major approaches competing for supremacy as the foreign policy towards Iraq. Vice President Cheney, and others including Secretary of Defense Rumsfeld and Paul Wolfowitz, advocated the use of military force to deal with Iraq, while Secretary of State Colin Powell preferred a more nuanced, diplomatic approach (Smith, 2008). These differences between significant members of the administration provided alternatives to the president and allowed him to choose between them.

Secretary of State Powell's position was based on more traditional approaches to foreign policy, where every diplomatic option is explored before force is used. If force was to be used, Powell believed a strong coalition, similar to what was done during the Gulf War in 1990, was necessary to generate overwhelming force to win the war quickly and decisively, while simultaneously planning for an exit from the conflict. The competing vision was advocated by a group known as the neo-conservatives (neocons), who believed that the U.S. needed to act for issues related to national security that was strongly tied to the theme of American exceptionalism and moral superiority. The advocates of this position argued that removing Saddam Hussein from power and replacing the Iraqi government with a democracy which would be friendly to the U.S would yield a more stable region. Vice President Cheney famously stated in a March 2003 interview on *Meet the Press* that "we will in fact be greeted as liberators," much as American troops were received in Europe during World War II.

The debate between the top advisors to the president was widely reported in the media and showed fissures in the Bush White House, as the cautious, thorough diplomatic position of Powell was rejected in favor of a military option action as supported by the neocon position advocated by Cheney, Rumsfeld, and Wolfowitz. The choice to launch the war in early 2003 created diplomatic problems, as several of America's traditional allies, including France and Germany, opposed the American action along with Russia and China. This opposition among three of the five permanent members of the U.N. Security Council prevented a U.N. resolution directly allowing the use of force to remove Saddam Hussein. The idea of American exceptionalism may have clouded the vision of some of the senior leadership in regards to the aftermath of the actual invasion, but the choice to go to war and spread American values was in compliance with a number of traditional American foreign policy themes and was accepted by the public.

The Bureaucracy

One of the most contentious issues when examining the decision to invade Iraq in 2003 is the role of the bureaucracy in providing information and preparing for the action. From the intelligence that was developed by the CIA and other intelligence agencies to the development of plans to invade Iraq and the preparation of post-war reconstruction plans, the foreign policy bureaucracy was intimately linked to the crisis. The two main agencies which focused on the proposed action against Iraq were the Departments of State and Defense, two preeminent actors in foreign policy. The Department of State controls the day-to-day diplomatic relations for the U.S., while the Department of Defense controls its military forces.

The Department of Defense was given the lead by the Bush Administration in shaping the actions toward Iraq. The fact that Defense was given the lead occurred for several very practical reasons: first, the initial stages of the actions towards Iraq would be based on military action, and second, the size of the Defense Department and the resources it had at its disposal and the number of people, both soldiers and support elements, dwarfed the capacity of the State Department. In addition, the Department of Defense was led by Donald Rumsfeld (with Paul Wolfowitz holding a major position as well); this leadership and oversight by two individuals who strongly supported the choice of invasion would ensure that President Bush's vision would be followed. The State Department would provide support to the military in terms of Foreign Service Officers and aid but the number of personnel that State could send to Iraq was limited, both due to the military nature of the foreign policy and the fact that the position of their leader, Colin Powell, had been rejected in the Executive Branch negotiations.

While the Department of Defense position was adopted, and it was given the lead in implementing the foreign policy, there was still internal disagreement within the agency as to how the U.S. military would actually fight the war. The debate between Secretary of Defense Donald Rumsfeld and many then-current generals and defense experts was over the makeup of the forces and the number necessary to achieve the foreign policy goals of President Bush. Rumsfeld believed that a smaller force could be used to quickly win the combat, while others argued that significantly more forces would be required to address the initial invasion and aftermath, a number similar to the 500,000 personnel used during the first Gulf War. In the end, Rumsfeld's policy won out and was the method of implementing the Bush foreign policy.

While there has been significant criticism that limited planning for the aftermath of the war with Iraq was undertaken, in fact, most bureaucratic agencies developed a plan to deal with the Iraq after the primary combat ended. "It is not the case that no one planned for post-Saddam Iraq. On the contrary, many agencies and organizations within the U.S. government identified a range of possible postwar challenges in 2002 and early 2003, before major combat commenced, and suggested strategies for addressing them. Some of these ideas seem quite prescient in retrospect, yet few if any made it into the serious planning process" (Bensahel, 2008 p. xvii). Elements within the Departments of Defense and State, among others, produced plans to address postwar Iraq, but issues and beliefs within the Executive Branch and within the White House provided no opportunity to push these ideas forward. A final limitation placed on post war planning was the limited role that the State Department had in the process (Bensahel et al. 2008) as it had been sidelined by its failure to influence the American course of action. These factors would come together to negate and almost reverse the impressive and decisive military victory at the outset of the conflict.

The Public

Public opinion and reaction to the possible invasion fluctuated between the 9/11 attacks and the start of the Iraq War. In a report issued by the American Enterprise Institute in 2007 (http://www.aei.org/docLib/20050805_IRAQ0805.pdf), multiple American public opinion polls showed that more than 60% of the American public favored military action toward Iraq. Another element which helped to maintain a strong level of support for the Bush Administration was the issue of Weapons of Mass Destruction (WMD). The given reason for invading Iraq was predicated on preventing Iraq from threatening the U.S. with WMDs. Four times between 9/11 and the start of the war in Iraq, a CBS poll asked if people believed that Iraq had weapons of mass destruction. The lowest reported belief that Iraq did have WMDs was 77% in September 2002 (AEI report 2007 p. 109). This high level of belief that Iraq possessed weapons of mass destruction supported the administration's argument that a state with WMDs was a threat to American security and needed to be stopped. The overall public level of support that the American population manifested for President Bush's positions allowed his administration to act with the full support of the American people in the early stages of the war.

In Conclusion

All foreign policy actions and decisions are affected by the amount of information that the state has about a given issue. The more informed U.S. foreign policy leaders are the better the decisions they make; unfortunately, a post-war examination of the decision to invade Iraq reveals a lack of clear intelligence. While strategic intelligence as to Iraqi military capability in a war against the United States was accurate, more detailed information about Iraq's possession of nuclear, chemical, and biological weapons were significantly less accurate, while the assessment of Iraq's ability to easily transition to democracy was overly optimistic at best (Byman 2008, p. 616-617). If clearer intelligence had been provided on the issue of WMDs, would this have changed the arguments and foreign policy made by the Bush administration? If a better understanding of Iraq was presented to policy makers prior to the war, would things have been done differently once the war was finished? While these questions can be debated in hindsight, the limits of understanding at the time of decision making are clearly visible. Policy makers are beholden to the quality of information brought to them; if that information is limited or flawed, it will impact the quality of the foreign policy decisions they make and the ways they choose to implement them.

A Civic Engagement Challenge—Becoming Involved in Foreign Policy Decisions

Two of the basic goals of this chapter are to de-mystify the U.S. foreign policy making process and to show that the ordinary American citizen has a real place in influencing how decisions are made and implemented. Students sometimes do not realize the impact they can have on a given issue of importance to them, especially so if that issue is international and seems both complicated and remote from any power they might have. Now that the reader has a better idea of how they fit into this process and who has the most influence, they can assert themselves into foreign-policy making in a number of ways.

"All politics is local" as the saying goes, and support or opposition for any U.S. foreign policy begins in a local arena, such as your university or local community. The civic engagement challenge for this chapter is for students to get involved with a local campaign to support or oppose an issue of U.S. foreign policy. This involvement can be from within a university-sponsored club or organization that promotes awareness or action, with a purposeful vote for a local or national candidate that supports your position, a protest, petition drive, phone call, or letter to your local representative. While students cannot right now hope to have the power to make U.S. foreign policy decisions, they most definitely can influence how those issues are perceived by their peers in the local community. So, recognize what international issue stirs a passion inside you, and get involved!

Discussion Questions:
1. What is a foreign policy and why is it important that each country has one?
2. Who are the primary actors in U.S. foreign policy?
3. What themes matter when discussing the content of American foreign policy?

4. The U.S. president is considered by most to be the dominant actor within the foreign policy process, but other actors have significant power to influence how policy is made. Who are these actors and how can they influence this process?

5. Given the events following 9/11 (including terrorism and wars in Afghanistan and Iraq), is foreign policy going to become easier or more difficult for the country to make?

References

Allison, G. & Zelikow, P. (1999). *Essence of decision: Explaining the Cuban missile crisis.* New York, NY: Longman.

American Enterprise Institute. 2007. AEI Public Opinion Studies: "Public Opinion and the War with Iraq" at http://www.aei.org/ docLib/20050805_IRAQ0805.pdf. Last Accessed July 21, 2010.

BBC. Bush approval ratings at http://news.bbc.co.uk/2/hi/6038436.stm Last Accessed July 21, 2010.

Bensahel, Nora. Olga Oliker. Keith Crane. Richard R. Brennan, Jr. Heather S. Gregg. Thomas Sullivan. and Andrew Rathmell. 2008. After Iraq: Prewar Planning and the Occupation of Iraq. Santa Monica, CA: Rand.

Byman, Daniel. 2008. An Autopsy of the Iraq Debacle: Policy Failure or Bridge Too Far? *Security Studies*: 17: 599-643.

Cable News Network. (2011). CNN. Retrieved from http://www.cnn.com/.

Central Intelligence Agency. (2011). CIA. Retrieved from https://www. cia.gov/index.html.

Department of Defense. (2011). U.S. Department of Defense. Retrieved from http://www.defense.gov/.

Dunn, D. H. 2003. Myths, Motivations, and 'Misunderestimations': The Bush Administration and Iraq. *International Affairs*: 79(5): 279-297.

Elovitz, P. H. (2008). Presidential responses to national trauma: Case studies of G. W. Bush, Carter, and Nixon. *Journal of Psychohistory,* 36(1), 36-58.

Greathouse, C. B. & Miner, J. S. (2010). *The U.S. and EU: Will competing strategic cultures enable future security cooperation?* [Unpublished manuscript].

Greathouse, C. B. & Miner, J. S. (2008). *American strategic culture and its role in the 2002 and 2006 versions of the national security strategy.* Retrieved from http://a-s.clayton.edu/ trachtenberg/2008%20Proceedings%20Greathouse-Miner%20 Submission%20PDF.pdf

Howell, W. G. & Pevehouse, J. C. *While dangers gather: Congressional checks on presidential war powers.* Princeton, NJ: Princeton University Press.

Kean, T. H., Chair, & Hamilton, L. H., Vice Chair. (2004). *The 9/11 report: The national commission on terrorist attacks upon the United States.* New York, NY: St. Martin's Press.

National Security Strategy of the United States. 2002.

Papp, Daniel S. Loch K. Johnson. John E. Endicott. 2005. American Foreign Policy: History, Politics, and Policy. New York, NY: Pearson Longman.

Rothkopf, D. J. (2005). *Running the world: The inside story of the National Security Council and the architects of american power.* New York, NY: Public Affairs.

Rosati, J. A. & Scott, J. M. (2010). *The politics of United States foreign policy*. Belmont, CA: Thomson Wadsworth.

Rourke, J. T. (2007). *International politics on the world stage.* New York, NY: McGraw Hill.

Shapiro, R. Y., Kumar, M. J., & Jacobs, L. R. (Eds.). (2000). *Presidential power: Forging the presidency for the twenty-first Century.* New York, NY: Columbia University Press.

Smith, M. A. 2008. U.S. bureaucratic politics and the decision to invade Iraq. Contemporary Politics: 14(1): 91-105.

Talbott, S. 2003. War in Iraq, Revolution in America. *International Affairs*: 79(5): 1037-1044.

Vice President Richard Cheney, *Meet the Press.* March 16, 2003

Woodward, B. (2008). *The war within.* New York, NY: Simon & Schuster.

Yergin, D. (1978). *Shattered peace: The origins of the cold war and the national security state.* Boston, MA: Houghton Mifflin.

Chapter Fifteen
Civic Engagement
Maria J. Albo

Learning Objectives
After covering the topic of civic engagement students should understand:

1. The role of political participation and public opinion on public policy outcomes.
2. The various ways individuals can participate in the political process.
3. The resources available for becoming an engaged citizen.
4. The influence of the Internet on civic engagement on the Millennial generation.

Abstract
This chapter will identify and explain how various forms of political participation influence government policy and facilitate an engaged citizenry. By offering comparisons of "engaged" v. "duty-based" citizenship, students will be guided through the process of political engagement from voting through contacting elected officials, and other examples of grassroots democracy. Finally, the link between the Internet and engaged citizenship for the Millennial generation will be discussed.

Introduction
In the United States as a representative democracy, our society expects and depends on citizen participation. We entered the 21st century more politically equal than ever before whereby virtually all United States citizens are entitled to vote and exercise their stake in society. However, researchers like Robert Putnam have argued that we are experiencing a serious decline in citizen participation. Putnam argues in his work, *Bowling Alone*, that Americans are suffering from a lack of **social capital,** which Putman defines as "connections among individuals –social networks and the norms of reciprocity and trustworthiness that arise from them" (Putnam, 2000, 19). Putnam asserts that declining social capital has resulted in the average American withdrawing from the political process. Because a democracy gets its power from the people, when individuals do not engage politically, it allows for politicians and special interests to

pursue their own agenda. Political participation is the only way to keep government accountable!

It has long been part of the American landscape to actively engage in civic affairs as the nature of direct democracy depends on citizen participation. As discussed in Chapter 4, schools traditionally have focused on the institutions of government and the importance of voting but overall civic education is lacking in schools. According to researchers Frischler and Smith, civic education in the United States is "merely knowledge of the institutional features of government: the function of local, state and national governments; the role of the legislative, executive and judicial branches; voting requirements, etc" (Fritschler & Smith, 2009, 8). While this understanding of the nuts and bolts of government is certainly important, it does not focus on how everyday people can influence their government. Much citizen involvement in political life happens on a local level and is a result of ongoing community involvement that truly impacts the political system and ultimately public policy.

Public Opinion and Public Policy

As previously discussed, when it is strong and clearly expressed, public opinion can influence public policy as national opinion tends to be very responsive to the public's demand for action.

While overall individuals have limited direct control over public policy, we entrust elected officials to carry out the "will of the people," which ideally refrains legislatures from making truly unpopular decisions. Consider the role of citizen participation in getting a local issue on the public policy agenda. Mothers Against Drunk Drivers (MADD) was founded in 1980 as a response to the death of thirteen-year-old Cari Lightner, who was killed by a serial drunk driver in Sacramento, California. Cari's mother, Candy Lightner, determined to avenge her daughter's death, began a national movement that would forever change the perceptions of drunk driving in the United States. At the time local attitudes viewed drunk driving as a trivial offence, and drunk drivers in popular culture were often depicted as comical rather than dangerous. MADD sought to change these perceptions and hold accountable individuals who choose to drive while intoxicated. MADD's effectiveness on public policy could not have been clearer. Within five years, hundreds of MADD chapters had been established nationwide (Graham, 2010, 123). MADD's advocates fought tirelessly with decision makers in Washington to reform drunk driving laws including raising the drinking age and instituting mandatory sentences for repeat offenders. These changes to public policy eventually swayed public opinion and criminalized drunk driving.

Influencing Public Opinion

A substantial factor in MADD's success was the group's ability to establish a network of citizens with a common purpose (to stop drunk driving). They expanded that network to include groups all across the country which were able to lobby in numbers and influence policy. Secondly, MADD members took the initiative to contact officials on their behalf and lobby for policy changes. MADD did not sit back and complain about drunken driving laws, nor did they simply go to the polls and vote for the candidate who promised to reform existing laws. Rather, as a group MADD initiated letter-writing campaigns, met with local and national officials, engaged in group protest when needed, and most importantly developed a network of likeminded citizens committed to a coming cause. It is this type of grassroots American effort that demonstrates the biggest influence individuals can exert over public policy.

Senator Bob Graham's book, *America: The Owner's Manual,* offers an insider's view on how to effectively participate in the political process. Senator Graham identifies the biggest obstacle in democratic participation as the perception that the average American has little influence in the democratic process. Many Americans believe that political influence is limited to the elite and special interest groups that seem to dominate the political landscape. Americans tend to suffer from low **political efficacy**, the idea that their participation in the political process can influence outcomes. Remember, when political efficacy is high, individuals are likely to engage in political matters while when efficacy is low, citizens refrain from political participation. In reality, many of our proudest political movements began with ordinary citizens bringing attention to issues, influencing their decision makers and ultimately influencing public policy.

Political Participation

There are various ways to become involved in the political process. Political participation can include voting, working on or contributing to a political campaign, writing letters to local government officials, or joining local civic groups committed to social and/or political causes. Researchers Sidney Verba and Norman Nie recognized there are numerous ways individuals take part in political matters and identified six categories of political participation along with an overview of individual characteristics typical of each group:

Inactives	Virtually never vote and are not involved in political matters.	Inactives are typically minorities, women, the young, and individuals with low socioeconomic status.
Voting Specialists	Vote regularly but have little participation in other aspects of political life.	Voting specialists are generally older and have strong ties to a political party.
Parochial Participants	Do not typically vote or engage in political matters but may seek government intervention on a specific issue. Generally highly involved in local community matters.	Parochial Participants tend to be minorities and citizens of low socioeconomic status.
Communalists	Do not vote regularly but are highly engaged in group and community activities aimed at solving social problems.	Communalists are usually of high socioeconomic status, white, Protestant, and well educated.
Campaigners	Vote regularly and are highly engaged in campaign activity. Highly partisan and very interested in political matters.	Campaigners are typically well educated, white and middle to high socioeconomic status.
Complete Activists	Vote regularly and are deeply involved in all aspects of social and political life.	Complete activists are typically well educated, white, and middle to high socioeconomic status.

(Verba & Nie, 1972, 81-84)

It is evident that demographics and individual **socioeconomic status**, defined as one's social position based predominantly on an individual's education, income and career, are closely related to political participation. Middle to upper class educated citizens are more likely to participate politically in all aspects of citizenship mostly due to the fact that their political efficacy is likely to be higher. However, it is important to note that it is Parochial Participants, typically of a lower socioeconomic status, who are most likely to be involved in local community affairs.

Responsibilities of Citizenship
Looking at the chart, it is important to note that while voting regularly is certainly important, it is hardly the only way to influence public policy. Both the Parochial Participants and the Communalists are highly involved in local matters but do not vote regularly. While visiting the polls on election day is truly the best way to influence government in a representative democracy overall, it is what citizens do in between elections that has the most impact in our communities (and on our everyday lives). Much of our formal schooling focuses on the nuts and bolts of government and encourages adherence to societal norms, a shared set of expectations about what people think people should do as good citizens (Dalton, 2008, 78). Yet very few of us are ever taught how to be an "engaged citizen" which goes beyond the traditional responsibilities of "duty-based citizenship" that is typically promoted in American public schools. **Duty-based Citizenship** encourages conformity and adherence to social norms while promoting basic activities such as registering with a political party, voting in all elections, donating to campaigns, and joining civic groups. **Engaged Citizenship** refers to a more active role in politics and local communities beyond simply voting and belonging to a political party. While duty-based citizenship has been on a steady decline, engaged citizenship appears to be on the rise. Russell Dalton of the University of California at Irvine argues that this shift is a good thing by "increasing political tolerance in America, which strengthens the foundation of our democratic process and encompasses norms of greater social concern and engagement" (Dalton, 2008, 22). Listed now are comparisons between duty-based citizenship v. engaged citizenship:

Duty-Based Citizenship Principles	Engaged Citizenship Principles
Vote in elections	Be active in voluntary organizations
Serve on a jury if called	Be active in politics
Always obey laws and regulations	Form opinion, independently of others
Men serve in the military when the country is at war	Support people who are worse off than themselves
Reported a crime that he or she may have witnessed	

(Table provided by Dalton, 2008, 21)

Engaged citizenship requires an active role in politics and the greater community beyond the traditional responsibilities of citizenship. Dalton notes that engaged citizens are more likely to be involved in continuous political action that challenges political institutions and promotes tolerance of different beliefs through action-based citizenship, including protesting and boycotting (Dalton, 2008, 88). He also argues that engaged citizenship is the most effective avenue of political participation, especially on the local level and for controversial political issues. Dalton notes, "citizen duty encourages Americans to show up on election day and participate in election campaigns. However, citizen duty discourages participation in protest and other continuous forms of participation" (Dalton, 2008, 22).

Engaged Citizenship

The principles of engaged citizenship go beyond "How a Bill becomes a Law," and questions "How can I participate effectively in the public life of my community?" (Putnam, 2000, 405). Engaged citizenship requires three things: electoral participation, political awareness, and civic activity. These categories are very broad to account for all the different ways individuals can take part in these various activities—for example, civic activity can encompass a wide range of activities from attending religious services to joining a sports league.

Electoral Participation

Electoral participation is arguably the most important component of engaged citizenship. While solely participating in elections is not truly the best way to influence public policy, citizens who participate in elections are most likely to participate in other aspects of engaged citizenship. The U.S. Immigration and Naturalization Service states, "The right to vote is a duty as well as a privilege" (1987:11). In the United States we depend on the electoral process to keep legislatures and other decision makers accountable to the public. To vote is to have a say in your government and the people in it who will make policy that affects your everyday life. Dalton asserts, "Participation is a prime criteria for defining the democratic citizen and his or her role within the political process" (Dalton, 2008, 2). In other words, participation is critical in order for a representative democracy to work effectively.

Despite the fact that as Americans we universally value our "right to vote" (see political socialization), the act of voting has been on a steady decline since the early 1900s. Senator Bob Graham asserts, "Although excitement surrounding the 2008 elections temporarily obscured concerns about our civic health, American democracy suffers from a pervasive lack of active participation among our citizens. For a variety of reasons, many of our fellow Americans view civics as a kind of spectator sport—something to be viewed from afar throughout the filters of media outlets and personalities" (Graham, 2010, xv).

The election of 2008 was monumental and unusual. Not only was this a historical election in terms of ideological and racial tipping points, it was also unprecedented in terms of young and minority voting. Despite the impressive record of 131 million people voting in the 2008 presidential election, where Barack Obama was elected the first African American President of the United States, roughly 75 million Americans (about 36%) of the adult citizen population did not vote (Hess & Herman, 2009, iv). According to the Pew Research Center, voters in the 2008 presidential election were uniquely diverse with 23.7% of voters who were non-white and 17.1% between the ages of 18-29 (Lopez & Taylor, 2009, p. 3). According to the 2009 report "Dissecting the 2008 Electorate: Most Diverse in U.S. History" a significant proportion of the increased turnout was driven by black women and young voters (Lopez & Taylor, 2009,ii). More than 2 million additional young people voted in 2008 than in the

2004 election (Lopez & Taylor, 2009, 6). Despite the impressive increased turnout, it is important to highlight data obtained from Project Vote which indicated that in 2008 out of 206 million adults, approximately 146 million self-reported they were registered to vote, but only 131 million actually voted on election day (Hess & Herman, 2009, 5). Therefore, while we certainly saw an increase in voter turnout, a substantial number of registered voters did not come through on election day.

How to: Voting
Step One: Determine voting eligibility
    If you are 18 years old and a United States citizen, you are eligible to vote. Check with your local voter registration office if you have been convicted of any felony offences, which in some states will ban you from voting.

Step Two: Register to vote
    There are numerous places where you can register to vote: the Department of Motor Vehicles (when renewing licenses), your local County Registration offices, post offices, and public libraries. In addition, many communities will hold registration drives on college campuses, at local high schools, or in area hospitals around election time. Registration is easy and only takes a couple of minutes.

    In some cases as a college student, you may want to declare your school address as your permanent residence. If you are planning on remaining in your college town for at least four years, it makes sense to establish residency and voice your opinion where you spend most of your time. Check with your local registration office for details on establishing residency for voter registration and for registration deadlines, as laws differ from state to state.

Step Three: Now what?
    Become informed about politics—research the candidates' stance on key issues and compare them with your thoughts and ideals. Discuss your feeling with a diverse group of people to gain new insights and challenge your preconceived notions. Remember to listen and be respectful of others' views at all times.

Step Four: VOTE!

Get out and vote! The General Election is always held on the first Tuesday in November of even numbered years. However, you must make an effort to keep up with local primary, runoff, and special election dates which typically have the worst turnout rate at about 15 percentage points lower than presidential elections (Hess & Herman, 2009, 14), which means that every vote is essential in these often-overlooked elections.

Political Awareness

The second component, political awareness, is critical in democracy because democracy depends on an informed electorate in order to function effectively. Dalton states that "the citizen's role in being sufficiently informed about government is to exercise a participatory role. The citizens should participate in democratic deliberation and discuss politics with other citizens, and ideally understand the views of others" (Dalton, 2008, 2). This advice clearly goes against conventional dogma that one should never discuss "religion and politics" with friends but rather these types of discussions may actually encourage future political participation by promoting awareness among your peers. Community organizations offer an exceptional opportunity to meet with likeminded neighbors and discuss issues facing our everyday lives.

Not surprisingly, as a nation we actually know very little about politics and seemingly the more information we have access to, the less we are informed about political matters. University of Maryland Professor William Galston revealed an important link between basic civic knowledge and citizen participation. Galston concluded that the more knowledgeable citizens are about political matters, the more likely they are to participate in political life. Galston states, "civic knowledge helps citizens understand their interests as individuals and as members of groups" (Galston, 2001, 223). Interestingly, Putnam notes, "the average college graduate knows little more about public affairs than did the average high school graduate in the 1940s" (Putnam, 2000, 35). Despite our exceptional advances in access to information, Americans today are less informed about political matters than they were fifty years ago. This trend is disturbing as politically knowledgeable citizens are more effective citizens. When individuals are knowledgeable about politics, they can better understand how policy decisions affect their interests and protect their interests when necessary.

Without basic civic knowledge it is difficult for individuals to understand political events and therefore they are likely to withdraw from political life altogether.

Civic Activity

The United States is a nation of "joiners." Group participation has a long history in the United States as volunteer organizations have historically reached out to citizens of diverse backgrounds and offered the opportunity to increase political efficacy by giving citizens a collective voice in their communities. "As America becomes more racially diverse, the demands for increasing social capital and fostering interracial understanding will become more pressuring. Voluntary civic associations should be a crucial instrument in achieving both of these goals—not only can they promote social capital and trust, they are ideal settings for fostering positive interracial contact" (Ha & Oliver, 2006, 24).

Putnam calls volunteer organizations "schools of democracy" and argues that these organizations are useful for developing essential skills for lifelong civic engagement and reinforcing community ties:

> *the most systematic study of civic skills in contemporary America suggests that for working class Americans, volunteer associations and churches offer the best opportunities for civic skill building, and even for professionals such groups are second only to the workplace for civic learning. Two-thirds or more of the members of religious, literary, youth and fraternal/service organizations exercised such civic skills as giving a presentation or running a meeting. Churches, in particular, are one of the few vital institutions left where low-income, minority and disadvantages citizens of all races can learn politically relevant skills and be recruited into political action.* (Putnam, 2000, 339)

Participation in religious life is another popular avenue for becoming involved in local communities and learning the necessary tools for effective political participation. Putnam asserts, "Faith communities in which people work together are arguably the single most important repository of social capital in American. Churches provide an important incubator for civic skills, civic norms, community interests and civic recruitment" (Putnam, 2000, 66). In addition, Putnam confirms that religiously active individuals are more likely to be politically active in their communities, have stronger social networks and participate in community organizations. Participation in religious organizations offers many opportunities to gain political skills such as public speaking, fundraising, administration, and leadership (Levitt, 2008, 778). Finally, religious participation is many times the only option for individuals of low socioeconomic status who lack additional resources available in middle class communities.

The Engaged Citizen: A Manual

Catherine Bolzendahl and Hilde Coffe state that citizenship entails both rights and obligations (Bolzendahl & Coffe, 2009, 765). Many of us would like to be engaged citizens but simply do not know how. We are busy and have limited time for community involvement in addition to our daily responsibilities. The consensus among educators is that students should be taught to be effective citizens, but they disagree on the best method. According to Frischler and Smith, "Most observers at some level agree with the idea that students should be effective citizens. But when it comes to specifying what, in practice, civic education actually means, this agreement often dissolves in heated controversy" (Fritschler & Smith, 2009, 8). The authors view civic education as having three components: a plan of study (curriculum), volunteerism to increase community participation, and access to extracurricular activities. University of Pennsylvania researchers have found that ongoing civic education appears to lead to higher political efficacy, which in turn leads to more engaged citizenship. According to the study, "This relationship makes intuitive sense: The more people believe their efforts to influence government will be rewarded with success, the more likely they will be to engage in such efforts" (Pasek, etal, 2008, 28).

Throughout your college career you will have the opportunity to engage in all three components of civic education. The core plan of study at most colleges covers all of the basics of American government and history necessary for basic civic knowledge. In addition, university life offers ample opportunity to participate in volunteer and extracurricular organizations where students can develop valuable skills necessary for engaged citizenship. From team sports to social groups to academic organizations, the college campus offers numerous opportunities to develop civic engagement skills. Taking these basic first steps as a college student can set you up for engaged citizenship throughout your life. "The researchers conclude that community service, political discussion and environmental conservatism are the basic first steps toward well rounded citizenship" (Tisch, 2010,7). Participation in the campus community can teach you valuable skills that you will be able to utilize in your future professional and personal life.

The following list provided by The Center for Information & Research on Civic Learning & Engagement (CIRCLE) shows basic ways that students become engaged citizens based on their level of involvement in their campus community:

> **Top Level:** community service, political and environmental discussions.
> **Intermediate Level:** political efficacy, willingness to contact officials, intention to vote, non-sporty extracurricular activities, conflict resolution skills.
> **Basic Level**: school engagement, school belonging, sporty extracurricular activities, school support, grades.
> (Tisch, 2010,7)

Practicing Democracy

Aside from campus life, the best way to become involved in political matters is to begin on the local level. While regular voting is essential, you will need to look beyond election day if you have a specific problem that requires personal attention. Remember, politicians in a direct democracy must be responsive to public opinion because that is what keeps them in office. Especially on the state and local level, individuals have a great deal of power to influence their government. While it may seem overwhelming or intimidating, contact with elected officials is truly the best first step toward handling problems in your community. However, you do not need to go at it alone. If you are upset about an issue it is likely that other members in your community are concerned as well. Remember that with collective action, ordinary citizens have had extraordinary influence on public policy. While a heartfelt effort from a single constituent can get an elected official's attention, a large number of letters (or a petition) almost guarantees notice.

There are a number of opportunities for direct participation, such as citizen initiatives and referendum that allow constituents to dictate specific policy directives to lawmakers. In addition, rallies, marches, and political protests are a surefire way to communicate your political directives. This type of participation must be used cautiously as there is a fine line between civic engagement and civic disobedience, though many of our most significant social changes were born of this type of grassroots democracy. If you choose to engage in this type of political participation, you must be aware of possible legal ramifications, including arrest and prosecution. As a general rule, despite which method of participation is chosen, the more constituents you can mobilize the greater the likelihood your issue will get noticed by politicians on various levels of government.

Pinpoint your go-to person

One of the keys to MADD's success was knowing the right people. Turning a policymaker into an ally is a critical step that should not be overlooked. Once you identify your problem you must establish jurisdiction—meaning you must determine if your issue is a federal, state, or local issue. Because state and local governments operate separately from the national government, it is likely that most issues affecting your day to day activities would fall under state or local jurisdiction. Ironically, it is on the state and local government level where traditional political participation (i.e. voting in elections) is the most lacking. Do not underestimate the importance of your local government. It is likely that even if they cannot help you solve your problem, they can put you in touch with the person who can. Remember, the national government generally only deals with issues of great national importance.

Once you have established jurisdiction it is essential to identify potentially important legislatures and staff members who can help you with your cause. According to Knecht, your list should include:

- Your senators and representatives—elected officials are constantly worried about public opinion because that is what gets them re-elected. Your elected officials want to hear from you about issues affecting their districts. Writing a letter to your local congressman is the best way to make your concern heard and potentially influence policy in your local community.

- Chairperson and ranking member in identified "key committees"—high level members in select committees can be invaluable. Committee members are likely to be sensitive to your concerns, especially if you represent a large constituency.
- Legislatures with a history of supporting your issue—elected officials sensitive to your issue can be great allies. This information is readily available via the Internet and can save you a great deal of time.
- Legislatures in leadership roles—legislatures in leadership roles are always interested in changes of public opinion, especially with larger constituencies. There is strength in numbers.
- Other potential allies—identify other powerful individuals within a political party or an interest group who may be helpful in promoting your issue.

(Knecht, 2005, 9-10)

Former Senator Graham emphasizes the importance of "Knowing the Decision Maker before you Begin to Lobby" and cautions that it is imperative to know who your decision makers are and what they believe in (Graham, 2010, 131). Much like you would shop around for the highest ranked computer or best performing car, you must research your legislatures and select the elected officials with the most power to help your cause. Graham recommends using the Internet and other research tools to investigate key information about your best choice for legislature. This information is critical in selecting your allies so you can focus your efforts on someone who you know will at least be somewhat interested in your cause. For example, you would not discuss your environmental concerns with a legislature who has voted against environmental protection bills in the past. Moreover, this approach will allow you to concentrate your efforts on individuals who are likely to want to assist you when you bring forth issues that coincide with the elected officials record and platform.

Contacting Elected Officials

Once you have determined who to contact regarding your problem, you must reach out to your elected officials and make your concerns known. Letters are typically the preferred method of communication with legislatures and offer a great opportunity to present your problem in a clear and concise manner.

Listed below are some general tips from Congress.org on how to write an effective letter:
- Your purpose for writing should be stated in the first paragraph of the letter. If your letter pertains to a specific piece of legislation, identify it accordingly, e.g., House bill: H. R. ____, Senate bill: S.____.
- Be courteous, to the point, and include key information, using examples to support your position.
- Address only one issue in each letter and, if possible, keep the letter to one page.

http://www.congress.org/congressorg/issues/basics/

Also, when addressing your letter, it is customary to refer to senators and representatives as "The Honorable" followed by their full name. For the salutation, you would use "Dear Senator" or "Dear Representative" depending on the situation. It is important to use proper headings and salutations even when sending emails to enhance your credibility as a citizen. Speaking of email—while electronic mail is gaining in popularity, it is important to note that letters by email do not have the same impact as a traditional letter, and it can be very difficult to convey tone. It is always a good idea to start with a traditional letter for maximum impact when reaching out to an elected official.

Meeting with an Elected Official
If you are lucky enough to score a face to face meeting with your elected official—congratulations! Now the real work begins. You only get one chance to make a first impression so keep the following tips in mind when visiting with important decision makers.

Before the meeting
In addition to your background research, make sure that you know the correct names, spellings, and pronunciations of all officials and staff members you will be interacting with. When you schedule your meeting, request only the least amount of time necessary to go over your entire

issue. Make sure you are dressed appropriately for meeting with an elected official. It is best to avoid clothing with any tears, tank tops, and open toe shoes (i.e. flip flops) when initially meeting with a government official. Do not bring any gifts to the meeting—it puts elected officials in an uncomfortable situation and is generally frowned on in government. Keep your group small—bring only essential members who are important in getting the message across.

At the meeting

Keep your presentation as brief as possible and discuss only the following: the problem you want to solve, possible solutions, and reasons why the official should support your proposal. Be ready to answer any questions about your issue with factual information. It is critical that you stay current on any late-breaking developments affecting your issue. You may want to take the time to type up your main talking points so if you run out of time the official can review them at a later date. You should practice your talking points prior to the meeting, especially if you are going as part of a group. Be respectful of the official's time and recognize non-verbal cues that the meeting has ended. Avoid temptation to ask for additional items or photographs.

After the meeting

Always follow up any face to face meeting with a handwritten thank you note. This action gives you an opportunity to reiterate your key points and provide your contact information. Keep in brief and regular contact via email with the decision maker's staff and acknowledge any action that has taken place on behalf of your issue. With certain exceptions, sweeping changes to public policy are just not possible. However, it is important to acknowledge little milestones along the way to keep up morale and reach your ultimate goal.

The above list was adopted from Mark Block, director of external relations for Newsweek (Graham, 2010, 137-139).

Persistence, consistency, and willingness are the keys to becoming an engaged citizen. Engaged citizenship is not something you do during election season; engaged citizenship means reaching out in your everyday life though following and participating in local elections (especially primaries), reading the newspaper, volunteering in your local community, and discussing current events with friends. Remember, representative democracy depends on your participation and individuals willing to put in the time and effort can make big differences in government.

Case Study—The Millennials and the Internet
The Internet may be the key to unlocking political engagement in today's young people as the web provides a universal tool for engaged citizenship. According to Galson, "the public's knowledge of institutions and processes is significantly higher than its knowledge of people and policies, perhaps because the former are more stable over time and require less monitoring" (Galson, 2001, 221). Engaged citizenship requires that an individual become and remain informed about political matters. The Internet provides unlimited access to information about politics, government, and policy issues. While base civic knowledge is essential, Galson notes, "Civic knowledge promotes political participation. All other things being equal the more knowledge citizens have, the more likely they are to participate in political matters" (Galson, 2001, 224). The Internet can be a useful tool in promoting lifelong citizenship, especially for the Millennial generation, our nation's youngest citizens born after 1982.

Generational changes and social changes are important themes throughout Robert Putnam's *Bowling Alone* as they are used to explain the decline in overall political participation in the United States since the 1960s. Putnam offers a number of possible explanations for this decline including general distrust of government since the Nixon administration, declining political party affiliation, and unstable social bonds. According to Putnam, "beneath the ups and downs of individual elections virtually all of the long-run decline in turnout is due to the gradual replacement of voters who came of age before or during the New Deal and World War II by a generation who came later" (Putnam, 2000, 33). Historically, older voters have always outnumbered younger voters, but unlike previous generations the younger voters were not replacing older voters. However, this trend may be reversing thanks to the Internet and the Millennials who have come of age in a perfect storm to revive civic engagement in the United States.

A growing body of research suggests that Generation Y, popularly referenced as the Millennials, may reverse this downward trend in political participation and become the next "Great Generation" actively involved in political matters. This trend is due to two factors: high political efficacy and the current political environment.

To better understand this idea, we must seek to understand the political climate of previous generations. The World War II generation (sometimes referenced as the "Greatest Generation") was influenced by significant historical events including the Great Depression, The New Deal, and a victorious war followed by long periods of economic prosperity. In contrast, the Baby Boomers' general experience, while positive in terms of economic prosperity, was plagued by political conflict including the Civil Rights Movement, the Watergate scandal, and Vietnam. Putnam argues that these negative experiences led to low political efficacy for the Boomers: "In political terms, this generation was indelibly marked by the events of the sixties—the civil rights movement (which happened while most of them were still in elementary school), the Kennedy and King assassinations, the trauma of Vietnam and Watergate. Perhaps with reason—they surely think so—they are distrusting of institutions, alienated from politics and (despite their campus flings of the sixties and seventies) distinctively less involved in civic life" (Putnam, 2000, 257). Moreover, this generation transmitted this alienation to their children, the highly individualistic Generation Xers, who grew up in an uncertain world economically and socially with no unifying moment to define their generation. Putnam explains, "in both personal and national terms, this generation is shaped by uncertainty, insecurity and the absence of a collective success story— no victorious D-Day or triumph over Hitler, no exhilarating, liberating marches on Washington and triumph over racism and war, indeed hardly any great collective events at all. For understandable reasons, this cohort is very inwardly focused" (Putnam, 2000, 259).

But the Millennials have a different story. Having witnessed the invention of the Internet, the horrific 9/11 attacks with the stunning demonstration of patriotism that followed, and the historical election of 2008 where the United States elected its first African American president, the Millennials are a confident, optimistic group with high levels of political efficacy.

Authors Neil Howe and William Strauss argue in "Millennials Rising: The Next Great Generation" that the Millennials, with the largest population cohort since the Baby Boomers, are the next "hero generation," a generation that rises after an era of society wide upheaval and distrust in the political system. The authors believe that this "generational cycle" is already evident with Millennials, specifically in a "can do" attitude and positive ethos. According to Howe and Strauss, "This generation will also be known for its hard work on a grassroots reconstruction of community, teamwork, and civic spirit. They're doing it in the realms of community service, race, gender relations, politics and faith" (Howe & Strauss, 2000, p.214).

Indeed the 2008 election demonstrated an increase in political participation with more than 2 million more young people between the ages of 18 to 29 voting compared to the 2004 election (Lopez & Taylor, 2009, p. 6).

The 2008 election was also unique in the use of the Internet among the candidates, particularly the victor Barack Obama. Winograd and Hais argue in their book, *Millennial Makeover: MySpace, YouTube, and the Future of American Politics,* that young people are twice as likely to use the Internet to gather information about politics. A 2006 survey revealed that 35% of young Internet users obtained most of their news about the 2006 election online (Wonograd & Hais, 2008, 164), while a late 2007 survey revealed that 42% of young people receive their political information from the Internet (Greenberg, 2009, 86). The democratic advantage in the last election was clear with Obama beating McCain in virtually all forms of political communication. The research overwhelmingly supports that the Internet is the vehicle to reach young voters. According to Greenberg, "young people own cyberspace. The tools of activism and communication are generated by this younger generation, and both progressives (using the blogosphere) and Democratic candidates (such as Barack Obama) have taken full advantage of this new way of conducting politics" (Greenberg, 2009, 78). Greenberg notes that Millennials passively receive information via the Internet (either by surfing or from friends); therefore, politicians need to make their presence on the Internet known and reach out to these voters rather than waiting for them to seek information.

The Internet is a crucial tool for politicians who want to secure the Millennial vote. The web also provides a comprehensive tool for engaged citizenship though numerous, free resources that empower voters to make educated decisions about their leadership. This rise in information availability combined with the political atmosphere surrounding today's college students has placed America on the way toward reversing the downward trends in political participation.

Discussion Questions
1. What is the role of public opinion in a representative democracy? How does public opinion influence public policy?
2. Identify various ways citizens can participate in the political process. What methods of political participation are the most effective? Why?
3. What resources are available for college students to become engaged citizens? How would you address a political problem in your community after reading this chapter?
4. What has been the impact of the Internet on civic engagement? Is it possible that the Internet could increase political participation?

References

Bianco, W. & Canon, D. (2009). *American politics today.* New York, NY: W.W. Norton & Co.

Bolzendahl, C. & Coffe, H. (2009). Citizenship beyond politics: the importance of political, civil and social rights and responsibilities among women and men. *The British Journal of Sociology,* 60(4), 763-791.

Dalton, R. (2006). The two faces of citizenship. *Democracy and Society,* 3(2), 21-23.

Dalton, R. (2008). Citizenship norms and the expansion of political participation. *Political Studies,* 56, 76-98.

Graham, B. (2010). *America the owner's manual: Making government work for fou.* Washington: CQ Press.

Ha, S. & Oliver, E. (2006). Examining the civic paradoxes of racial segregation. *Democracy and Society,* 3(2), 23-29.

Hess, D. & Herman, Jody. (2009). Representational bias in the 2008 Electorate. Retrieved from http://www.projectvote.org.

Hocutt, M. (2005). Indoctrination v. education. *Academic Questions*, 35-43.

Howe, N. & Strauss, B. (2000). *Millennials rising: The next great generation.* New York, NY: Vantage Books

Fritschler, A. L. & Smith, B. L. R. (2009). Engagement in civic education remains weak. *Forum.*

Feldman, L., Jamieson, K., Pasek, J., & Romer, D. (2008). Schools as incubators of democratic participation: Building long term political efficacy with civic education. *Applied Development Science*, 12(1), 26-37.

Galston, W. (2001). Political knowledge, political engagement and civic education. *Annual Review of Political Science,* 4, 217-234.

Greenberg, A. (2009). A generation apart: Young voters and the 2008 presidential election. *The Hedge Hog Review,* 11(1), 74-87.

Knecht, I. (2005). Citizen lobbying: Building relationships to influence policy. *National Center for Victims of Crime,* Summer/Fall 2005.

Levitt, P. (2008). Religion as a path to civic engagement. *Ethnic and Racial Studies,* 31(4), 766-791.

Lopez, M. H. & Taylor, P. (2009). *Dissecting the 2008 electorate: Most diverse in us history.* Washington, DC: Pew Research Center

Putnam, R. (2000). *Bowling alone: The collapse and revival of American community.* New York, NY: Simon & Schuster.

Winograd, M. & Hais, M. (2008). *Millennial makeover: MySpace, YouTube and the future of American politics.* Piscataway, NJ: Rutgers University Press.

Youniss, J. (2005). Much to learn about new agents of political socialization. *Human Development*, 48, 356-362.

Center for Information & Research on Civic Learning and Engagement (CIRCLE). Tufts University. Jonathan M. Tisch College of Citizenship and Public Service. April 2010.

About the Authors

Ms. Maria J. Albo, instructor of political science, earned an M.P.A. from North Georgia College & State University. She has published a peer-reviewed journal article on public policy relating to illegal immigration and teaches several sections of American Government every semester.

Dr. Ross C. Alexander, associate professor of political science, possesses a Ph.D. in political science from Northern Illinois University with specializations in public administration, American politics, and political theory in addition to an M.P.A. from Arizona State University. He has published several peer-reviewed journal articles addressing public administration, state and local government, and information literacy. Dr. Alexander currently teaches courses in American Government, American Political Theory, State and Local Government, Political Leadership, Senior Seminar in Political Science, Leadership and Organizational Theory, Public Budgeting and Public Personnel Administration. He has been teaching the survey course in American Government for 12 years and is very familiar with the trends and textbooks in the field.

Dr. Carl D. Cavalli, associate professor of political science, earned an M.A. and Ph.D. in political science from the University of North Carolina at Chapel Hill with specializations in American politics, comparative politics, and political theory. He has published a book on Presidential-Congressional Relations in addition to peer-reviewed journal articles addressing American Government. Dr. Cavalli currently teaches the following courses: Presidency, Congress, Legislative Process, Political Parties and Elections, Road to Congress, Road to the White House, and American Government, which he has been teaching for over 25 years. Dr. Cavalli is an expert in the field of American politics.

Dr. Barry D. Friedman, professor of political science, earned M.B.A., M.P.A., and Ph.D. degrees in political science from the University of Connecticut, with emphases in public administration, American politics, and public policy. He has authored numerous books and articles in the fields of federal regulation, non-profit administration, and public policy. Dr. Friedman teaches courses on Public Management, Public Policy Analysis, Politics and Bureaucracy, Ethics, Statistics, Senior Seminar in Political Science, Introduction to Political Science and American Government, which he has been teaching for 25 years.

Dr. Craig Greathouse, associate professor of political science, earned a Ph.D. in political science with specialties in international relations and comparative politics from Claremont Graduate University in addition to an M.A. in Political Science from the University of Akron. Dr. Greathouse has published peer-reviewed journal articles addressing European foreign policy. His teaching experience includes the following courses: Introduction to the European Union, International Political Economy, International Relations Theory, Global Issues and American Government.

Dr. Jonathan Miner, associate professor of political science, possesses a Ph.D. in international studies with specializations in foreign policy, international law and organizations, and comparative politics from the University of South Carolina in addition to an M.A. in Political Science from the University of Iowa and J.D. from Drake University. His publications focus on foreign policy and Middle Eastern politics. Courses Dr. Miner teaches include International Law, Foreign Policy Process, Global Issues, Middle East Politics, and Research Methods.

Dr. Brian M. Murphy received M.A. and Ph.D. degrees in political science from Miami University. Prior to his current position as Dean of the College of Liberal & Applied Arts at Stephen F. Austin State University, he was Co-Director of the European Union Center for the University System of Georgia, which was housed at Georgia Institute of Technology, as well as professor of political science at North Georgia College & State University. His administrative positions at North Georgia included head of the Department of Political Science & Criminal Justice, Director of the Honors Program, Coordinator of International Programs, and Associate in the Office of Academic Affairs. From 1997-2007, Dr. Murphy directed the University System of Georgia's program on European Union Studies. In 1998, he was appointed General Secretary of the Transatlantic Information Exchange Service, a program launched by the European Commission and United States Information Agency. In 2006, Dr. Murphy was appointed to a strategic planning committee for the University System of Georgia to prepare higher education in the state to leverage competition in the global economy. Dr. Murphy continues to serve as a Senior Fellow at the Southern Center for International Studies.

Dr. K. Michael Reese, professor of criminal justice, possesses a J.D. from the University of Alabama, an LL.M. from Emory University, and a Ph.D. from Georgia State University in Higher Education with a cognate in Law. Dr. Reese practiced law in both the private and public sectors for a number